In Praise of Maoist Economic Planning

Living Standards and Economic
Development in Sichuan since 1931.

Studies on Contemporary China

The Contemporary China Institute, based at the School of Oriental and African Studies (University of London), was established in 1968. Throughout its existence, it has been a national focus for research and publications on twentieth-century China. This new series, which is edited at the Institute, seeks to maintain and extend that tradition by making available the best work of scholars throughout the world. Future volumes will embrace a wide variety of subjects, including China's social, political, and economic change, intellectual and cultural developments, and foreign relations.

In Praise of Maoist Economic Planning

Living Standards and Economic
Development in Sichuan since 1931.

CHRIS BRAMALL

CLARENDON PRESS · OXFORD

1993

Oxford University Press, Walton Street, Oxford OX2 6DP
Oxford New York Toronto
Delhi Bombay Calcutta Madras Karachi
Kuala Lumpur Singapore Hong Kong Tokyo
Nairobi Dar es Salaam Cape Town
Melbourne Auckland Madrid
and associated companies in
Berlin Ibadan

Oxford is a trade mark of Oxford University Press

Published in the United States
by Oxford University Press Inc., New York

British Library Cataloguing in Publication Data
Data available

Library of Congress Cataloging in Publication Data
Bramall, Chris.
In Praise of Maoist Economic Planning
Chris Bramall.
p. cm. — (Studies on contemporary China)
Includes bibliographical references and index.
1. Szechwan Province (China)—Economic conditions. 2. China—
Economic policy—1976– 3. Income distribution—China—Szechwan
Province. 4. Regional disparities—China—Szechwan Province.
5. Famines—China—Szechwan Province. I. Title. II. Series:
Studies on contemporary China (Oxford, England)
HC428.S9B7 1993 338.951'38—dc20 92–44066

ISBN 0–19–828790–9

1 3 5 7 9 10 8 6 4 2

Typeset by Best-set Typesetter Ltd., Hong Kong

Printed in Great Britain
on acid-free paper by
Bookcraft (Bath) Ltd
Midsomer Norton, Avon

To Marion

Preface

This book is an evaluation of economic development in China's most populous province between the Nanjing decade (1928–37) and the 'liberalization' programme initiated in 1978. Much of it discusses the changing distribution of incomes and capabilities between locations within Sichuan. The famine that followed the Great Leap Forward is also discussed in some detail. Although much of this is necessarily descriptive, the book's main aim is to analyse and to explain the achievements and the failures of the Maoist regime. Its conclusions are much more positive than has been the norm in recent years.

In writing it, I am greatly indebted to Bob Ash, Terry Byres, Liu Minquan, and Iain Macpherson for their trenchant critical comments and their encouragement. I have also benefited from the suggestions and advice of Alan Hughes, Wing-shing Tang, the late Ken Walker, and Zhang Xunhai, as well the participants in the Third World Economic History and Development Group's London Conference (September 1988) and the Cambridge Research Group on the Chinese Economy. An anonymous referee also helped to make this a far better book than it would otherwise have been. I owe a special debt to Peter Nolan. His influence has been immeasurable and his enthusiasm infectious. I cannot imagine how this work would have been conceived, let alone completed, without him.

I should also like to thank the Contemporary China Institute for its kindness in publishing an earlier paper of mine on Sichuan; Charles D'Orban of the Library of the School of Oriental and African Studies for keeping me abreast of the flood of recent publications on the province; the Economic and Social Research Council for financial assistance during the early stages of this work; the British Council for funding a year in China; the Master and Fellows of Sidney Sussex College in the University of Cambridge for a Research Fellowship that enabled much of my research to be carried out; and the Economic Research Institute, Chengdu, for its hospitality during a research visit to Sichuan. Finally, I am indebted to Sarah Barrett for her superb copy-editing, and to members of the editorial department at Oxford University Press for their meticulous care in readying the book for publication.

This book is in no sense the last word on economic development in Sichuan. It is scarcely the beginning of the beginning. Accordingly, the responsibility for any errors and misinterpretations lies even more heavily than usual upon the shoulders of the author. I accept it entirely.

C. M. B.

Cambridge
August 1992

Contents

Romanization		x
Abbreviations		xi
Administrative Divisions		xii
Weights and Measures		xiii
List of Tables		xiv
List of Figures		xviii
1.	Maoist Economic Development, Its Critics, and Sichuan	1
2.	Sichuan's Development Record	27
3.	The Roots of Backwardness	55
4.	The Theory and Measurement of Income Distribution	115
5.	The Spatial Distribution	139
6.	An Analysis of Spatial Trends	175
7.	Poverty and Inequality in Sichuan's Villages in the 1930s	215
8.	Poverty and Inequality in Sichuan's Villages in the 1970s	259
9.	Famine	281
10.	Food Availability Decline and Institutional Change	305
11.	Conclusion	335
Appendix		341
References:		357
	Chinese-language Sources	357
	Western-language Sources	365
Index		381

Romanization

The romanization used in this book is in general the pinyin form. However, some pinyin versions, e.g. Xizang for Tibet, are neither well known nor easily recognized, and therefore the traditional form is used instead. Chinese names are cited Chinese-style, with the family name first. Some of the proper names frequently encountered are as follows:

Pinyin form	Traditional Western form	This book
Beijing	Peking	Beijing
Chengdu	Chengtu	Chengdu
Chongqing	Chungking	Chongqing
gaoliang	kaoliang (sorghum)	gaoliang
Guomindang	Kuomintang	Kuomintang
Jiang Jieshi	Chiang Kaishek	Chiang Kaishek
Mao Zedong	Mao Tsetung	Mao Zedong
Nanjing	Nanking	Nanjing
Qing	Ch'ing	Qing
tong oil	tung oil	tung oil
Sichuan	Szechwan	Sichuan
Xizang	Tibet	Tibet
Yangzi = Changjiang	Yangtze	Yangzi

Abbreviations

CBR	crude birth rate
CCP	Chinese Communist Party
CDR	crude death rate
'Grain'	includes pulses and tubers unless otherwise stated
KMT	Kuomintang
n.a.	not available
NARB	National Agricultural Research Bureau
NDMP	net domestic material product or national income (*guomin shouru*)
neg.	negligible
NVAIO (GVAIO)	sum of NVAO and NVIO (or GVAO and GVIO)
NVAO (GVAO)	net (gross) value of agricultural output
NVIO (GVIO)	net (gross) value of industrial output

Administrative Divisions

Chinese administrative divisions have no true Western equivalents. However, the use of pinyin in this context would make much of this book unreadable to a non-specialist without constant reference to the glossary. I have therefore used the standard Western equivalents, of which the most common are summarized below. Less common terms are explained when used. Prefecture and autonomous prefecture names are identified in the Appendix; italicized county names denote the name of the prefecture.

This book	Pinyin form
autonomous county	*zizhixian*
autonomous prefecture	*zizhizhou*
autonomous region	*zizhiqu*
city	*shi*
commune	*gongshe*
county	*xian*
district	*qu*
prefecture	*diqu*
production brigade	*dadui*
production team	*dui*
province	*sheng*
township	*xiang*
village	*cun*

Weights and Measures

I should have liked to have avoided the use of Chinese weights and measures. However, some pre-1949 Chinese units are of uncertain size and, in any case, the conversion of units increases the possibility of error. Accordingly, I have use the pinyin equivalent throughout. Where the prefix *shi* is used in the context of the 1930s, it refers to a market, or standard, unit used throughout China. This prefix is very rarely applied to post-1949 measures. If no prefix is used, pre-1949 units are local measures and their metric size is given wherever I have been able to identify it. All post-1949 measures are standard, all-China measures.

The Western equivalent of common post-1949 Chinese measures, and pre-1949 standard measures, are given below. Others are given in the text.

Pre-1949 pinyin	Post-1949 pinyin	Western equivalent
shi	*shi*	'market' prefix
shi shi	*shi*	100 litres
shi dan	*dan*	50 kilograms
shi mu	*mu*	0.0667 hectares
shi jin	*jin*	0.5 kilograms
yuan	*yuan*	1 Chinese dollar

List of Tables

1.1.	Sichuan's Relative Backwardness in the 1950s	12
1.2.	International Population Densities in 1984	16
1.3.	Rural Modernization in Sichuan since 1978	24
1.4.	Output of Selected Producer Goods in Sichuan, 1931–1943	25
2.1.	Macroeconomic Trends in Sichuan, 1931–1978	29
2.2.	Macroeconomic Performance of Sichuan and China	31
2.3.	Trends in Daily Food Consumption in Sichuan after 1931	34
2.4.	International Expenditure and Savings Patterns	36
2.5.	Anthropometric Data	40
2.6.	Height of Boys Aged Seven in Urban China, 1979	41
2.7.	Industrial Output Growth in Sichuan after 1952	43
2.8.	Industrialization Levels in China and Sichuan, late 1970s	44
2.9.	Trends in Consumption after 1952 in Sichuan	47
2.10.	Sichuan's Trade Balance, 1952–1978	48
2.11.	Trends in Capabilities in Sichuan	50
2.12.	Infant Mortality Rates in Developing Countries	52
3.1.	The Economy of Sichuan in Peace and War, 1931–1945	74
3.2.	Sichuan's Economy in the 1950s and the Late Maoist Period	79
3.3.	Farm-Sector Performance in the 1950s	84
3.4.	Fixed Investment in Sichuan after 1965	100
3.5.	Trends in Living Standards in Sichuan, 1975–1990	104
3.6.	Growth of Farm Output and Inputs in Sichuan, 1978–1987	106
3.7.	Fixed Investment in Transport and Communications in Sichuan	110
5.1.	NVAIO and Net Peasant Incomes by County, 1985	146
5.2.	Pork Consumption and NVAIO by Prefecture, 1980s	147

5.3. Spatial Differentials in Comparative Perspective 150

5.4. Inequalities within China's Provinces in the 1980s 158

5.5. Prefectures Ranked by NVAIO Per Capita, 1939–1943, 1982, and 1985 160

5.6. Basic Needs and NVAIO per capita by County, 1982 162

5.7. The Relative Dispersion of Incomes by County, 1939–1985 164

5.8. The Absolute Dispersion of Average Per Capita County Incomes, 1939–1985 166

5.9. Absolute Spatial Inequality in Sichuan, 1978–1982 167

5.10. Trends in Provincial Output Per Capita at 1978 Prices 168

5.11. Absolute and Relative Spatial Poverty in Sichuan, 1939–1982 170

5.12. Growth of Real Per Capita NVAIO in Poor Prefectures, 1952–1982 172

5.13. Summary of Long-Run Spatial Trends 173

6.1. NVAIO Per Capita and Trends in Population Density 181

6.2. Spatial Inequalities in Industrialization 186

6.3. Output of Commune and Brigade Enterprises by County, 1976 187

6.4. Trends in Crop Yields in Shifang 197

6.5. Material Production Costs in Jiangsu's Farm Sector 198

6.6. The Share of Cash Crops in Sown Area, 1931–1984 200

6.7. Procurement Prices in Sichuan, 1952–1978 202

6.8. Value Added per *Mu* by Crop Type in Sichuan, Late 1970s 203

6.9. Use of Modern Inputs by Location, 1977 207

6.10. Farm Sector Modernization in Sichuan by 1980 208

6.11. Grain Production Per Capita in Sichuan 209

6.12. Dispersion of Per Capita Grain Production by County 210

6.13. Correlation between Grain Production and NVAO 211

6.14. Investment and Agricultural Performance in Jingyan 213

7.1. Landholdings of the Landlord Class by County, mid-1930s 218

7.2. Landownership by Class, before Land Reform 219

7.3. Average Farm Size in Sichuan, mid-1930s 223

7.4.   Rents as a Share of Output in Sichuan and China, 1930s   226

7.5.   Incomes by Caste in Liangshan, early 1950s   231

7.6.   The Tax Burden in Sichuan during the 1930s   234

7.7.   Percentage of Landlord-Owned Arable Land by Landlord Type, 1935   236

7.8.   Landownership per Warlord Household, 1935   237

7.9.   Percentage of Farm Households in Debt in Sichuan, 1930s   239

7.10. Mortgage Interest Rates in Sichuan, mid-1930s   240

7.11. Retail Food Prices in Chengdu and Chongqing, 1928–1940   248

7.12. The Fiscal Deficit of Liu Xiang's 21st Army, 1928–1933   250

8.1.   Rural Gini Coefficients for LDCs in the 1970s   260

8.2.   Collective-Income Differentials in Guanghan County, 1977–1978   261

8.3.   Spatial Variation in Capabilities within Sichuan, 1983   265

8.4.   Within-County Income Distribution in Sichuan, 1983   266

8.5.   Net Per Capita Incomes by Household Type, 1978–1984   272

9.1.   Per Capita Food Consumption in Sichuan, 1931–1936 and 1937   283

9.2.   Official Estimates of Population, 1935–1945   284

9.3.   Production of Rice, 1931–1938 and 1956–1963   285

9.4.   Retail Prices of Milled Rice and Corn by Region, January–June 1936   290

9.5.   The Great Leap Famine in the Provinces   293

9.6.   Estimates of Crude Death Rates in China, 1957–1963   295

9.7.   Demographic Trends in Sichuan and China, 1955–1964   296

9.8.   True Excess Mortality in Sichuan: Some Alternative Estimates   297

9.9.   The Spatial Impact of the 1958–1962 Sichuan Famine   301

10.1. Grain Availability in Sichuan, 1955–1964   307

10.2. The Collapse of Output   314

10.3. Food Availability during the Leap in Sichuan and China   317

10.4. Grain Output, Yield, and Area in Shifang during the Leap   318

10.5. Accumulation in Sichuan and China, 1957–1963   323

10.6. The Share of Net Sichuan Grain Exports in Output, 1954–1963   325

10.7. Procurement Prices, 1957   331

List of Figures

1. The Provinces of China, 1978   14
2. Population Density in Sichuan, 1982   17
3. Main Cities, Rivers, and Railways of Sichuan, 1978   20
4. Counties and Cities of Sichuan, 1985   140
5. Net Industrial and Agricultural Output Value Per Capita
   by County in Sichuan, 1939–1943   149
6. Net Industrial and Agricultural Output Value Per Capita
   by County in Sichuan, 1982   157
7a. Famine Survivors from the Leap in Sichuan   286
7b. Famine Survivors from the 1930s in Sichuan   287
8. Net Industrial and Agricultural Output Value Per
   Capita, 1985   352

1

Maoist Economic Development, Its Critics, and Sichuan

The Literature

A substantial literature on Maoist economic development now exists in the wake of the progressive release of systematic economic data after 1978. Although considerable doubts remain over many of these statistics, it is recognized that, at their best (for example, the 1982 population census), Chinese figures bear comparison with those issued by other third-world countries. Moreover, whatever their flaws, the internal consistency of State Statistical Bureau data is such that most Western economists have been content to use them as at least the foundation of their analysis. On the basis of these figures, some Western academics have been content to write off Maoist economic development as a complete failure. However, a characteristic of the best work of social scientists has been a strenuous attempt to present a balanced appraisal of the Maoist record. Three good examples of this are the work of Carl Riskin, Mark Selden, and Peter Nolan.

Carl Riskin (1987; 1990*a*; 1990*b*) has paid due tribute to the successes achieved in China during the Maoist era. He has noted that the Maoist experience demonstrates the ability of centrally planned economies to grow rapidly and to meet the basic needs of their populations (1987: 3–4). Moreover, partly as a result of the establishment of an effective system of rural relief, health care, and sanitation, China was able to attain a level of life expectancy in excess of the norms achieved by poor countries at comparable levels of per capita income. Maoist investment in rural infrastructure was essential for the output growth achieved during the first five years of 'reform' in the 1980s (Riskin, 1990*b*: 51, 57). And the regime proved remarkably adept at smoothing out, and in some respects eliminating, class-based income inequalities.

Riskin nevertheless emphasizes a number of flaws in Maoist theory and practice. In general terms, Mao's failure was his inability to devise an alternative to Soviet-style central economic planning on the one hand and to market capitalism on the other. This underlying difficulty is evident across a wide range of economic indicators. For example, per capita foodgrain availability remained stagnant during the late Maoist period and fell well below subsistence during the Great Leap Forward (Riskin, 1987: ch. 6; 1990*a*). High rates of investment were partially offset by a secular rise in the marginal capital–output ratio, especially in the urban industrial sector. More-over, the *overall* record on income distribution was rather un-distinguished, mainly because of the preoccupation with intra-rural and intra-urban class-based income inequality. In some respects—for a leadership that had made revolution in the name of the peasantry— the greatest failure lay in the widening of the income gap between the rural and urban sectors. Despite a wage freeze for most of the 1960s and 1970s, the divergent trajectories of agricultural and industrial labour productivity led to an inexorable increase in the differential. Moreover, the Maoist development strategy paid scant attention to the persistence of large interlocal (or spatial) differentials in liv-ing standards. Although provincial differentials may have narrowed (Riskin, 1987: 229), 'Inequality between [rural] localities was un-doubtedly preserved and even enhanced by restrictions on migration from poorer to richer villages' (p. 237). Most importantly of all, rural poverty persisted into the late 1970s. Indeed, Riskin places great store by the reduction in poverty that occurred after 1978:

A reduction of over 100 million in the number of absolutely poor people in only seven years must be celebrated as a feat of major importance that *accomplishes exactly what economic development is supposed to but often does not*: improve the condition of the most disadvantaged members of society. (Riskin, 1990*b*: 53; emphasis added)

Like many market socialists, and in the spirit of Deng Xiaoping's own slogan, 'Poverty is not socialism', Riskin thus places a great deal of ethical weight on the criterion of absolute poverty reduction.

Riskin's objective, of course, is to explain as well as to describe poor Maoist economic performance. In this he follows the spirit of the overarching Chinese slogan of the early 1980s, 'Readjustment and reform'. He argues that part of the Maoist failure is attributable to bad planning and, especially during the Cultural Revolution, to the absence of central planning (Riskin, 1987: ch. 11). These 'structural' failures, as he calls them, were numerous. Most obviously, the share of accumulation in national income was excessive, and in consequence per capita consumption was squeezed. Within the heavy industrial sector, the energy and transport subsectors were neglected. Services, commerce, and non-productive investment (notably housing) likewise received a very low priority. Nevertheless, Riskin is sceptical about the idea that 'a return to command planning without Maoism was a viable substitute for systemic reform' (1987: 281). Systemic reform, involving a movement towards a much more market-orientated system of resource allocation, was also needed because of the sheer complexity of allocating resources by means of central planning in an increasingly mature economy (p. 4).

There is nothing very neoclassical in this appraisal. In particular, Riskin's analysis makes it abundantly clear that 'the market' is in no sense a sufficient response to the challenge of economic development. Similarly clear is his view that improved economic planning would have led to improved performance in the 1980s, even in the absence of systemic reform.

There are many similarities between this and the analysis of Peter Nolan (1988; Nolan and Dong, 1990*a*; 1990*b*). Nolan argues that the Maoist approach to economic development should be seen as essentially Stalinist, and points to the emphasis on heavy industry, the dominant roles played by state industry and collective farms, and the neglect of foreign trade. The outcome was not unlike that in the USSR, and compares unfavourably with the development records of the East Asian Newly Industrializing Countries after 1950. The Soviet famine of the early 1930s has its counterpart in the Chinese famine of the early 1960s. Living standards in China improved little in the long run, and the presence of regional concentrations of rural poverty in the late 1970s showed the degree to which spatial inequalities persisted. Rates of growth were modest, and many indicators of productivity show either stagnation or a trend decline. Like Riskin, Nolan gives a great deal of emphasis to the poor Maoist record on poverty:

Most Chinese peasants under Mao, despite some improvements since pre-1949, still lived in abysmal poverty . . .   (Nolan, 1988: 10)

Redistribution per se can only go so far in alleviating mass poverty. Growth is essential to take mass living standards beyond a certain level and it is this which must be the overriding goal for a country still at China's low level of development. Equality in poverty, albeit somewhat reduced poverty, is not the most desirable condition.   (Nolan and Dong, 1990*b*: 129).

This should not be taken as an espousal of the precepts of neoclassical economics. Rather, Nolan advocates a Bukharinist approach to development, founded upon a 'strong' (even an authoritarian) state which controls the 'commanding heights' of the economy and which does not hesitate to provide poverty relief, education, and health care for the population. Such a form of 'enlightened despotism' comes close to describing the achievements of the Chinese economy under Mao's direction prior to 1955, but on which the Maoists failed to build in the 1960s and 1970s.

Nolan's assault on the systemic failures of late Maoism is stronger than that of Riskin. Nolan too singles out a number of essentially structural failures in Maoist economic planning, such as the neglect of transport, energy, and consumption. Furthermore, as much of his work is focused on the rural sector, Nolan points to the way in which the intersectoral terms of trade were biased in favour of the urban industrial sector, in that the price paid by the state for the purchase of farm products was well below marginal cost. As a corollary to this analysis, he suggests that the shift in the terms of trade in favour of the farm sector in 1979 did play an important role in promoting the explosive farm sector growth of the early 1980s (Nolan 1988: 77–81). However, he downplays the role of structural failure and, further, suggests that apparent structural failure was *caused* by systemic factors. For example, rising marginal capital–output ratios necessitated higher rates of investment to maintain acceptable rates of output growth. Moreover, in so far as a higher investment share implies stagnant per capita consumption, and given that work incentives depend upon a secular increase in the supply of consumption goods, a vicious circle ensues (p. 55). In addition, whilst recognizing that collectivization *per se* does not make famine inevitable or ensure an absence of material incentives within villages, Nolan suggests that it makes both much more likely, in that there is no countervailing force to act against the will of the state. An independent peasantry, by contrast, is much better able to resist and avoid such outcomes.

Collectivization, indeed, is seen as the principal systemic failure of the Maoist period, given the overwhelming importance of the rural sector in the economy. But other factors played a part, notably the curbs imposed on the growth of non-farm petty commodity production. The failure to allow rural industry to develop contributed significantly to continued peasant poverty, and the absence of such industry in turn reduced the degree of competition faced by state-owned industry. Thus Nolan suggests that many of the successes of the early 1980s stemmed from decollectivization, and that the growth of rural industry was instrumental in the reduction in absolute poverty that occurred over the same period.

Mark Selden's work shares many common features with that of Nolan and Riskin (Selden, 1988; Friedman, Pickowicz, and Selden,

1991). He explicitly lists the developmental achievements of Maoist China as the elimination of property-based inequalities, the reduction of intralocal income inequality, the development of heavy industry via high accumulation, the elimination of foreign control, a slight increase in per capita farm output and per capita urban incomes, and significant gains in nutrition and life expectancy. However, these were offset, especially during the last two Maoist decades, by failures which included stagnation of living standards at a low level, widening urban–rural differentials, persistent rural poverty, growing spatial inequality, stagnant farm and industrial productivity, and the long-run decline of the service sector (Selden, 1988: 15–17). The devastating impact of the famine which followed the Great Leap Forward is also stressed. The poor performance of the Maoist period is contrasted with that of the East Asian NICs, and the Chinese record is viewed as not so vastly superior to that of India when China's famine deaths are considered.

In some respects, however, Selden is much more critical of the Maoist regime. Spatial inequalities, he argues, not only persisted but widened (Friedman, Pickowicz, and Selden, 1991: pp. xviii, xxii). This was partly because some villages and localities received favourable treatment from central government but also, and perhaps more importantly, because the suppression of the market eliminated a range of income-earning opportunities for poor areas. In consequence, villages not only declined in relative terms but also absolutely, at least in Hebei province's Raoyang county. Selden also stresses the coercive aspect of the late Maoist regime, suggesting that the centralization of power at a national and, in particular, at a local level led to the arbitrary exercise of force in the service of entrenched vested interests.

The centrality of state power and leadership preferences in socialist China made the nature of state goals and organizations decisive. There were no institutional checks on arbitrariness, coercion and abuse of power . . . [it] rendered patriotic supporters in the countryside victims of an unmitigated disaster . . . the party, which eliminated property-based structures of inequality, institutionalized its own stratified inequalities. (Friedman, Pickowicz, and Selden, 1991: 282, 285)

Moreover, despite its anti-feudal rhetoric, the Maoist regime unwittingly preserved aspects of the old order towards which the peasantry looked for a refuge from the exercise of state power (Friedman, Pickowicz, and Selden, 1991: 269–70).

Like Nolan and Riskin, Selden suggests that the blame for Maoist failures resided within the system itself. 'Mobilizational collectivism' in particular is singled out for its role in suppressing the market and for making the exercise of coercion possible (Selden, 1988). However, Selden has more recently suggested that even the pre-1955 economic structures of the early Maoist honeymoon were less conducive to development than many had previously thought. The notion that the New Economic Policy of the early 1950s—what might almost be called Chinese Bukharinism—was ideal is dispelled by the gradually emerging reality of rural life during that period.

We found an early strain in socialist dynamics and structures that eventually, as it grew stronger, produced brutal outcomes. These seeds were planted well before 1949 in such systemic factors as a security force set to crush, arbitrarily and mercilessly, those dubbed counter-revolutionary, and a notion of socialism that treated all accumulated wealth as resulting from exploitation. Mao did not suddenly go wrong with the injustices of the 1957–58 anti-rightist campaign or the economic irrationality of the Great Leap. (Friedman, Pickowicz, and Selden, 1991: 273)

Themes and Problems

One theme that merges in the work of Riskin, Nolan, and Selden is the persistence of large spatial concentrations of absolute poverty in the Chinese countryside in the late 1970s. It cannot be denied that any country that fails to eliminate the most obvious aspects of poverty— inadequate supplies of food, clothing, and housing—remains under- developed (though how much weight we should ascribe to this is another matter; see Chapter 5). Moreover, it is universally acknowl- edged that poverty in this sense did remain at the time of Mao's death. However, it is not clear that it is entirely fair to blame the Maoist regime for failing to *eliminate* absolute poverty. The issue of whether the status of counties where average per capita incomes were below a poverty line before 1949 improved after the Revolution seems at least to be worth considering. There is very little on this in the writings of Selden, Nolan, and Riskin; instead, the emphasis was on how much remained to be done. One of the intentions of this book is therefore to discuss the extent of the transformation in spatial aspects of poverty in the long run.

A second theme in the writings mentioned above is that spatial inequalities showed little sign of diminution, and perhaps even widened, during the Maoist period. That is a surprising conclusion, given the emphasis placed on balanced growth (in the regional sense amongst others) in some of Mao's speeches, especially in the mid-1950s. Relatively little systematic work has been done on this, and it deserves a detailed examination.

A third undercurrent in the work of Nolan, Riskin, and Selden is the limited attention paid to non-material components of living standards. To be sure, national trends in capabilities such as life expectancy, infant mortality, and literacy are given considerable weight. However, the *distribution* of these capabilities receives scant attention. That is particularly problematic because one can argue that, if an area enjoys a high level of life expectancy, it ought not to be described as poor even though food consumption or per capita income is very low. In all this, of course, I have been heavily influenced by the work of Amartya Sen and the emphasis he has placed on measures other than opulence as a direct guide to living standards. Nevertheless, it needs to be said at once that it is difficult to treat this issue with the importance it deserves because of a grave lack of data. My intention in this book is merely to say as much as is possible given these data constraints, rather than to make an implicit ethical judgement that poverty is best described and measured in terms of food availability and disposable income. As will become clear, however, it is my view that we need to give much more weight to trends in capabilities in evaluating the Maoist record, and rather less to measures of opulence (see in particular Chapter 2).

Any evaluation of Maoist performance requires a counterfactual: how might the Chinese economy have performed after 1949 with a different system of economic organization or with a different set of planning priorities?

One counterfactual is to assume that a Nationalist government remained in power after 1949, and that it pursued policies similar to those of the Kuomintang in Taiwan. Some have suggested that the outcome would have been similar. Indeed, Rawski has argued that the Republican Chinese economy performed well in terms of growth and that, because markets were competitive, factors of production were paid close to the marginal products such that the income inequalities that did exist did not imply injustice (Rawski, 1989). Given the political instability and external threats during the Nanjing Decade, Rawski concludes that this record ought to be viewed as impressive. Moreover, the growth of the Chinese economy after 1978 ought to be seen as a continuation of the Republican pattern.

Riskin, Selden, and Nolan have little to say about the performance of the Republican economy, although in general they are less impressed than Rawski (see Riskin, 1987: ch. 2, for example). Comparisons between Maoist performance and the development records of

Taiwan and South Korea are drawn, but in general they are wary of making an explicit comparison. That is hardly surprising, given the difficulties inherent in comparing a country as large and diverse as the People's Republic with the much smaller economies of South Korea and Taiwan, which in any case enjoyed favourable economic links with the USA and Japan. Instead, they tend to compare performance under Mao with that of the 1980s, and suggest that many of the successes of the Dengist regime could have been achieved much earlier.

Obviously, this is one way of proceeding. However, there are dangers involved. The difficulty is that one needs to pay very careful attention to the constraints. For example, it has been suggested that British economic growth during the Industrial Revolution was actually very slow (Crafts, 1985). That is especially so in purely statistical terms when compared with the records of modern developing countries. However, the enormous gulf between the technologies available, and the very fact that Britain was the first industrial nation, makes it an unfair comparison. In the Chinese context, two issues need to be addressed. First, one must examine the extent to which China's military and diplomatic isolation constrained her growth, especially as the situation was radically different after 1978. Second, it needs to be considered whether the growth of the 1980s was dependent upon the earlier achievements of the Maoist regime. The standard Feldman-type growth models that coloured the thinking of planners in state socialist countries suggest that consumption growth will be slow in the short run but that the gains from a high investment share will be evident in the long term; and perhaps China had reached that stage by the 1980s. This book will therefore pay considerable attention to the global constraints on Chinese performance in the Maoist era, and also to the extent to which growth in the 1980s was a function of an infrastructural legacy.

Another respect in which the book seeks to build upon certain aspects of the work of Riskin, Selden, and Nolan is by making an explicit comparison of the condition of the Chinese economy in the Republican period with its condition by the late 1980s. Of course, these issues are not entirely neglected by this distinguished troika, but in general their analyses are rather unsystematic. For instance, when the extent of poverty in the late 1970s is discussed, it is usually compared with the norms for developed countries. Similarly, very little work has been done on trends in opulence and capabilities in the long run. The late 1950s are often used as a bench-mark by which to measure consumption and life expectancy in the late 1970s, but there are strong arguments for looking at the situation in the 1930s if we are interested in the precise achievements of the Maoist regime taken as a whole. Only when income distribution is discussed has the position in the 1970s been compared with the 1930s. But even here, a good deal of work needs to be done, not least because (as will become clear below) much of our data on the 1930s are unsatisfactory. For all these reasons, this book aims to make an explicit comparison between late Maoist and Republican China.

If description of trends is important, explanation is central, and it is here that the differences between this work and those of others is most marked. Riskin, Selden, and Nolan acknowledge that some of the failures of the Maoist period are attributable to poor or non-existent planning, notably during the period of the Cultural Revolution. However, the principal cause of poor performance was systemic. The suppression of virtually all forms of market activity in rural and urban sectors had adverse effects upon the growth rate, and therefore both per capita consumption growth and poverty reduction suffered. This book will argue that this interpretation is ill-founded. There were indeed failures during the Maoist period, but these were structural rather than systemic. The system of central planning, I shall suggest, served China rather well.

Unfortunately it is impossible to address all these issues at a national level. The main difficulty lies with the quality of the data for the 1930s (Bramall, 1989*a*). We know very little about GDP per capita and about consumption because of the poor quality of the statistics collected by the National Agricultural Research Bureau on farm output in the late Republican period. Grave doubts, in particular, surround estimates of cultivated and sown area. It is possible to estimate GDP per capita for the 1930s (Liu and Yeh, 1965; Yeh, 1979; Rawski, 1989). However, it is implausible that the biases and data problems of the 1930s were the same in every province. Accordingly, the only way to proceed is to look at the data on each province separately. As far as income distribution data are concerned, no national data exist. Roll's pioneering work (1980) excluded many provinces, covered a single year, and was based upon a series of more or less heroic assumptions. In any case, as is inevitable when the emphasis is on the estimation of overall Gini coefficients, almost nothing is known about the spatial distribution of income. In such circumstances, the delineation of *national* patterns of spatial inequality and poverty from scratch is an impossible task.

Accordingly, this book addresses the issues raised above at a provincial level. Only in this way are the issues manageable. Chapters

2 and 3 look at trends in provincial averages, and try to explain the trends observed. Chapters 4–8 look at distribution (mainly in terms of income but not exclusively so) and how it changed between the 1930s and the late 1970s. The issues of spatial and intralocal income distribution are discussed separately. Chapters 9 and 10 consider at the famine of the early 1960s, discussing both its extent and its causes.

The Case for Sichuan

The province chosen for this analysis of living standards is Sichuan. In making this choice, I was mindful of two considerations. First, I did not want to choose a province with manifest locational advantages. This effectively ruled out China's coastal provinces. These all enjoy significant transportational advantages in terms of coastal shipping, and benefited disproportionately from foreign investment before 1949; some, notably Guangdong, enjoyed significant trade with Hong Kong. On the other hand, I did not wish to select an incredibly backward area of the mainland such as a north-western province or Tibet. Not only was there a long legacy of backwardness to be overcome after 1949 in such areas, but physical geography is anything but conducive to economic development. In particular, the terrain is very rugged— imposing severe transport costs—and water is scarce, so that agricultural development is difficult to achieve. It seems unrealistic to expect an economic miracle to have taken place in areas such as these, even over the course of several decades. It would be equivalent to expecting Britain's Industrial Revolution to have taken place in the Cairngorms.

Instead, I was looking for a province that was close to the China norm in terms of its economic and physical geography, and in terms of its economic history. Of course, it is impossible to find a truly representative province—only China itself is representative of China—but in the end I selected Sichuan.

This is an area in the south-west of China which borders on Tibet. Its surface area is close to that of France, and its population in 1990 was 107 million. In other words, we are talking of what, by European standards would be a large country. Compared to some other parts of China, Sichuan is disadvantaged. There was little foreign investment and little industrialization prior to the Revolution—there was under ten miles of railway within its boundaries in the late 1940s—and there are very few areas of flat land within the province. The western part of the province is part of the Himalayan plateau, and its average elevation exceeds 3,000 metres. The eastern half is a basin consisting of low hills and shallow valleys, the whole surrounded by mountains. It is one of the cloudiest parts of China.

On the other hand, Sichuan does have some advantages from a developmental perspective. By far the most important is that her soils and climate are admirably suited to farming. Winters are very short, with up to 340 frost-free days per annum in much of eastern Sichuan, and rainfall is heavy throughout the year. As a result the province has long enjoyed the title 'granary of heaven' (*tianfu zhiguo*). Despite all this, it was one of the poorer parts of Republican China. Accordingly, it is precisely in provinces like Sichuan that one would expect to see some evidence of economic development after three decades of Maoist rule.

Some idea of Sichuan's relative standing in the early 1950s may be gleaned from Table 1.1. In the case of NDMP p.c., which is a reasonable proxy for GDP p.c., Sichuan was well below the national average in the early 1950s. The same is true for the degree of urbanization. The degree of industrialization is, by contrast, much closer to the Chinese average, which partly reflects the wartime industrialization of the Kuomintang. In terms of the crude death rate, Sichuan's average was somewhat superior to the national average, and actually below that registered in Jiangsu and Zhejiang. It is therefore difficult to generalize about Sichuan's relative standing, except to say that her base was considerably higher than for the north-western provinces but on the whole lower than that attained by the coastal provinces by the early 1950s.

It was in the name of poor provinces such as Sichuan that the revolution was made. At least, that is the impression that is created by some of Mao's speeches, most notably in his 'On the Ten Great Relationships':

In the past our industry was concentrated in the coastal regions. . . . About 70% of all our industry, both light and heavy, is to be found in the coastal regions and only 30% in the interior. This irrational structure is the product of history. The coastal industrial base must be put to full use, but to even out the distribution of industry in the course of its development we must strive to promote industry in the interior . . .   (cited in Selden, 1979: 317)

Of course, theory and practice are not identical. Nevertheless, this does suggest that it was Mao's intention to improve the relative standing of the hinterland. It is therefore not unreasonable to use a part of the Chinese interior as a case study of Maoist economic development in action.

TABLE 1.1. *Sichuan's Relative Backwardness in the 1950s*

	NDMP p.c.[a]	CDR[b]	Urban share[c]	Industry share[d]
Hebei	122	11.6	9.7	17.2
Shanxi	131	13.0	9.4	14.6
Nei Mongol	199	12.7	12.8	8.3
Liaoning	268	8.5	29.0	44.1
Jilin	164	9.2	23.9	25.4
Heilongjiang	253	10.8	28.8	29.3
Jiangsu	112	11.8	12.5	19.3
Zhejiang	121	11.2	12.7	10.0
Anhui	102	13.0	7.7	7.9
Fujian	121	9.0	18.8	18.2
Jiangxi	115	13.6	10.4	13.5
Shandong	99	12.4	4.7	16.2
Henan	92	12.7	7.6	15.0
Hubei	114	12.0	10.4	15.0
Hunan	92	14.0	7.9	11.1
Guangdong[e]	125	10.3	17.5	22.3
Guangxi	77	13.7	9.1	19.9
Sichuan	83	10.0	8.0	14.1
Guizhou	72	8.3	7.2	15.3
Yunnan	94	15.5	4.8	11.9
Shaanxi	116	10.4	10.5	13.5
Gansu	114	11.4	9.6	7.0
Qinghai	143	11.8	11.6	5.9
Ningxia	115	11.3	12.0	4.1
Xinjiang	211	14.9	13.3	11.4
Mean	130	11.4	12.4	15.6
Sichuan as % of mean	64	88	65	90

[a] NDMP p.c. (net domestic material product per capita) is in current yuan, and is the average for 1953–7. From Zhongguo guojia tongjiju (1987) and LSTJ (1990).

[b] CDRs (crude death rates) are per 1,000 and are an average for 1954–7. From LSTJ (1990).

[c] Urban share is the share of the urban population in total population in 1952 except for Fujian (1954), Shandong (1953), Henan (1954), Hubei (1953), Guangdong (1953), Guangxi (1953), and Qinghai (1953). Data from LSTJ (1990) except Shandong, Guangdong, and Qinghai, which are taken from ZGRKTJNJ (1988: 275).

[d] Industry share is the share of industrial output value in NDMP at current prices in 1952. From LSTJ (1990).

[e] The Guangdong data exclude Hainan except in the case of the urban population share.

Sichuan: Physical Geography

The province of Sichuan lies in the south-western part of China and borders on Tibet (Fig. 1). Its capital city is Chengdu and its surface area is equivalent to that of France.

The province divides into two distinct halves. In the eastern part lies the Sichuan (or, by virtue of its soil colour, Red) Basin. This is one of the most fertile areas of China, and well deserves its classical title of *tianfu zhiguo*. Mountains of 2,000–3,000 m. in height separate the Basin on every side from the rest of China, and one consequence of this is an abundance of cloudy days and the local saying *Shu quan fei ri* (in Sichuan, dogs bark at the sun). The climate of the Basin is subtropical. The temperature rarely falls below zero, and on average there are up to 340 frost-free days per year in the eastern part of the Basin. Further north and west around Chengdu, winter lasts longer, and double rice-cropping is impossible unless plastics are used to provide protection against frost during early spring. During the summer, the average temperature for the provincial capital is three to four degrees below the average for eastern China, but it can climb as high as 44 °C in Chongqing, hence its status as one of three 'furnaces' of China (the other two being Nanjing and Wuhan). The terrain is undulating for the most part, and the only significant area of plain is to be found around Chengdu, on the north-western fringe of the Basin.

The physical geography of western Sichuan is very different (Ren, Yang, and Bao, 1985). This area in turn divides into two distinct subregions. To the south and east, on the Yunnan–Guizhou plateau, the elevation averages 1,500 m. and the climate is tropical. Winters are therefore warm, but the elevation ensures that the summers are cool. Thus Kunming, capital of Yunnan province, is usually called 'the city of eternal spring', and conditions in south-western Sichuan are similar. A wide range of tropical flora can be found, and double-rice cropping is a simple matter. In consequence, the valleys of south-western Sichuan, particularly the Anning river valley, are the most fertile in the province.

To the north, however, conditions are altogether more inhospitable. Topographically, the bulk of western Sichuan lies on the Himalayan plateau and has an average elevation of more than 3,000 m. Here is to be found the province's highest mountain, Gongga *shan*, which rises to 7,590 m. and dwarfs the much better-known Emei mountain (3,099 m.) on the south-western edge of the Sichuan Basin. The valleys do enjoy up to 200 frost-free days per annum, and therefore farming

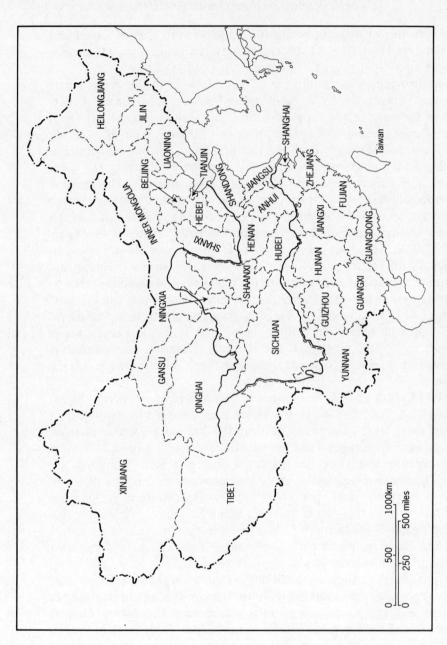

FIG. 1. The Provinces of China, 1978

is commonplace during the summer. However, the available arable area is small, and therefore animal husbandry and forestry are more important to the economy. Western Sichuan is also notable for its great rivers and their deep gorges. The western border of the province rests on the Jinsha ('the river of golden sands') which is the upper part of the Yangzi. Two other great rivers run parallel and close to the Jinsha at this point, the Salween and the Mekong.

Sichuan: Economic Geography

The historical evolution of Sichuan's population before 1953 is shrouded in mystery. For the early seventeenth century, it has been estimated at 5 million, although it fell following the collapse of the Ming dynasty to perhaps 3 million (Smith, 1988). Until recently, it was accepted that population increased thereafter to reach 44 million by the middle of the nineteenth century. However, Skinner (1987) suggests that this is an overestimate; his revised figure is 28.5 million. Between then and 1953, the trend is unclear. Official estimates put the province's population at 52 million by the early 1930s, but this is an underestimate (Bramall 1989a: app. A3); the true figure was probably closer to 56 million. In 1953, the first modern census established that the population (using the post-1955 boundaries) was 65.7 million. From then on it increased rapidly, rising to more than 104 million by 1987.

By international standards, the province's population density falls into the middle of the range (Table 1.2). Nor is Sichuan exceptional by the standards of other Chinese provinces. Many of those of eastern China have population densities which are far higher; that of Jiangsu exceeded 600 persons in 1986. But other parts of China, notably Tibet and the north-west, are much less densely settled; Tibet's population was no more than 2 persons per km^2 and Xinjiang's, at 9 persons, was little higher.

Population density within the province follows elevation very closely (Fig. 2). The average density for western Sichuan in 1982 was 22 persons per km^2, but for the Sichuan Basin it was far higher, at 371 persons. The most densely settled area was the Chengdu plain; in some of the counties close to the provincial capital, there were more than 900 persons per km^2. The central Sichuan Basin was not far behind, with an average density of more than 500 persons.

Ethnically, more than 95% of the population in the 1980s are Han Chinese. Of the ethnic minorities, the two most significant are the Yi

TABLE 1.2. *International Population Densities in 1984*[a]

Country	Density per km^2	Country	Density per km^2
Bangladesh	681	LICs[b]	
Japan	323	(excluding China and India)	32
West Germany	246	USA	25
United Kingdom	230	Sub-Saharan Africa	16
India	228	Australia	2
Sichuan (1982)	175	Mauritania	2
China (1986)	110	Botswana	2
France	100	Mongolia	1

[a] Population data include urban residents. Population densities in city states such as Hong Kong and Singapore was much higher still.

[b] LICs = low-income countries according to the World Bank's classification.

Sources: International—World Bank (1986*b*: 180); China—ZGTJNJ (1987: 91); Sichuan—ZSSWY (1984: 18).

(or Lolo), numbering over 1.5 million at the time of the 1982 census, and some 900,000 Tibetans. These two ethnic groups are concentrated in the south-western and the north-western parts of the province respectively. For example, the Tibetan share in the total population of Aba and Garze prefectures was more than 60% in 1982, whilst the Yi accounted for 45–50% of Liangshan prefecture's inhabitants. An additional area where ethnic minorities dominate is the south-east corner, where the Tujia and Miao peoples together numbered almost 1 million in 1982, or 15–20% of Fuling prefecture's population.

Even in the early 1990s, Sichuan's economy is dominated by her rural sector. The urban population in 1982 accounted for just over 14% of the total population, though Chinese definitions of urban are decidedly problematic (ZGTJNJ, 1983: 106). This was below the Chinese average (21%) which is itself quite typical for a low-income economy (World Bank 1986*b*: 240), although international differences in the definition of 'urban' undermine the usefulness of this comparison. There are four major cities in contemporary Sichuan. Of these, two are relatively minor: Panzhihua (formerly Dukou) in the south-western corner and Zigong on the Yangzi river. Some 1.4 million persons lived in these two in 1982. However, the key urban

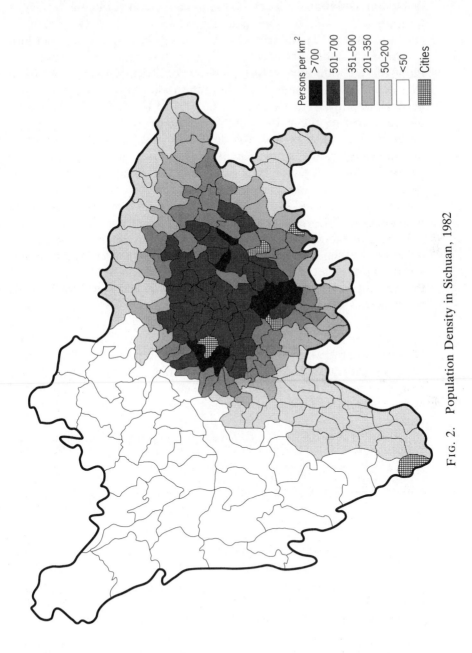

Persons per km²

■ >700
■ 501–700
▦ 351–500
▦ 201–350
▨ 50–200
□ <50
▦ Cities

Fig. 2. Population Density in Sichuan, 1982

centres are Chengdu and Chongqing. Each has a current population (excluding counties under the administrative control of the cities) of more than 2.5 million. Chengdu, famous for its silk for two millennia and visited by Marco Polo, is the provincial capital and cultural centre. Late nineteenth-century Western visitors were amongst its most fervent admirers (Hosie, 1897; von Richthofen, 1903; Bird, 1985) and the city retains its allure in the 1980s. Since 1949, it has also become an important industrial centre. But the industrial capital of Sichuan, and of the entire south-western region, is Chongqing. Its development, much of which is due to its position at the confluence of the Yangzi and Jialing Rivers, dates from the Tang and Song dynasties. However, the process of modern industrialization began only when the city was opened to foreign commerce (1876), accelerating during the Second World War when it became the national capital following the fall of Nanjing in 1939.

If the province's level of urbanization is still limited, the same can no longer be said for its transport infrastructure. But that was not so during the late Qing and Republican eras. On the one hand, the province was physically isolated from the rest of China by its mountainous periphery. Chengdu was linked by road to the Wei valley and Xi'an to the north but this commercial artery was in poor condition by the end of the nineteenth century. Moreover, in the absence of a trans-provincial railway, the only route by which freight could be profitably transported was the Yangzi River. At best, this journey was hazardous because of the strong current and submerged rocks that characterize the Yangzi Gorges between Sichuan and Hubei:

I have found that many of the deterrent perils which are arrayed before the eyes of travellers about to begin a journey are greatly exaggerated and often vanish altogether. Not so the perils of the Yangtze. They fully warrant the worst descriptions which have been given of them. The risks are many and serious, and cannot be provided against by any forethought. (Bird, 1985: 110)

Moreover, before the first successful passage by a powered vessel (1909), the journey upstream was immensely slow and therefore expensive in terms of manpower. According to Morrison (1985), the journey upstream required thirty of thirty-five days. One consequence of this was that famine relief was almost impossible:

The freight on rice and wheat from Hupeh or Hunan to various places in Sz'-chwan would, according to their distance from Chung-king-fu, amount to between one and three times the prime cost of those articles in ordinary years. Besides, from the time a famine is really felt in Sz'-chwan, it would require from three to six months to provide various portions of the province with imported grain, even if a sufficient number of boats were immediately on hand and the whole required stock of grain lay ready for shipment . . . (von Richthofen, 1903: 167)

These problems of *interprovincial* transport had been largely solved by the 1970s. This was partly due to the construction of railways linking Sichuan with the rest of China to north and south. It also reflected the blasting of submerged rocks in the Gorges and the raising of the water level upstream of the Gezhouba dam. The passage of the Yangzi is now a simple matter for powered craft. Some problems remain, notably a lack of shipping capacity; only 60% of demand was being met in the late 1970s (Zhang and Ceng, 1984). But no longer can one regard Sichuan as isolated.

Improvements in *intraprovincial* transportation have been less spectacular (Fig. 3). Compared to many countries, and in terms of both population and surface area the province is a country-equivalent, Sichuan is significantly disadvantaged in being land-locked. That is important because island nations, such as Taiwan and Japan, and coastal provinces of China such as Zhejiang and Jiangsu, are able to rely upon coastal shipping for transportation between *provincial* centres. In the pre-railway age this was of immense importance, given the extremely high cost of overland transportation. Of course, transportation in late-nineteenth-century Sichuan was not impossible. The province's name means 'Four Rivers', and it is true that these, as well as the Yangzi, were important commercial arteries, but it is all too easy to exaggerate their significance. Along the river corridors commerce flourished, but not so in the hinterland: as has been noted, most of eastern Sichuan is undulating rather than flat, and the movement of goods was thus extremely difficult and expensive. Moreover, little was done to supplement these water-courses before 1949. The only railways within the province were two short coal-carrying lines near Chongqing. Chengdu could only be reached by small junks, and even on the Chengdu plain the development of canals was almost non-existent. In short, there was no early modern transport revolution in the province.

By the 1970s, the situation had improved immeasurably. Chengdu was linked to Chongqing by rail in the early 1950s, and the trunk railways linking the province with Kunming, Guiyang, and Xi'an also helped intraprovincial transport. Moreover, the road network was expanded enormously after 1949. By 1981, only one county (Derong) was not accessible by road, and the length of the total network increased by a factor of 9 between 1949 and 1981 (ZSSWY, 1984). Symbolically, however, the construction of a pair of ultra-modern

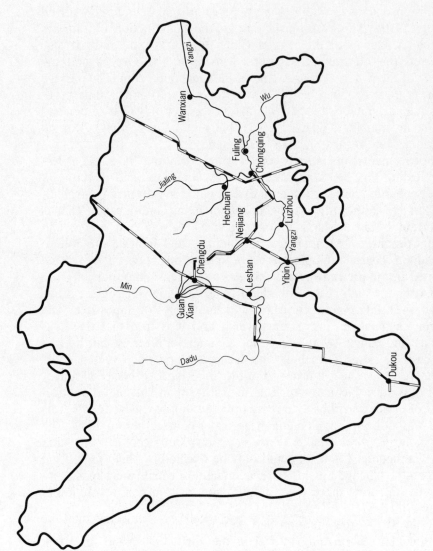

Fig. 3. Main Cities, Rivers, and Railways of Sichuan, 1978

road bridges over the Yangzi and Jialing rivers at Chongqing was at least as important. Even so, the increase in the movement of freight within the province was not spectacular except during the 1950s. 24.7 billion tonne-kilometres of freight were moved in 1978, compared to 9.6 billion in 1957, over a period when population increased from 70 to 100 million (SCTJNJ, 1985: 297). Part of this slow increase reflected national restrictions on private commerce, but it is significant that the movement of freight increased by only 50% between 1978 and 1985 at a time when the province's real NDMP increased by almost 90% (Zhongguo guojia tongjiju, 1987: 343). As a result, the share of transport and communication in NDMP fell from 3.4% in 1978 to 2.5% in 1985 (p. 342). This share was also below the national averages of 3.9% and 3.6% in 1978 and 1985 respectively (ZGTJNJ, 1987: 53).

This extensive investment in infrastructure involved long gestation periods, but one can conceive of Maoist infrastructural investment as shifting out the production possibility curve. By the late 1970s, when most of this investment had been completed, there was extensive scope for rapid output growth. Without this infrastructural legacy, the rapid economic growth of the early 1980s would have been impossible.

Sichuan: Political Change

The boundaries of contemporary Sichuan correspond closely to those of the province during the nineteenth century. However, significant changes took place between 1911 and 1955, including the creation of the new province of Xikang out of western Sichuan and eastern Tibet. In many respects, this was merely a recognition of the existence of an area of territory that was outside the control of both provincial and national government although its boundaries corresponded closely to the old Tibetan province of Kham. Its existence was formally recognized in 1939, and it functioned until 1955 as a fully fledged province. In that year, the two halves of Sichuan were reunited and the territory west of the Jinsha River was returned to Tibet.

These formal boundary changes are much less significant than the political upheavals that followed the 1911 Revolution. In the late Imperial era, Sichuan was firmly under the control of the Emperor who ruled via an appointed governor-general (Adshead, 1984). The latter was also responsible for civil and military administration in neighbouring Guizhou province, on the Tibetan border, and in parts of Yunnan and Hubei. The collapse of the Empire ushered in a period of shifting warlord factions, whose internecine struggles extended to confrontation with elements of the Red Army (in the early 1930s). This struggle for provincial hegemony, broken only by a brief period of armed neutrality between 1928 and 1932, continued until the end of 1934 (Kapp, 1973). In December of that year, the leading warlord was forced by the strain of civil war and continual fighting with Red Army units in northern Sichuan to appeal to Chiang Kaishek for assistance. 1935 therefore saw the gradual reassertion of Nanjing-based Kuomintang control in the province.

The province's fortunes rose briefly following the beginning of the war against Japan, with Chongqing, as national capital, playing host to a stream of Western soldiers and politicians during the Second World War. After VJ day, however, the Kuomintang government returned to Nanjing, and hence the province slipped out of the headlines. It briefly served as a Kuomintang redoubt in 1948 and 1949, but was soon abandoned in favour of Taiwan. Chengdu fell to the Red Army in December 1949, one of the last cities of mainland China to be 'liberated'.

After 1949, political change in Sichuan seems to have followed the national pattern fairly closely. As Goodman (1986) has argued, there is little evidence of the provincial separatism that was a characteristic of the Republican era. But that is not to suggest that Sichuan replicated national trends precisely. She was slower than most provinces to collectivize in the mid-1950s and yet, under the leadership of Li Jingquan, institutional radicalism (the establishment of the commune and the downgrading of material incentives) was much greater during 1958–62. There also appears to have been severe fighting during the 'Cultural Revolution' (1966–8) on the streets of Chengdu and other provincial cities (Mathews, 1971). The pendulum swung in the opposite direction in the 1970s. Zhao Ziyang was appointed as provincial party secretary in 1975, and under his direction a gradual transition to a market-oriented economy took place. Sichuan was by no means one of the first provinces to decollectivize (in the sense of restoring the *household* as the principal organizational unit in the countryside) but it was in the van of the more general movement away from central planning in the countryside (Bramall, 1989*a*).

Sichuan: Phases of Industrialization

Agriculture has remained the dominant economic sector in Sichuan throughout the twentieth century. However, little is known about its quantitative aspects in either the late Qing or the early Republican periods. The conventional wisdom is that Sichuan prospered during the Imperial twilight (Adshead, 1984). But this interpretation is not very convincing. Almost nothing is known of trends in population, yields, and sown area; in addition, Adshead pays too little attention to the famines that occurred in 1872–3 and at the end of the century. As for the early Republic, little is known of the economic history, although Kapp (1973) has shed much light on the politics of the period.

Trends in total and per capita farm output between 1931 and 1978 are discussed in some detail in Chapter 2 (see also Bramall, 1989*a*). We anticipate that discussion somewhat by examining Sichuan's unimpressive growth record, particularly compared with performance *after* 1978. The main features of the post-1978 period are summarized in Table 1.3.

Although a number of problems have emerged since 1984, including stagnant grain output, declining investment in rural infrastructure, and growing income differentials, the magnitude of Sichuan's transformation is undeniable. Key elements in this process were decollectivization, a shift in the intersectoral terms of trade towards the farm sector, and the removal of restrictions on rural commerce. Together, these had the effect of revitalizing the farm sector and promoting the growth of collectively owned rural industry. That this growth was able to take place without any sustained increase in infrastructural investment demonstrates the considerable unexploited potential of the rural sector during the late Maoist era.

The process of industrialization in the province falls into five periods. The first period of growth occurred following the opening of Chongqing to foreign trade. Modern factory industry was established for the first time during these years, though salt production at Zigong has a much longer history (Zigong shi jingji yanjiusuo, 1985; Peng and Chen, 1985; Zelin, 1988). Most of the new industries produced consumer goods (such as matches and textiles) but not all; for example, a power-generating company was founded in 1905 (Fu, 1983). However, the development of a producer goods sector was far more rapid during the next two phases of industrialization in 1928–32 and 1937–45. In both cases, this pattern was determined by the exigencies of war. During the relatively stable years of warlord government at the end of the 1920s, heavy industry developed apace in Chongqing. For example, the famous Minsheng company was founded in 1925, specializing initially in shipping but gradually diversifying into coal-mining (and associated rail lines) and machine-tool production (Kapp,

TABLE 1.3.   *Rural Modernization in Sichuan since 1978*

	Agr. output growth[a] (% p.a.)	Grain output p.c.[b] (kg.)	Net peasant income p.c.[c] (currect yuan)	Crude death rate[d] (per 1,000)	Rural ind.[e] (%)
1978	13.9	329	127	7.0	9.2
1979	9.0	344	156	6.9	9.7
1980	9.2	350	188	6.8	10.0
1981	4.0	349	221	7.0	10.1
1982	11.6	383	256	7.6	10.4
1983	4.1	398	258	7.1	10.0
1984	9.3	403	287	7.1	11.4
1985	2.8	376	315	7.3	12.2
1986	3.6	380	338	6.9	13.6
1987	2.5	375	369	7.0	14.3
1988	1.7	366	449	6.6	15.6
1989	1.0	381	494	7.3	15.6

[a] Agricultural output growth is measured by the growth of the net value of agricultural output at comparable prices. Rural industrial output value is excluded. Calculated from data in LSTJ (1990: 694).

[b] In terms of unprocessed grain. Calculated from data in LSTJ (1990: 690, 700).

[c] From LSTJ (1990: 720).

[d] From LSTJ (1990: 690).

[e] Refers to the share of township and village (*xiangcun*) industrial output value in the gross value of provincial industrial output, both at constant prices. Calculated from data in LSTJ (1990: 704).

1974; Zheng, 1983). Chongqing's first waterworks and cement plant also date from this period (Wen, 1983; Ning, 1983).

During the Second World War, the process continued, along with some limited import-substitution for consumer goods. The trend in industrial production is evident in Table 1.4.

The process of modern industrialization was, however, concentrated in Leshan and Baxian prefectures; they provided 65% of total 1942 provincial coal production. Traditional handicraft production continued to dominate in the counties of the middle Basin and around Chengdu, though silk and other export products suffered following the closure of the Yangzi in 1937.

TABLE 1.4.   *Output of Selected Producer Goods in Sichuan,*
1931–1943

Commodity	Output	
	1930s	1940s
Coal (000 tons)	673 (1931–7)	2,540 (1942)
Iron (000 tons)	20 (1934)	128 (1942)
Salt (000 tonnes)	371 (1931–6)	464 (1937–43)

Sources: Coal—1931–7: Bramall, (1989*a*: app. A6). 1942: Zhou (1946*b*: 108). Iron—1934: Bramall (1989*a*: app. A6). 1942: Zhou, Hou, and Chen (1946*b*: 109). Salt—Zigong shi jingji yanjiusuo (1985: 212).

The fourth phase of industrial development took place during the 1950s. Net industrial output measured at 1952 prices increased at an average annual rate of 24% (Zhongguo guojia tongjiju, 1987: 343) and the spatial distribution of industry changed as a concentrated effort was made to develop industrial production in and around Chengdu. During the 1960s, attempts were made to establish Sichuan as a strategic area that might provide a base for resistance in the event of an American (or Soviet) attack on eastern China. This period of 'Third-Line' construction (Naughton, 1988) was particularly notable for the development of Dukou as a steel and a national rocket-launching centre. Despite these developments, industrial production grew only slowly in the late 1960s, mainly because of disruption associated with the 'Cultural Revolution'. Indeed, net industrial output (at 1957 prices) fell by 33% in 1967 and by a further 51% in 1968. However, growth accelerated again during the fifth phase (1971–5). During this, the Fourth Five-Year Plan, net industrial output growth (at 1970 prices) averaged 16% per annum (Zhongguo guojia tongjiju, 1987: 343). In essence, this reflected the continuation of 'Third-Line' construction, this time largely undisrupted by political change.

Nevertheless, despite an acceleration in the pace of industrialization after 1949, agriculture remained the dominant sector (in terms of share in value-added) in the late 1970s. Net industrial output remained low by both international and Chinese standards.

2

Sichuan's Development Record

Introduction

The province of Sichuan occupies an illustrious position in Chinese history. She was the repository of the values of the Han dynasty during the period of the Three Kingdoms (third century AD) and a refuge for scholars fleeing from Chang'an during the disintegration of the Tang dynasty in the tenth century; she was home to the great Tang poets, Li Bai and Du Fu. Above all, Sichuan was the Heavenly Kingdom, enveloped in mist and surrounded by mountain walls but blessed with abundant rainfall and a warm climate, truly a land of peace and plenty.

Such at least is the legend. The reality of life in Sichuan, even during the supposedly halcyon days of the late Qing Empire (Adshead, 1984), was altogether different:

Szechuan is a rich and superb province of boundless resources, and I believe from what I saw and heard, that the trading and farming classes are very well off, and are able to afford many luxuries, but I certainly saw several over-crowded regions of the 'Red Basin', where the condition of the people deeply moved my sympathy and pity, for a docile, cheerful, industrious, harmless population, free, as rural poverty is apt to be from crime and gross vice, is giving the utmost of its strength for a wage which never permits to man, wife, or child the comfortable sensation of satiety, and which when rice rises in price changes the habitual short commons into starvation.   (Bird, 1985: 243)

Conditions in the 1930s and 1940s were allegedly even worse:

Walled off by mountains through which the Yangtse Gorges were still the only entrance, Szechuan in 1937 was a backwater where the old unregenerate ways of China's civil war period survived.   (Peck, 1941: 146)

In the brothels and opium houses of Szechuan, all sorts of opium could be had, from the very fine Yunnan quality to the dross the huakan bearers smoked; and the sordid story of opium was linked with greed of the warlords, their need for money to finance their private wars. Szechuan, the wealthiest province of China, had the poorest people, multitudes in rags, because of decades of tyranny and decades of opium-growing.   (Han, 1982: 112)

The purpose of this chapter is to assess the reality of such claims and, more importantly, to sketch the province's development trajectory between the 1930s and the late 1970s. It considers macroeconomic trends first, before moving on to a discussion of agricultural and industrial performance and ending with an analysis of trends in capabilities.

Macroeconomic Trends

It is difficult to establish macroeconomic trends between the 1930s and the late 1970s with any precision because of the poor quality of data for Republican Sichuan.[1] However, the general trends identified in Table 2.1 are reasonably reliable. They show real per capita output growing at an annual rate of between 0.6% and 1.4% (depending upon which set of relative prices are used). Although this rate of progress is unspectacular, one would be hard put to describe it as long-run stagnation. In comparative perspective, Japanese GDP per capita grew at about 2.1% per annum between 1889 and 1938 (Minami, 1986: 43), whilst at the height of Britain's Industrial Revolution (1801–31) the annual growth rate was only 0.5% (Mathias and Davis, 1989: 30). Of course, Sichuan's record is poor when compared against that of the East Asian NICs and Japan since the Second World War, but then her growth was interrupted by Japanese invasion and the closure of the Yangzi River to trade (1937–45) and by the final stages of the titanic struggle for supremacy between the Kuomintang and the Chinese Communist Party (1945–9). In that context, the province's growth record must be viewed as eminently respectable.

In some respects, a more relevant comparison is between Sichuan and China during the Maoist era, not least because the Revolution had been made in the name of the poor peasant: where in China were there more of these than in the backward and impoverished provinces of the south-west? More importantly, Maoist *policy* aimed explicitly to achieve this end. Thus the system of planning sought to avoid reliance on a 'trickling down' to the western region over the course of several decades; rather, the fruits of Maoist growth in eastern China would be swiftly distributed to the poor and needy provinces of the hinterland to allow them to develop their own industry. This would be accomplished by the redirection of capital. In this process, the rich metropolitan areas of the eastern seaboard would be heavily taxed

---

[1] For a discussion of these and other issues, see Bramall (1989*a*).

TABLE 2.1. *Macroeconomic Trends in Sichuan, 1931–1978*[a]

	1931–6	1975–8	Annual growth (%)[b]
Population (millions)	56.0	96.0	+1.3
At 1952 constant prices			
GDP (million *yuan*)	4,636	14,799	+2.7
GDP per capita (*yuan*)	83	154	+1.4
At 1957 constant prices			
GDP (million *yuan*)	5,644	15,115	+2.3
GDP per capita (*yuan*)	101	157	+1.0
At 1978 constant prices			
GDP (million *yuan*)	8,291	18,213	+1.8
GDP per capita (*yuan*)	148	190	+0.6

[a] These data do not allow for post-1949 boundary changes whereby a part of the pre-1949 province of Xikang was incorporated into Sichuan. However, the population of this predominantly pastoral area was only 1.5 million in 1982, and therefore the impact on growth trends is negligible.

[b] Growth rates are based upon endpoints (1934 and 1977 respectively) only.

Sources: Population—Bramall (1989*a*: 60); GDP estimates—Bramall (1989*a*: 30–1).

and the revenue redistributed by central government. In addition, the cream of the intelligentsia would place their skills and knowledge at the disposal of rural sector, in many cases by sharing the life, toil, and hopes of the peasant. With the old Confucian disdain for manual labour eradicated, and capital movements determined by social rather private rates of return, backward provinces like Sichuan would at last begin to develop.

The classic statement of these ideas was Mao's speech 'On the Ten Great Relationships' of April 1956. This emphasized the need for continued economic development in coastal areas; it is one of Mao's less radical speeches, in that the emphasis throughout is on balance ('walking on two legs'). Nevertheless, here was a clear commitment to the needs of the interior, and there is little doubt that many aspects of national policy were directed to this end. For example, Shanghai was allowed to retain only a very small proportion of its tax revenue for reinvestment before 1980, with the lion's share being siphoned off for allocation by the central government. Some 15 million youths were 'sent down' into the countryside after 1966, and a 'hardship premium' was paid on top of the normal wage rate to attract workers from eastern China to the nascent industries of the west.

However, the most obvious example of Maoist concern for the provinces of the interior is manifested in the programme of 'Third-Front' construction begun in 1964 (see also Naughton, 1988):

The 'third line' construction in Sichuan province started on a large scale in 1964, right after the three years of national economic calamities. To build the 'third line' in south-west China was a decision of strategic importance made by the Party Central Committee and the late Comrade Mao Zedong in the 1960s. During the following decade, a number of major railroads were completed, linking Chengdu with Guiyang, Chengdu with Kunming, Wuhan with Chongqing, and Changsha with Guiyang. In addition, the Panzhihua iron and steel base was completed and went into operation; and a batch of industrial and mining enterprises were set up on virgin soil in Sichuan, Guizhou, and Yunnan provinces. During that period the total investment in Sichuan came to 39.3 billion *yuan*, which was 74.9 percent of the total state industrial investment in Sichuan before 1981—52.62 billion *yuan*. There were altogether over 250 heavy industrial enterprises which were either newly built, expanded, or transferred from China's coastal cities.   (Lin and Gu, 1985: 186)

One might reasonably expect the product of this type of economic strategy to have been a provincial growth rate in excess of that achieved nationally. That this was not the outcome is manifest in Table 2.2.

The Chinese economy in aggregate, despite starting from a higher base, outperformed that of Sichuan as measured by NDMP per capita; whilst the province's per capita real growth rate was around 2.5%, the Chinese average was a full 1% higher per year. This was not because of relatively faster provincial population growth; in fact, Sichuan's population grew at only 1.56% over this period compared to the national rate of 1.96%. When one disaggregates the output trend, it is evident that Sichuan was outperformed in respect of *both* industry and agriculture. Real net industrial output value grew at marginally less than 10% for China as a whole, whereas for Sichuan it averaged 8.8%. Net agricultural output value in real terms declined in both cases, but the fall was greater for Sichuan: in the province, the decline was at a rate of 0.35% per annum compared to 0.25% per annum for China (although, given the poor quality of the underlying data, this contrast is insignificant).

In terms of macroeconomic performance, we can therefore conclude that Sichuan performed perfectly respectably compared to many developing countries but less well than the Chinese economy as a

TABLE 2.2. *Macroeconomic Performance of Sichuan and China[a]*

	NDMP per capita[b] (comparable *yuan*)		Growth per annum (%)
	1953–7	1976–80	1953–7 to 1976–80
Sichuan	75.4	127.9	+2.3
China	126.3	272.8	+3.4

[a] The endpoints chosen for this analysis are 5-year averages. This is in order to avoid bias resulting from harvest fluctuations or other real and monetary shocks. The use of 1949–52 data has been avoided because per capita output levels were abnormally low as a result of war and civil war, whilst post-1980 data take us well into the era of reform; before 1981, when decollectivization began in earnest, the Chinese economic system remained Maoist in its essentials. The reforms of the late 1970s were mainly structural rather than systemic.

[b] NDMP is at comparable prices, and growth rates have been calculated between endpoints only.

Sources: calculated from data on total NDMP and on population given in LSTJ (1990: 2, 6, 690, 694).

whole during the Maoist period, even though there was considerable scope for catching up.

Agriculture and Food Consumption

At a sectoral level, the performance of agriculture was a particular cause for concern. Zhao Ziyang, for one, was aware of many of the failures in the agricultural sector:

The slow progress of agricultural production is a glaring problem in our province. The state has built many factories in Sichuan, which was a strategic decision made by Chairman Mao. Nevertheless, the development of our agriculture lags far behind industrial growth. Compared with 1965, industrial production in 1975 went up by 160 percent, while grain output increased less than 30 percent. This situation must be rapidly rectified. (Zhao Ziyang, translated in Shambaugh, 1982: 23–4)

This analysis is confirmed by the historical record. During the 1930s, the province was essentially self-sufficient in grain. During the

1950s, Sichuan even became a substantial net exporter, playing a critical role in meeting the grain deficits of other provinces by exporting an average of 3.18 billion *jin* of grain (*maoyiliang*) per annum between 1953 and 1957 (ZSSWY, 1984: 148); Sichuan was contributing almost one-third of all interprovincial transfers by 1957 (Walker, 1984: 88). Yet by the late 1970s, the position had been reversed. Sichuan was not only no longer a grain exporter but was forced to import grain from other provinces, on average 0.4 billion *jin* during the 5th Five-Year Plan (1976–80) (ZSSWY, 1984: 148). The capacity of her grain subsector to meet demand was therefore, by this measure, some way below that of the subsector during the Republican period.

This decline is paralleled by the provincial record on food consumption. Food availability was undoubtedly severely restricted during the 1940s in urban centres such as Chengdu and Chongqing. This reflected a combination of Japanese bombing of supply routes and warehouses and labour shortages in the farm sector because of conscription and heavy demand from the construction industry. Throughout most of the 1930s, however, harvests were good and opium cultivation complemented rather than substituted for food production. In consequence, an average of around 2,500 Kcal of food per capita were available for human consumption during the early 1930s. That was well above the notional subsistence requirement of 2,000 Kcal, and it compares favourably with late Meiji Japan. For the latter, Nishikawa cites evidence showing that military rations contained 2,580 Kcal (Nishikawa, 1988: 440), and that average peasant consumption in the 1890s in Yamaguichi prefecture averaged about 2,000 Kcal (p. 438).[2] Moreover, the levels achieved in Sichuan in the 1930s exceeded those in many parts of contemporary South Asia. According to Naseem, more than 70% of Pakistan's rural population consumed less than 1,995 Kcal per capita per day in 1971–2 (cited in Burki, 1988: 75). As for India, a survey covering rural areas in nine states put average (unweighted) calorie consumption at 2,366 Kcal in 1979. The range of consumption was considerable, with Uttar Pradesh averaging only 1,983 Kcal compared to 2,751 Kcal in Karnataka, and in six of the nine states the figure fell below 2,500 Kcal. Nor was 1979 an unusually bad year. Over the years 1975–82, the 1979 average was exceeded only in 1980 and 1981 (Ramachandran, n.d.: 279).[3]

---

[2] This last figure at face value suggests that the Sichuan estimates are implausibly high if one accepts the conventional wisdom that Japan has the status of a development model. However, it should be noted that Nishikawa's estimates for Japan are for grain only, and exclude calories derived from sake, vegetables, vegetable oil, meat, fish, and fruit. He tends to dismiss these other items as insignificant, but it is unlikely that the aggregate was trivial.

[3] The 9 states were Kerala, Tamil Nadu, Karnataka, Andhra Pradesh, Maharashtra, Gujarat, Madhya Pradesh, West Bengal, and Uttar Pradesh.

Chinese estimates of calorie consumption in Sichuan in the late 1970s and early 1980s suggest a situation very similar to that prevailing during the Republican period. On the basis of peasant and urban consumption, income, and expenditure surveys, energy consumption per capita per day was put at 2,834 Kcal and 3,042 Kcal in 1978 and 1982 respectively (Liu, 1988: 370). A national nutrition survey conducted in 1982 arrived at somewhat lower estimates, putting peasant calorie consumption per capita at 2,693 Kcal per day and that of workers and university students at 3,345 and 3,229 Kcal respectively (Liu, 1988: 369).

Unfortunately, these estimates are of scant reliability. The survey data used for the first set of estimates were biased towards high-income areas and refer to 1978, which is very unrepresentative of the mid-1970s (see Bramall, 1989*a* for a discussion). I roughly estimate rural per capita daily grain consumption to have been 480 *jin* in 1978, significantly lower than the survey figure of 517 *jin*. My estimates for 1975, 1976, and 1977 would be about 15% lower still.[4] As for the 1982 data, these clearly fall outside the period of interest to us. In any case, it seems implausible that the average university student consumed as many as 3,200 Kcal per day by then.

More generally, my own estimates of food consumption suggest that *at least* 2,000 Kcal were available during the Maoist twilight in Sichuan; Table 2.3 shows food consumption as estimated from output data for a wide range of foods. However, this is an understatement of true consumption because these data are not comprehensive. Calories derived from fruit, fish, other animal fats, eggs, and especially vegetables must have added at least 200 Kcal per capita per day to the totals in both the 1930s and the late 1970s.

However, even if these revised figures give no hint of a subsistence crisis in the late 1970s, there is no denying the substantial trend fall, nor the deterioration in the quality of the diet compared to the 1930s. The fine-grain share remained approximately constant at just over 60%, but this hides a steep decline in calories derived from rice, which fell from 1,325 to 973 Kcal. To some extent this was compensated for by an increase in calories derived from tubers, particularly sweet potatoes. However, these latter are regarded as an inferior good by most Sichuanese, and this process of substitu-

---

[4] Using available estimates of grain production per capita (SCJJNJ, 1986: 285) and non-food use of grain estimates for 1984 (Nongcun yanjiuzu, 1986: 588) (this source estimates that about 26% of grain was used for industrial, seed, feed, and waste purposes and this does not include that part of the grain ration (*kouliang*) used by households for seed and feed; quite how large this latter was in 1984 is difficult to determine), and allowing for higher urban than rural consumption, I estimate human grain consumption in rural Sichuan as being about 480 *jin*.

TABLE 2.3. *Trends in Daily Food Consumption in Sichuan after 1931*

	Energy (Kcal)		Protein (grams)	
	1931–6	1975–8	1931–6	1975–8
Rice	1,325	973	23	17
Wheat	222	277	7	9
Corn	256	283	6	7
Gaoliang	70	13	1	neg.
Other grains	96	45	3	1
Sweet potatoes	54	220	1	3
Potatoes	neg.	45	neg.	1
Soya beans	83	20	7	2
Broad beans	99	18	7	1
Field peas	71	22	5	2
Sugar	40	15	0	0
Vegetable oil	71	39	0	0
Peanuts	45	8	2	neg.
Meat	77	83	3	3
TOTAL	2,509	2,061	66	46
Percentage shares by food types				
Fine grains	62	61	46	57
Coarse grains	17	17	16	19
Tubers	2	13	1	7
Pulses	10	3	29	10
Others	10	7	7	8

Source:
Energy—Bramall (1989*a*). The figures presented here for 1931–6 are my estimate E, i.e. they are calculated from corrected data on cultivated area and population.
Protein—calculated from data in Bramall (1989*a*) and protein content of different foods given in Piazza (1983: 7).

tion provided tangible evidence for them of how far their diet was deteriorating. The proportion of energy derived from both pulses and others also shows a marked decline.

Trends in protein consumption, as with food energy, show a clear decline between the 1930s and the late 1970s; late Maoist consumption was therefore little better than two-thirds of the level attained before the Revolution. In addition, the quality of protein intake had declined. Proportionately, more came from tubers and fine grains and less from protein-rich foods such as soya beans. None of this is particularly surprising given the much greater emphasis placed on raising grain and tuber production after 1949, but even so the fall in the share of proteins contributed by pulses—from 29% to 10%—still seems remarkable.[5]

These long-run trends in consumption patterns find confirmation in those income and expenditure surveys that are available.[6] These are helpful as guide to trends in food consumption because, in general, the share of expenditure on food in total expenditure is negatively correlated with real income although the relationship can clearly never be linear except over part of the income range (Engel's Law). Accordingly, if real income increased significantly over time in Sichuan, we would expect to see a fall in the food share in total expenditure. In *urban* Chengdu in the late 1930s, expenditure on food as a percentage of total expenditure varied a great deal across social classes. For the military–official–educational class, of which 30 families were surveyed, it averaged 31.7% of total expenditure in 1937 (Hu, 1943*a*: 16).[7] For the 63 families designated as members of the merchant–storekeeper class, the food share in total expenditure was little different at 34.2% (Hu, 1943*b*: 193). However, the claim of food on total expenditure for the labourer–pedlar class was altogether greater. For the 120 families surveyed, the average figure was 63.3% (Hu, 1943*c*: 225). This range understates the true dispersion of food consumption shares, however: the three classes surveyed covered only about 61% of the population of Chengdu (on the basis of 1934 occupational data—Yang and Hu, 1939: 32). The major omission seems to be the great urban underclass of casual labourers, the unemployed, and the destitute. Thus the 63.3% figure quoted for the labourer–pedlar class is probably closer to the median than to the higher end of the range.

---

[5] Tubers fall within the scope of the term 'grain' as used during the Maoist period. So does soya, but evidently this did not ensure a high level of production of the latter.

[6] The reliability of such surveys is questionable. Survey size is small, and post-1949 efforts, using the *dianxing diaocha* (typical example) rather than random sampling methods, are biased towards high-income locations. Moreover, it is not clear how far food grown on small plots of private land is included in the estimates of food consumption. In consequence, survey data is useful only as a check on the broad magnitudes of food consumption over time.

[7] These are the class titles used in the original survey conducted under the auspices of the University of Nanjing.

By comparison, the share of food expenditure in total expenditure on average in Sichuan's urban centres in 1980 was 58.1% (SCTJNJ, 1984: 310). For Chengdu, the figure was 57.8% (Chengdu shi renmin zhengfu jingji yanjiu zhongxin, 1987: 61) and for Chongqing it was 55.1% (*Chongqing nianjian*, 1987: 344). Given that food prices were well below marginal costs because of subsidization in the late 1970s, and that very low house rents made more income available for expenditure, perhaps on food—both of which would tend to raise the food share in total expenditure—these data may well understate the true fall in the food share over time. But we cannot be certain that real incomes increased in the long run, because urban income elasticities of demand for food in Sichuan in the early 1980s were still very high. According to a 1983 survey, the staff and worker income elasticity of demand in Chengdu and Chongqing was 0.71 for food (ranging from 0.31 for grain to 1.26 for eggs) and in the smaller cities of Zigong and Dukou it was 0.75 (*Sichuan sheng jingji yuce shiliji*, 1986: 223). It is therefore probably unwise to reach any firm conclusion given these incomplete and unsatisfactory data, except to say that there is no evidence of either a big fall or a big increase in the share of food expenditure over time.

TABLE 2.4. *International Expenditure and Savings Patterns (% of Total Expenditure)*

	Sichuan[a]	China[a]	USA	Japan	GB	
	1978–80	1978–80	1979	1979	1860	1914
Food	71.8	64.2	16.5	25.2	67.1	63.6
Clothing	11.2	12.6	6.9	7.2	7.3	7.0
Fuel	5.3	6.4	n.a.	n.a.	4.9	4.2
Housing	3.1	5.9	20.3	17.4	14.6	14.1
Daily items	6.3	8.2	6.4	6.2	n.a.	n.a.
Recreation and services	2.5	2.7	8.2	9.0	n.a.	n.a.
Others	0	0	41.7	35.0	6.1	11.1
Average savings propensity	5.4	13.1	n.a.	n.a.	n.a.	n.a.

[a] Data on Sichuan and China are for peasant expenditure only.

Sources: China—ZGTJNJ (1983: 499); Sichuan—ZSSWY (1984: 226); USA, Japan—Wang (1985: 274); GB—Wilkinson (1988: 182).

We can also compare the expenditure patterns of Sichuan's peasants in the late 1970s with those of the peasantry elsewhere in China. If a region is poor, one would expect to find a relatively higher proportion of total expenditure going on food to maintain subsistence levels of consumption. One might even expect to find vindication of the classical/Kaleckian savings function in which 'workers do not save'. These presumptions are borne out if one compares the expenditure patterns, and average savings propensities, of Sichuanese and Chinese peasants in the late 1970s (See Table 2.4).

The percentage of total peasant expenditure going on food was more than seven percentage points higher in Sichuan than in China as a whole, and infinitely greater than in modern Japan or the USA. Yet, as the historical data for the UK indicate, these coefficients are not particularly remarkable. Nor are they unusual compared with those of contemporary LDCs although, as Kueh points out (1988: 649), they are certainly towards the bottom end of the range. In the Chinese context, therefore, Maoist Sichuan emerges as a very poor province. In 1978, the share of food in total expenditure was higher there than in any other Chinese province. In 1979 Sichuan was second to Ningxia, and in 1980 it was the joint leader with Yunnan (Kueh, 1988: 664).[8]

As far as calorie consumption is concerned, Sichuan's national standing was quite favourable if one considers either 1978 or 1982. In 1978, the official national estimate of calorie consumption is 2,311 Kcal (ZGTJNJ, 1983: 509).[9] For Sichuan the figure was 2,332 Kcal (Bramall, 1989*a*), an understatement of true consumption because it excludes vegetables, dairy products, and fruit. By 1982, average provincial peasant per capita daily energy consumption had risen to 2,693 Kcal (Liu, 1988: 368) compared to a national figure of 2,707 Kcal (ZGTJNJ, 1983: 509). According to a detailed 1983 survey which covered 65 counties in different parts of China, the population of the three Sichuan counties included (Wenjiang, Cangxi, and Quxian) averaged calorie consumption of 3,041, 3,105, and 2,693 Kcal per day respec-

---

[8] These Engel coefficients are somewhat misleading, at least if one accepts that food consumption is price-elastic. The high food shares in total consumption for Sichuan in the late 1970s at least partially reflect good harvests and consequent lower food prices. Thus the food share in total expenditure in Sichuan fell both absolutely and compared to other provinces following the poor harvests in the province during 1980 and 1981, when e.g. grain production per capita stagnated at around 350 kg. per capita (SCJJNJ, 1986: 285–6). The same general point applies in comparing Engel coefficients in market and centrally planned economies, because a feature of the latter is that food prices are typically well below marginal cost. In some respects, therefore, a high Engel coefficient is a mark of the success of a planned economy. Nevertheless, this does not alter the general conclusion that the high Engel coefficient for Sichuan indicates that it was one of the poorest provinces in China.

[9] Piazza's estimate (1986: 73) is a little higher at 2,413 Kcal.

tively. Given that the last two were relatively poor counties by Sichuan standards, these levels of consumption are very high and significantly above the national average of 2,615 (Chen *et al.*, 1990: 582).

To be sure, the use of 1978 data is misleading because Sichuan enjoyed an unusually good harvest in that year. Moreover, estimates for 1982 and 1983 obviously reflect the rapid growth in grain output (in particular) that took place in the early 1980s. If instead we use an average for 1975–8, the Sichuan figure is only 2,061 Kcal (Bramall 1989*a*: 19) compared to the national average of 2,287 Kcal (Piazza, 1986: 73). In short, with respect to nutrient availability, Sichuan's performance probably fell somewhat below the national average for the late 1970s.

The most interesting question, of course, is whether food consumption in Sichuan was adequate. Some Chinese academics have taken a pessimistic view even of the *higher* levels of energy intake estimated from the surveys discussed above:

According to a 1982 national nutrition survey, worker and university student average daily energy consumption basically met health requirements but rural per capita daily energy consumption of 2693.45 Kcal fell below this requirement. At the same time that big increases in energy consumption were being achieved, the proportion of calories derived from protein—9.99, 10.23 and 10.02% in 1957, 1978 and 1982 respectively—had hardly changed over twenty-five years and was below the health requirement of 10–14%. (Liu, 1988: 370)

However, it is difficult to take this analysis seriously. There is little point in quoting calorie consumption to two decimal points, and it is equally hard to accept the notion of a 'normal requirement' of more than 2,700 Kcal in the absence of peculiar assumptions about activity rates or population age and sex composition. It is true that this figure is not untypical of some of those mentioned in the more recent Chinese literature. Kueh, for instance, cites a source giving a national urban and rural combined per capita daily requirement of 2,600 Kcal (Kueh, 1988: 655–7). But World Bank estimates of Chinese requirements are a good deal lower than this; energy requirements were put at 2,160 Kcal per day in 1979 (World Bank, 1983: 119) and 2,360 in 1983 (World Bank, 1986*b*: 234). Moreover, World Bank estimates for other low-income countries in 1983 are also much lower than the 2,600–2,700 'norm' for China. The estimate for India is 2,200 Kcal, 2,300 Kcal for Kenya, and just over 2,200 Kcal for Sri Lanka (1986*b*: 234). The same appears true of protein consumption. The per capita daily protein requirement for China for 1979 was estimated at 35 grams by the World Bank (1983: 120), well below Sichuan's actual daily consumption, which averaged 46 grams during 1975–1978.

This is inconclusive, however, because defining 'requirements' is not a simple procedure. Such requirements depend upon the sex ratio, activity rates, and physical size of the population. Thus the food energy requirement for a woman doing very light work has been estimated as 2,200 Kcal per day, whereas 4,000 Kcal are needed by a man doing very heavy physical work (Chen *et al.*, 1990: 17). This is important for two reasons. First, estimates of requirements require a great deal of information, not only about population sex and age composition, but also about activity rates; reliable data on this latter for China are very difficult to come by. Second, we can hardly assume that activity rates remain constant over time. If we assume that activity rates increased significantly after 1978 because of decollectivization— a routine assumption for most economists working on China—the improvement in nutrition that apparently occurred between 1978 and 1983 may be more notional than real. It also needs to be said that the critics of the Maoist regime cannot have it both ways. Critics usually argue that late Maoism 'failed' because its work-force was under-employed in collective farms *and* because calorie supply was in-adequate. But if underemployment was endemic, activity rates would have been correspondingly lower and with them calorific require-ments. In this perspective, calorie consumption per capita per day in Sichuan in the late 1970s of about 2,050 begins to look much more impressive.

We must also recognize that height and body weight may accom-modate itself to notional inadequacies in the quantity and quality of calories provided. Accordingly, the anthropometric data are in some respects a better guide as to the adequacy of nutrition. Unfortunately these data are rather patchy. The fullest information available is for Chengdu and Chongqing school children, and relates to changes be-tween the mid-1950s and 1979. As Piazza points out in his discussion of the Chongqing data, this information is somewhat suspect. Only school children are included (thus excluding illiterates, proportionately more of whom almost certainly came from low-income families), the sample is restricted to a big urban centre, and, most dramatically of all, all unhealthy children were excluded (Piazza, 1986: 133–7). Nevertheless, as he rightly concludes, it is unlikely that the long-run *trend* is distorted by this type of treatment, although that is probably not true in the case of Chengdu because the data there were collected in 1958, at the height of the Great Leap Forward, rather in the less

TABLE 2.5.   *Anthropometric Data*

	Chengdu		Chongqing	
	1958	1979	1956	1979
Heights (cm.) of Chengdu and Chongqing children aged 17				
Male	162	166	160	166
Female	153	156	151	156
Weights (kg.) of Chengdu and Chongqing children aged 17				
Male	49.3	53.2	48.6	53.2
Female	46.7	48.2	44.6	48.2

Sources: Piazza (1986: 210–25); Liu (1988: 362).

troubled year of 1956. The broad results can be seen in Table 2.5.

These data show a clear improvement in the height and weight of urban seventeen-year-olds, although the increases are by no means startling and the average, 5 ft. 6 in., male seventeen-year-old was still small in the late 1970s by Western standards. In comparison with the situation in England during the Industrial Revolution, the heights attained by 1979 were somewhat below that for Sandhurst entrants in 1841, which averaged 172 cm. (Floud, Wachter, and Gregory, 1990: 177). However, they did exceed the average for working-class boys employed in English factories in 1833; the figure for them was only 159 cm. (p. 173).

Moreover, the heights of Sichuan's children seems to have lagged somewhat behind the national average, as Table 2.6 demonstrates. The Sichuan record, as represented by boys aged seven living in Chengdu, was far from being dismal. Chengdu boys were taller at that age than their counterparts in Liuzhou city in Guangxi and those living in Changchun in Jilin. However, these two estimates are rather anomalous. It seems remarkable that a prosperous city such as Changchun should lag in this respect—and located in Manchuria at that—and Liuzhou is not really comparable with the others because it is not a provincial capital. More significantly, perhaps, the Chengdu figure was considerably lower than the urban national average and well below the levels attained in Nanjing, Shanghai, and—especially—Shenyang in the late 1970s.

TABLE 2.6.　*Height of Boys Aged Seven in Urban China, 1979*

City	Province	Height (cm.)	Source
Changchun	Jilin	116.6	Cao (1988: 373)
Liuzhou	Guangxi	117.4	Hong (1988: 358)
Nanjing (1975)	Jiangsu	120.4	Du (1987: 316)
Shijiazhuang	Hebei	120.6	Wang (1987: 424)
Shanghai	Shanghai	122.6	Hu (1987: 327)
Shenyang	Liaoning	128.7	Song (1987: 301)
Chengdu	Sichuan	118.7	Liu (1988: 362)
CHINA URBAN AVERAGE		121.2	ZGRKNJ (1985: 346)

Trends over time for the rural population are much more uncertain. A 1982 survey found that Sichuan's adult urban males were no fewer than 8 cm. taller than their rural counterparts (Liu, 1988: 364), and this rural average of only 160 cm. (5 ft. 3 in.) for an adult male seems remarkably low by international standards. Nevertheless, it is possible that there was some improvement compared to the 1950s because, by Asian standards, such a height is not unprecedented. In late Meiji Japan, for instance, the average height of army recruits fluctuated between 156 and 158 cm. (Hanley, 1988: 465).

In sum, our examination of trends in food consumption suggests that the hypothesis of declining food consumption leading to nutritional inadequacy is not supported by any of the evidence. There is evidence that food consumption per capita declined between the Republican and late Maoist periods in Sichuan. Nevertheless, when food availability is compared to a notional food requirement, and when the anthropometric data are taken into account, there is nothing to suggest chronic undernutrition.

Industrial Performance

It was noted in the previous section that food consumption probably declined between the Republican period and the late 1970s. However, it was at least partially offset by Sichuan's impressive rate of industrialization. Measured at 1978 prices, the share of industry in GDP averaged 29% between 1975 and 1978; using 1952 relative prices, which were much more favourable for industry, the share was no less than 52%. In both cases, the contrast with the 1930s was pronounced: those industrial and mining sectors on which we have information contributed perhaps 2% of GDP during the last decade of the Republic (Bramall, 1989*a*: 30–1). In terms of the increase in physical output, Table 2.7 is arguably more reliable in that it avoids the use of Chinese price data which were related neither to marginal private nor to marginal social costs in any systematic fashion.

The increases in production shown in Table 2.7 are spectacular: coal production grew tenfold, steel production by a factor of 48, and a chemical fertilizer industry was created from scratch. Such trends are fully consistent with the 9% growth rate of real industrial output value identified earlier. Even allowing for the province's very low base in 1952 (by which time wartime industrialization had increased it beyond the level of the 1930s), this growth record bears comparison even with those of post-war Japan and the East Asian NICs.

Indeed, one can hardly overestimate the extent of Sichuan's industrial transformation. Before 1949, Chengdu was a rather sleepy provincial capital, her only industry of the handicraft variety. By 1978, the city walls had come down, the Min River was spanned by a series of modern road bridges, and parts of the old city had been demolished. The environmental costs were considerable, but by the end of the Maoist period Chengdu was ringed with modern factories and fast approaching the status of industrial metropolis, employing more than a million workers by 1980 (Chengdu shi renmin zhengfu jingji yanjiu zhongxin, 1987: 670). Similarly Chongqing. In the early 1940s, this sprawling city had been the industrial centre of south-west China for half a century. Yet her industrial base was negligible: water continued to be carried by hand from the Yangzi River, and immediately before the war with Japan she possessed no more than 583 factories employing a very modest 18,700 workers. A working class barely existed to exercise the minds and attention of the local clandestine CCP branches, and it is unlikely that factory conditions unduly distracted high-ranking CCP visitors such as Zhou Enlai in the early 1940s. For even in 1944, at the height of Chongqing's industrial development and the apogee of the city's international fame, there were still only 2,382 'factories' (Sichuan sheng Zhongguo jingji shi xuehui, 1986: 96–120). By 1982, Chongqing's work-force exceeded 1.4 million (ZGTJNJ, 1983: 49). Moreover, the horizons of the peasantry had been broadened. In the 1940s, they gazed in amazement at the tractors and buses that the war brought. By the late 1970s they were driving them with aplomb.

TABLE 2.7. *Industrial Output Growth in Sichuan after 1952*

Product	1952	1978
Steel (000 tonnes)	50	2,380
Coal (000 tonnes)	3,370	37,940
Cement (000 tonnes)	40	4,550
Electricity (million kWh)	300	13,900
Chemical fertilizer (000 tonnes)	0	1,110
Cloth (million m.)	156	518
Yarn (000 tonnes)	23	100
Bicycles (000)	0	4
Sugar (000 tonnes)	55	126

Source: LSTJ (1990: 706–7).

It is therefore relatively unsurprising that many of Sichuan's economists have regarded this period in the province's history as one of great success:

There is a sound industrial foundation and the output of major products has more than doubled. Since liberation the province has invested the sum of 40.1 billion *yuan* in its capital construction and has initially established an industrial foundation characterised by relatively full categories of sectors and a certain degree of production capacity and a certain level of technology. By the end of 1983, there were 46,000 industrial enterprises of various kinds in the whole province and these enterprises employed about 3.38 million staff members and workers. The province has not only set up industrial enterprises in each of its counties, but has also set up a number of large backbone enterprises with advanced technology and equipment—the products of which are important for the whole nation, including the Panzhihua iron and steel mill, the Emei machinery plant, the Xindu machinery plant, the number 2 heavy machinery plant, the Dazu automobile plant, the Dongfang boiler plant, the Dongfang motor plant, the Dongfang steam turbine plant, the Ziyang locomotive plant, the Sichuan chemical plant, the Luzhou natural gas plant, the Sichuan vinylon plant and the Emei cement plant. . . . In the past, the province could not produce chemical fertilizer, plate glass, special kinds of rolled steel, automobiles, tractors, equipment for power stations, large mines or metallurgical plants, electrical products, chemical fibres, bicycles, sewing machines and wristwatches. But now it has the capacity to carry out batch production of these products. (Xin *et al.*, 1984: 30)

Nevertheless, the province's industrial performance was disappointing in several respects. For one thing, Sichuan continued to lag behind the national norm in terms of the degree of her industrialization. It was noted earlier that the national rate of industrial growth exceeded that achieved by Sichuan, and this meant that the province lagged well behind the national average in terms of absolute per capita output. Table 2.8 here is instructive. Only in the case of chemical fertilizer did per capita output in Sichuan exceed the national level by 1976–80, which is in itself an indication of the extent of the province's backwardness in that it was a key agricultural input. Even Chongqing, her industrial heartland, was dwarfed by the great industrial cities of the east coast. Shanghai employed 4.75 million staff and workers in 1982 (ZGTJNJ, 1983: 45), almost double the combined work-forces of Chongqing and Chengdu. Chongqing may indeed have dominated the Chinese south-west, but it was to shop on Shanghai's Nanjing and Huaihai Roads that the knowledgeable Sichuanese aspired.

Zhao Ziyang, for one, was aware of many of the failures in the province's economic development:

Weakness in the basic industries is another contradiction that needs to be resolved urgently in our effort to speed up Sichuan's construction. Sichuan now has a fairly large industrial production capacity, but it is short in supply of electricity and fuel. As a result, raw materials, including steel products, cannot meet the needs of civilian industry or defence industry, both in terms of variety or quantity. This prevents a considerable portion of industrial operations from running at full capacity and also impedes the process of

TABLE 2.8. *Industrialization Levels in China and Sichuan, late 1970s: Average Per Capita Industrial Production, 1976–1980*

	Sichuan	China
Steel (tonnes)	0.023	0.031
Coal (tonnes)	0.373	0.604
Cement (tonnes)	0.043	0.067
Electricity (kWh)	140.301	263.032
Metal-cutting machine tools (no.)	0.00009	0.0002
Chemical fertilizer (tonnes)	0.010	0.009
Cloth (m.)	5.244	11.563
Bicycles (no.)	0.00008	0.010
Sugar (tonnes)	0.001	0.002

Sources: Sichuan—SCJJNJ (1986: 293–5); ZSSWY (1984: 260–6); ZGRKNJ (1985: 522). China—ZGGY (1985: 43–57); ZGRKTJNJ (1987: 89).

agricultural mechanisation. Therefore we must emphasize fighting the two battles of agriculture and basic industries. (Zhao Ziyang, translated in Shambaugh, 1982: 23–4)

Industrial and mining enterprises in Sichuan are backward in technical equipment and production technique. They lack a full line of production capacity, and their labor productivity remains at a low level. To develop the province's industry at high speed and establish as quickly as possible a relatively complete industrial system, we must, aside from building some necessary factories of advanced technology as required by the state plan, mainly rely on tapping the potentials of existing enterprises, devoting great effort to their technical transformation in order to revamp their backward operation and raise the labor productivity by a big margin. Scientific research in industry must revolve around industrial, technical transformation. Research efforts must focus on certain key problems in order to resolve them in earnest and push production forward. (Zhao Ziyang, translated in Shambaugh, 1982: 48)

To some extent, Zhao's commentaries were conditioned by political considerations. The first piece, written for *Hongqi*, was much in accord with Hua Guofeng's rhetoric in the mid-1970s, and in particular his insistence on the simultaneous development of industry and agriculture. The (second) *Sichuan Ribao* article, and in particular its emphasis on technology, was much more in accord with the emerging Dengist assessment of the ills of the Chinese economy. Furthermore, the problems faced by Sichuan were hardly unique but shared by many parts of China.

Nevertheless, there is unquestionably an important kernel of truth in Zhao's belief that the province remained rather backward in the late 1970s, and this emerges more clearly with respect to certain specific industrial sectors:

. . . our province's light spinning industry has a very weak foundation and has developed slowly. If one compares Sichuan with various coastal provinces, it can be seen that the province lags behind in virtually every area, including equipment, technology and craftsmanship. The textile spinning industry is historically underdeveloped and there is no evidence of the usual process whereby cottage production is replaced by modern industry. In addition, the light spinning industry has been in a state of disequilibrium ever since Liberation. In the thirty years since Liberation, we have developed—at the same time as developing heavy industry—a number of light spinning enterprises designed to fill a variety of gaps within the industry and there can be no question that the light spinning industry has developed to some extent. But up until the present, with the exception of an extremely small number of modern enteprises, the overwhelming majority of firms in Sichuan's light spinning sector lag a long way behind in the areas of capital equipment, technology and craftsmanship. Many of the latter use a combination of modern and traditional methods of production, making do with whatever is available. . . . It can also be seen from analysing the state of Sichuan's light spinning industry that it has not made the most of certain advantageous conditions over the last thirty years. For example, the technical transformation fund available for the industry has not been used for this purpose but instead for increasing capital construction; the slogan "uproot, change and transform" is only rhetoric. Linked with this problem is a deficiency of trained personnel and poor management. Not only are specialist managerial and technical personnel lacking but also those that are available are unevenly distributed throughout the province. Indeed one could go so far as to say that some collective enterprises have no technical personnel at all. In short, the number and quality of technical personnel is not up to the level required by production. Even the Sichuan silk industry, which is of national importance, has no specialist training institute while the food processing and other industries are in an analogous position.   (Gan and Yang, 1984: 219)[10]

A more general problem with China's industrial development was her relatively underdeveloped consumer-goods sector. This was equally true of Maoist Sichuan. As was demonstrated in Table 2.7, the rate of growth of output of producer goods was significantly faster than that of consumer products. This is also apparent from the composition of industrial output. During the period 1953–7, the share of light industry in total gross industrial output value averaged 67%; for 1976 to 1980, the average was only 44% (LSTJ, 1990: 705).

However, it needs to be said that the relatively poor performance of consumer-oriented industry did not lead to stagnant levels of consumption, as Table 2.9 demonstrates. It is true that cotton-cloth consumption was no higher in 1978 than it had been in 1957. However, it is noteworthy that cotton-cloth consumption per head actually fell after 1978 and despite rising incomes. This is due to rising consumption of synthetic cloths, a process that began before 1978. As for the other commodities listed, definite increases took place between the late 1950s and the late Maoist period. Although one cannot describe 5.4 pairs of leather shoes per 100 persons in 1978 as lavish provision, it still represented a level of consumption almost seven times that achieved in 1952.

Moreover, the ownership of consumer goods in rural areas shows a definite trend increase after 1954. In that year, there were a mere 0.02 bicycles per 10,000 peasants; by 1978, the figure had risen to 8.51 per 10,000. Over the same time horizon, the ownership of wrist-watches increasased from 0.08 to 11.75 per 10,000 and that of sewing machines from 0.09 to 9.46 per 10,000 (Nongcun yanjiuzu, 1986: 512). Again,

---

[10] All translations, unless otherwise credited, are mine.

TABLE 2.9. *Trends in Consumption after 1952 in Sichuan:*
Per Capita Consumption Levels—Peasants and Non-Peasants Combined

	Sugar (kg.)	Cotton cloth (m.)	Leather shoes (pairs per 100 persons)	Domestic coal (kg.)
1952	0.7	3.4	0.8	16.3
1957	1.2	5.7	2.7	39.3
1962	1.2	2.4	3.5	65.9
1965	1.5	5.3	n.a.	53.3
1966	1.8	6.0	n.a.	50.2
1970	1.5	6.2	n.a.	44.7
1975	1.5	5.5	3.6	52.1
1978	1.9	5.7	5.4	57.2

Source: SCSHTJZL (1989: 138).

Sichuan's peasants were hardly affluent by 1978, but definite gains had been made. All this suggests that declining food consumption per head, especially after 1957, is *not* indicative of trends in consumption as a whole, although it is the former that has received most attention.

The province was able to achieve this sustained growth in consumption levels despite the inadequacies of her light industry by importing consumer goods from eastern China. According to an official party source:

the proportion of products selling on urban and rural markets in 1981 supplied from outside the province was 32% compared to 10.9% in 1952. The share of inflows for various commodities supplied in 1981 was sugar 54.4%, cigarettes 41.4%, cotton cloth 40.7%, knitting wool 64.9%, sewing machines 78.6% and bicycles 89.5% ...   (ZSSWY, 1984: 510)

Sichuan's growing reliance on imports from other parts of China by the late 1970s is summarized more generally by the data in Table 2.10. These make a mockery of those who suggest that interprovincial trade was negligible during the late Maoist period. On the contrary, poor provinces like Sichuan ran net trade deficits with the rest of the country, and relied by implication on capital inflows to finance the deficit. In one sense, of course, these deficits are an indication of Sichuan's poor industrial performance in the light industrial sphere, but in another sense there is evidence here of regional specialization. While provinces like Sichuan concentrated on the development of the 'Third-Front' heavy industrial base which would provide the means to

TABLE 2.10.   *Sichuan's Trade Balance, 1952–1978*

	1952	1957	1966	1978
Gross commodity imports (selected items)				
Cigarettes (000 cases)	64.2	106.7	251.4	212.6
Cotton clothing (000 pairs)	157.4	746.2	2,893.9	5,246.0
Underclothing (000 pairs)	1,034.5	7,627.3	10,442.4	15,695.8
Cotton cloth (million m.)	43.4	203.0	233.8	198.9
Sewing machines (000)	n.a.	2.4	34.7	170.9
Bicycles (000)	1.1	9.0	25.3	217.6
Wrist-watches (000)	10.2	75.8	165.8	582.7
Radios (000)	n.a.	3.2	86.4	93.9
Gross commodity exports (selected items)				
Vegetable oil (million *jin*)	4.9	44.4	48.2	29.7
Pigs (000 head)	n.a.	862.7	749.0	828.8
Salt (000 tonnes)	83.2	142.1	128.4	56.1
Tea (000 *dan*)	40.7	11.8	92.2	178.4
Silk (000 m.)	n.a.	640.0	855.3	6,785.6
Import and export value (million yuan*)*				
Exports	249	1,039	672	731
Imports	208	649	1,557	2,024
BALANCE	+41	+390	−885	−1,293
BALANCE AS % OF NDMP	+1.1	+5.3	−7.4	−6.3

Sources: SCJJDL (1985: 106); NDMP from LSTJ (1990: 693).

sustain the population of eastern China in the event of an American attack on China's traditional industrial heartland, the eastern provinces provided the consumer goods and capital inflows to support rising consumption levels in the interior.

Moreover, although it is true that producer goods contribute little directly to consumption in the short term, an exclusive focus on consumption and disposable income is an unsatisfactory guide to the long run. Of course, there is no one-for-one link between output and disposable income in any given period. But over the long run, the link is much closer because the production of capital goods—steel, machine tools, and cement—today makes possible the production of consumer goods tomorrow. Furthermore, short-run levels of production of consumer goods can be a very misleading guide to long-run living standards, in that they cannot be maintained in the absence of investment. To be sure, investment may be unproductive, but it is more than arguable that investment contributes just as much to living standards as does consumption. It is for this very reason that GDP is used by most economists as the most reliable guide to non-welfare aspects of the living standard. From this perspective, the relatively poor performance of the light industrial sector is less significant than many have suggested. In both Sichuan and China, the development of heavy industry during the Maoist period laid the foundation for the explosion of the production of consumer goods during the 1980s.

Taken as a whole, it is difficult to argue that industrial performance was anything less than impressive before 1978. Of course there were problems; several industries were technologically backward, the light industrial sector was performing less than ideally, and the overall rate of growth was somewhat below the national average. Nevertheless, the rates of growth achieved in the producer-goods subsector were high, and in achieving these rates of increase the foundation for future consumer-good production was being created. In the short term, consumption levels increased by virtue of growing imports from other parts of China.

Capabilities

Capabilities—the term is of course Sen's—are extremely difficult to measure. It is usual to proxy them by looking at a range of functionings—that is, the achievements of a population. But it is evident that achievements and potential are two quite distinct concepts. Most obviously, a person may choose suicide at forty even though he or she has the capability to live to be seventy. In general, however, functionings serve reasonably well. The terms will therefore be used interchangeably in what follows.

The most remarkable feature of Sichuan's economic development since the mid-1930s is the astounding improvement that has taken place—*despite declining levels of food consumption*. This conclusion is true of a wide variety of indicators, some of which are summarized in Table 2.11.

Male life expectancy increased from perhaps 30 years at birth during the 'Nanjing decade' to 59 years by 1973–5 and to 63 years by 1981. Female life expectancy reached 61 years by the early 1970s and stood at 65 by 1981. The narrower, but arguably at least as important, measure of rural infant mortality fell from perhaps 200 per 1,000 live

TABLE 2.11.   *Trends in Capabilities in Sichuan*

	1930s[a]	1973–5	1981
Life expectancy (years at birth)			
Male	30	59	63
Female	n.a.	61	65
Infant mortality (per 1,000 live births)			
Rural	200	n.a.	43
Illiteracy (% of population aged 12 and over)			
Rural	80	n.a.	34
Urban	n.a.	n.a.	12

[a] The data for the 1930s are in every case problematic. These figures should be taken as indicating rough orders of magnitude, no more. For a discussion, see Bramall (1989a).

Sources: Bramall (1989a: 33–40) for the 1930s; ZGRKNJ (1985: 1065–6); Liu (1988: 130–1); ZGRKTJNJ (1988: 473–5).

births in the 1930s to 43 by 1981. Of women sampled in the retrospective 1982 fertility survey, 90% of those born in peripheral rural areas of the Upper Yangzi macroregion in 1935 were illiterate, compared to only about 30% of those born in the mid-1960s. Virtually none of the female 1981 urban population born in the mid-1960s was illiterate (Lavely *et al.*, 1990: 77). Sichuan's rate of rural illiteracy fell from more than 80% in the 1930s to about 32% by 1981. In some cities, infant mortality was as low as 14 per 1,000 live births. Moreover, it is significant that infant mortality rates exceeded 100 in only 20 of Sichuan's counties, whereas the provincial average was probably double that in the 1930s.

The province still lagged some way behind the national average in respect of certain types of capability by the late 1970s. Male life expectancy of 62.9 years was below that of all but five of China's provinces; the same was true of female life expectancy. A similar general picture emerges from the 1973–5 National Cancer Survey. For the four counties on which data on infant mortality are available (Shifang, Wenjiang, Cangxi, and Quxian), the rates recorded were 50, 91, 75, and 104 respectively (Chen *et al.*, 1990: 98; *Shifang xian zhi*, 1988: 4–38). These were in excess of the national average and well above the rates for 1981. Nevertheless, massive progress had been made compared to the 1930s. Moreover, it is worth noting that the counties on the Chengdu plain (Wenjiang and Shifang) were little better in respect of infant mortality than the other two (suggesting that the benefits of growth were widely dispersed), and, further, that female infant mortality was well below that for males in all three counties.

Nevertheless, it is interesting and perhaps significant that the province did not lag behind in all respects. Rural illiteracy in Sichuan in 1981, standing at 34%, was actually below the national average and less than in a number of more prosperous predominantly rural provinces such as Jiangsu (37%), Shandong (39%), and Fujian (40%) (ZGRKTJNJ, 1988: 474–5). In this respect at least, Sichuan had managed to catch up with the national average. It is wise to bear this in mind before concluding that Maoist emphasis on the need to eliminate differentials between coastal areas of China and the hinterland was mere rhetoric.

Sichuan's achievement (and that of Maoist China) is clearest when her record is contrasted with that of other comparable developing countries. India provides the most obvious example. By 1982–4, the national infant mortality rate in rural areas of India averaged 114 per 1,000, compared to a mere 43 per 1,000 in Sichuan. Perhaps more significantly, given that Sichuan is a 'poor' province by Chinese standards, the highest figure for an Indian state was that for Uttar Pradesh, which stood at 163 (Jain and Visaria, 1988: 96). Even Kerala, the Indian state with the lowest rural infant mortality rate, could do no better than match Sichuan by the early 1980s. Moreover, the secular decline in India was much less marked. In the 1930s, the national infant mortality rate stood at about 180 per 1,000 live births, and its decline largely halted between the early 1960s and 1975 (Jain and Visaria, 1988: 128). According to a recent World Bank report (1989: 54):

The overall death rate has fallen only gradually in India and the infant mortality rate has declined even less rapidly. . . . Official estimates for 1985 show a nearly five-fold differential in infant mortality between Kerala (31) in the South and Uttar Pradesh (142) in the Central Region. However, surveys carried out in 1987 under the auspices of the Family Planning Foundation found infant mortality rates well above 250 in impoverished pockets of Uttar Pradesh and Madhya Pradesh and tribal areas of Orissa.

The same is true if one puts these rates in broader international perspective (Table 2.12). Despite the relatively low level of real GDP per capita attained in China and Sichuan by the early 1980s, their infant mortality rates were incredibly low. China in fact was 84th if

TABLE 2.12.   *Infant Mortality Rates in Developing Countries*

Country	Year	Infant Mortality Rate
India	1988	98
Ethiopia	1988	153
Bangladesh	1988	118
Nigeria	1988	104
Pakistan	1988	108
Indonesia	1988	84
Egypt	1988	83
Very high U5MR[a]	1988	127
High U5MR	1988	83
Rural Sichuan	1981	43

[a] Very high U5MR (under-5 mortality rate) indicates the median infant mortality for all countries with an under-5 mortality rate in excess of 170. High U5MR is for countries with a rate between 95 and 170. The criteria for selection for this table were a U5MR in excess of 95 and a population of over 40 million.

Source: UNICEF (1990: 76).

the UNICEF countries are ranked from highest to lowest in terms of their under-five mortality rates for 1988 (which was little different from that for the early 1980s).

It is evidence from countries such as China that has led to A. K. Sen's emphasis on capabilities as a measure of living standards (Sen, 1981; 1987; Dreze and Sen, 1989). He has argued that the traditional focus of much of the development literature on opulence and commodity entitlements is misplaced. At best, measures such as food availability, the ownership of goods, and commodity consumption provide an oblique guide to living standards. The case of Maoist Sichuan in many respects provides a perfect illustration of Sen's arguments.

Indeed, the remarkable feature of Sichuan's development that has emerged in this chapter is how little growth in living standards, as conventionally measured, took place. It is true that industrial production grew rapidly, and that the consumption of a range of consumer products increased steadily, albeit from a low base. Yet perhaps the most interesting conclusion is that food consumption declined in calorific terms between the Republican period and the time of

Mao's death. Moreover, a significant deterioration in the quality of food consumed occurred over the same time horizon. In conventional assessments of development, this amounts to failure. Even for economists like Riskin, it is a source of concern, the usual argument being that if food consumption had grown more quickly, living standards would have been higher. Riskin, for example, suggests that poor protein quality was a severe problem, and notes a 37.1% rate of stunting in Sichuan as evidence of malnutrition. He argues:

Part of the reason for this emphasis [on raising living standards by Deng after 1978] is the slowness with which living standards rose during the two decades before the beginning of the economic reform movement in the late 1970s. With continued poverty went chronic hunger . . .   (Riskin, 1990a: 331)

Yet the evidence for capabilities relating to Sichuan suggests that this is misleading. It is doubtful at best to talk here of 'chronic hunger'. Riskin's stress on protein quality deficiencies is not substantiated, and the data on stunting usually come from small and unrepresentative samples. If activity rates were low on collective farms prior to the early 1980s, nutritional requirements may well have been lower for a given class of weight and height than in the 1930s. Moreover, it is far from obvious that we should talk of 'slowness' in growth of living standards, given the phenomenal improvements that took place in life expectancy, literacy, and infant mortality in the long run. It is not that Riskin is unaware of trends in capabilities; however, he continues to emphasize food consumption even though, despite a long-run decline, energy and protein availability in the late 1970s were probably adequate.

This is *not* to say that Sichuan had 'succeeded' in terms of living standards by 1978. One obvious sign of this was that life expectancy rose from 62.9 and 64.9 for men and women respectively in 1981 to 66.7 and 68.7 by 1987 (SCSHTJZL, 1989: 53). Many economists writing on China have concluded that much of this was due to the (undoubted) increases in per capita agricultural output that took place between 1978 and 1984. There may be some truth in this. However, and even putting aside likely changes in activity rates and hence calorific requirements, it is not clear that general increases in per capita food availability were decisive. This is because a number of other positive factors were at work in the 1980s. For example, the post-1978 leadership adopted a strongly poverty-focused strategy designed to address the worst aspects of continued regional absolute poverty (Delman, Ostergaard, and Christiansen, 1990). These local improvements in food availability were undoubtedly much more important than the direct impact of higher production levels on the Chengdu plain and the Yangzi valley. Moreover, and despite decollectivization, significant qualitative improvements took place in rural health care, especially in respect of inoculation. As a result of China's rising inoculation rate, she received an award from the United Nations which, via its World Health Organization, had played a key role in designing and monitoring China's immunization programme.[11]

In short, there is reason to suggest that too much attention has been paid in recent years to the failure of the late Maoist regime to achieve dramatic improvements in per capita food availability. The key conclusion seems to be that food consumption was generally sufficient to allow remarkable improvements in life expectancy to take place. This is not to suggest that rising food consumption cannot contribute to improvements in living standards, or that such improvements played no part at all in continued increase in life expectancy during the 1980s. However, a myopic emphasis on general measures of food availability seriously distorts the record of Maoist Sichuan in respect of living standards. Sichuan's record was not flawless, but it was extremely good.

[11] *Beijing Review*, 3–9 June 1991, p. 21.

3

The Roots of Backwardness

The Impossibility of Development?

Sichuan is not Tibet, with its high mountains, enormous distances, and extreme temperatures. Nor does Sichuan suffer from the shortages of water that plague Gansu and much of the Chinese north-west. And any comparison between the province and the icy wastes of Manchuria can only be favourable to the former. In general Sichuan enjoys a favourable inheritance. Much of this stems from the heavy rainfall and lowering clouds that cast such a Stygian gloom over the province. In agriculture, this abundance of water provides good conditions for rice cultivation and it is not surprising that this is the key farm crop. If, by the 1970s, this resource was not being exploited to the full it was because of a lack of complementary inputs such as plastics and electricity (for pumping) and, to a lesser extent, chemical fertilizer. Moreover, the potential for hydro-electricity generation is vast because of the superabundance of broad, fast-flowing rivers. Much recent attention has concentrated on the idea of building a dam in the Gorges of the Yangzi but there is enormous scope for smaller scale projects, especially in western Sichuan. According to Smil, some 61% of potential hydro-electricity is to be found in the south-west but only a fraction of this had been tapped even by the late 1970s (Smil, 1988: 24–30). In addition, there are extensive coal deposits underneath the Sichuan basin. And yet, despite this abundance, the province suffers from crippling power shortages.

Moreover, it is easy to ignore how much potential for industrial development existed in Sichuan even in the early 1930s. Sichuan's highly developed farm sector, epitomized by the area around Chengdu irrigated by the famous Du River dam (*Dujiangyan*), provided a solid foundation upon which an industrial sector could establish itself. Moreover, there are many rivers running through the province which act as conduits for the shipment of goods. These favourable preconditions, and the small fixed-capital requirements of household enterprises, allowed light industry to flourish, and in consequence the province was well served by an extensive handicraft sector making products as diverse as silk, cotton, bamboo products, lacquerware, and processed foodstuffs. As a result, Sichuan's labour force had acquired a considerable range of skills by the early 1930s. It is traditional skills such as these which, in countries as varied as Vietnam and Hungary, have led in the immediate aftermath of 'destalinization' to the rapid establishment of small-scale hairdressing, spinning and weaving, and restaurants. The classic Chinese illustration of this is to be found in Zhejiang's Wenzhou municipality since 1978 (Nolan and Dong, 1990*a*).

Furthermore, in evaluating Sichuan's developmental possibilities, one can hardly ignore one of the current themes in the development literature: that raising consumption levels in a poor country or region can boost growth rates because it raises the quality of the labour force. In other words, for a poor country, the difference between mass consumption and investment in terms of its impact upon growth rates is negligible. None of this is new. The notion of efficiency wages is to be found in Marshall's writings, and was restated by Kalecki in his wide-ranging critique of the 'Stalinist' system; and the 'basic-needs approach' was a hallmark of the writings of, *inter alia*, Streeten during the 1970s. Such notions have only gained wide currency amongst economists because of theoretical formalization during the 1980s. Nevertheless, novel or not, this insight allows a devastating attack upon 'heavy industry first' strategies of industrialization.

Of course, Sichuan was not poised on the brink of 'take-off' in the early 1930s. This does not reflect any pessimism about light industrialization *per se*. Rather, the essential preconditions for any sort of investment—political stability—transparently did not exist in the province during the Republican era. Despite periods of relatively stable warlord rule, the medium-term prospects were at best uncertain. Indeed, it is by no means impossible that political stability was both a necessary and even a sufficient condition for some form of 'take-off' in the Sichuan of the 1930s.

However, this idea that little more than an 'enabling state' adopting an essentially Smithian approach is sufficient for development seems implausible. To be sure, the market provides a formidable engine for growth, but only when supplemented by a state able both to create the infrastructural preconditions for industrialization (the 'developmental state') and to atone for any instances of entrepreneurial failure. The state must also ensure that any income differentials which emerge during the growth process are kept within bounds. The classic illustrations of such a path of development are now increasingly well known, and include Taiwan, South Korea, and, most obviously, Japan, though only in the first of these was income distribution relatively equal in the early stages of development; as Wade has suggested, the East Asian miracle has rested on an amalgam of developmental state and extensive competition (Wade, 1990). Finally, the limited success enjoyed by Sri Lanka, once the epitome of the basic-needs approach to economic development, in the long run sheds a great deal of doubt upon the viability of a consumption-focused programme of growth.

The reality of Sichuan's position in the early 1930s is best judged with reference to the advantages enjoyed by these successful developers. In this perspective, the province's inheritance in the early 1930s was altogether less impressive. Most obviously, it is difficult to think of an area comparable in size to Sichuan and far from the coast which has successfully embarked upon a programme of industrialization. The records, for example, of Afghanistan, Czechoslovakia, Uganda, Zambia, and Botswana are inauspicious. Of course, all these nation-states have endured problems of various kinds, including invasion, civil war, tribalism, and imperialism, but it is still surprising that not one of them has become an advanced industrial nation *if* being land-locked is really no obstacle to economic development. Moreover, even if one looks at the great success story of the USA, it is note-worthy that even now the states of the mid-West remain primary producers, and that per capita incomes lagged behind the national average over the period 1880–1950. For example, the area designated by Easterlin as West North Central increased its per capita income level to a peak of 97% of the national average in 1900, owing to an initial exploitation of the open frontier and mining opportunities; but as industrialization proceeded elsewhere, the region fell back to averaging around 85% of per capita national income (Easterlin, 1971).[1] This is hardly an example of stagnation, of course, but it does give an indication of the problems involved in developing a continental hinterland even when population density is low (in sharp contrast to Sichuan) and natural resources abundant. Finally, the contrasting geography of Sichuan and the coastal economies of Japan, Taiwan, and South Korea hardly needs to be underlined.

In addition, it is important not to forget how primitive the province's industry was in the early 1930s. To be sure, in a modern sense, Sichuan's agriculture was also backward. Nevertheless, yields were high by the international standards of the time and, as has been seen, the sector was capable of generating a surplus above subsistence food requirements. However, the technological gap between Sichuan and

[1] Comprising the states of North Dakota, South Dakota, Minnesota, Iowa, Missouri, Kansas, and Nebraska.

the modern factories of the Western economies was enormous. Even more significantly, the province's industry lagged well behind that of eastern China. Whatever the costs of imperialism may have been for Sunan, the Pearl River delta, and southern Manchuria, the long-run legacy was favourable. Of course, a proportion of fixed assets had either been destroyed during the war or, as in the case of Manchuria, removed by the Soviet Union. Of course, the road and rail network was in ruins. But much of this damage was superficial. Factory sites needed to be restored rather than constructed anew. Railways required new rails and rolling stock rather than the construction of embankments and cuttings from scratch. More importantly, many of the skilled workers and trained technical personnel had come through the war unscathed, precisely because they had been evacuated to Sichuan. Just as the arrival of these evacuees had made wartime industrialization possible in Sichuan, so their departure led to stagnation. For although they left behind tangible evidence of their presence in the form of fixed capital assets, the asset legacy constituted at best a very weak foundation from which to launch an industrial revolution. There is, in fact, not a shred of evidence to suggest that the province was on the verge of 'take-off' at any point before 1949.

Perhaps most significantly of all, given its importance in ensuring effective competition and facilitating the exploitation of the economies of scale that derive from product specialization, the transport sector was woefully underdeveloped. In 1944 (the year in which wartime production peaked), 28% of industrial fixed capital was to be found in the chemicals subsector, 24% in metallurgy, and 15% in mechanical engineering. The combined share of textiles and food-processing was a mere 21%, which gives an idea of the heavy-industry orientation of Sichuan's wartime industrial sector (Sichuan sheng Zhongguo jingji shi xuehui, 1986: 105). However, although much had been accomplished during the war years to develop industrial capacity, and even to exploit the coal reserves around Chongqing to power the new factories, transport remained sadly neglected. For example, work on the Chengdu–Chongqing railway, which was planned eventually to link the provincial capital with Wuhan by running alongside the line of the Yangzi River, had begun as early as 1903 but was still not completed by 1945. There was no other railway operating in the province except a short mineral line near Chongqing. If anything, road transport was in an even worse state. The Imperial road network was decaying even in Isabella Bishop's time (Bird, 1985) and the exigencies of war did little to improve the situation, although the road network continued to expand in size during the 1930s and 1940s (Pai, 1939).

It was not simply that the level of funding was low. Of central government expenditure on economic construction and development between 1939 and 1944, the share of transport never fell below 65% and reached a peak in 1940 of 80% (G. Q. Zhang, 1986: 83). The real problem was that the projects which had priority were of little *post-war* relevance to the provincial economy. The road network in Yunnan linking Sichuan with the Burma road was logical in the circumstances of that war, but it lost most of its relevance after 1945 because Burma was never going to be a major trading partner even if the costs of shipping freight via Yunnan had been lower. The air-bases constructed south of Chengdu and for Chennault's US bomber squadrons in Yunnan were of even less post-war relevance.

Finally, the deficiencies of Sichuan's waterways have passed into legend. The main Yangzi artery linking Sichuan and eastern China was also the most perilous. One Chinese account summarizes the transport situation thus:

Road transport was well described in the phrase 'The road to Shu is hard, harder than going to the heavens' while river transport on the Changjiang, Jialing and other rivers was menaced by dangerous shoals and submerged reefs; these factors severely hindered the development of modern industry. (Gu, 1985: 480)

These observations are confirmed by estimates of the share of transport in national income in the early 1950s. During the 1st Five-Year Plan (1953–7), the share of transport averaged less than 3% in Sichuan (Zhongguo guojia tongjiju, 1987: 342) compared to about 4.2% for China as a whole (ZGTJNJ, 1987: 53). The very extent of Sichuan's inherited backwardness in the transport sphere ensured that economic development would be a slow process in the early stages.

In the light of these considerations, it can be argued that economic development in the long run in Sichuan was conditional on a programme of infrastructural development in the short and medium term. This was the only way to ensure the achievement of the long-run goal of improving living standards. The province's infrastructure was so backward, and its inherited economic geography so unfavourable, that a massive programme of investment was a necessary precondition for economic development.[2] The gestation periods involved were inevitably long, and therefore only during the decade of explosive growth ushered in by 1978 did the programme come to fruition. Alter-

---

[2] This argument is, of course, a variant on the model put forward by Feldman and others for the Soviet Union in the 1920s. The key difference between it and the strategy followed by South Korea and Taiwan is that the last two have placed far more emphasis on infrastructure, and on the development of the subsectors of heavy industry servicing that infrastructure, than did the Soviet Union.

natively, one can express the argument in neoclassical terms. The Maoist period can be conceived of as shifting the production possibility frontier outwards. The Dengist reforms allowed the provincial economy to move 'on to' the production frontier and hence exploit the capacity created in the previous three decades. Consumption might have been raised more quickly before 1978 by adopting a somewhat different economic strategy, even given the strategic constraints outlined below, but only at the price of a much slower rate of long-run growth.

Accordingly, some of the criticism that naturally results from a consideration of the development indicators outlined in the previous chapter is misplaced. Sichuan faced enormous obstacles in setting out upon the road to economic development, and that needs to be remembered before concluding too uncritically that her development record was one of failure. The growth that occurred in the province during the 1980s would have been impossible without the infrastructure that had been so painstakingly created by the Maoist state. The rest of this chapter shows how Maoist economic policy did contribute to a long-run improvement in living standards, even though it was necessarily subordinated to other goals during much of the period.

Planning: Theoretical Issues

It is axiomatic for many that the task of economic development is made more difficult by attempts at central planning. This hypothesis has of course gained in popularity following the movement towards a more market-oriented economy that has taken place in China and in Eastern Europe since the mid-1980s. In China, the key events have occurred since 1978 and have involved decollectivization, greater autonomy for urban industry, the removal of restrictions on the growth of privately owned rural industry, market determination of a number of commodity prices, the gradual creation of stock, money, and labour markets and the encouragement of foreign investment. In the former USSR, the post-Gorbachev era promises much by way of liberalization in the economic sphere (even if as yet little concrete has been achieved).

This attack on planning is not new. 'Liberal' critics of this approach to economic management, such as von Mises, Robbins, and Hayek, have been voicing their disapproval ever since the founding of the USSR. Its novelty lies in the fact that many who were previously defenders of the system now number themselves amongst its critics.

The death of 'socialism' in previously centrally planned economies has prompted a rethink by many on the Left in Western Europe. Central to the opposition of these Western 'revisionists' is the notion that China and the USSR are not, and never have been, 'socialist' in the sense of being forged by democratic processes and responsive to popular needs. In both countries, it is argued, the state has been despotic. Its objective has been the imposition of uniformity rather than the promotion of consumer choice. It has placed too much emphasis on the reduction of relative inequality instead of the elimination of absolute poverty. It has neglected efficient resource allocation in favour of bureaucratic regulation.

The aims of the reforms in both China and the USSR have been set out by prominent economists. Of China, Ma Hong has written (1983: 93, 95):

The present system of economic management in China is a highly centralized one which relies primarily on administrative methods of management. It was basically copied from the Soviet Union during the latter period of Stalin's leadership. China's experience over the past 32 years has revealed many defects in this model. . . . With such an economic structure and managerial methods, socialist commodity production cannot develop rapidly. The sluggishness of the economy and the poor economic results are very much related to the defects in the present economic structure.

Aganbegyan's views on the USSR are not dissimilar (1988: 20):

All other efforts to transform the economy are now coming up against the absence of solutions to the problems of management in the workings of the economic mechanism. At present this mechanism encourages extensive and impedes intensive development. It further complicates the problem by making scientific and technological progress unprofitable and failing to guarantee advantage to those who raise the quality of production. It encourages new construction but makes work on technical reconstruction unprofitable.

The essence of the critique of planning is twofold. First, it is argued, planning leads to allocative inefficiency. The virtue of the market, it is said, is the invisible hand which guides its operation and thereby produces order out of chaos. The result is an allocation of resources which is 'efficient' in the sense that no improvement is possible; that is, no agent can be better off without another being worse off. Unsurprisingly, especially because these conclusions can be given elegant mathematical expression, such a notion has tremendous appeal:

I should like to record that it is a major intellectual achievement. One must be far gone in philistine turpitude not to appreciate the quite surprising nature of this result, or to be unmoved by the elegant means by which it is proved. It establishes the astonishing claim that it is logically possible to describe an economy in which millions of agents, looking no further than their own interests and responding to the sparse information system of prices only, can still attain a coherent economic disposition of resources. (Hahn, 1984: 114)

However, few neoclassical economists have ever claimed—certainly not Hahn—that economies achieve such a state. The conditions required for the existence of a general competitive equilibrium, including the presence of a continuum of seriatim contingent future markets and the absence of agents possessing market power, are so strict that such an outcome is highly implausible. The issue is rather one of second best, in which it is argued that market failures are likely to be less than state failures resulting from interventionist government policies. According to Friedman and Friedman (1980: 51–2):

Government measures also have third-party effects. 'Government failure' no less than 'market failure' arises from 'external' or 'neighbourhood' effects . . . As a result a government attempt to rectify the situation may very well end up making matters worse rather than better—imposing costs on innocent third parties or conferring benefits on lucky bystanders. To finance its activities it must collect taxes, which themselves affect what the taxpayers do—still another third party effect.

Other areas of 'state failure' which have attracted attention in the last two decades include the development of state bureaucracies that quickly develop interests and objectives of their own, and the development of rent-seeking behaviour (particularly corruption).

It should be noted, however, that Friedman and others are *not* suggesting that there is no role for government. But intervention should be limited to those cases where clear benefits are likely and, even here, the onus of proof must be on the proponents of intervention. Whilst this leaves many issues unresolved—no Marxist has ever advocated intervention except where she has expected clear benefits to arise—Friedman's position becomes clear when he lists those countries that he believes correspond to his ideal. These include modern Hong Kong and nineteenth-century Great Britain, the USA and Meiji Japan. Nevertheless, their methods of economic management are evidently far removed from those prevailing in the USSR or China.

The second major criticism of central planning is that it serves to prevent dynamic efficiency by discouraging technical progress. Thus the strength of the market economy lies not in its (supposed) static efficiency but in its ability to generate invention and innovation. The work that has most influenced Western thinking here is that of Schumpeter, who saw the individual entrepreneur as the key agent in the innovation process:

innovations in the economic system do not as a rule take place in such a way that first new wants arise spontaneously in consumers and then the productive apparatus swings round through their pressure. We do not deny the presence of this nexus. It is, however, the producer who as a rule initiates economic change, and consumers are educated by him if necessary; they are, as it were, taught to want new things, or things which differ in some respect or other from those which they have been in the habit of using. (Schumpeter, 1951: 65)

Yet for Schumpeter the key player in the development process, the introducer of 'new combinations of productive means', is not motivated primarily by short-run material gain:

in no sense is his characteristic motivation of the hedonist kind . . . activity of the entrepreneurial type is obviously an obstacle to hedonist enjoyment of those kinds of commodity which are usually acquired by incomes beyond a certain size because their 'consumption' presupposes leisure. Hedonistically, therefore, the conduct which we usually observe in individuals of our type would be irrational. (p. 92)

[Instead, for the entrepreneur . . .] First of all, there is the dream and the will to found a private kingdom, usually, though not necessarily, also a dynasty. . . . Then there is the will to conquer: the impulse to fight, to prove oneself superior to others, to succeed for the sake, not of the fruits of success, but of success itself. . . . Finally, there is the joy of creating, of getting things done, or simply of exercising one's energy and ingenuity. (p. 93)

Schumpeter explicitly denies that he is glorifying the entrepreneur (p. 90 n.). However, it is difficult to see his description in any other light. Moreover, he is quite explicit on the need for entrepreneurship:

possibilities of profit are powerless and unreal if they are not supported by the entrepreneur's personality. . . . We may go still further. The fact that economic systems without development may exist teaches us that individuals who are capable and inclined to carry out such innovations may even not exist at all. (p. 197)

In this Schumpeterian perspective, the slow rates of growth achieved in planned economies stem from the absence of a 'heroic' entrepreneurial class. This is in turn a product of the economic system. Indeed, the literature on planned economies now abounds in illustrations of how centralized economic planning acts as a break on innovation, diffusion, and entrepreneurship. The essential argument is that budget constraints are 'soft' and hence there is no profit incentive to innovate. In addition, planning targets focus on output quantity rather than technical progress and risk-taking, and tight controls on income distribution and inherited wealth preclude the possibility of creating a dynasty which Schumpeter identified as being so important.

This argument receives support from the record of the Soviet Union, which is widely held to have been worse on innovation and diffusion than on invention and the development of scientific knowledge:

The proposition that the Soviet economic system is the source of major constraints on Soviet technological performance is not the sort of proposition that lends itself to rigorous hypothesis-testing. . . . On balance, however, there are strong grounds for believing that in a medium-developed or highly-developed country, an administrative economic system of the Soviet type will tend, other things equal, to generate slower technological innovation and diffusion than a capitalist market economy of the West European or North American type. (Hanson, 1981: 49)

Comparatively little work has been done for China, but many see her experience as not dissimilar from that of the USSR. According to Nolan, one of the problems faced by a planned economy is that its institutional structure leads to the rapid diffusion of useless technologies:

collectives can act as a medium through which both good and bad techniques can be disseminated. In a free market setting, inappropriate new technologies will simply not be purchased or be used experimentally only by a small segment of the peasantry. Enormous nationwide errors become a real possibility with collective farms, especially when operating together with an administratively planned industry which has few incentives to produce products that peasants really want. (Nolan, 1988: 36)

Even amongst those who have in the past been sympathetic to economic planning, doubts have been raised about its impact upon technical progress. The argument here is relatively sophisticated. It has been suggested, in the context of the Soviet Union, that planning worked reasonably well during the 1930s and 1950s when substantial quantities of under-utilized inputs, such as virgin land and under- or unemployed labour, were available. Growth then was a simple matter of increasing the rate of growth of total factor inputs, and the planning system was rather good at that. But since the 1960s, it is argued, the Soviet Union's growth rate has slowed because of a gradual tailing off of input growth and, crucially, the failure of the system to generate growth in total factor productivity. A consensus has thus emerged that planning is more useful in the early rather than the later stages of economic development. In the later stages of development, there is no longer scope for factor input growth, and the system of central planning is incapable of generating rapid factor productivity growth. Or, to use the Lewis terminology (1954), the supply of labour is no longer 'unlimited'.

An example of this line of thinking comes from the writings of Aganbegyan who argues that *perestroika* and *glasnost* are a necessary condition for a successful transition from extensive to intensive development:

One of the hardest problems to solve in the acceleration of the socio-economic development of the country, is that this must be achieved in circumstances of a falling growth of natural productive resources . . . The limited increases in extensive factors in economic growth cannot be relied upon to achieve acceleration of the socio-economic development of the country. The economy must move decisively and rapidly to intensive development and to the acceleration of efficiency through better use of resources . . . (Aganbegyan, 1988: 67, 76)

A further illustration comes from the work of Gomulka. He has argued in a rather unorthodox fashion that command economies are able to achieve high rates of innovation in the short term by virtue of their immense capacity to channel investment and labour resources into such areas. One of his examples supporting this hypothesis is the Soviet Union in the 1950s. In that decade, the USSR had an impressive innovation record because, although the lag between invention and innovation was longer in most cases than in the West, the sheer volume of invention taking place, reflecting the enormous investment in science, education, and R & D, was such that the volume of innovation was also high.

However, Gomulka also argues that it is not possible to sustain such an effort in the long run; something has to be done eventually to improve static efficiency:

A country which has a highly inefficient economic system may still enjoy a high innovation rate provided . . . that the country is prepared to com-pensate for that inefficiency with larger quantities of labour and investment resources . . . This is the reason why in an economy such as that of the Soviet Union, low static efficiency need not be inconsistent with high dynamic efficency . . . However, the Soviet method of compensating for allocative inefficiency and innovation resistance with larger conventional and innovation inputs would cease to be feasible as a way of sustaining a high innovation rate once the initial reserves of these inputs have been exhausted, and, consequently, when the output and investment growth rates have declined substantially. (Gomulka, 1986: 52, 53)

Taken together, the arguments presented above constitute a wide-ranging critique of central planning that depends neither on flimsy theoretical foundations nor on a belief that any intervention *per se* is bad, but rather on the historical experiences of the USSR and China. Seen in this light, the problems of Sichuan are merely part of a more general problem. Economic development in the province failed not because she was in any important sense unique but because she was hampered by the very same system of central planning that stymied national economic development.

These arguments against planning, though strongly argued and often made, are not convincing. One of the interesting aspects of the Gomulka formulation is the recognition that an LDC may initially suffer from endemic under-utilization of factors of production, and therefore that a 'mobilizational' role for planning may indeed exist. This seems particularly relevant in the case of Sichuan precisely because conditions neither in the 1930s nor in the early 1950s were comparable to those in the Soviet Union on the eve of *perestroika*. The latter had already experienced fifty years of rapid economic growth, and therefore the notion that the scope for resource mobilization was limited carries a little more conviction (though by no means enough, as will be argued shortly); but for Sichuan, stagnation of per capita output had been the norm. Accordingly, there is no doubt that great scope for the mobilization of 'surplus' labour existed in the province if only some effective planning body could be established. In this respect, the conclusions drawn by Brown and Li from a survey of farm activity on Mount Emei during the late 1920s are interesting:

The winter months are practically idle ones as far as the farm operations are concerned. There is nothing remunerative done on the farms during the winter months, and, unless the operator travels miles away to timbered areas, he has nothing productive to do. Any occupation which would give him work during the winter months, as well as in June and July, would help him financially without curtailing any of his present farm occupations. (Brown and Li, 1926: 1067–8)

Moreover, the labour force available for productive activities increased very quickly after 1949 in Sichuan as throughout China. The total employed labour force grew from 32.6 million according to the census of 1953 to 54.0 million by that of 1982 (Liu, 1988: 250). Much of this reflected the rapid growth in the province's population, but there is also some evidence that the participation rate increased, especially during the 1950s when there were labour shortages. According to official data, the rural labour force as a percentage of the rural population increased from 42.0 in 1949 to 44.9 by 1957 (Liu, 1988: 277). Those critical of central planning will doubtless argue that this labour could have been absorbed, principally by means of inter-sectoral migration *à la* Lewis, via the operation of the market. However, such an optimistic outcome is improbable. Even supposing that a market demand for labour had existed, obstacles to migration posed by the inadequacies of the transport network and information flows would have been significant. Moreover, it seems highly likely that a large percentage of any labour that did migrate would merely have found itself under- or unemployed in shanty towns of the type that litter the urban periphery in Latin America.

A more fundamental objection to the Gomulka hypothesis is that there is still a mobilizational role for planning even in a mature economy. On a purely empirical plane, it is rather paradoxical that economies such as those of Sweden or West Germany have been characterized by progressively greater planning as the 'level' of economic development has increased. It may well be true that there are likely to be relatively few unemployed resources at a given moment in time (at least if some sort of policy of demand management is being pursued), but it hardly follows that there are no under-employed inputs. It is more plausible to assume that all market economies are characterized by large sectoral differences in factor productivity, precisely because different rates of invention and innovation, as well as changes in the pattern of demand across sectors, are constantly occurring. It follows that the sectoral reallocation of inputs can *always* raise factor productivity, even though there is comparatively little *intrasectoral* static inefficiency; and if one accepts that static *intersectoral* inefficiency exists in a market economy, the case for planning is made. An example of this is provided by the recent experience of the UK economy, which entered the 1970s with her traditional sectors such as textiles, shipping, mining, and steel in obvious decline. Aggregate productivity and output growth rates could have been raised almost as a matter of arithmetic by the transfer of capital and labour to chemicals, electronics, and financial services.

Of course, market signals have led to some such intersectoral transfers, but it is very hard indeed to claim that the pace of transfer has been optimal, in terms either of the time-span or of the social costs incurred. There are a number of obvious reasons for this which include limited information, high mobility costs, and the need for a substantial proportion of the labour force to be retrained. Doubtless a neoclassical economist would point out that the bureaucracy needed to effect such transfers would be immensely inefficient and would have been 'hijacked' by rent-seeking coalitions with goals of their own. Some of this is undeniable, though it is as well perhaps to remember that the notion of a state pursuing its own interests independently of those of 'society' follows from the *assumption* of self-interest imposed in all neoclassical paradigms rather than from any weight of empirical evidence. Moreover, one must not be blind to the bureaucratic problems faced by multinational enterprises, remarkably few of which rely upon market forces to determine intra-enterprise resource allocation. Further, the alleged costs of planning need to be set against the immense static costs incurred in the 'market solution', which invariably include unemployment, alienation, higher mortality rates, industrial unrest, and deskilling. It is far more likely in reality that the cost of 'market failure' in terms of intersectoral resource allocation far outweigh the costs imposed by the establishment of a state apparatus with the objective of accelerating the intersectoral transfer. This conclusion is very much conditioned by the real successes achieved by the Ministry of International Trade and Industry (MITI) in Japan and the French Commissariat du Plan.

Nor is the notion that planned economies are incapable of generating technical progress at the same rate as market economies persuasive. Schumpeter has rightly drawn our attention to the role of entrepreneurship in generating technical progress, but he also argued strongly that there were economies of scale in innovation, that the creation of large firms was essential, and that private-sector monopolies did have important advantages in this respect. One way of achieving this end was by means of the creation of large, state-owned, firms; and, partly for this reason, Schumpeter believed that capitalism would evolve into socialism. An alternative policy solution is for the state to encourage the merger of medium-sized private enterprises, as in much of Western Europe in the 1970s. In addition, it is difficult to see how successful innovation and diffusion can be accomplished without an educated and informed work-force whose time horizon is at least medium-term. One important type of market failure is indeed a limited supply of information, production of which is sub-optimal because many of the benefits are social rather than provate. According to Chakravarty (1987: 43–4):

Inability to carry out the technological transfer so widely regarded as necessary for initiating growth-promoting changes would appear to lie also at least partially in the sphere of information failure—that is, the inability to assess the social value of a particular piece of information. It is extremely doubtful whether the problem can be resolved only in price-theoretic terms. Considerable direct investment in appropriate forms of human capital appear to be necessary too, as the Japanese and Korean experience would suggest.

It is also important to recognize that the inability of a planned economy to generate rapid invention or innovation does not constrain economic development, because all that matters is the ability of the state to exploit the backlog of innovations that all late starters enjoy. Provided the state is capable of the rapid diffusion of new products and processes, a rapid rate of technical progress is possible. This point has recently been made by Amsden in the context of South Korea. For her, late industrializers—that is, economies beginning their development during the twentieth century—rely almost entirely upon diffusion because neither invention nor innovation is necessary:

If industrialization first occurred in England on the basis of invention, and if it occurred in Germany and the United States on the basis of innovation, then it occurs now among 'backward countries' on the basis of learning. (Amsden, 1989: 4)

Planned economies are uniquely placed to exploit these potential gains from learning, in that they can either order firms to adopt a particular type of product/process or they can manipulate relative prices to achieve the same result. Of course, this line of argument is not decisive. It has sometimes been argued, for example, that price adjustment to serve static and dynamic ends is impossible, because it must involve an iterative process of negotiation between enterprise and government which is both time-consuming and complicated. Moreover, as was noted earlier, other economists like Nolan have alleged that administrative diktat may lead to the rapid diffusion of the 'wrong' processes and products.

Ultimately, therefore, the empirical evidence must be decisive in determining whether the process of diffusion is accomplished successfully or unsuccessfully within a planned economy. Many Western economists, as noted earlier, have interpreted the evidence for the Soviet Union in particular as showing that planned economies do indeed perform badly in this regard. However, many writers, this one included, are not convinced. The difficulty is that much of the evidence rests on distinctly tendentious foundations, because the estimation of the rate of technical progress taking place in an economy is extremely difficult. Most of the studies on the Soviet Union have relied upon Cobb–Douglas and CES aggregate production functions with technological progress being calculated as a residual. But this type of measurement is useless.[3] There is no case for associating the residual with technical progress; a whole host of other factors enter into it, most notably economies of scale. Indeed many, like Kaldor, have argued that technical progress and capital formation are inextricably intertwined, and therefore that it is impossible to differentiate between shifts in, and movement along, a production frontier. Furthermore, precise measurement of the residual is impossible, especially for command economies where remarkably little useful information is available on the precise magnitude and quality of capital and labour inputs. These types of argument are particularly strong for the defence sector. For obvious reasons, it is impossible to measure the rate of technical progress in that sector and, given the vast importance of this in command economies, it follows that estimates of technical progress based on the civilian sector understate the overall rate of technical progress. It is entirely realistic to argue that economies like the Soviet Union enjoy a rapid rate of technical progress. Their difficulty is that much of it takes place in the military rather than the civilian sector.

Finally, the allegation that planned economies are necessarily characterized by immense static inefficiency in terms of resource allocation is bogus. The contention that *intrasectoral* static efficiency is higher in a planned than in a market economy is essentially unsubstantiated. Those who write on the subject of 'planning failure' seem oblivious to the waste that is endemic under a market system. Much of this is ignored because of a persistent tendency to equate 'profit' and 'surplus'. As Baran pointed out many years ago (1957), the latter greatly exceeds the former because of the vast quantities of unproductive labour endemic to capitalism: unemployment, advertising, marketing expenditure, and corporate hospitality, to say nothing of the army of supervisory staff paid to force workers and peasants

---

[3] For a lucid summary of many of the issues involved, see Henin (1986: ch. 7). An indication of the problems involved in measuring productivity growth in the Chinese context is provided by the recent work of Chen *et al.* (1988). They show that the value of the capital stock of Chinese state industry during the Maoist period has been overstated in earlier works. This enables them to demonstrate that total and partial factor productivity growth was also much better than previously thought—which requires in turn a more positive appraisal of Maoist economic development. As these new estimates themselves remain problematic, the episode illustrates the dangers involved in basing a regime assessment on the flimsy foundation of production function analysis.

to produce surplus value (Pagano, 1985; Bowles, Gordon, and Weisskopf, 1984). Nor should we forget the direct costs of religion in terms of the diversion of labour and investible funds to 'unproductive' uses. All these are commonplace in 'capitalist' societies, whether they be the Western European economies of the nineteenth century or modern America. None of Marx's original insights into these problems have dulled with the passage of time. Moreover, whilst it is true that central planning in Sichuan, China, and elsewhere has made some important mistakes when it has come to 'picking winners' (the same is true of the limited planning exercised in West Germany, France, and the United Kingdom since the last war), the record of multinational corporations and landowners is hardly any better. These are not trivial issues when one realizes that these activities are not 'small' relative to the size of the economy. They are simply less well publicized.

In short, there are enormous advantages to be had from economic planning. In the very early stages of development, the scope for the mobilization of underemployed and unemployed factors of production is particularly large; but even when the economy matures, intersectoral redeployment of factors remains essential if an economy is to remain competitive, and the process of transfer can be accelerated by means of state intervention. In addition, it is by no means clear that planned economies are inefficient either in terms of their static allocation of resources within sectors or in their ability to generate rapid technical progress. Of course, allocation is Pareto-inefficient, but then so it is in a market economy; and when it comes to second best—how does an imperfect system of planning compare to an imperfect market?—the former does rather well.

It has to be remembered, however, that the evidence is decidedly difficult to interpret. Moreover, it seems more than probable that the experience of countries may differ enormously. Accordingly, it is not enough to rely on evidence from the Soviet Union and elsewhere to make the case for the effectiveness of planning in the Chinese context. The case for planning as a spur rather than an obstacle to economic development in Sichuan must ultimately rest neither on theory nor on the experience of other countries and regions but on the experience of the province itself. The hypothesis that planning served Sichuan well will only hold up if the evidence on that province supports it. To put the point even more baldly: it is all very well to talk about the advantages in principle of planning for Sichuan. We really need evidence for a period in the province's recent history in which economic planning both was tried and was effective. But even more than that is needed. It must also be shown that periods of failure in Sichuan's post-1931 development were not due to planning. To all these issues we now turn.

How Not to Plan: Sichuan During the War Years

The first time that planning was tried in the province was between 1937 and 1945, when Sichuan served as the centre of the resistance offered to the Japanese. Located far from the coast and surrounded by mountains, the province was an ideal strategic rear area and almost invulnerable when defended by an adequately equipped and motivated army; but equipment was also needed and in 1937, whilst it seemed likely that the Western powers would ultimately be drawn into the war against Japan, the only way that it could be provided was by means of indigenous industrialization. With that end in mind, modern machinery and skilled labour was transferred from the coast via the Yangzi to Sichuan. Within the province itself, a sustained effort was launched to develop both heavy industry and to satisfy basic consumer needs.

The scale of this programme was not insignificant, especially in view of the difficulties involved:

Even in ordinary times, transportation facilities in the interior were extremely inadequate, many of the bridges were unable to bear heavy traffic and the Yangtze river was inaccessible to large steamships during part of the year. The section from Ichang upwards to Szechuen was particularly difficult for the movement of such bulky things as machinery. Traffic on the Yangtze river at the end of 1937 and during the early months of 1938 was already crowded with archives of the Central Government to Chungking. To make matters worse, this was the low-water season, and the river was unnavigable to big steamships. (Chin Feng, Vice-Minister of Economic Affairs, cited in Chi, 1939: 5)

Despite these problems, some 40,000 tons of machinery was transferred to the interior (Chi, 1939: 5). By March 1942, 120,000 tonnes and 446 factories had been moved to the interior, of which 90,000 tonnes and 214 factories went to Sichuan (Sichuan sheng Zhongguo jingji shi xuehui, 1986: 103). Of the 2,371 factories operating in Sichuan at the end of 1944, only 98 had been founded before 1937 and no less than 609 were founded in 1942 alone (p. 108).[4]

---

[4] An operation was classified as a factory by the KMT's Ministry of Economics between 1932 and 1937 if it used powered machinery and either employed more than 30 workers or

There is little doubt that these and other war-time developments were a consequence of central economic planning rather than the efforts of the private sector. Only 165 of Sichuan's 1,654 enterprises were run by the central government in 1942, but these accounted for 63% of total industrial asset value (p. 104). Substantial loans were also granted by the state to private enterprises (*China Handbook 1939–45*: 376). Moreover, planning extended beyond the industrial sphere. Against the advice of American 'experts', who believed that price controls were unenforceable in China, they were introduced in 1938 and again in 1943. An even stronger indication of the extent of government intervention was in the field of farm taxation. This took three forms. First, a number of systematic land surveys designed to identify true cultivated and sown area in order to estimate the tax base were introduced. Secondly, land tax was levied in kind rather than in cash, thus reversing traditional practice. Thirdly, forced loans to be paid in the form of grain were instituted. These measures were in response to the hyperinflation of the 1940s, and were designed to ensure a stable food supply for Chongqing's swollen urban population. For example, in Sichuan between July 1944 and June 1945, 19.3 million *shi dan* of rice were collected (taxation and forced loan combined), which amounted to more than a sixth of total rice production (*China Handbook 1939–45*: 199)—hardly an insignificant amount.

However, these measures failed. Indeed the Chinese economy in general, and that of Sichuan in particular, performed spectacularly badly during the war years. Some of the relevant data are summarized in Table 3.1.

As the first column shows, prices fluctuated markedly during the 1930s without showing any definite trend. And the price level even fell in the first years of war. But thereafter, fuelled by high levels of military spending, the inflation rate accelerated to reach hyperinflationary standards by the end of the war. The price controls mentioned above and designed to stem this tide failed completely because of endemic corruption, and because the inadequate transport network led to sharp intraprovincial price variations and hence abundant scope for highly profitable commodity speculation (Eastman, 1986: 596–9). The immediate consequences were the gradual collapse of the market economy and significant changes in the distribution of income. Some groups were beneficiaries, including the Chongqing stonecutters, many relatively small-scale farmers (especially before land tax was levied in

owned assets greater than 10,000 *yuan*. Presumably this definition was also employed during the war years.

TABLE 3.1. *The Economy of Sichuan in Peace and War, 1931–1945*

Year	Price index[a] Food (1937 = 100)	Real wage indices[b]			Agriculture: Output and stocks		
		Stonecutters (Jan.–June 1937 = 100)	Workers (Jan.–June 1937 = 100)	Professors (1937 = 100)	Grain output[c] (million *shi dan*)	Pigs[d] (000 head)	Buffalo[d] (000 head)
1931	116	n.a.	n.a.	n.a.	n.a.	n.a.	n.a.
1932	106	n.a.	n.a.	n.a.	247.5	n.a.	n.a.
1933	73	n.a.	n.a.	n.a.	245.1	n.a.	n.a.
1934	51	n.a.	n.a.	n.a.	236.5	n.a.	n.a.
1935	58	n.a.	n.a.	n.a.	222.8	11,944	2,595
1936	95	n.a.	n.a.	n.a.	200.5	10,278	2,365
1937	100	104	102	100	207.7	9,176	2,106
1938	95	194	155	95	224.1	8,307	1.988
1939	142	348	118	64	228.2	8,616	1,926
1940	490	208	80	26	198.3	8,653	1,875
1941	1,748	126	55	15	181.1	8,712	1,808

TABLE 3.1. (cont.)

| Year | Price index[a] | Real wage indices[b] | | | Agriculture: Output and stocks | | |
	Food (1937 = 100)	Stonecutters (Jan.–June 1937 = 100)	Workers (Jan.–June 1937 = 100)	Professors (1937 = 100)	Grain output[c] (million *shi dan*)	Pigs[d] (000 head)	Buffalo[d] (000 head)
1942	3,992	211	50	12	179.2	8,380	1,790
1943	12,100	231	42	14	192.2	8,384	1,761
1944	45,929	n.a.	43	n.a.	197.8	8,166	1,770
1945	154,168	n.a.	37	n.a.	n.a.	n.a.	n.a.

[a] The index for 1931–7 covers the retail price of milled rice only and comes from Zhongguo nongmin yinhang (1941: 507). The post-1937 index is for wholesale prices and covers all foods, weighted by the share in expenditure. The data come from various editions of *Economic Facts*. Both indices are for Chengdu only.

[b] Chongqing's stonecutters were the only group of industrial workers to experience an increase in real wages during the war, mainly because there was such high demand for air-raid shelter construction; data from Epstein (1949: 10). The column headed 'Workers' covers Chongqing's industrial workers; the source is Xu (1983: 115). The professorial real wage index is for Chengdu-based academics; the source is Y. Y. Wang (1943: 209).

[c] This covers only the 4 major crops—rice, wheat, corn, and sweet potatoes. Sweet-potato output is expressed in grain equivalent terms in the total, using the conversion ratio of 5 kg. of sweet potatoes = 1 kg of grain (the post-1963 CCP conversion norm). Output data refer to unprocessed grain, and constitute 3 year moving averages, and are based upon official estimates of sown area. Sources: Xu (1983: 54–7); *China Handbook 1937–43*: 561–629.

[d] 3-year moving averages. Sources: Xu (1983: 299); *China Handbook 1937–43*: 579–86.

kind), and commodity speculators; but the industrial working class and those on fixed incomes suffered disproportionately. By the end of the war, real wages were barely one-third of their level at the beginning. Although the impact of this on living standards was blunted by subsidies in kind—many workers received at least one meal per day from their employers—it could not cushion the blow completely.

A factor contributing to the inflationary process and hence to the decline in real wages was the poor performance of the agricultural sector. As the last three columns in Table 3.1 show, the output of the principal grains and the size of the animal stock declined steadily between the late 1930s and the end of the war. These trends were not unrelated. Grain output was adversely affected by high rates of taxation, compulsory loans, and labour shortages. This in turn reduced the availability of feed, and hence animal numbers fell. It is just possible that per capita animal numbers and grain production held up well during the war years if one accepts the assumption that the province's population declined because of the conscription of Sichuanese peasants to fight outside the province; precise data on population trends during these years is signally lacking, but, in view of what we know of the influx of refugees, workers, and government employees into the province, this seems unlikely.[5]

Even in the industrial sector, the achievements of wartime planning were transient. There were, admittedly, genuine gains early on. The number of Sichuan's factories which used power-driven machinery increased from 115 pre-war to 1,654 by 1942 and to 2,382 by 1944. Moreover, much of this new industrial development was in the heavy industrial sector, whereas pre-war industry was dominated by the handicraft sector. As a result, some 66% of assets owned by factories using powered machinery were concentrated in the chemical, machine-building, and metallurgy subsectors by 1944 (Sichuan sheng Zhongguo jingji shi xuehui, 1986: 96–120). These trends are reflected in those output data available to us. For example, salt output at Zigong (the main salt-producing centre) increased from about 370,000 tonnes in the 1930s to around 500,000 tonnes by 1940–2 (Zigong shi jingji yanjiusuo, 1985: 212). Neijiang, the leading sugar-producing prefecture, increased its output of white sugar from about 12 million *jin* in the late 1930s to 22 million in 1940 (M. H. Wang, 1985: 193–4). Production of coal quadrupled between the early 1930s and 1942 (Zhongguo guomin zhengfu zhujiju tongjiju, 1936: 25; Zhou, Hou,

---

[5] For some recent Chinese estimates of Sichuan's population, see Liu (1988: ch. 2) and Li (1989: ch. 7).

and Chen, 1946*b*: 108) and iron output increased sixfold (Zhou, Hou, and Chen, 1946*b*: 108–9; Freyn, 1941: 419) between 1934 and 1942.

However, this programme of industrialization quickly ran out of steam. The number of new enterprises reached a peak of 609 in 1942, but by 1944 this had fallen back to 290 (Zhou, Hou, and Chen, 1946: 108). Even more seriously, the incidence of enterprise 'death' was very high, and the total fell quickly during 1945. Moreover, output peaked in the early 1940s and then declined; for example, Neijiang's white-sugar production was only 8.3 million *jin* by 1945 and exhibited a clear trend decline after 1940. Salt production at Zigong peaked even earlier in 1939, and then also gradually declined. The reasons for this are several. First, returns to commodity speculation increased sharply after 1938, whilst those in manufacturing declined (see the table in Eastman, 1986: 196). Secondly, government spending on the industrial sector declined as a percentage of non-defence expenditure from 62% in 1937–8 to 33% in 1939 and only 13% by 1944 (G. Q. Zhang, 1986: 81–3). Instead, much of this expenditure was switched to interprovincial transport and, in the last years of the war, to the development of north-west China, from which Sichuan's industry gained little. Loans for industrial purposes were also increasingly difficult to obtain.

The essential fragility of the Nationalist wartime economy is under-lined by the events of 1944. By then, one might have conjectured, the military effort would have been strengthening progressively as initial teething problems were overcome and new weapon-creating capacity came on stream. Yet Chiang Kaishek's troops were so badly equipped, motivated, and led that they were contemptuously swept aside in the last great Japanese offensive of the war, Operation Ichigo. This led to the fall of Chennault's American air-bases in the Guilin area; indeed, Chongqing itself was highly vulnerable to a Japanese drive from the south by December 1944. Fortunately for the Nationalists, the success of American naval operations in the western Pacific and the ac-companying continuous drain of Japanese manpower and airpower precluded effective exploitation of Ichigo's initial success. It was as well, for by then Chiang's regime teetered on the verge of ruin.

Thus the war years saw the first attempt at economic planning in Sichuan's history. By all criteria it was a failure. The war was won by the Americans and lost by the Japanese; Mao and Chiang alike were irrelevant. The Nationalist economy lurched from crisis to crisis, sustained only by lavish injections of Western aid. Industrial output collapsed and agricultural output declined. The income distribution shifted violently against Sichuan's (admittedly small) industrial working class. Price increases reached hyperinflationary levels.

Yet there is nothing in Sichuan's wartime experience that convincingly shows that planning *per se* was at fault. If planning was characterized by anything during these years, it was by flaws in its implementation. Most obviously, the aim of planning was not economic development. Chiang's overwhelmingly aim was to maintain his authority intact and to gradually establish a military machine capable of overwhelming the Communists in the civil war that would inevitably follow the defeat of Japan. In consequence, essential (in the eyes of Western advisers and CCP observers) economic and military steps were simply not taken. For many American observers, but notably Stilwell and Wedemeyer, the Chinese economy could be made to function effectively if its direction was in their hands rather than in those of the Peanut and his coterie, and while one may disagree with some of Stilwell's sentiments, few would argue that Chiang was the ideal leader in either peace or war. Accordingly, Sichuan's wartime tribulations reflect the incompetence of its leadership rather than any fundamental flaw in the theory and practice of economic planning.

Successful Planning: The 1950s

In sharp contrast to the province's wartime experience, and her experience between 1958 and 1975 (which is the subject of the next section), is her development record during the 1950s. Sichuan's successful performance during these years rests upon her adoption of a system of economic planning. Trends in some of the more important indicators are summarized in Table 3.2.

It is evident from these figures that economic performance during the 1950s was overwhelmingly superior to what followed, a conclusion that is reinforced by the fact that the Great Leap Forward débâcle is excluded from the post-1958 period in this comparison. If we compared the 1950s with the entire 1958–78 period, the comparison would be even more favourable to the latter. As it is, growth rates during the 1950s were at least double those achieved subsequently.

Of course, none of this is conclusive; two questions in particular need to be answered. To begin with, is it correct to describe the economic system in operation between 1953 and 1958 as planning? Secondly, and crucially, is there any evidence that economic performance during this period was successful because of—or despite—central

TABLE 3.2. *Sichuan's Economy in the 1950s and the Late Maoist Period*[a]

Sector	Annual growth rates (% p.a.)	
	1952/4–1956/8	1962/5–1975/8
NDMP	10.8	5.8
Agriculture	5.1	2.4
Industry	21.7	10.6
Grain output per capita	3.1	1.0

[a] NDMP (or national income), agriculture, and industry figures are for output value measured using a linked series of constant price data (which the Chinese call comparable prices). Grain figures are based on (unhusked) volume data per head of total population.

Sources: Grain—SCJJNJ (1986: 285); others—Zhongguo guojia tongjiju (1987: 343).

economic planning? Moreover, is there anything to support the counter-factual proposition that performance would have been better still without central planning?

The answer to the first is unequivocal. Sichuan's economy was planned during the 1950s. It is, of course, true that some assets were owned neither by state nor collective for much of the 1953–8 period; private ownership persisted into the late 1950s in both urban and rural sectors. It is also true that some have tended to describe the model of the 1950s as Bukharinist and therefore in some sense as different from mature central planning; but none of this is enough to lead one to the conclusion that the economy of Sichuan (or China) was dominated by market forces. Crucially, the commanding heights of the industrial sector, and infrastructure, were under public ownership; the procurement of grain was a state monopoly; and most prices, certainly the most important ones, were fixed by the state. This latter is particularly important because the most basic feature of the Smithian and subsequent conceptions of the market is price determination by the interaction of private agents. Moreover, one cannot describe the mechanism of price determination as market socialism (in the sense that the Chinese state mimicked the functioning of the Walrasian auctioneer such that prices were *de facto* determined by demand and supply). Manifestly that did not happen. Finally, it is as well to remember that to describe an economic system as Bukharinist is in no sense the same as calling it a market economy, as Nolan, amongst others, has emphasized.

The second question requires more careful analysis, and is best answered by looking at industrial and agricultural sectors separately. The performance of the latter is particularly controversial. The old 'Maoist' view was that agricultural performance was good throughout China during these years in the sense that per capita output was rising; the essential cause was the gradual introduction of collective institutions in the countryside. In the long run, it was argued, a sustained increase in productivity required mechanization, which in turn required both the amalgamation of small peasant land holdings if economies of scale were to be exploited and the mobilization of a 'surplus' above necessary consumption to feed the urban population as well as provide raw materials for industrial development. Moreover, such large-scale farm units needed to be collectively owned, both to avoid centrifugal differentiation ('polarization') and full to mobilize underemployed farm labour, not least the labour of women.

These ideas are summarized in Mao's speech on co-operatives of July 1955:

[some] comrades fail to understand that socialist industrialization cannot be carried out in isolation from agricultural cooperation. In the first place, as everyone knows, China's current level of production of marketable grain and industrial raw material is very low, whereas the state's need for them is growing year by year . . . if our agriculture cannot make a leap from small-scale farming with animal-drawn farm implements to large-scale mechanised farming . . . we shall run into formidable difficulties in our socialist industrial-isation and shall be unable to complete it. . . . In the second place, some of our comrades have not given any thought to the connection between the following two facts, namely, that heavy industry, the most important branch of socialist industrialization, produces tractors and other farm machinery, chemical fertilizers, modern means of transport, oil, electrical power etc., for agricultural use, but that all these things can only be used, or used extensively, on the basis of large-scale co-operative agriculture . . . (Mao, 1971: 405–6)

As is clear to everyone, the spontaneous forces of capitalism have been steadily growing in the countryside in recent years, with new rich peasants springing up everywhere and many well-to-do middle peasants striving to become rich peasants. On the other hand, many poor peasants are still living in poverty for lack of sufficient means of production with some in debt and others selling or renting out their land. If this tendency goes unchecked, the polarisation in the countryside will inevitably be aggravated day by day. . . . There is no solution to this problem except to . . . carry out co-operation and eliminate the rich-peasant economy and the individual economy in the countryside so that all the people will become increasingly well off together. (pp. 411–12)

The decade of the 1950s saw a gradual institutional trend towards this ideal as mutual aid teams became commonplace, and were supplanted in turn by lower- and higher-stage co-operatives. By the end of 1956, the latter form of organization, involving collective ownership of means of production and distribution according to work, was firmly established as the norm throughout China. Inevitably there were some teething problems, and most peasants had to be led into collectives by a mixture of threats and bribes administered by a relatively small group ('vanguard') of dedicated revolutionaries. For all that, collectivization was far more peaceful than in the USSR in the late 1920s and early 1930s (Nolan, 1976).

Some of this, in particular the relatively impressive farm performance and the essentially peaceful character of collectivization, is common ground with the revisionists (Nolan, 1976; Selden, 1982; Friedman, Pickowicz, and Selden, 1991), although it has been argued that the output of minor crops fell considerably (Nolan, 1981). However, the revisionists take issue with the view that collectivization was functionally necessary, and argue strongly that farm performance would have been better still without the transition to full collectivization. This argument is based upon two assumptions. The first is that land reform, and the relatively primitive but voluntary co-operative forms of organization that had emerged by 1954, had led to a remarkable reduction in pre-1949 income inequality, *and* that there is no evidence of the re-emergence of such inequalities in the period after land reform and before collectivization. This stemmed from the availability of cheap loans from credit co-operatives, progressive land taxation, and co-operative arrangements for the sharing of indivisible farm inputs such as carts and draught animals. The second assumption is that the process of collectivization, precisely because it was not truly voluntary, dampened peasant enthusiasm and led to the widespread slaughter of pigs. In addition, collective emphasis on grain production may have led to increases in per capita grain output, but the impact of this upon peasant incomes was partially offset by reduced production of 'minor' crops. Ultimately, this was a consequence of central planning. The need to guarantee the supply of grain to deficit areas, particularly the urban centres of eastern China (see Walker, 1984), necessitated the neglect of minor crops, and this was reflected in the relative price structure.

This view that planning in general and collectivization in particular led to an adverse effect on farm performance is summarized by Selden (1988: 80–2):

The most acute rural problems and obstacles to effective co-operative formation and rural development were not those of class polarization or exploitation but the general poverty of the countryside, the limited availability of improved means of production and skilled technical and administrative personnel, the tension generated by high targets, low state prices, and extractive, centralizing policies of the five-year plan, and the organizational difficulties associated with large-scale cooperation.

However, this is not very convincing. At a general analytical level, it is problematic as to whether the Chinese system of progressive taxation and elementary co-operative forms would have prevented class polarization. It is possible to tax agriculture in an LDC, but it is very difficult to do so in a manner that is both progressive and yet still able to raise a significant volume of revenue (because progressive income taxation is relatively easy to evade). Indeed, one of the arguments for collectives is that they facilitate tax revenue collection. As for co-operatives, the problem is that they can easily be 'captured' by a small number of articulate and well-educated individuals or by tightly knit clan associations, who can then use the co-operative to further their own economic interests. Co-operatives thus serve to encourage polarization, as Lenin had pointed out (Bramall, 1991). To some extent, these problems can be circumvented by the growth of rural industry. Indeed, it is arguable that rural polarization failed to re-emerge in Taiwan after land reform because poor and/or landless peasants were able to participate in the rapid growth of non-farm industry. However, this was not really a viable strategy for China because of strategic factors, which necessitated the rapid development of heavy industry.

Moreover, the empirical evidence warrants at best scepticism about the revisionist analysis. This focuses on trends between 1952 and 1954, and on the evolution of collectives after 1958, in an attempt to show that polarization was not occurring under the post-land reform institutional framework and that, in any case, the subsequent experience with collectives indicates that they were not the solution but part of the problem. However, the 1952–4 period is far too short to enable one to say anything conclusive about polarization, and post-1958 difficulties reflected a whole constellation of factors, ranging from strategic constraints to the discrediting of the whole collective approach as a result of the Great Leap Forward and the Cultural Revolution.

As far as Sichuan is concerned, there is no doubt that the farm sector suffered from a number of problems in the mid-1950s, and it is surely no accident that these difficulties coincided with the 'high tide' of collectivization. It is particularly interesting to compare 1954 with 1955. Between these two years, per capita grain production fell from 577 *jin* to 568 *jin*, and the number of pigs per capita fell from 0.32 to 0.28, with the total number of pigs falling from 21.4 to 19.1 million (SCJJNJ, 1986: 285). Moreover, 1955 saw the rapid introduction of elementary co-operatives instead of mutual-aid teams; there were 9,400 of the latter at the end of 1954, and 174,000 by the end of 1955 (ZSSWY, 1984: 207).

Yet it is uncertain how much should be read into this. A grain output fluctuation (and grain output affects feed availability and hence pig numbers) of this order of magnitude is explicable in terms of poor weather, and does not necessarily indicate anything about the impact of institutional change *per se*. Furthermore, it is surprising that there was no fall in the number of draught animals if collectivization was really so bitterly resented. After all, it was this that did occur on a large scale in the Soviet Union in the late 1920s and early 1930s. In contrast, the numbers increased steadily in Sichuan throughout the 1950s. In addition, the microeconomic evidence is unclear on whether the collective movement provoked widespread resistance in Sichuan; certainly there is little in Endicott's work (1988) on Shifang (admittedly an unrepresentative area) to support such a conclusion.

Most importantly, trends in farm performance *after 1955* suggest that the new system of collectives was working rather well. This is plain if we compare the early 1950s and the late 1950s (Table 3.3). In general, Sichuan's farm sector seems to have performed rather better than the national norm. This may have been partly due to good weather, although evidence on this for Sichuan is hard to find. It may also be that the process of collectivization was rather more gradual in the province than elsewhere. As Goodman has noted (1986: 70), only 7% of Sichuan's households were in higher-stage collectives by June 1956, compared to a national figure of 63% although the differential was non-existent by November of that year. Nevertheless, neither national nor provincial data suggest that collectivization was a disaster.

Of course, one would not wish to accept these data too uncritically. Although it is something of an article of faith amongst sinologists that the data for the First Five-Year Plan are the best collected on China before the early 1980s, the very extent and pace of institutional reform in the countryside during the period must cast doubt upon this conventional wisdom. In any case, the late 1950s average includes

TABLE 3.3. *Farm-Sector Performance in the 1950s*

	Grain per capita (kg, unhusked)		Pig stock (million head)		NVAO per capita (comparable *yuan*)	
	China	Sichuan	China	Sichuan	China	Sichuan
1952–4 (av.)	283	276	95.9	17.5	59	43
1955	299	285	87.9	19.1	62	45
1956–8 (av.)	304	312	121.7	23.7	63	49

Sources: Sichuan—SCJJNJ (1986: 283–5); LSTJ (1990: 690, 693–4). China—ZGTJNJ (1989: 30, 87, 1988); LSTJ (1990: 1, 6, 12).

data for 1958, which must be suspect in view of the disintegration of the system of statistical collection that was occurring during that and subsequent years. More positively, it is interesting that much of the evidence—on Sichuan at any rate—published after 1978 tends to support the notion that collectivization was successful even though it is in conflict with the policies of *decollectivization* pursued in the early 1980s. In sum, therefore, there are grounds for concluding that, although collectivization involved transition costs, its medium-term impact was less damaging than some have suggested.

As far as the relationship between technical progress in agriculture and planning is concerned, there is no question that Nolan is right when he argues that planning can lead to the rapid dissemination of inferior techniques; the experience throughout China during the 1950s with the infamous double-wheeled and double-bladed plough was unfavourable.[6] It seems highly unlikely that such a technology would ever have been adopted by peasants operating within a market economy. On the other hand, it is dangerous to generalize about technical progress on the basis of a few examples. That becomes particularly apparent when we recognize that many successful instances of technical progress occurred within the farm sector in the 1950s. In Sichuan, these included the rapid diffusion of new sugar cane and wheat varieties, a trend towards deep ploughing and close planting, and the introduction of powered threshers and sprinklers. In

[6] Sichuan's experience was similar. According to an account cited in Endicott (1988: 41), the plough required 3 buffalo to pull it and even then it sank into the mud.

Longchang, Rongchang, and Neijiang counties, veterinary stations were established to reduce the number of diseased pigs at the end of 1955. The effect was to reduce the death rate from over 10% to under 4% by 1957 (*Longchang wenshi ziliao xuanji*, 1986: 71–3).

Most important of all was the modernization of methods of irrigation. Before 1949, paddy-fields located high on mountain slopes relied on rainfall for irrigation because of the absence of pumping equipment. This meant that such fields had to remain flooded during the winter (the dry season) and therefore multiple cropping was impossible; but the diffusion of pumping equipment and small-scale hydroelectricity stations after 1949 began to change this situation. By 1955, 4,130 hectares were mechanically irrigated compared to only 330 before 1949, essentially because of an increase in the number of pumping stations from 3 to 54 over the same period (Afanas' yeskiy, 1960: 70). Of course, all this constituted a small beginning, but it does show that planning was not necessarily incapable of generating technical progress; and in historical perspective it is difficult to argue that technical progress was slower after 1949 than it had been in the preceding century—quite the contrary.

Finally, the role played by the planners in altering the relative price structure should not be overlooked. As Chakravarty has argued (1989: 6–7):

in regard to instruments, there are reasons to believe that planners sometimes took the view that relative prices were *fixed*, thereby choosing to rely more on 'planning by direction' rather than through the 'market', even when it is indeed possible and probably even desirable to do so. If prices are assumed as fixed, they are accordingly ruled out as instruments of policy, thus elevating quantity type instruments to a commanding position in planning contexts.

One of the most interesting features of the Chinese experience has been that agricultural performance has been best when the relative price structure has been deliberately altered in that sector's favour. Sichuan's experience is little different from the national norm in this respect. Impressive performance in terms of per capita output growth during the 1980s occurred at a time when agricultural product prices were increasing at an average rate of 6.8% per annum (1978–85) compared to industrial price increases of 1.4% per annum (SCJJNJ, 1986: 307–8). There were important institutional changes also taking place of course, and therefore the correlation between relative price increases and improved agricultural performance is not evidence of causality. Nevertheless, the evidence is highly suggestive, especially when the experience in earlier periods is considered. For example, farm performance was poor between 1965 and 1978 when industrial product prices were stagnant, but farm product prices also increased by barely more than 1% per annum, with much of the increase occurring in 1966. And, of most interest for our purposes, agricultural product prices increased on average by 4.8% per annum between 1952 and 1958 whilst industrial product prices showed no change. The link between deliberate manipulation of the intersectoral terms of trade and successful agricultural performance may not be proven—but there is nothing to suggest rejection of the hypothesis.

Planning success in Sichuan during the 1950s was most apparent in the arenas of industry and infrastructure. Some infrastructure did exist in the province before 1949. Many irrigation networks pre-dated the Qing dynasty, the rivers provided important commercial arteries, and the frenzied construction of the 1940s halted and probably reversed the declining quality of the Imperial road network. Nevertheless, the province's position was hardly enviable, especially since it remained in large measure isolated from China's eastern provinces. Trade was possible via the Yangzi River or by road over the Qinling mountains and hence on to the Longhai railway and Xi'an. But it was hardly a simple or profitable matter to indulge in transprovincial trade, and it was these difficulties that provoked Li Bai's famous poem 'The Road to Shu'. Moreover, in an economic sense, Sichuan's isolation made little sense, because it prevented the effective exploitation of provincial comparative advantage; for example, Sichuan could have specialized in grain production whilst the great cities and the prosperous counties of the lower Yangzi specialized in the production of industrial commodities and cash crops respectively.

Much of the infrastructural investment in Sichuan during the 1950s was designed to make possible the exploitation of this very trading opportunity. The most obvious indication of this is the scale of the investment in railway building. Fixed investment in railways during the First Five-Year Plan in Sichuan totalled 610 million *yuan*; this amounted to approximately 75% of the total volume of fixed investment in transport and communication, or 23% of fixed investment in the province during that period.[7] The first part of this scheme was to link the eastern basin with Chengdu and hence concentrate available grain surpluses at a single centre. This was a relatively simple task, because most of the work on the Chengdu–Chongqing railway had

---

[7] Fixed investment here refers to that undertaken by provincial and national governments only. It takes no account of private or co-operative fixed investment, which was especially significant in the farm sector.

already been completed before 1949; indeed, the track would have been completed during the war but for shortages of high-quality steel. Accordingly, the railway was soon brought into service; it was opened to traffic on 1 July 1952. The next phase was to link this intraprovincial railway with the remainder of China. The only way to do this was to build a new 670 km. line northwards from Chengdu towards Baoji, across the fearsome obstacle posed by the Qinling mountains in southern Shaanxi to reach the Wei River valley. As these mountains rise to heights in excess of 3,000 m., this project was one of the most difficult attempted in world railway history. Its cost (fixed investment only) was 1.2 million *yuan* per kilometre, or more than three times that of the Chengdu–Chongqing railway (Gao, 1987: 73). Nevertheless, the project was successfully completed on 13 July 1956 (though it was not fully operational until December); thereafter, for the first time, the province enjoyed a reliable means of communication with the rest of the country.

The other area of infrastructure which attracted heavy investment was energy. This sector received fixed investment to the value of 350 million *yuan* (13% of the total), the bulk of which was allocated to electricity generation although a third was invested in the coal industry. It is not clear precisely how effective any of this was, but there is no doubt that energy production rose sharply during the 1950s; total output in 1952 was only 3.4 million tonnes, but by 1957 it had reached 7.8 millions, and it rose even more quickly in 1958 and 1959 as small-scale coal-mines were opened in rural areas. Simultaneously, provincial electricity generation increased from 2.5 million kWh in 1952 to 6.8 million by 1957 (SCJJNJ, 1986: 293). This rapid growth suggests that, whilst this investment may have been less than optimally allocated, it was none the less sufficiently effective to generate rapid output increases.

Compared to infrastructure, investment in industry was rather downplayed. Of the 156 major projects built in China during the First Five-Year Plan with Soviet assistance, only 6 were allocated to Sichuan; and of the 694 smaller-scale projects, the province's share was only 16. Both figures far from adequately reflect the province's share in the national population, and neither represents any concerted attempt to enable the poor provinces of western China to catch up with the norm in eastern China. Nevertheless, given the relatively small industrial base that Sichuan possessed in the early 1950s, this industrial investment was of great significance. Moreover, it is very difficult to believe that the sectors in which the investment took place—predominantly heavy industry—would have received the same priority under a market system. In a closed economy, the pattern of industrial development will be determined by the pattern of short-run income elasticities of demand. Such elasticities are difficult to estimate, but it seems likely that they were relatively high for light industrial products and low for capital goods such as steel and machinery in Sichuan during the 1950s. As a result, the emphasis placed upon heavy industrial development in the province during the 1950s may well have involved static losses in allocative efficiency. In long-run perspective, however, it is hard to believe that the investment allocation resulting from planning was 'wrong', for ultimately rapid provincial development was dependent upon a growing output of heavy industrial products. Moreover, it is not as though the cost of this programme was any obvious decline in living standards; the evidence, scanty and unreliable though it is, suggests that food consumption and real income rose during the decade.

The closest international parallel here is with post-war Japan and the role played by the Ministry of International Trade and Industry in essentially ignoring her short-run comparative advantage in relatively labour-intensive products and concentrating instead upon the production of chemicals and cars, where the country's long-run comparative advantage was believed to lie. It is certainly not obvious that this pattern of development in Japan's case was wrong, given her phenomenal post-war growth record. Nevertheless, the issue is controversial. One can, for example, pose the counterfactual that growth would have been faster still in the absence of MITI or, following Kosai and Ogino (1984), that comparative advantage had already shifted to heavy and chemical industry by the 1950s and therefore MITI was simply copying what the market would have done anyway. Nevertheless, given that South Korea followed a similarly successful approach, and that the sustained 10% per annum rate of growth of GDP achieved by Japan has rarely been matched, let alone exceeded, the negative counterfactual is not very compelling.

None of this is to imply that the allocation of fixed investment by the state within the industrial sector during the 1950s was optimal. It was not. For example, fully 31.5% of fixed investment went into the machine-building sector. This was higher than the average during both the 1958–80 period and the Sixth Five-Year Plan (1981–5), 29.3% and 27.7% respectively (Gao, 1987: 478–9). Furthermore, the share going to the chemical industry (5.2%) seems surprisingly small in view of the importance of plastics and chemical fertilizers to the provincial economy. Nevertheless, in other respects the pattern of investment

allocation seems to have been well conceived. If we compare investment allocation between 1953 and 1957 with investment allocation
during the entire 1949–85 period, the sectors receiving significantly
greater priority in the 1950s were electricity generation, light industry,
and coal-mining. The sector receiving significantly less priority in the
1950s was metallurgy.

Planning in Sichuan during the 1950s, therefore, seems to have
worked well. Of course there were technological failures. Of course
the process of collectivization was imperfect. Of course, in retrospect,
some aspects of industrial investment allocation seem to have been ill
conceived. And of course planning involved some short-run allocative
inefficiencies. Nevertheless, the progress made by the provincial
economy on the eve of the Great Leap Forward was phenomenal.
That is especially so when one compares it with the progress made
during the 1930s. That decade had seen the beginnings of modern
industrial development, of which the 16.5 km. railway carrying coal
between Beibei and Baimiaoyu north of Chongqing was the orna-
ment, but it is difficult to describe this progress as other than pitifully
small. The province remained in effective economic isolation from
eastern China. Poppy-growing and opium smoking were alike endemic. Modern industry accounted for less than 5% of provincial
GDP. The year 1937 saw a severe famine in northern Sichuan. The
warlords remained, their power in eclipse but still a potent check
on the Kuomintang's freedom of manœuvre in political and military
spheres.

The contrast between the 1930s and the late 1950s is overwhelming.
By 1958, the province was firmly integrated into the national economy,
owing to the herculean efforts of her railway engineers and the
blowing up of obstacles to navigation in the Yangzi Gorges. Per capita
output of steel, coal, and electricity, without which economic modernization was impossible, far exceeded the peak levels of the 1930s and
was growing. The percentage of cultivated area irrigated by pump,
canal, and reservoir instead of rainwater had increased substantially.
Enormous institutional changes in the countryside had been brought
about without famine, and a sustained mortality reduction had been
achieved. Consumption levels were certainly no higher (and probably
somewhat lower on average) than during the 1930s, but the sheer
scale and pace of industrialization was a promise of substantial improvement in the not too distant future. Moreover, even during the
1950s, the quality of life was improving thanks to income redistribution and health care, whilst cultural horizons were expanding in step

with burgeoning educational provision. Sichuan was by no means a developed country by the end of the 1950s, but a great deal had been accomplished.

Strategic Imperatives: Late Maoist Planning, 1958–1975[8]

Chinese central planning reached its apogee, in terms of public ownership of the means of production and price control, in the twenty years after 1958. During this period, per capita grain consumption stagnated although industrial production continued to increase quite quickly and the trend in capabilities after 1962 was favourable. However, the era was launched inauspiciously by the Great Leap Forward, which in Sichuan alone consigned more than ten million peasants to a premature death (see Chapter 9). There was nothing quite to match this catastrophe in the years after 1962, but equally there was little by way of compensation. Long-run performance was by no means disastrous, but was signally inferior in many respects to that achieved during the first decade of Maoist rule.

Explaining poor performance is an altogether more interesting task. If we begin by considering the agricultural sector, the proximate explanation of poor performance was low labour productivity. In terms of grain, per capita output reached 600 *jin* in 1957 and 1958 in Sichuan, yet by the early 1970s it had fallen back to around the 550 *jin* mark (SCJJNJ, 1986: 285). In the entire 1959–75 period, only once did grain production per capita exceed 600 *jin* (in 1966, when it reached 609 *jin*). There is no evidence that this disappointing trend reflected diversification within the agricultural sector; per capita output of non-grain products was also stagnant. It is true that the number of pigs per capita stood at 0.41 in 1974 and 1975, somewhat higher than the 1957 and 1958 levels of 0.36, and the share of aquatic products in GVAO (constant prices) actually tripled between 1957 and 1975 (*Sichuan yuye jingji*, 1985: 55); but vegetable oil production, the crucial non-grain consumption good, was only 10 *jin* per capita in 1974–5, compared to about 12 *jin* in the mid-1950s (SCJJNJ, 1986: 285).

When it comes to isolating the *underlying* explanation of poor agricultural performance, it is easy to blame the system of economic

---

[8] 1975 is designated as the terminal date because it marks the appointment of Zhao as provincial party secretary and the gradual beginnings of liberalization.

planning in general, and collectivization in particular. For China as a whole, neoclassical accounts take this line. Market socialists take a more balanced view and recognize that some of the problems of the Maoist period could have been avoided. Nevertheless, the planning mechanism and the institutional framework *per se* is still made to bear the greater part of the blame:

This analysis suggests that one cannot conclude precisely the degree of responsibility of collective institutions *per se* for China's relatively poor agricultural performance pre-1978. Excessive, heavy-handed state intervention exacerbated the problems. . . . However, it seems unquestionable that a major part of the problems encountered by the rural economy pre-1978 is attributable to the institution of the collective farm *per se*.   (Nolan, 1988: 79)

In Sichuan's case there are many examples of apparent institutional failure. For example, the province's forests were owned largely by state farms in the late 1950s. However, profitability was not an important target, and for that reason wholesale deforestation was encouraged during the Great Leap Forward by the urgent energy demands of rural iron- and steel-smelting. None of that would have happened under a system of private ownership. Rural iron- and steel-making was unprofitable, and rapid deforestation yielded few net social benefits because of the resultant erosion of mountain slopes. One illustration of the problems caused in this last respect is as follows:

According to an investigation conducted in Nanjiang *xian*'s Yangba commune which is located at an altitude of over 1,200 metres . . . the area afforested in 1957 was 15,800 *mu*, about 43% of land area. But between 1958 and 1963, the entire commune in an indiscriminate and disorderly manner felled approximately 10,000 *mu*. . . . This reduced afforested area by 63.3% and the volume of available timber reserves by 98%. . . . The felling of trees also led to substantial soil erosion and to a deterioration in the quality of cultivated land; the area of cultivated land enjoying high and stable yields fell from 54% of the total in 1957 to 33% in 1963.   (ZKCDY, 1980: 202)

Nor is this an untypical instance. In the province as a whole, afforested area fell from 160 million *mu* in 1949 to only 110 million *mu* by 1979. In the central 58 counties, average afforested area was only 4.5%, and in 19 of these it was down to 1% (Xie, 1984: 206).

Another example of the allegedly adverse impact of central planning was the attempt to introduce double rice-cropping throughout Sichuan instead of the normal winter crop. This amounted to a reversal of the pre-1949 practice, but because the policy was propagated via collectives, double rice-cropping spread quickly after 1965.

As a result, the area that was double rice-cropped increased from 540,000 *mu* to 3.95 million *mu* by 1977 (*SAG*, 1986: 40). As late as the early 1980s, this slow progress was bemoaned by Sichuan's agronomists:

the double-crop paddyfield area in Sichuan remains very low (8 percent) and output of double-cropped paddy amounts to only 12 percent of total paddy output. This provides a striking contrast to the situation in provinces, regions (and cities) in south China that produce mostly two crops of paddy. (*SAG*, 1986: 51)

Yet this pattern of cultivation had not been practised before 1949 because it made very little sense in terms of profitability. This was eventually noted in the Agricultural Yearbook of 1981 (*SAG*, 1986: 174). By 1982, the provincial newspaper was talking of the 'blind development of double rice crops' such that 'the advantages obtainable from intermediate rice were damaged' (*Sichuan Ribao*, 1982: 38) and as early as January 1979, Fei Xiaotong condemned double rice-cropping in the following terms:

For instance, a few years ago, province leaders—without discussing it with peasants or considering local conditions—had ordered all the communes to grow one crop of wheat and two crops of rice a year instead of one. They called this an advanced experience successful in other provinces. The result was disastrous. Continual autumn rains in some areas of Szechuan cause low temperatures and a shortened period of sunshine. This, in addition to a shortage of labor and fertiliser, delayed planting the second crop of rice and crops were either poor or failed altogether. The peasants had told the provincial leaders point-blank, "Your order is foolish. Three crops will yield even less than two." Back came the arrogant answer: "Growing three crops or not is a question of political line!" The peasants were furious. Multiplied many times, this was the situation in Szechuan's agriculture under the gang of four. (Fei, 1979: 61–2)

Unsurprisingly, decollectivization, combined with offical opposition to generalized double rice-cropping in the early 1980s, led to a big reduction in its extent. By 1983 the 1977 figure of 3.95 million *mu* had fallen to 800,000 *mu*, or some 1.6% of paddy-field, with remaining double-cropping areas heavily concentrated in the southern part of the Sichuan Basin and in the Anning River valley area of Liangshan prefecture (Gan, 1986: 70).

It is noteworthy in retrospect how petty were many of the policies pursued in the agricultural sector. One instance of this was the attempt during the late 1960s to prevent peasants from breeding fish in paddy-fields as a means of supplementing their protein-deficient diet. The official rationale was that such sideline pursuits led to class differentiation in the countryside and also diverted labour from grain production. As a result, the slogan 'Paddy-fields are only able to grow rice' was actively promulgated, and the total output of fish grown in paddy-fields fell from 5.3 million *jin* in 1965 to only 3.7 million by 1971 (*Sichuan yuye jingji*, 1985: 160–1). Again, this is an example of collectives allowing the rapid dissemination of an inappropriate policy, with fearful results. As a measure designed to raise rice production, the measure was misguided because the *absence* of fish actually reduced paddy-field fertility and hence yields. Surveys conducted in the Chengdu area in 1976–7 showed that rice yields were reduced by as much as 20% (*Sichuan yuye jingji*, 1985: 137–8).

The problems afflicting the industrial sector by the late 1970s because of failures of the system of economic planning were seemingly at least as severe as those affecting agriculture. Indeed, one of the great paradoxes of the development of industry in Sichuan (and in China, for that matter) was that heavy industry received the lion's share of state investment and yet suffered from the most intractable problems by the late 1970s. Perhaps the most celebrated of these problems was that posed by energy shortages. As has been mentioned previously, the south-west in general, and Sichuan in particular, is blessed with abundant hydroelectricity potential because it has a very large number of fast-flowing rivers; in per capita terms, Sichuan's hydrogeneration capacity per capita is probably the greatest in the world (Smil, 1988: 120). The Sichuan basin also has abundant coal reserves and small quantities of natural gas. Yet by the late 1970s, the province was facing severe shortages and the future seemed bleak:

at the moment, the province's natural gas potential is still unclear with output falling every year. Pressure has begun to accumulate to develop the province's coalfields but unfortunately the prospects are not particularly bright; a number of old mines are on the verge of exhaustion while in a number of new mines workable reserves are not yet completely proved.   (Xin, 1984: 179)

These difficulties are traced by Sichuan's economists to failures in the decision-making process and in central planning:

During the 1970s, although the geological structure of natural gas reserves was still uncertain, it was decided that Sichuan must make natural gas her principal energy source. At the same time, investment in the coal industry was reduced and the construction of a number of coal-mines was halted. But it is now known that natural gas reserves are far below the estimates made at that time. Increasingly in recent years, the imbalance between energy supply and demand has led to an intensified programme of gas drilling, but many new wells have produced only water or a small volume of gas. From 1979 onwards, natural gas production has steadily declined. This large shortfall in natural gas output has forced many factories to halt or to reduce production. Moreover, many of the enterprises using natural gas were high-volume, high-value, and large-profit producers. In 1979, 16 firms each produced more than 100 million *yuan*'s worth of output, and of these 14 used natural gas. Of the 39 firms with an output value of between 50 and 100 million *yuan*, 29 used natural gas.   (Gu, 1985: 484)

The energy problem in the rural sector was equally acute. After initial experiments during the Great Leap Forward, it was concluded by the mid-1960s that biogas generators would relieve the most pressing problems. A popularization campaign therefore began in the 1970s, and the number of generators in operation grew from 30,000 in spring 1974 to 4.3 million by the end of 1977 (Smil, 1988: 54). This attracted UN attention and encouraged attempts to promote the technology in other LDCs. But the technology proved far less robust than had been hoped. Not only did the operation of the digesters need very careful attention, but their construction needed to be perfect. As neither was achieved in practice, the programme rapidly lost momentum after 1977 (Smil, 1988: 62).

Most seriously of all, in view of the staggering volume of investment committed to it, the programme of 'Third-Front' construction launched after 1965 for predominantly strategic reasons (on which more later) yielded few direct economic benefits. A major problem was what Gu calls the 'sheep shit' arrangement of enterprises (Gu, 1985: 484) in which factory workshops were scattered across narrow mountain gullies. Such a dispersion made it very difficult to co-ordinate production, and necessarily involved high transport and comunication costs. Moreover, because much investment that supposedly added to enterprise fixed assets, and thence to enhanced productive potential, was actually used for infrastructure construction and the digging of air-raid shelters, perhaps 20% of notional productive capacity was imaginary. In addition, few of the 'Third-Front' facilities were complete by the late 1970s, and as a result they were unable to produce any output. According to a 1978 survey, some 11.3 billion *yuan* was needed to make such facilities operational. That was an enormous sum when it is recognized that severe opportunity costs were involved; it was estimated in the same year that 5 or 6 billion *yuan* was needed to bring social infrastructure such as housing, schools, and medical facilities up to the national norm (Gu, 1985: 484–5). This evidence suggests that the vast investment in heavy industry undertaken in Sichuan after 1949, and particularly after 1965, produced at best marginal economic benefits in even the medium term.

Some of the failures of light industry and transportation also seemingly have their origins in the system of economic planning. For example, river transport was neglected despite the very high level of demand:

Since the development of the railway in Sichuan, river transportation has been neglected. At present, passenger craft are inadequate in number, merchant shipping is obsolete, and new lightweight craft are too small so that an increasingly sharp conflict between commodity supply and transport capacity is developing. Export capacity is currently able to satisfy only 60% of demand and the total volume of transport capacity is less than in 1957. (Zhang and Ceng, 1984: 158)

The problems of the spinning industry illustrate in microcosm the difficulties faced by the light industrial sector as a whole by the end of the 1970s:

It can be seen from an examination of the condition of Sichuan's light spinning industry that it has not made the most of certain advantageous conditions over the last thirty years. For example, the technical-transformation fund available for the light spinning industry has not been used in this way but instead used to increase capital construction; the slogan 'Uproot, change, and reform' is only a formality. Linked with this problem is a deficiency of technical personnel and poor management; not only are specialist managerial and technical personnel lacking, but also those that are available are unevenly distributed throughout the province. Indeed, one could go as far as to say that some collective enterprises have no technical personnel at all. . . . Even the Sichuan silk industry, which is of national importance, has no specialist training institute.   (Gan and Yang, 1984: 219)

This catalogue of 'planning failures' is lengthy. It is also misleading. One difficulty in blaming the most spectacular failure of the period, the famine of the early 1960s, on planning is that the chaos that reigned during the Great Leap Forward can hardly be called a planned economy. The most obvious feature of the 1958–62 period is the *collapse* of economic planning in any systematic sense. This were due to the combined effects of the administrative decentralization of 1958 and the emasculation of the State Statistical Bureau, upon which the party was dependent for reliable statistical information for planning purposes. These issues are discussed extensively in Chapters 9 and 10, but even a superficial examination reveals that the failures of this period were due to the absence, rather than to the inherent nature, of central economic planning.

It is also rather misleading to take the accounts of Sichuan's economists at face value when it comes to evaluating the worth or otherwise of the system of economic planning. There were very con-

siderable pressures upon China's academic economists writing during
the late 1970s to provide evidence and a theoretical rationale for the
new market-oriented policies being introduced by Zhao Ziyang and
Deng Xiaoping during the late 1970s. They were not expected to be
objective but rather to serve the political aims of the party; and,
although these types of arguments are difficult to prove, one cannot
help but feel that this influenced their writings.

This emerges more clearly when one tries to decide how significant
some of the planning failures mentioned above really were. Double
rice-cropped area at its peak only amounted to 8% of total rice-sown
area. The share of total aquatic products at its own zenith (1961) was
0.5% of GVAO (SCJJNJ, 1986: 282–3). And even if we accept that
erosion is directly attributable to systemic failure *per se*, it is hard to
believe that this had major consequences for farm production during
the 1960s and 1970s. In any case, if forestry depletion had been 'left to
the market', the rate of erosion would probably have been at least as
fast, the only likely difference being that wood would have been used
for purposes other than iron and steelmaking.[9]

Furthermore, it is unclear that Sichuan's performance between 1958
and 1975 was particularly bad in terms of technical progress, allegedly
one of the major failings of central economic planning. Although the
rate of technical progress was less than optimal during the 1960s and
1970s, one could say that of every economy, including Japan. Moreover, on examining the Chinese record on technical progress, one
cannot but be impressed by the achievements of the Maoist period.
The military field saw the development of nuclear weaponry and
the technology which has enabled the construction of land- and sea-
launched inter-continental ballistic missiles during the 1980s. In the
civilian field, perhaps the most notably success was the construction of
a road and rail bridge over the Yangzi River at Nanjing during the
1960s, even though a number of Soviet experts had concluded that it
could not be done. However, the major achievements were in the
field of agriculture. The farm economy was backward during the
1930s (although anything but technologically stagnant), and the rural
landscape had been changed out of all recognition by the late 1970s
as the 'green revolution' package of improved water control, high-
yielding varieties, and chemical fertilizers became widely available.

---

[9] The optimal policy was probably a forestry subsidy. In its absence, the free market
would have led to a rate of deforestation that was too fast because its full social costs—in
terms of the impact of erosion-induced silting on lowland irrigation systems and hence
agricultural yields—would not enter into the decison-making process of private, forest-
owning agents. Its impact would, of course, been spread over a longer period than was the
case with deforestation occurring during the Leap.

The period of the Cultural Revolution (1966–76) was damaging to this effort, but it is evident in retrospect that it was not sufficient to halt technological modernization. As for industry, one can do worse than simply list those commodities that were not being produced at all in the early 1950s and yet were being produced in substantial quantities by the late 1970s. This list includes chemical fertilizers, pesticides, small-scale electricity-generating equipment, oil, and vehicles.

Nevertheless, as has already been seen, the results in terms of living standards of this creative effort were rather disappointing. Hence the argument: if such investment was taking place, and if modernization was in train, how else can poor performance be explained except in terms of systemic failure? The difficulty with this proposition is that it fails to distinguish between the issue of systemic failure on the one hand and that of the allocation of investment across sectors and subsectors on the other. The poor performance of the agricultural and light industrial sector during the Maoist years can be attributed directly to inadequate inputs.

Two types of evidence support this conclusion. To begin with, these two sectors were starved of investment inputs during the Maoist years. It is true that traditional attempts to estimate intersectoral flows have concluded that the farm sector was a net recipient after the Great Leap Forward. The intersectoral terms of trade moved strongly in favour of agricultural products; with 1950 = 100, the index for 1957 stood at 164 and had climbed to 277 by 1975 (SCJJNJ, 1986: 307–8). Moreover, there is no question that the volume of modern inputs provided to the farm sector increased sharply after 1965 (see Chapter 8). Indeed, in the more prosperous parts of the province, the application of chemical fertilizer per hectare was fast approaching the levels prevailing in Japan and Taiwan. This was in response to an increase in use from about 1 kg. per rural inhabitant in 1957 to 21.5 by 1975 (ZSSWY, 1984: 186; Liu, 1988: 74). However, whether this trend was large enough when relative sectoral productivity growth rates are considered is questionable. It certainly is the case that industrial productivity rose much more quickly than implied by the decline in industrial product prices (Dong, 1982; Riskin, 1987), and if one accepts that decreasing returns to scale to the traditional farm package set in the more prosperous parts of the Sichuan Basin after 1949, it follows that an enormous effort was needed to modernize Sichuan's agriculture. Secondly, the improved performance of the farm sector after 1978 can be traced in substantial part to the injection of new current inputs to complement existing fixed capital; these issues are discussed below.

We must also consider the problems of heavy industry. For whilst some may agree with the proposition advanced above that light industry, agriculture, and infrastructure were denuded of funds, they do not accept that increased input provision is a *sufficient* condition for improvements in performance. This perspective is based on the view that heavy industry was not starved of inputs and yet still it performed badly. Would not the redirection of those inputs to other sectors have led to the same result in the absence of systemic reform? In other words, did not the solution to Sichuan's problems of the 1970s require *both* a reallocation of investment *and* the replacement of the visible hand of the planners by the invisible hand of the market to ensure intrasectoral allocative efficiency?

The most convincing answer to this question is that economic transformation did not require the latter. The underlying truth of Maoist economic development in Sichuan is not that economic policy failed to increase living standards, but rather that it was subordinated to other ends. Rising living standards did not feature high on the policy-making agenda because the overriding economic and political objective was nothing less than to make China into a great power. To that goal *all* economic and social policies of the 1960s and 1970s were subordinated. Heavy industry 'failed' in Sichuan to provide the necessary volume of inputs for the farm and light industrial sectors because it was orientated towards satisfying military and strategic targets. To the detail and consequences of this policy orientation we now turn.

China's strategic situation affected Sichuan more than any other province because it was Sichuan that was singled out as the focus of the 'Third-Front' programme. This ambitious project was launched in 1964/5 partly because the Sino-Soviet split of 1960 meant that China's security would henceforth depend upon her own efforts; no longer could she shelter behind the Soviet Union's nuclear and conventional umbrella. It was also conditioned by the initiation of the United States' bombing campaign against Vietnam, which began in August 1964 after attacks on US warships operating in the Gulf of Tonkin. As China was Vietnam's staunchest ally, this brought home the possibility of raids on China itself. Additionally, Sichuan was uniquely suited by location and by history to function as a strategic rear area from which resistance could be continued even in the event of the loss of large tracts of eastern China. In locational terms, it possessed what was signally lacking as far as the industry located along the east China coast was concerned, namely distance from American bomber bases in Taiwan, South Korea, Japan, and the Philippines, as well as carrier-based aircraft operating from the South China Sea. As the American nuclear threat was predominantly based on strategic bombers at the time, this was no idle consideration. Furthermore, Sichuan's location was advantageous in that the distance over which arms had to be transported to Vietnam would be short. Similarly, it would make it easier to supply the Chinese troops entrenched along the disputed Himalayan frontier with India. Finally, history made the choice of Sichuan inevitable. Not only had the ancient kingdom of Shu provided a haven for refugees fleeing from the north, but it had served as the redoubt of the Kuomintang during the Second World War.

The impact of the 'Third-Front' programme on Sichuan has been summarized thus:

Most of Sichuan's industry was established after 1965. Beginning in 1965, because of the international situation and with the approval of the Central Committee, Chairman Mao made the strategic decision to begin large-scale industrialization in the Chinese interior. During the fifteen years between 1965 and 1979, the State invested a total of 10 billion [*baiyi*] *yuan* in Sichuan, three-quarters of all investment in the province between 1949 and 1979. Of these 10 billion, three-quarters was invested in heavy industry, defence industries, and railway construction. During this period more than 250 large and medium-sized projects were launched as part of a unified national deployment plan. . . . The production of most mining and industrial enterprises was oriented towards national requirements, and was geared both towards the promotion of capital construction and towards going to war. These factors determined the present structure of Sichuan's industry. (Gu, 1985: 480)

The figure quoted here for the scale of investment should probably not be taken too literally; *baiyi* almost certainly means simply a very large sum. This is because we know that investment far exceeded this figure in Sichuan during the period in question. An official party source (ZSSWY, 1984: 488) puts total state investment between 1950 and 1981 at 54.562 billion *yuan*, and this is confirmed by other materials (SCJJNJ, 1986; Gao, 1987).

Table 3.4 gives a better indication of the true scale of the invest-ment effort. State fixed investment alone seems to have accounted for more than 20% of provincial NDMP during the Third and Fourth Five-Year Plans. By way of comparison, this exceeded the *total* investment share in GDP achieved by either the American or the British economy during the 1970s.

Precisely how much of this was directed towards strategic goals is uncertain. Investment in armaments production is invariably included in the machine-building total, and the only figure specifically on the defence sector readily available is for total fixed investment in defence

TABLE 3.4. *Fixed Investment in Sichuan after 1965*

	Sectoral shares in state fixed investment[a]				SFI/NDMP[b]
	Machine-building	Other heavy industry	Light industry	Transport	
1953–7	11.9	24.2	1.9	29.9	9.5
1958–62	17.5	54.3	1.6	14.1	18.1
1963–5	19.9	40.1	0.6	13.6	11.8
1966–70	20.7	39.2	1.3	24.8	24.7
1971–5	21.7	45.6	1.7	12.6	20.7
1976–80	14.4	45.8	0.6	7.2	12.6
1981–5	9.6	36.3	1.0	8.3	8.6

[a] These figures are for *jiben jianshe* or fixed investment only. This is a narrower definition than *jilei* (accumulation) because it excludes working capital. During the 'Third-Front' period, fixed investment typically accounted for some 75% of total investment.

[b] State fixed investment as a % of NDMP.

Source: Gao (1987: app.).

industry for the entire 1950–1981 period (ZSSWY, 1984: 489). This was put at 8.506 billion *yuan*, with only 2.345 billion going into civilian machine-building over the same period. However, this definition ignores the extent to which transportation, construction, and heavy industrial investment was overwhelmingly oriented towards the needs of the military sector. According to Gu (1985: 482), some 50% of steel products and more than a third of electrical machinery was geared towards defence requirements. The importance of strategic considerations—compare this to the paltry sums allocated to light industry in the previous table—in determining investment patterns is remarkable.

This places the supposedly 'irrational' pattern of heavy industrial development in a rather different perspective. Of course new factory workshops were widely dispersed across the countryside: it was an elementary precaution against air attack. Of course the major industrial project of these years, the enormous Panzhihua integrated steel complex, was built in what was, in narrowly economic terms, a bizarre setting. Not only is the city located in the depths of south-western Sichuan, far from the major centres of population, but the topography is extremely difficult. There is little flat land available, and therefore the city is built on steep mountain slopes and straddles both banks of the Jinsha *jiang* (which in turn necessitated a vast investment in bridges to link the two parts of the city together). However, the military advantages were self-evident; Panzhihua was much less vulnerable to air attack than if it had been located in Chongqing, and it was also far closer to the Vietnamese border. Of course the investment effort of the Maoist period is not reflected in living standards: most of it was being used to produce steel and armaments. Of course civilian shipping was neglected, for Sichuan became an alternative base for units of the Chinese navy. Even the commune, often derided when analysed from an economic perspective, served strategic goals, in that each was large enough to support an effective militia unit and to exploit economies of scale in political education.

The success or otherwise of this grand strategic design will always be a matter for debate, even when evaluated against the targets it set out to achieve. Those Chinese writers that discuss the defence aspects of Sichuan's industrialization conclude that its success is obvious. It did allow China to create an industrial base that could have survived a limited nuclear strike. Moreover, China by the late 1970s possessed a credible nuclear deterrent capability as well as a much-enhanced capacity to supply the needs of conventional forces:

At Liberation, the People's Government in Sichuan inherited only seven seriously damaged munitions factories from the old China. . . . these could only produce 7.9 mm. rifles, 60 and 120 mm. mortars (and shells), light and heavy machine-guns, flame-throwers, and hand-grenades. . . . Between 1965 and 1980, a brief fifteen-year period, tens of new weapons systems were produced. On 24 June 1970, the first batch of nuclear fuel was successfully extracted in Sichuan. On 26 November 1979, her first successful intercontinental ballistic missile flight took place. In 1980, the first type-33 submarine built in Sichuan was launched.   (Gao, 1987: 136, 137)

Western assessments, of which there are few as yet (but see Naughton, 1988; Kirkby and Cannon, 1989), are much less charitable:

It is the magnitude of the commitment that throws doubt on the reasonableness of the strategy. While the immediate threats faced by the Chinese were real enough, the development of industry in the Third Front was a long term project that could not be expected to bear fruit for ten or more years: consider the fifteen year process of building the Panzhihua steel complex in relation to the initial threat posed by the American presence in Vietnam during the mid-1960s. . . . Thus, it is not the Third Front strategy per se that is irrational, but rather the scale on which it was carried out. (Naughton, 1988: 372–3)

To be sure, in retrospect, much of this expenditure was wasted, but then that is always so with defence programmes operating close to scientific frontiers. Obvious Western examples of 'waste' include continued expenditure on Britain's atomic-bomb project during the Second World War even when it was obvious that the American project was far ahead, the expenditures undertaken by the US to make operational the B1 ('stealth') bomber and the MX ICBM, and the problems afflicting the Shuttle programme. It is easy to criticize these projects with hindsight and point out that the same results could have been achieved more quickly and cheaply, but it is never so easy at the time. Moreover, to appreciate the problems China had to overcome in developing her own nuclear capability, one only has to think about the primitive conditions that were the norm in the 1930s. Most Sichuan peasants was still using wooden ploughs, and even Chongqing, the industrial centre of the whole south-western region, was dependent upon water drawn by bucket from the Yangzi River. Electricity was an alien concept, and warlord troops were often armed with muskets. Yet despite this legacy of backwardness (Sichuan, of course, was anything but unique in these respects), China possessed a nuclear arsenal by 1963 and she is now a superpower.[10] It is difficult to see how transformation on such a scale could have been accomplished without a prodigious effort and without many wrong turns.

Moreover, it is not easy to single out projects that were plainly absurd when seen in military perspective. Concrete air-raid shelters under the streets of Chengdu and Chongqing did make it easy for Sichuan's population to survive a limited nuclear strike or carpet bombing. Railways were needed to supply armaments to Vietnam. Steel and concrete were required in enormous quantities if these and other projects were to be realized. Of course many plants were incomplete by the late 1970s, but that was because the urgency had gone out of 'Third Front' programme following Nixon's visit to Peking. Furthermore, the Politburo could hardly have expected such an outcome when the programme was launched during the 1960s.

If there is a conclusion to be reached on economic planning during the period from 1958 to 1975, it is that it was successful in achieving its objectives, and that the opportunity costs incurred were largely unavoidable. Plainly it did not succeed in raising per capita consumption, but it should not be judged by that criterion. It is easy for Western economists to argue that the revealed preferences of the

---

[10] Khrushchev's embargo on the transfer of Soviet nuclear secrets in the late 1950s also hindered the Chinese programme.

planners made little sense in narrowly economic terms, and the planning system itself is an even more obvious target for criticism; but the reality of this period is that the planning system did not fail: it was remarkably successful in achieving the goals that it was set.

Moreover, it is ironic that Western academics are so critical of the programme, when it requires no great leap of imagination to reach the conclusion that the limited improvement in certain aspects of living standards in Sichuan between the 1930s and the 1970s owed more than a little to Western imperialism. Western (and Soviet) 'interference' in China during the nineteenth and early twentieth centuries led ultimately to nationalist fervour. This desire for China to 'stand up' was echoed increasingly in the policies of the CCP and its active role in the war against Japan. It may be that this was more important than any other single factor in sweeping the CCP to power in 1949. Indeed, it is one of the great paradoxes of modern Chinese history that a party calling itself Nationalist was defeated on the very issue of nationalism by a party calling itself Communist. After 1949, the main objective of the CCP, with massive popular support, was to ensure that never again would China be a mere pawn in world affairs, with a place at the conference table (Versailles, Casablanca) but no real power. The hostility of the USA, and later the USSR, only convinced the Party of the objective's importance. Defence industrialization in Sichuan followed almost as a matter of course.

The evidence on Sichuan leads only to the conclusion that planning was remarkably successful in achieving the objectives laid down by the CCP. The system proved itself well able to guarantee rapid growth of inputs in the key defence sector and, despite these prior claims, the rate of civilian technological progress was by no means negligible. Of course there were some failures during the post-1958 period, of which the famine induced by the Great Leap Forward is the most notable. However, a direct causal link between failure and central economic planning *per se* is conspicuous only by its absence.

Garnering the Fruits: Sichuan since 1975

The strongest support for the hypothesis that planning was a success rather than a failure in Sichuan comes from the province's experience after 1975. Some of the post-1975 achievements in terms of living standards are summarized in Table 3.5. Moreover, it has become almost an article of faith amongst the majority of those who write on contemporary China that these impressive achievements owed

TABLE 3.5. *Trends in Living Standards in Sichuan, 1975–1990*

	Late Mao	Late Deng
Life expectancy (at birth)[a]	59.8 (1973–5) 64.4 (1981)	68.0 (1987)
Infant mortality (per 1,000)[b]	79.4 (1973–5) 57.7 (1981)	n.a.
Crude death rate (per 1,000)[c]	8.1 (av., 1975–8)	7.1 (1990)
Grain consumption (kg. per capita)[d]	204 (av., 1975, 1978)	242 (av., 1984–7)
Pork consumption (kg. per capita)[d]	8 (av., 1975, 1978)	19 (av., 1984–7)
Bicycle ownership (per 100 households)[e]	8.9 (1980)	41.8 (1988)
TV ownership (per 100 households)[e]	0.2 (1981)	25.6 (1988)
GDP per capita (comparable *yuan*)[f]	238 (1978)	569 (1989)

[a] 1973–5 (national cancer survey) and 1981 (census): Liu (1988: 151); 1987: SCSHTJZL (1989: 53).
[b] 1973–5 (national cancer survey) and 1981 (census); Liu (1988: 130).
[c] 1975–8 (registration data); SCSHTJZL (1989: 55). 1990 (census data): *Beijing Review*, 17–23 Dec. 1990, p. 23.
[d] SCSHTJZL (1989: 138).
[e] Ibid. 139–40, 502. For rural households only.
[f] Calculated from comparable price indices of GDP and population in LSTJ (1990: 690, 692).

virtually everything to the 'spontaneous' growth of the market economy. State 'interference' in the market mechanism was vastly reduced as the farm sector was decollectivized, and as restrictions upon the operation of private enterprises in industry and commerce were removed. This 'bonfire of controls', it is argued, played the critical role in inducing the extraordinary dynamism that was the hallmark of the Chinese economy in the 1980s.

However, the successes of the post-1975 period need to be seen in a broader perspective. In particular, it needs to be recognized that external circumstances inevitably condition a country or region's economic strategy. The external environment faced by China after the mid-1970s was altogether more benign than during the 1960s following the *rapprochement* with the USA and, more recently, with the Soviet Union. Moreover, the nuclear programme had been brought to fruition. Even if there is a sharp downturn in China's strategic position, her nuclear arsenal gives her a formidable deterrent capability. In consequence there is less need for a crash programme of development. Of course her nuclear capability will have to be periodically up-graded, but the marginal costs involved are likely to be relatively slight, given that key infrastructure is now in place. Taken together, these factors allowed the redirection of investment to civilian goals for the first time since the 1950s, with beneficial effects on economic performance.

Furthermore, it is at least arguable that the growth of the market was not 'spontaneous' but a consequence of a deliberate change in government policy. At a political level, the writings and speeches of Zhao Ziyang—supported by his deeds in allowing private-sector activities in agriculture, commerce, and handicraft industry to flourish—were important in creating a favourable set of private-sector expectations. Much more important, however, was the decision to raise procurement prices for farm products in 1979 by more than 20%. As the impact of this increase for urban consumers was cushioned by subsidies, the net effect was the emergence of a sizeable fiscal deficit in the late 1970s. This policy of demand expansion was massively important in the reform process. The sudden increase in peasant purchasing power provided a direct stimulus to the establishment of rural industry to meet this new demand. Moreover, the increase in the size of the profits retained by farm households allowed them to invest in new farm inputs and thus accelerate the process of farm modernization. In many respects, of course, the process quickly became self-supporting, but recognition of that should not lead us to downplay the very positive role of the state in initiating this virtuous circle.

However, neither liberalization nor demand management would have proved successful without the existence of supply-side slack. Whilst the Maoist period may not have seen big increases in per capita consumption in Sichuan, it did produce a massive increase in the stock of fixed capital in both farm and industrial sectors. The real tribute to the pre-1975 Maoist strategy, which emphasized investment rather than consumption, is therefore that it made subsequent growth possible. The experience of China and Sichuan during the 1980s serves not as an indictment but as a vindication of heavy industry-biased strategies of economic development for very poor developing economies.

In agriculture, for instance, the 1980s saw at last a conjuncture of abundant inputs of chemical fertilizer and properly irrigated paddy-field. The latter was one of the great achievements of the Maoist period, the former an area of relative neglect (in favour of the defence sector). Input growth after 1978 is shown in Table 3.6.

This growing use of modern inputs in isolation was not enough, for the key feature of the 'green-revolution' technology is that it is a package, with irrigation playing an integral role. As Chapter 6 indicates, the expansion of the irrigated area was one of the great successes of the Maoist periods.

The importance of fixed capital in the farm sector receives confirmation from the slowdown of agricultural output growth, particularly grain production, after 1984. Of course, poor farm-sector

TABLE 3.6. *Growth of Farm Output and Inputs in Sichuan, 1978–1987*

	Machine power (billion watts)	Chemical fertilizer (kg. per hectare)[a]	Area tractor-ploughed (% of arable land)[b]
1978	4.65	128.5	15.0
1979	5.81	151.4	14.8
1980	6.65	165.8	11.8
1981	7.26	181.2	11.0
1982	7.63	180.5	11.5
1983	8.14	205.5	9.6
1984	8.66	204.8	9.1
1985	9.33	211.5	8.1
1986	10.13	247.1	8.3
1987	10.88	234.0	8.2
1988	11.66	237.2	8.8

[a] Measured in terms of nutrient (or effective) weight per cultivated hectare.

[b] The decline in tractor-ploughed area stems from the reductions in farm size associated with decollectivization rather than the 'inappropriateness' of mechanization in farming *per se*. It is difficult to mechanize paddy production, as the experience of Japan and Taiwan indicates, but we must not forget that non-rice farming is very important in the province.

Sources: SCJJNJ (1986); ZGTJNJ (1987; 1988; 1989).

investment performance—little more than 5% of peasant expenditure was on fixed capital by the mid-1980s (NYJJWT, 1986)—was not due to supply-side bottle-necks alone. Continued uncertainty over property rights has done nothing to encourage fixed investment by peasant households. But the relative price structure is perhaps even more important, in that the rate of profit to be earned from grain production was low relative to that obtaining in other economic activities. Watson (1989: 126) summarizes this interpretation thus:

In economic terms, though, prices are obviously the key issue. They influence not only state resources and investment choices but also both household and co-operative behaviour. As producer independence grows, so does the significance of the signals received through the structure of prices. Getting the prices right is thus as important for agricultural investment as is further structural reform.

However, these arguments are perhaps a little too sanguine. It is *not* clear that investment will be optimal in a market economy with a proper system of property rights subject to relative price incentives. The United Kingdom's experience during the 1970s indicates that private-sector investment responds only slowly to market prices even when these embody subsidies; part of this price inelasticity of investment demand may ultimately derive from entrepreneurial failure, and during the recovery of the 1980s, big increases in manufacturing profitability have been only partially reflected in increased fixed investment (Green, 1989). In any case, investment in infrastructure will always be sub-optimal in a market economy because it is a public good unless some effective (but implausible) system of co-operatives can be established. There are therefore grounds for believing that the Maoist system was much better than its Dengist successor at inducing investment in fixed capital in the farm sector.

Moreover, we should not underestimate the long-run impact of Maoist expenditure on crop research and agrarian science and technology. Many of these innovations would have come to fruition in the 1980s with or without the market-oriented reforms of that decade. Stone (1988: 819–20, 821) concluded:

There is no question that the rate of growth of staple food production, greater than during the Maoist period, has been extremely rapid for a large country and that, in view of the decline in foodgrain sown area, the success is completely attributable to yield growth, one of the basic indicators of technical change. Yet growth for staple crops disaggregated, and particularly for the most fertilizer-responsive crops, was already accelerating prior to 1978. This was largely due to three groups of factors: (1) the rapid spread of short-stature wheat and rice varieties, the most successful double-crop hybrid corn varieties, and varietal change based on crosses of Chinese and imported sweet potatoes coupled with extension system successes related to these introductions; (2) rapid development of water control in the late 1960s and early 1970s, especially in north China, based primarily on tubewell and reservoir construction; and (3) the accelerating growth in supplies of chemical fertilizers, the input still critically inadequate fully to achieve the yield potential of the short-stature, fertilizer-responsive varieties throughout China's major producing areas . . . much of the credit for post-Mao growth in food-grain yields must go to initiatives undertaken during the Maoist period.

These arguments are as true for Sichuan as they are for China. Many of the province's successes in the agricultural sphere, such as the use of chemical fertilizer, electrification, new seed varieties, and a vast increase in the irrigated area, are documented in Chapter 6.

The industrial sector also benefited from the enormous investment that had taken place under Mao. This was most obvious in the way that military installations were increasingly converted to civilian use. A good example is the use of Chengdu's air-raid shelters to house shops selling textiles and other consumer goods. More significant was the reorientation of defence industries away from military and towards civilian products. Of course, capital is not putty and cannot be remoulded at will to cater for market demand; but it is evident that Sichuan's defence industries did move a long way in this direction during the early 1980s. During the Sixth Five-Year Plan period, 51% of bicycles, 100% of cameras, 38% of washing-machines, and 72% of refrigerators produced in the province were made in defence industries (SCJJNJ, 1987: 257). By 1985, 41% of the gross output value of Sichuan's defence industries was accounted for by civilian products, compared to 13% in 1980 (p. 258). Between 1979 and 1983, the gross value of civilian products produced by defence industries increased by no less than 44% per annum (Gao, 1987: 158). More-over, the policy of 'defence–civilian integration' (*zhunmin jiehe*) pursued actively from the late 1970s onwards led to a growing vertical integration of civilian and defence plants to produce a single finished product (pp. 157–8). At a microlevel, the shipping industry is an example. The shortages in this sector mentioned earlier have been partially relieved during the late 1970s and early 1980s by exploiting the capacity of the naval facilities established as part of the Third-Front programme in Chongqing, Fuling, and Wanxian after 1965:

In recent years, with the position of the national economy improving, China's shipping industry has adopted as a guiding principle the slogan 'Give priority in the Chinese interior to export promotion and to a variety of management forms in the shipping industry'. Under the direction of these guiding principles, Sichuan's shipping industry has achieved good results. In the last few years, the value of civilian products as a proportion of the gross output value of the shipping industry has succeeded in growing every year, from 12% in 1979 to 24.9% in 1980, 36.1% in 1981, 40% in 1982, 50.2% in 1983, and 56.8% in 1984.   (Gao, 1987: 147)

Of course, some of these figures are so high as to be rather hard to believe. It is possible that identical products have been reclassified as civilian after 1978, possibly because of their use by rear-echelon troops that have also be reclassified as civilians. In any case, the area is a definitional nightmare. Is, for example, a cotton vest produced in a defence factory and sold to a soldier for his personal use, whether on duty or not, a military or a civilian product? Nevertheless, and these difficulties notwithstanding, it seems plausible that there has been a significant reorientation after 1975.

More generally, it is difficult to see how the explosive growth of the 1980s could have been achieved in the absence of the heavy investment in energy and transportation that had taken place between 1949 and the late 1970s. That is not to pretend that transport and energy problems are in any sense solved. After all, there seems to be a general consensus amongst academics and Chinese officials that these are the two bottle-necks *par excellence* in the economy at present; moreover, a significant proportion of new investment has been allocated to these sectors during the 1980s. For instance, the massive road-building scheme in and around Chengdu during the late 1980s has involved the construction of multi-lane highways and accompanying new road bridges. However, the fact that the inherited infrastructure was inadequate for the explosive growth of the 1980s does not mean that it served no useful purpose. Without the heavy Maoist investment in infrastructure, it is difficult to believe that *any* growth would have taken place. The emergence of bottle-necks in an economy growing in real terms at 10% per annum over more than a decade is remarkably unsurprising. To be sure, a greater investment in energy and infrastructure could have been made during the Maoist period, but the worth of that which *was* undertaken was self-evident during the 1980s.

An indication of the extent of investment in transport is presented in Table 3.7. The importance of investment in the transport and communications in the First Five-Year Plan is particularly marked, and there is some evidence here of declining priority after 1957. However, the share was by no means small in the late 1960s and early 1970s and, even more significantly, there was a vast increase in the absolute sums involved. In the case of railways, for example, fixed

TABLE 3.7. *Fixed Investment in Transport and Communications in Sichuan (million current yuan)*

	1953–7	1958–62	1966–70	1971–5	1976–80	1981–5
Railways	610.2	531.8	2,696.4	1,170.9	274.7	356.6
Roads	147.5	221.4	355.4	297.0	273.4	368.6
Rivers	14.7	91.5	34.0	101.5	101.1	296.6
Air	1.3	20.6	29.9	16.1	20.9	79.9
Communications	31.0	49.8	98.3	100.9	76.2	184.7
TOTAL	804.6	973.4	3,214.0	1,735.3	900.6	1,295.7
SHARE (%)[a]	30.0	14.1	24.8	12.5	7.2	8.2

[a] 'Share' is the % share of fixed investment and communication in total provincial fixed investment.

Source: Gao (1987: 418–20).

investment during the late 1960s was more than four times the level of the First Five-Year plan. Furthermore, if infrastructure had been neglected during the late Maoist period, one might reasonably have expected to see a sudden surge in the early 1980s, but that did not happen. The railway network has changed little in its extent during the 1980s (some 2,800 km.), yet the volume of freight increased from 17.7 billion tonne/km. in 1978 to 35.2 billion tonne/km. in 1988 (LSTJ, 1990: 709). The road network increased in extent by 14% between 1982 and 1988 (ZGTJNJ, 1989: 396; 1983: 300) yet the volume of freight increased by 78% over the same period (LSTJ, 1990: 709). By the late 1980s the need for further infrastructural investment was increasingly evident from the degree of congestion, but this does not alter the fact that the inheritance from the late Maoist period was at least adequate to support the surge in production that occurred in the early Dengist period.

More generally, it is important not to ignore the impact of the Maoist years on the quality of the labour force and the implications that this had for post-1975 economic development. Illiteracy in Sichuan, as elsewhere in China, fell dramatically between the 1930s and the late 1970s (Bramall, 1989a: 37–40) and it is difficult to believe that the consequences were unfavourable. It is transparent that the data need to be heavily qualified, and of course there must be doubts about how far the type of education received in the Maoist school was ideally suited to the task of modernizing a poor farm economy. Nevertheless, it is difficult to envisage a country being able to embark upon the path of modern economic growth without a literate population. Indeed, one of the problems with the post-1978 pattern of development has been a decline in school attendance in some areas because rural industry providing an abundance of jobs for even children has developed apace.[11] To some extent, higher incomes have made it easier to finance education in the countryside, and it is likely that firms will pay increasing attention to work-force training in the future. Moreover, the decline in absolute numbers to some extent reflects a fall in the number of children of school age.[12] Nevertheless, the overall trend is potentially disturbing, and throws into sharp relief the achievements of the Maoist years.

---

[11] I am grateful to Atsuko Kobayashi for drawing my attention to trends in Zhejiang and Jiangsu in this regard in the late 1980s.

[12] I should like to thank Peter Nolan for reminding me of this point.

Summary

It is a great fault of much of the literature seeking to evaluate the performance of 'socialist' regimes that it neglects to pose the most important counterfactual. Whilst it is true that such economies have fallen well short of achieving a Pareto-efficient resource allocation during their periods of central planning, their likely performance in its absence remains a legitimate area of enquiry. It is at least conceivable that the market outcome could have been even worse when one pays due regard to the absence of clearly defined systems of property rights pre-planning, the external threats that many such have faced during the twentieth century, and their unfavourable economic geography. As has often rightly been said in defence of China, her development record bears comparison with that of India since 1947. Moreover, one must be careful not to draw the wrong conclusion from the 'de-Stalinization' that has taken place in Eastern Europe during the late 1980s. There is a widespread popular perception that planning has failed, given the gulf in living standards between East and West. However, this arguably reflects the impact of *glasnost* on aspirations rather than poor performance *per se*. If the East does lag behind the West, at least part of that must be due to the relatively primitive economic systems that existed there before the advent of planning. And much of the remaining 'achievement gap' reflects the strategic threat posed by the West which forced these countries to devote a large proportion of low per capita levels of GDP to defence.

These arguments are particularly relevant to any assessment of Sichuan's economic performance. It has been suggested in this chapter that the nature of the system of Maoist economic planning does not explain the province's modest record on living standards over the half-century after 1931. The periods when trends were least favourable, namely wartime and during the Great Leap Forward, reflect in large measure the *absence* rather than the presence of effective economic planning. The years between the early 1960s and 1975 were not marked by conspicuous economic success; but, in view of the military threat offered by the USSR and the USA, it is hardly surprising that investment was diverted from civilian to military sectors, and it was central planning that made this diversion possible. After Mao's death, when there was no significant external threat, the improvement in consumption levels was marked. Moreover, there is a good deal in Sichuan's development experience to suggest that planning can successfully ensure the attainment of relatively narrowly defined economic objectives. For example, trends during the 1950s show just how much can be achieved by economic planning in a poor economy, and Sichuan's phenomenal performance since 1975 is a tribute to the success of the Maoist system in providing an infrastructural foundation in energy, irrigation, transport, and heavy industry. All this was achieved in a geographical environment inimical to rapid economic development, and despite the legacy of backwardness that was the province's inheritance. It is a record of which Sichuan should be proud.

4

The Theory and Measurement of Income Distribution

The Notion of Exploitation

Marxists argue that a given income distribution can be evaluated using the principle of exploitation. Exploitation, however, is difficult to define. Marx's own definition (1954: 209) was as follows:

> During the second period of the labour-process, that in which his labour is no longer necessary labour, the workman . . . expends labour-power; but his labour, being no longer necessary labour, he creates no value for himself. He creates surplus-value which, for the capitalist, has all the charms of a creation out of nothing . . . The rate of surplus-value is . . . an exact expression for the degree of exploitation of labour-power by capital . . .

This definition is based upon the labour theory of value, however, from which many modern Marxists disassociate themselves. Hence some alternatives have been suggested, notably Roemer's game-theoretic definition (1982):

> . . . feudal exploitation is equivalent to the neoclassical concept of exploitation: a producer is exploited if he is not being paid his marginal product. . . . A coalition is feudally exploited if it can improve its lot by withdrawing under these rules: the coalition can take with it its own endowment.   (pp. 20, 199)

> Marxian (or capitalist) exploitation arises from barriers to opportunities which agents face as a consequence of their restricted access to the alienable, nonhuman means of production. . . . the test for capitalist exploitation amounts to equalising every agent's access to society's alienable property in constructing the hypothetical alternative.   (pp. 21, 202)

However, it is not clear that the notion of exploitation can be rescued by redefinition, because there is no explanation here of *why* the distribution of means of production is what it is and why access rights to property should be equalized across agents. The Marxist approach is therefore incomplete because it lacks a proper theory of justice. Roemer concludes as follows:

What power the expropriation theory appears to have come from another assumption, not stated, that the capitalist starts out with a monopoly on the ownership of the means of production, unjustly acquired; it is the injustice of that monopoly which leads us to believe he has no claim to the product of the labourer. As Cohen says, in his own criticism of the expropriation theory: 'If it is morally all right that capitalists do and workers do not own the means of production, then capitalist profit is not the fruit of exploitation; and if the pre-contractual distributive position is morally wrong, then the case for exploitation is made.' . . . The central ethical question, which exploitation theory is imperfectly equipped to answer is: what distribution of assets is morally all right.   (pp. 278, 281–2)

Roemer's argument is not fully convincing. It may well be that the principle of exploitation is not in itself a sufficient condition for an evaluation of a given income distribution, but then Marx never made the claim that the theory of exploitation was a theory of justice—quite the contrary. One of the strengths of his approach is that it emphasizes the importance of the study of historical processes. At a (very) bare minimum, Marxism is exploitation plus history, not exploitation alone. If we need to explain why the distribution of means of production took the form that it did in a given historical epoch, and if we also need to judge whether that distribution was just as a precondition for judging an income distribution using the notion of exploitation, so be it. Moreover, we can at least break down the issue into two analytically separate questions. On the one hand, we have the question of measurement: what was the degree of exploitation and how did it change over time? On the other, there is the more fundamental question: was the degree of measured exploitation unjust? This latter issue falls outside the scope of this book, which addresses only the first of these two issues.

There are other, more practical, difficulties in the application of the theory of exploitation. One is the need to regard modes of production as unique, and to believe that transition is effected instantaneously between modes by means of revolution. This Marxist approach, it is alleged by the critics, fails to take account of the coexistence of, for example, feudal and capitalist relations of production in different localities within a given country at a specified moment in time. Therefore, the notion of exploitation is unhelpful because one must first specify the unique mode of production prevailing in a given period, and this ensures that any analysis is halted in its tracks at the first hurdle. For example, was the Russian economy capitalist or still feudal after the Emancipation of 1861? As Rudra (1988: 483) puts it with regard to India:

there has been . . . an excess of discussions on what has come to be known as the debate on the 'mode of production in Indian agriculture.' In this debate, which has been inconclusive and very largely sterile, the focus has been on the name to be given to an assumed single mode of production.

To some extent, the issue can be circumvented by accepting that modes of production coexist. This, indeed, is the solution to the impasse taken by many Marxists, including Mao. He made no attempt to suggest that China was capitalist by the Republican period. Quite the contrary: for him, China during the 1930s was undergoing a transitional stage between the feudal and capitalist modes of production; elements of the two were to be found side by side in the countryside. It was clear that exploitation was universal and not of vast significance, whether the process of compelling surplus labour was called capitalist or feudal. The crucial point was that, because both modes involved exploitation, there could be no suggestion of a high degree of equality in the villages.

Thus Mao's writings on conditions amongst the peasantry in Hunan province make a distinction between proletarians and semi-proletarians, and explicitly state: 'There is as yet little modern capitalist farming in China' (1971: 18). Chinese society was characterized not by a single but by multiple contradictions:

There are many contradictions in the course of development of any major thing. For instance, in the course of China's bourgeois-democratic revolution, where the conditions are exceedingly complex, there exist the contradiction between all the oppressed classes in Chinese society and imperialism, the contradiction between the great masses of the people and feudalism, the contradiction between the proletariat and the bourgeoisie, the contradiction between the peasantry and the urban petty bourgeoisie on the one hand and the bourgeoisie on the other. . . . [however] . . . no change has taken place in the nature of the *fundamental* contradiction in the process as a whole, i.e. in the anti-imperialist, anti-feudal, democratic-revolutionary nature of the process (the opposite of which is its semi-colonial and semi-feudal nature) . . .   (Mao, 1971: 99, 103; emphasis added)

Lenin was even more explicit on the need to avoid dogmatism:

Of course, infinitely diverse combinations are possible of this or that type of capitalist evolution and only hopeless pedants could set about solving the peculiar and complex problems arising merely by quoting this or that opinion of Marx about a different historical epoch. (Lenin, 1957: 9)

This is an inadequate solution, however, because if one accepts that feudal and capitalist modes occurred simultaneously, there is an immediate aggregation problem. If feudal and capitalist exploitation coexist, does a 1% rate of feudal exploitation and a 1% rate of capitalist exploitation sum to an aggregate 2% rate of exploitation? Or is capitalist exploitation qualitatively different from feudal exploitation? Moreover, there is no single non-labour factor of production. Exploitation can stem from the concentration of ownership of land, financial capital, industrial capital, draught animals, and even slaves. Is it not possible, indeed likely, that the ownership of some of these will be more concentrated than that of others? Does it not follow that the degree of exploitation suffered by a given peasant household will differ depending upon the type of means of production involved? How, then, does one measure the net degree of exploitation? Is usury the same as landlordism?

An illustration of the problems involved is Patnaik's (1976) attempt to measure the degree of exploitation in India. This is unsatisfactory because, as Rahman (1986) points out, Patnaik looks merely at *labour* exploitation when the process is multi-faceted. Furthermore, households may be both exploited and exploiting at one and the same time. Even small households in modern India and Tsarist Russia employed servants of some sort, yet it does not (presumably) follow that they are therefore exploiters. Moreover, not surprisingly, any attempt at a 'netting' approach is anathema to many, including Rudra (1988: 490): '"Netting" is an arithmetic operation: numbers can be netted by subtracting a number with a negative sign from a number with a positive sign. But I do not know how a relation of exploitation can be netted.'

In practice, these problems can be circumvented. Indeed, from the perspective of the 'revolutionary in the field', these objections carry little weight. 'Netting' was a necessity during the Chinese land reform movement in the late 1940s and early 1950s. Thus the 1947 Basic Agrarian Reform Law (drawn up by Mao) explicitly recognized different forms of exploitation, all leading to conditions of destitution amongst the peasantry and landless labourers:

China's agrarian system is unjust in the extreme. Speaking of general conditions, landlords and rich peasants who make up less than ten percent of the rural population hold approximately seventy to eighty percent of the land, cruelly exploiting the peasantry. Farm labourers, poor peasants, middle peasants and other people, however, who make up over 90 percent of the rural population hold a total of approximately only 20 to 30 percent of the land, toiling throughout the whole year, knowing neither warmth nor full stomach. . . . In order to change these conditions, it is necessary, on the basis of the demands of the peasantry, to wipe out the agrarian system of feudal and semi-feudal exploitation.   (quoted in Hinton, 1966: 615)

Moreover, as Huang rightly argues (1975: 158), the process became even more refined with practice: 'The analysis embodied in the Land Reform Law of 1950 had been profoundly reshaped by the realities of the Chinese countryside . . . In the process, revolutionaries had in fact taken into account many of the exceptional phenomena to which Western liberal scholarship had referred.'

One cannot, of course, pretend that there was anything 'objective' or 'scientific' about the process. Class boundaries were arbitrary and, as the accounts of writers like William Hinton make clear, ideology and the perceptions of neighbours counted for a good deal, especially in the marginal cases. Even so, *some* measure of exploitation was devised and successfully applied.

All this poses immense difficulties for the modern researcher on Sichuan (and on China) because of the information required. We need to know what the degree of exploitation was in the 1930s and the 1970s. We need to know what qualitative data were used in arriving at judgements on marginal cases; it is not something to be taken on trust. Resolution of these issues is manifestly a difficult task even if all the relevant information is available, but in Sichuan's case such data are not available. Some surveys of the degree of exploitation were carried out in the early 1950s.[1] However, nothing systematic was undertaken during the periods that interest us. During the 1930s, the CCP was in no position to carry out such work except in parts of northern Sichuan. During the 1970s, such work was held to be unnecessary because exploitation had been 'abolished' by the Revolution of 1949. Notions of exploitation under socialism (see Roemer's (1982) concept of socialist exploitation) were anathema to provincial and national leadership alike. Moreover, no attempt was made in either period to apply the concept to the spatial distribution of income.

Accordingly, and despite the undoubted merits of the notion of exploitation as a theoretical device, it is impossible to apply to Sichuan. We must use the data that are available to us, and that means reliance on income statistics.

Income Distribution: The Western Orthodoxy

Until relatively recently, most Western economists used a relative-income approach to place a given income distribution in historical

---

[1] Detailed data drawn from surveys conducted in ethnic minority areas in Sichuan in the 1950s have been published. See ASL (1985), GSL (1985), LSL (1985).

and comparative international perspective. When the World Bank's
Development Report cites data on income distribution, it uses figures
on the share of income accruing to the various fractiles of the
population—a relative-inequality approach. However, it is being
increasingly well recognized that there is no overriding reason why we
should restrict ourselves to the use of percentage shares, Lorenz
curves, and the associated Gini coefficient. Alternatives include the
coefficient of variation, the variance of the logarithm of incomes,
Theil's entropy index and his L measure, the Atkinson index, and
Sen's index of poverty.[2]

How should we choose between these measures? In one sense, the
choice is purely technical, with each measure suffering from a number
of limitations. The variance, for example, is not mean-independent,
and the variance of log-income does not satisfy the (generally
accepted) Pigou–Dalton condition that any transfer from a poorer
person to a richer person, *ceteris paribus*, always increases the index
(Sen, 1973: 27). In fact, the distribution becomes non-concave at high
income levels, such that a transfer from a rich to a less rich person
causes an increase in inequality. Additionally, it is useless if there is a
person in the distribution whose income is zero (Anand, 1983: 308).
As for the Lorenz approach, this provides only an ambiguous result
when two Lorenz curves cross, while the Gini coefficient cannot
be decomposed additively into spatial and intralocal components
because of overlapping (Anand, 1983). The Theil entropy index is
non-intuitive (why choose this particular way of measuring the income
distribution?—Sen, 1973) and is also most sensitive to inequality at
the upper end of the income range (Fields, 1980: 109), a property
which is not necessarily desirable.

A more fundamental quandary, however, brings us back to the
normative problem that many Western economists would prefer to
avoid—justice. All of the measures outlined above are based on very
different welfare functions, which themselves reflect an assessment
by the user of which measure of distribution is most relevant in a
particular context. Four general classes of welfare function are dis-
tinguishable. The first is the relative-income approach, which involves
a consideration of the entire distribution and the computation of a
global measure of inequality such as the Gini coefficient. Implicit here
are the twin assumptions that the middle of the distribution is as
important as the upper and lower ends and that persons are more
concerned about their relative, rather than their absolute, income

---

[2] For a summary of these, see Sen (1973), Atkinson (1975), or Cowell (1977).

status. By contrast, the relative-poverty criterion concentrates on the poorest segment of the population and its position relative to the mean. Thus if the average income per capita of the poorest (say) 20% increased by 5% over a year whilst mean per capita income increased by 10%, that is seen as an increase in relative poverty. This change in the social norm is seen as increasing the deprivation of the poor.

This emphasis on relative status is not universally accepted, and an absolute approach has often been advocated instead. The absolute-poverty approach contrasts sharply with the relative one in stressing the absolute (real) income received by the poor. The illustration of the relative-poverty criterion cited above would be interpreted not as a decrease but a clear increase in welfare because the poor are absolutely better off; the fate of the rest of the population is irrelevant in this view. Moreover, there is no denying that such an approach is influential. For example, many of the families interviewed by Townsend's team in Britain saw the poverty of the late 1960s as much less 'real' than that of the 1930s (Townsend, 1979), just as famine in sub-Saharan Africa or the Indian subcontinent appears to have a greater capacity to shock than the poverty of many black Washingtonians.

The counterpart of the absolute-poverty criterion is the absolute-income approach. By this is meant the use of a measure of dispersion which is *not* mean-independent. Underlying the idea is the notion that a fraction of the population may experience greater dissatisfaction if the absolute difference in income between them and some other group is growing—even if their relative position is simultaneously improving. For example, a 10% increase in a wage of £100 represents a much smaller absolute increase than a 5% increment to a wage of £1,000, even though it is relatively greater. As with absolute poverty, the absolute income approach can hardly be rejected out of hand. In Britain during the 1970s, incomes policies under which a maximum percentage figure was stipulated were bitterly resented, on the grounds that they allowed the absolute-income disparity between manual and professional employees to increase.

There are many difficulties in deciding which of these four is best. There is, of course, the very general problem of devising a satisfactory theory of justice. Not everyone accepts the idea that a reduction in any of the four measures mentioned constitutes an 'improvement' in the distribution. To those who see equality and liberty as polar opposites, an increase in inequality is most definitely not an improvement because it necessarily implies a sacrifice of the latter. Moreover, it is unclear whether many Marxists would regard poverty amongst a previously rich stratum as undesirable, although the idea 'feed the poor, starve the rich' seems to me to be as unjust as its converse. However, we can put this issue aside on the same grounds on which we avoided any decision on an ethical judgement as to how a given degree of measured exploitation should be appraised, namely, that the issues of measurement and evaluation are logically separate. However, a further problem arises if the four measures of distributional change do not move in the same direction over time. Unfortunately that will often be the case, because economic development, if the term is to have any meaning, involves both growth and structural change, and such development, as Fields (1980) has pointed out, often results in a rise in the Gini coefficient (increase in relative inequality) and a fall in the share of the bottom 40% (rising relative poverty) as well as a simultaneous reduction in absolute poverty. If one believes that absolute poverty is 'what matters', the Gini coefficient is a very misleading indicator of distributional change.

Fields has in mind in this example a particular type of dualistic economic development, with an economy divided into a stagnant traditional sector and an expanding (in terms of employment) modern sector. In development's initial stages, the income share of the lowest fractile of the population falls because this fractile does not share in 'modern-sector enlargement growth'. At the same time, the enlargement of the modern sector raises its share in total income and therefore raises the Gini coefficient; unchanged *intrasectoral* inequality is assumed throughout. There is also a simultaneous reduction in absolute poverty because of migration from the traditional to the modern sector. That is, some people who were previously poor are now rich; from an absolute-poverty perspective, that is a Pareto improvement and therefore to be welcomed (Fields, 1980: 52–3).

In an attempt to reconcile the relative-inequality and absolute-poverty approaches, Fields proposes what he calls a 'general welfare function' (pp. 36–40). In that this incorporates GDP per capita, poverty, and relative inequality as components, it is difficult to criticize (except in that it stresses opulence at the expense of capabilities). However, one of the conditions imposed upon the function is much less acceptable:

... when an increasing fraction of the economically active population is drawn into an enlarged modern sector, then, other things being equal, relative inequality should be no greater than before. Because the wage differential between modern and traditional sector workers is held constant, this is hardly an unreasonable property.

[It follows that] . . . For modern sector enlargement growth, the conventional relative inequality measures do not 'correctly' measure relative inequality, if the 'correct' definition of relative inequality in dualistic development is the intersectoral income difference or ratio (or a monotonic transformation thereof).

[Therefore] . . . the falling share of the lowest 40% and rising Gini coefficient that arise in this case are statistical artifacts without social welfare content. (Fields, 1980: 39, 55, 56)

Unfortunately, it is the Fields welfare function that is the artefact. Fields's approach is *arguably* correct (that is, if one believes that the absolute-poverty approach is the 'right' one), but it by no means commands unanimous support—which presumably is the purpose of a *general* welfare function. The difficulty in the example Fields quotes is that relative poverty is increasing. If population mean income is increasing and only a part of the population are sharing in this growth, this arguably constitutes a fall in the welfare of those left behind. It is *not* true that some agents are better off and no others worse off (a Pareto improvement) if the incomes of the newly rich enter negatively into the utility functions of the poor ('envy'). Moreover, the increase in the mean implies a change in the social norm, and with it comes an inability on the part of those whose previous (pre-growth) style of living was in accordance with the then social norm to participate in the new society. In other words, the process of growth that Fields describes involves an increase in social deprivation for the poorest members of society. Growth has led to an increase in relative poverty. Of course, one might argue that those not sharing in the growth process might see their welfare as enhanced because of an increased expectation of future income increments for themselves. But one might equally argue the converse. The essential point remains: an ethical judgement is required here which must be subjective.

Moreover, Fields does his case little good by proclaiming: 'Personally, I am most concerned about the alleviation of economic misery among the very poorest' (p. 57). How does this attempt to seize the moral high ground conform with an admission that 'Rawlsians would be indifferent to this type of growth' (p. 54) and the confession that the bottom 40% does not gain at all from the process? It does not. Fields has done us a great service by showing how the process of economic development can affect the distribution of income, and has clarified the way in which various measures of distribution respond to such economic change; but his 'general welfare function' amounts to nothing more than a renewed plea for the use of absolute-poverty measures.

Nevertheless, Sen argues that we should not see the search for a general welfare function as akin to the quest for the Holy Grail:

this does not make the exercise of poverty assessment in a given society a value judgement. Nor a subjective exercise of some kind or other. For the person studying and measuring poverty, the conventions of society are matters of fact (what *are* the contemporary standards?), and not issues of morality or of subjective search (what *should be* the contemporary standards? what *should be* my values? how do I *feel* about all this?).   (Sen, 1981: 16)

However, this does not help matters. First, if a long-run comparison is being made, one needs to answer the question: *which* set of preferences? For example, should one use the social preferences of the 1930s or those of the 1970s in evaluating long-run changes in welfare in Sichuan? Secondly, it is impossible to use the Sen approach in practice because we have no means of knowing the preferences of 'the population' in either the 1930s or the 1970s; and even in cases where we can ask people directly, it is uncertain whether they will reveal their true preferences. Moreover, it can hardly be assumed that preferences are determined exogenously; governments may be able to impose preferences, or at least influence them, by means of propaganda or simply the suppression of information. Thirdly, is it necessarily the case that we should accept revealed preferences, especially if they involve discrimination by a majority against an ethnic minority? Why should national preferences be sovereign? Moreover, suppose one wishes to make international comparisons of income distribution, perhaps in order to decide which countries are in most need of international aid. Will not the revealed preferences of populations vary?

An illustration of the complexity of these issues is provided by the fate of European Jews during the 1930s and 1940s. What were the preferences of the German people during this period? Is the view of the majority of Germans the only consideration? Did their views change over time? For example, a majority might have favoured discrimination yet recoiled from genocide. If Germany had not declared war, would it have been ethically correct for other countries to have intervened to prevent the Holocaust? This is an extreme example but it does illustrate how problematic the Sen approach is. The best that can be said is that the use of any of the four general categories mentioned above is less demanding of information than the notion of exploitation; here, at any rate, we do not face the tricky problem of measuring labour time, socially necessary or otherwise. It is much easier to ask someone about their level of income than their level of exploitation. More relevantly, too, for a historical study, there is far more information available on income distribution than on exploitation.

How, then, do we proceed to analyse spatial distribution if the notion of a general welfare function is illusory?[3] In one sense, there is no difficulty. We can analyse the data using relative and absolute measures of both poverty and inequality. However, suppose the measures move in different directions or, less seriously, the extent of change varies between measures? The best solution is perhaps the simplest. Let us give equal ethical weight to each of the four approaches and then adopt a majority rule so that, if three or four of the measures move in the same direction, we can conclude that the distribution 'improved' or 'worsened'. If two measures move in one direction and the other two in the opposite direction, let the sum of the percentage increases be decisive. Thus if relative poverty and relative inequality each fall by 50% whilst absolute poverty and absolute inequality each increase by 10%, it will be concluded that the income distribution became more equal. Of course this method is unsatisfactory, but so too is every conceivable alternative, unless one is prepared to advance a theory of justice on which there is no consensus.

The Intralocal Distribution

The National Agricultural Research Bureau (NARB) collected data on many economic magnitudes during the 1930s, but income was not one of them. Vermeer (1982: 1) summarizes the general dearth of data:

Statistical data on income distribution in rural China before 1949 are not accurate enough to allow for anything other than superficial generalisations about rural inequality. During the Republican period, Chinese economists and social scientists in their rural surveys collected data on landholding, production, ownership of production means, rents, taxes, family size—but rarely on income.

Moreover, many applied studies have been content with all-China generalizations. Those provincial studies that do exist for the 1930s— Ash (1976) on Jiangsu, Myers (1970) on Shandong, Huang (1985) on north China, and Vermeer (1988) on Shaanxi—are not necessarily applicable to the experience of and conditions in Sichuan in the same

---

[3] The *intralocal* distribution presents special problems of measurement. See the discussion in the next section of this chapter.

decade. Most obviously of all, it had the largest population of any Chinese province, covered an area the size of modern France, and boasted an astonishing variety of physical geography within its frontiers. That suggests that there is a very real danger of drawing misleading conclusions for the province *in toto* from the experience of a few untypical localities.

In addition, Sichuan's countryside was hardly a watchword for peace and rural tranquility during the 1930s. It is true that the beginning of the decade saw uneasy armed neutrality prevailing between rival warlord forces, but that soon gave way to bitter conflict. The political landscape was further complicated by the arrival of CCP forces in the south-east, the north, and the west. These in turn attracted Kuomintang forces from eastern China to Sichuan and led to extensive military operations in the mid-1930s. Political hegemony did eventually pass to Chiang Kaishek and his Nanjing government, but there was barely time to assume the mantle of authority before the Japanese invasion in 1937. This closed the Yangzi, thus severing the province's principal commercial link with the outside world, and led to an influx of eastern personnel and eastern capital which served to end Sichuan's economic isolation and accelerate her economic development.

This is not to suggest that other Chinese provinces were a model of political stability. Manifestly, they were not. The CCP and Kuomintang forces that arrived in Sichuan in the 1930s came from other parts of China, not from another planet. Moreover, warlordism was not a Sichuanese speciality. Even so, the combination of these shocks was to alter the distribution out of all recognition between 1911 and 1931, only for the events of the 1930s and early 1940s to change it once more. The outcome of these influences can only be traced by detailed evaluation, not by the application of the all-China trend.

Moreover, the specification of the mode of production that was the norm in Sichuan is a perilous exercise, and that makes the application of grand theory particularly problematic. Consider 1934. In that year, Zhang Guotao's CCP forces occupied part of northern Sichuan and were in the midst of land reform. Mao's forces to the west were embarked upon a similar task, and neither commander's attitude towards the landlord class was exactly conciliatory. For want of a better term, we can style this mode of production as socialist. On the Chengdu plain, many households participated extensively in the market-place and wage labour was far from uncommon. Their mode of production was essentially capitalist. Elsewhere in the Sichuan Basin, and on its periphery, the role of the market was much less apparent. The bulk of production was used to meet subsistence needs. Industry was underdeveloped, wage labour was less in evidence, and transport difficulties were legion. To stretch a point, we might describe the mode of production there as feudal. It certainly was not capitalist. In Liangshan prefecture in the south-west, slavery was commonplace: a regular trade therein took place with neighbouring Han areas. Clearly, the mode of production here was slavery. In short, in a single year, four modes of production coexisted. The situation in Sichuan was therefore very different from that in the more advanced, homogeneous, Han provinces of eastern China.

All these considerations show the difficulties involved in trying to apply a general theory of distributional change in a specific provincial context; but if income data are sparse, and the experience of other provinces is unhelpful, how *do* we measure intralocal distribution in Sichuan?

Maoist Perspectives

Much Maoist analysis of village income distribution in the China of the 1930s centres on inequalities in landownership as a guide to poverty and inequality.[4] Those with small landholdings were typically poor, and vice versa. However, few studies confine themselves exclusively to landownership. All have noted that there was no clearly defined and enforceable system of property rights. Incomes were therefore determined in large measure by political and military power. As power was unequally distributed, it was inevitable that incomes would also be so. This notion is well expressed by Dore who, in the Japanese context, distinguishes between two types of landlord:

The first is typically one who acquires control of a territory by military conquest . . . he is lord and master in every sense; he draws produce from the cultivator by virtue of his monopoly of violence; political control and economic exploitation are one and indivisible and there is no conceptual distinction between rents and taxes.   (Dore, 1965: 378)

This characterization in turn evidently owed much to Lenin's outline (1957: 192) of the essential features of feudalism:

---

[4] This term is used rather reluctantly because it is difficult to generalize about a disparate group of writers, and because 'Maoist' is particularly value-laden. However, some convenient shorthand form is necessary. By it are meant those who believe that the Chinese income distribution was unequal by international standards and that the differentiation of the peasantry was increasing. These ideas derive from Lenin's work on the Russian peasantry (1957; 1959). In the Chinese context, they were taken up by the CCP, and Western writers who I believe take a basically Maoist view include Ash (1976), Esherick (1981), and Huang (1975; 1985).

. . . a condition for such a system of economy was the personal dependence of the peasant on the landlord. If the landlord had not possessed direct power over the person of the peasant, he could not have compelled a man who had a plot of land and conducted his own husbandry to work for him. Hence there was required 'extra-economic coercion'. . . The form and degree of this coercion may be the most varied, ranging from the peasant's serf status to his deficiency of rights in the social estate.

The antecedents of Roemer's notion of feudal exploitation are clear from this description, as is the a priori relevance of the analysis to the Republican economy. If one were to try to identify the principal feature of that period, political instability would be the most obvious choice. At no point between 1912 and 1949 was China either politically united or peaceful, these years being marked by a perpetual struggle for supremacy between warlord, Kuomintang, and CCP forces.

But how did inequalities in power and ownership of land lead to income inequalities?[5] According to the Maoists, when capitalist relations of production (freely mobile wage labour) begin to appear in the countryside, the differentiation of the peasantry becomes centrifugal (Shanin, 1972). If a household could create (or inherit by means of a favourable location) a 'surplus' (the difference between output and some notion of 'necessary' consumption) for itself which was larger than that possessed by other households, that surplus would become cumulatively greater over time. The peasantry thus 'disintegrated' over time into capitalist and proletariat households.

This process of centrifugal differentiation reflected the impact of several factors. First, small farms with a large surplus because of (say) differential fertility were able to use it to buy more land. As economies of scale are the norm by assumption, this purchase would not only raise total surplus but also increase the rate of surplus per unit land by reducing costs of production.

Secondly, increases in farm size gave large farms a growing degree of monopsony power. This enabled them to 'exploit' (that is, extract surplus value from) landless farm workers and small-scale owner-operators who supplemented their income from farming with wages from farm labour. In addition, supposing that the landowner did not wish to operate his land as a managerial farm, he also enjoyed monopoly power in the tenancy market. Thus Maoists argue that high rents were the rule in rural areas during the transition phase because landowners were faced with a large number of unorganized would-be

---

[5] The following arguments are very general, having been put forward in the context of many LDCs, not just China. The debate between Maoists and neo-populists also differs little between countries.

tenants. This same economic power also enabled landlords to impose exploitative contracts upon their tenants, involving such practices as rent deposits, short-term tenure, and rents that were invariant with harvest fluctuation.

Thirdly, the surplus was used to finance the purchase of capital inputs. Even if the level of technology was primitive, land productivity could be increased by purchasing 'traditional' inputs such as organic fertilizer, by irrigation, and by the use of animals to supply motive power. However, if 'modern' inputs had been available—which for Lenin meant machinery, rather than the 'Green Revolution' package emphasized by modern Maoists in which high-yielding varieties and chemical fertilizers are combined with mechanized irrigation and tractorization—the process of differentiation would have proceeded even more quickly because of the relatively greater impact on productivity.

Fourthly, the concentration of a surplus amongst a small number of households enabled them to exercise monopoly power in rural money, input, and product markets. Bhaduri (1977), for example, has pointed out that Indian landowners typically face little competition in the money market because the formal banking sector is underdeveloped or even nonexistent in the early stages of development. When there is such limited competition between suppliers of credit, borrower collateral is essentially non-marketable. This allows landowners, acting as money-lenders, systematically to undervalue collateral so that, in the event of default, the landowner will make a clear net asset gain from the transaction because the value of outstanding debt is less than the true value of the collateral. Moreover, the 'personal' relationship between lender and borrower—they often have the same place of residence and the borrower may be an employee or a tenant of the landowner—means that the lender is in a stronger position to recover collateral than, say, a bank in the urban sector. These twin considerations of collateral undervaluation and ease of collateral 'recovery' provide a strong motive for the lender to precipitate default. One way of doing this is for the lender to deliberately impose a high interest rate. According to Bhaduri (1977: 352): 'The rate of interest is . . . seen to operate as a conventional device in the hand of the rural money-lender for accumulating assets, through the transfer of undervalued collateral deliberately brought about by a large-scale default.'

Similarly, large landowners are able to dominate input and product markets. Their surplus can, for example, be held in the form of hoarded grain which can be used both to raise the price and to realize speculative profits by releasing it on to the market at the right moment (usually in the period leading up to the next harvest). Alternatively, they can decide to buy capital inputs in bulk and then resell these to the peasantry at an inflated price. This emphasis on the market power of landlords is a feature of the work of Griffin (1974).

In summary, Maoists stress the totality of the domination of the rural economy by the landlord class, whether in land, labour, credit, input, or product markets, with dominance in each case resting on a combination of ownership of the means of production and political and military power. An initial unjust advantage leads to cumulative increases in differentials between rich and poor households in the countryside. The only way the process can be halted and reversed is by means of a revolution led by the peasantry and urban proletariat. Land reform will narrow differentials in the short run, but the only long-run solution is held to be collectivization.

The Neo-Populist Critique

There is a very different view of the countryside to be found in the writings of the neo-populists (Chayanov, 1966 edn.; Shanin, 1972; Scott, 1976; and, in the Chinese context, Buck, 1937; Myers, 1970; 1982; 1986; Elvin, 1973; Brandt, 1989). In essence, they deny the relevance of any *static* analysis of ownership of the means of production. Where subsistence rather than market-oriented production persisted, co-operation within the villages acted to redistribute both income and means of production:

The rural families struggling to make a living in their villages did not depend solely upon contracts; they also cooperated with each other. . . . It took two forms. The first involved only a few households, which shared their land, labour, or farm capital for short periods when seasonal demand was greatest. . . . The second form involved many households in a village— sometimes in several villages—grouped together and bearing the costs of undertaking a certain enterprise . . . the most important activity requiring large-scale cooperation was probably water control. (Myers, 1986: 248–9)

They also argue that, in locations where political stability was the norm, there is no need to analyse the way markets operate in determining the degree of static inequality because factors of production were invariably paid their marginal products:

The large number of buyers and sellers that haggled over prices suggests that price competition was intense . . . In general, these competitive product markets seem to have allowed rural families to obtain fair prices, because buyers and sellers never held sufficient economic power to fix prices for very long. (Myers, 1986: 233–4)

Moreover, in *both* market and subsistence sectors, the social mobility of households was considerable. Over time, poor households became prosperous and rich households became poor. In neoclassical language, endowments were periodically redistributed such that successive Pareto-efficient price vectors were associated with different income distributions. The key factor here was partible inheritance:

Large landowners formed the backbone of local elite power in villages or market towns. Yet they were not a permanent caste-like group; their large, extended families rarely maintained their position in the community for more than a generation or two before being replaced by other families . . . The reason for this was the custom of partible inheritance, which divided the land and household property among the sons, while providing some security for aged parents. This custom was practised by all households, large or small, wealthy or poor, located either north or south . . . (Myers, 1986: 240–1, 243–4)

Chinese rural society in the nineteenth and the early twentieth century was thus one of the most fluid in the world, lacking any of the status or caste restraints which typified late pre-modern Japan or India. (Elvin, 1973: 258)

Although these writers in general avoid lyrical characterization of the Republican countryside, they argue that the primary problem was that of absolute poverty, itself a consequence of low levels of technology and skills. Seen in long-run historical perspective, this was a direct consequence of the closed nature of Qing society and its inability to foster domestic invention and innovation. It follows from this portrayal that the role of commercialization was positive in its impact. Some neo-populists have recently gone further and argued that commercialization also served to narrow those inequalities that did exist. According to Brandt, for example, the growing commercialization of the Chinese economy between the 1890s and the early 1930s led to a reduction in income inequality:

Rising real wages, a growth in off-farm opportunities, and new non-agricultural sources of incomes all helped to reduce the role of landowner-ship in income distribution. I believe the successively lower measures of inequality for landownership, cultivated area, and incomes reveal the equalizing tendencies these forces had between the 1890s and 1930s. (Brandt, 1989: 173–4)

During the 1920s and 1930s, these trends were slowed down (and perhaps halted) by a short-run crisis that stemmed from four factors: a

fall in the level of aggregate demand, a change in the structure of that
demand, the growth of warlordism and political instability, and a
series of natural disasters (Myers, 1986). Indeed, the true 'crisis' of
the Chinese economy dates from 1931 according to these writers, with
Eastman (1988) going so far as to talk of the 'myth' of peasant
immiserization before 1931. All are, however, in agreement that the
principal obstacles to economic development lay in the sphere of
political instability, both internal and external, and that Maoist notions
of class-based antagonism were inaccurate:

... the weakness of class consciousness among the peasantry [is] illustrated
by the comparative rarity and traditional nature of the social movements
directed against the wealthy. . . . Of the representatives of the elite, it was the
official, not the landlord, who was the most common target. The spontaneous
orientation of peasant action suggests that the peasantry of Republican China
were more conscious of state oppression than of class exploitation.   (Bianco,
1986: 301)

Thus there was little intrinsic injustice in the Chinese countryside.
Inequality was reduced by co-operation, and was in any case seen to
be of less importance than poverty by villagers. Poverty itself was held
to be a consequence of external 'interference' in the harmonious
operation of the village economy, combined with long-run technological stagnation. One task for Western scholarship is, therefore,
to use available studies of rural poverty to generalize about its extent
in China and in Sichuan during the 1930s. Most neo-populists are, for
example, quite happy to rely upon Buck's work (1937) as a guide to
the situation in Sichuan before the disturbances of the 1930s. More
importantly, they argue, we should concentrate on both describing
and explaining Republican China's technological stagnation—rather
than ceaselessly arguing about the irrelevant issue of inequality,
except perhaps in the spatial context.

In one respect, the entire neo-populist theory (and its neoclassical
offshoots) serves as a useful corrective to the Maoist vision. At least
there is a recognition here that there were forces at work which
tended to narrow, rather than to widen, differentials in the Chinese
countryside. These centripetal tendencies are largely ignored by
the Maoists. Nevertheless, the neo-populist interpretation remains
unconvincing.

Whilst not doubting that co-operation between households did take
place, it is not apparent that this was of great significance in reducing
inequalities. Given that poverty was widespread, and means of production scarce, it seems likely that co-operation was little more than a
veil covering a reality of intense conflict between households. That

must have applied especially to public goods such as timber, water, and common grazing land. Without access to these inputs, even sub-sistence was unattainable, and there was no certainty that co-operative membership would guarantee that inputs were available when needed. Popkin, for example (1979: 30), concludes very generally about peasant societies that

peasants see in one another sufficient uncertainty or threat to make social interactions difficult. Moreover, the range of persons for whom peasants make sacrifices (or for whom they do not keep strict accounts) is narrow and generally limited to family units that cook and eat together and that pool many of their day-to-day resources.

Moreover, it is a mistake to conceive of co-operatives as funda-mentally democratic institutions.[6] Marxists have always objected to 'reformist' bodies of this sort on the grounds that they are quickly taken over by the rich and powerful, and that they therefore serve the interests of a small and privileged segment of the community:

Why were the plans of the old co-operators, from Robert Owen onwards, fantastic? Because they dreamed of peacefully remodelling contemporary society into socialism without taking account of such fundamental questions as the class struggle, the capture of political power by the working class, the overthrow of the rule of the exploiting class. (Lenin, Jan. 1923, in Lenin, n.d.: 364)

To be sure, Mao himself saw co-operatives as a decided improve-ment upon private farming but his overall interpretation is close to the Leninist orthodoxy, as his 'On the Question of Agricultural Co-operation' (31 July 1955) makes clear:

As everybody knows, we already have . . . a revolution which took the land from the landlords and distributed it to the peasants in order to free them from the bondage of the feudal system of ownership. But this revolution is past and feudal ownership has been abolished. What exists in the countryside today is capitalist ownership by the rich peasants and a vast sea of private ownership by the individual peasants. As is clear to everyone, the spontaneous forces of capitalism have been steadily growing in the countryside in recent years, with new rich peasants springing up everywhere and many well-to-do middle peasants striving to become rich peasants . . . If this tendency goes unchecked, the polarisation in the countryside will inevitably be aggravated day by day . . . There is no solution to this problem except . . . [to] . . . carry

---

[6] Claude Aubert has suggested to me that Taiwanese co-operatives can be so described, at least when compared against Chinese collectives under Mao, but I remain sceptical.

out cooperation and eliminate the rich-peasant economy and the individual economy in the countryside so that all the rural people will become increasingly well-of together.   (Mao, 1971: 411–12)

This view was not merely an expression of paranoia. As Huang has shown, the allocation of taxation between households within China's villages was determined by the headman and the village council. Although the allocation was generally progressive, the very fact that taxation was levied at all on landless households during the 1930s was both a violation of tradition and an example of the use of political power to serve sectional ends (except where landless households did possess substantial quantities of means of production other than land; a household could be both landless and rich) (Huang, 1985).

Secondly, there is a lack of evidence on China to substantiate the neo-populist mobility claims. That is particularly worrying because much of the evidence on relatively well-documented Tsarist Russia used to substantiate the claims is unconvincing. In particular, there must be doubts about both the representativeness of the studies cited by Shanin (1972; 1985) and his interpretation of them. He makes no mention of whether social mobility affected the middle stratum of households or bottom and top ends; this is important because many would argue that mobility in the middle of the distribution is less significant than either the decline of the very rich or the rise of the very poor. Moreover, of his original 13,880 household sample, 4,586 had disappeared by 1900. Only 663 were identified as extinct, the balance either emigrating or disappearing without trace. This strongly suggests that any conclusion must be tentative because the analysis is very sensitive to the treatment of disappearance. As it is, Shanin argues (1972: 228) that the extent of disappearance *reinforces* his conclusion of substantial mobility. That may be true, but it is equally possible that many of these untraced households also became extinct. Doubtless such untraced extinction is a form of mobility, but it is hardly upward.

Furthermore, the argument relating to partible inheritance neglects the possibility of an expansion of wealth by means of marriage, or by inheritance from a branch of the family without heirs. Unless it is proposed that the bulk of marriages transcended social strata (unlikely in the extreme), this mobility argument loses much of its force. Finally, the mobility argument is at best a long-run hypothesis. The length of Shanin's dynamic study is half a lifetime but even this seems far too short a span during which a substantial estate could be reduced to mere fragments. Those who hypothesize partition as an important

factor evidently have in mind a rural society which is relatively un-
stratified to begin with. Accordingly, the argument may (just) be
applicable to the *peasantry*, but it does not show how partition helps
to eliminate land-based differentials between the peasantry and the
landed gentry/aristocracy. Of course, these issues require investigation in the specific context of Republican Sichuan before they can be
dismissed, but this Russian evidence does not suggest a promising
outcome.

The third flaw in the analysis of Myers, Brandt, and the rest is its
strong neoclassical component. It is frequently asserted that markets
in China approximated to the model of perfect competition.

Examples of highly imperfect product and factor markets in rural China
abound in the literature. Yet, as Albert Feuerwerker noted several years ago,
few studies document these common assumptions about local markets. I
agree. Certainly the data on rural product and factor markets for the early
twentieth century examined in this book reveal those features usually associated with competitive market conditions: many buyers and sellers, freedom
of entry and exit, mobility of resources, and so forth. . . . Huang's work
excluded, however, the consensus now emerging is that markets in the late
nineteenth and early twentieth centuries worked reasonably well and were
relatively free from the kinds of distortions so common to other low-income
countries.   (Brandt, 1989: 10, 147)

Myers has gone further even than this and suggested that few
economies have ever approached perfect competition more nearly
than late Imperial China (Myers, 1989: 641).

Unfortunately, this analysis fails on two counts. First, the empirical
evidence is highly problematic. Brandt attempts to show that the data
support what he calls 'revisionist views' (1989: 148). However, his
resurrection of that hardy perennial, J. L. Buck's data sets, is misconceived: Buck himself recognized how biased his results were.
Moreover, the Japanese Mantetsu surveys of the late 1930s (also used
by Brandt; see Huang, 1985 for a full discussion of these materials)
were necessarily compiled under very unusual circumstances. They
provide insights, but one ought not to generalize about China from
such an unrepresentative sample. It also needs to be said that Brandt
is dismissive of those materials which do not support his conclusions.
Chuan and Kraus (1975), for example, 'actually suggest the possibility
that the Yangtse was less commercialized in the 1920s and 1930s
than it was two hundred years earlier' (Brandt, 1989: 182). Chuan
and Kraus do have a case—for example, Sichuan was virtually self-
sufficient in foodstuffs in the 1930s largely because of political instability

within and outside the province (X. M. Zhang, 1939; Lu, 1936). However, Brandt insists throughout his book that commercialization steadily increased over time and especially after 1890. He *may* be right, but there is a good deal of evidence that needs to be explained away for his claim to carry conviction.

The second problem is rather more general, and centres on the broad contours of Chinese political economy during the early twentieth century. For markets to be perfectly competitive, one strictly needs perfect certainty (or, alternatively, a continuum of seriatim contingent future markets), a 'large' number of agents (strictly an infinity), and zero transaction costs. It is not claimed that this is literally true, of course, but China is supposed to have been closer to this ideal than most other LDCs. One then recalls the absence of mass education, basic public services, and transport infrastructure in Republican China; Sichuan, although the size of France, had nothing more than a mere 16.5 km. of coal-carrying railway in the late 1930s. One recalls the warlordism and civil war of the 1920s and 1930s. One remembers the persistence of slavery and even cannibalism in western Sichuan, and one marvels at Brandt's notion of 'mobility of resources' when the vast majority of Chinese women tottered on their bound feet. Brandt may wonder at the lack of detailed documentation of market imperfections, but realities such as these have been quite sufficient for the rest of us.

Measurement: A Summary

This chapter has tried to show that the question of the measurement of income distribution can in general be separated from the question of its evaluation. However, it cannot be wholly excluded without reverting to something akin to the majority voting rule that was suggested for use in evaluating the spatial distribution. The difficulty is that ethical considerations colour the choice both of the *type* of statistic to be used to measure income distribution and the *evaluation* of trends in any statistic used. An example of the first type of choice is whether one uses a relative-inequality measure in preference to an absolute-poverty measure. An example of the second is, supposing one is using an inequality measure, whether an increase or decrease in the Gini coefficient constitutes an improvement or otherwise in the distribution. This chapter has largely avoided issues of the latter type and concentrated on those that relate to the former. The objective is to measure changes in the distribution, not determine their desirability.

With that end in mind, the notion of exploitation was considered first. There is much to be said for this type of approach, but it is difficult to see that it is of relevance to historical issues unless data on the degree of exploitation have already been collected. In general, it is too demanding of information to be widely applicable. There followed a discussion of the statistical treatments of income distribution employed in the Western-style literature. These have been grouped into the four categories of absolute inequality, relative inequality, absolute poverty, and relative poverty. It has been suggested that Fields's attempt to devise a 'general welfare function' which satisfactorily takes into account all four is unsuccessful unless one adopts a particular ethical stance. This has been avoided by assuming a majority rule.

This chapter should not, however, be read as an affirmation of the general Maoist approach to measurement. The neo-populist claims relating to mobility and the competitive nature of markets and co-operation all need to be examined in the case of Sichuan rather than neglected as 'wrong' on a priori grounds. It is certainly not enough to assume that markets are uncompetitive and to restrict our analysis to the distribution of landownership. In fact, *neither* Maoist nor neo-populist analysis of income distribution carries conviction. Both methods of measurement are flawed, in that they fail to take into account a number of key influences. The Maoists are too ready to ignore factors working towards the elimination of inequalities over time; their interest is only in influences making for centrifugal differentiation. For their part, the neo-populists pay inadequate attention to considerations which markedly weaken the mobility arguments that form the core of their interpretation: the possibility of co-operation serving as a veil for competition and greater inequality, the impact of marriage on the size of estates, and the very strict conditions needed to obtain the neoclassical conclusion. All these issues will be addressed in the following chapters.

5

The Spatial Distribution

Changes in the pattern of spatial differentials at the level of the county between 1931–6 and 1975–8 can be observed by estimating the net value of industrial and agricultural output (NVAIO) per capita for 1939–43 and for 1982.[1] These data are summarized in the Appendix, and they are used here to chart the evolution of spatial inequalities at the county level within Sichuan over time. This chapter discusses the pattern of differentials in the early 1940s, and proceeds from there to a similar examination of the 1982 data. The final section brings together these two periods and assesses the extent of distributional change in the long run, using a number of elementary measures of statistical dispersion. We begin with the literature, and move from there to data problems.

Previous Scholarship on Differentials in the 1940s

Since the 1960s, a good deal of research has been undertaken on spatial inequalities in Republican Sichuan (Skinner, 1964–5; Myers, 1967; Rozman, 1982; Smith, 1988). Most of this starts from the proposition that living standards can be proxied by the extent of marketing activity, an approach pioneered by a number of Japanese scholars. It is also implicit in the celebrated work of G. W. Skinner.

According to Skinner, the Upper Yangzi macroregion—of which the Sichuan Basin is the predominant but not the only component—was much less commercialized than eastern China. He describes the growth process as one of intensification (in which the size of marketing areas tended to fall over time) rather than modernization (in which the size of marketing areas tends to fall): 'It will be noted to begin with that no significant modernization of the rural economy had

---

[1] County-level data are also provided in the Appendix for 1985, and some of these data are discussed in the present chapter. However, the primary purpose is to compare trends between 1939–43 and 1982.

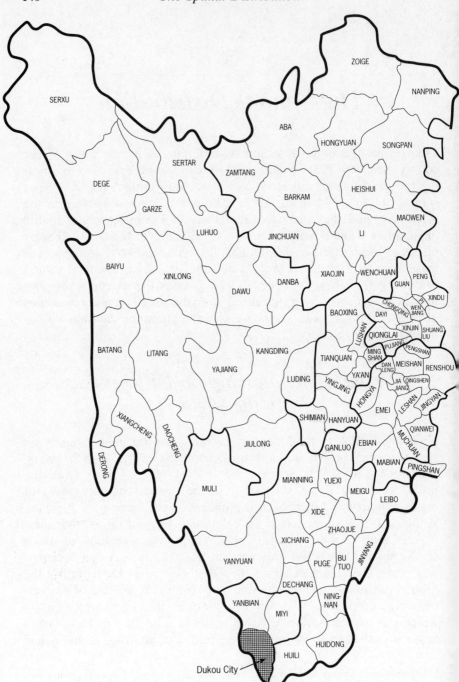

FIG. 4. Counties and Cities of Sichuan, 1985

occurred in either zone of the Basin . . . The Szechwan countryside of 1948 was in this regard far behind rural Shantung in 1911' (Skinner, 1964–5: 225, 226).

The commercialization process was itself dependent upon rising population density and improvements in the transport infrastructure. In general, the initial intensification phase is brought about by rising population density, whereas the era of modernization is ushered in by a transport revolution, especially in overland transport. Although he believes that it is wrong to talk of a transport revolution having occurred in the Upper Yangzi macroregion, Skinner believes that one can distinguish between core and peripheral areas of the region on the basis of transport innovations; the dividing line between the two was the point beyond which river steamers could not pass. More precisely, when population density is held constant, the extent of commercialization evident in counties located in what Skinner calls the Central Riverine Zone (broadly, the Yangzi and its tributaries) is significantly greater than in peripheral counties (Skinner, 1964–5: 223–6). The simplicity of this approach is attractive. Developed counties are marked by a high degree of commercial activity which derives initially from population density and, increasingly during the modern era, from improvements in transport networks. Therefore, according to Skinner, the Central Riverine Zone consisted of 68 counties and periphery of 88 counties in the Upper Yangzi macroregion in 1948.

However, Skinner's delineation of spatial differences is not compelling. First, his analysis is restricted to counties in the Sichuan Basin and therefore excludes the mountainous areas in the western part of the province. Secondly, the choice of 1948 for a base year is rather odd, especially because he views his theory as 'applicable in any particular region only to periods during which major catastrophes were avoided' (1964–5: 196). No definition of catastrophe is provided, but presumably the conflict between warlords and CCP in northern Sichuan in the early 1930s, the famine of 1936–7, the establishment of the national capital at Chongqing between 1939 and 1945, the hyperinflation of the 1940s, and the imminent collapse of Nationalist rule in 1948 are not to be classified as 'normal'. It is therefore distinctly questionable to infer that, because the Sichuan of 1948 lagged behind the Shandong of 1911, Sichuan in particular and the Upper Yangzi macroregion in general was much less developed than eastern China. In other words, the comparison is very much biased in favour of Shandong. To expect commercial activity to have remained at a high level in the circumstances prevailing in Sichuan during the 1930s and 1940s is at odds with everything that is known about the impact of hyperinflation; a universal consequence is the growth of barter which, because of its high transaction costs relative to those of a monetary economy, leads to a decline in commercial activity. It is therefore difficult to see much purpose in the employment of 1948 data.

A third difficulty is that commercialization is at best a rather oblique guide to living standards. To be fair to Skinner, his work does not aim to chart spatial differences in living standards *per se*. However, this is certainly implicit in his writings and needs to be scrutinized. To be sure, there is a long neo-Smithian and indeed Marxian (some of Marx's writings explicitly portray imperialism as a pioneer of capitalism) tradition in which the opening up of traditional societies to Western commerce leads to the development of the forces of production and hence to growth in per capita incomes. Recent exponents of this interpretation in the Chinese context are Brandt (1989) and Rawski (1989). However, there is hardly a consensus of optimism. Marxist *dependencia* writers have always portrayed trade as immiserizing, and one does well to remember that Marx himself saw imperialism as progressive only in the very long run. Moreover, in respect of China, Phillip Huang (1990: 77) has argued that commercialization in China prior to the 1980s led to involutionary growth:

the Ming–Qing period did see substantial growth in the delta's rural economy, in the sense of an absolute increase in the levels of output and output value . . . But close examination will show that this growth was attained at the cost of declining returns per work day. . . . It was *growth without development or involutionary growth . . .*

Given this ongoing debate, it is more useful to look at living standards directly wherever possible rather than to rely upon commerce as a proxy.

Fourthly, the causal processes that Skinner has in mind as determinants of development are unpersuasive. This is not to deny that population growth and infrastructural development can provide a positive dynamic; but to put supreme emphasis on these alone during the Republican period is rather misleading. Skinner himself acknowledges that the counties of the Chengdu plain—which is part of his periphery—are exceptions, but there is an argument for looking in more detail at what might be characterized as a leading sector or a growth pole of Sichuan's economy. Smith (1988) has to some extent substantiated the Skinnerian interpretation by providing some evidence of a long-run shift in the demographic and commercial centre of the province towards the Chongqing area. However, such conclusions are very sensitive both to the data used and to the periods chosen. As

much of Smith's analysis is based upon unadjusted—and therefore highly unreliable—data collected during the 1930s, a degree of
scepticism is warranted. Furthermore, even if the late nineteenth-
century did see the rise of Chongqing, the agricultural sector's share
in GDP was so large even in the 1930s that it is to the Chengdu area
that we should look for signs of modernization.

The Chengdu plain is, of course, particularly interesting because, as
it falls outside the Central Riverine Zone, there was little transport
modernization before the Revolution of 1949. Nevertheless, the extent
of commercialization using Skinner's measure was far in advance of
that of core districts. Skinner seems to take the view here that the
area's 'extraordinary fertility' ensured high population density and
therefore ensured a high level of commercialization, irrespective of
inadequate transport networks (Skinner, 1964–5: 224). If that is so, it
seems to cast a good deal of doubt on the notion that we should assign
central importance to transport infrastructure as a determinant of
living standards. Of course, the Chengdu plain might have reached a
high-level equilibrium plateau based on agricultural development
beyond which it could not advance without industrialization-facilitating
transport modernization. However, the growth of household industry
in the late nineteenth and early twentieth centuries makes this an
uneasy conjecture. It seems rather more sensible to conclude that
Skinner overstates the importance of transport in the development
process.

We are left with a theory that sees commercialization and, by
implication, living standards as a function of population density.
Unfortunately, this is very problematic. Skinner argues that 'When
density of population is held constant, local variations in these natural
features are to all intents and purposes controlled' (p. 224); by natural
features, he means local topography, land productivity, and climate.
But this will only be the case if migration is of such a magnitude as to
equalize population densities between counties. That in turn implies
that migration costs are insignificant, and that the information sets of
would-be migrants are extensive enough to encompass differences in
real earnings between locations as well as differences in the probability
of employment. But if the world is characterized by uncertainty rather
than by risk (using the terms in the Keynesian sense)—or, more
concretely, by the fact that peasants knew little of the world outside
their own district—this seems rather unlikely.

In any case, land productivity is hardly a natural factor, and this
leads on to the observation that the process of economic development
in Sichuan in the 1930s was not a consequence of the unfettered

operation of market forces. A crucial dynamic was provided by warlord-led industrialization in the Chongqing area in the 1930s mentioned earlier. A further stimulus was provided by the establishment of the national capital there by the Kuomintang in the 1940s. Both had important effects on the demand for farm products and factor markets. In other words, the extent of commercialization that Skinner found in 1948 in the Central Riverine Zone can be legitimately viewed as largely independent of population density. Similarly, one cannot assess the position of areas of the northern Basin in the 1940s without reference to the establishment there of a CCP base area in the 1930s.

One is therefore left with the impression that the delineation of the spatial economy of Sichuan provided by Skinner is questionable, and that his explanation of its emergence is at best incomplete. In any case, nothing of significance has been written on the evolution of the province's spatial economy *after* the great Revolutionary divide, or on the degree to which Maoist development led to a narrowing of the distinction between the core and the periphery. The remainder of this chapter seeks to remedy that deficiency.

Some Data Problems

The following analysis of spatial differences in living standards between counties and its evolution over time relies in the main on per capita net output value as a proxy for income. Although the use of per capita NVAIO as a substitute for per capita disposable income is much to be preferred to the use of GVAIO because it at least is a measure of value added, it is still unsatisfactory in several respects. First, it omits a number of important economic sectors, most notably commerce, transport, and construction, and there is no evidence that value added from these was equally distributed across counties. Secondly, NVAIO incorporates fixed investment and is therefore an imperfect guide to short-run disposable income. Thirdly, NVAIO does not adequately reflect the impact of taxation, subsidies, and extra-county financial remittances. Nevertheless, despite the force of these criticisms, NVAIO still appears to serve as a good proxy for peasant income levels. This can be seen by comparing NVAIO per capita and net peasant income per capita in some of the counties close to Chengdu in 1985 (Table 5.1).

Despite differences in the type of price used and all the problems with NVAIO per capita just identified, there is little question that NVAIO serves as a reasonable proxy for incomes. The only excep-

TABLE 5.1. *NVAIO and Net Peasant Incomes by County, 1985*

County	Net peasant income per capita (current *yuan*)	NVAIO per capita (constant 1980 *yuan*)
Wenjiang	433	399
Pi	457	432
Xindu	492	496
Peng	404	389
Guan	399	424
Chongqing	438	376
Dayi	443	366
Qionglai	428	396
Pujiang	417	349
Xinjin	435	371
Jintang	310	272
Shuangliu	381	382
Correlation coefficient: $r = 0.80$		

Sources: Incomes—Chengdu shi renmin zhengfu jingji yanjiu zhongxin (1987: 675–6); NVAIO—Appendix.

tions are the semi-urban districts of Chengdu and Chongqing, where NVAIO per capita data vastly underestimate per capita income. In Chongqing's Shapingba district, 1984 net peasant income per capita was 535 *yuan* (CAY, 1985: 266), yet 1985 NVAIO per capita was only 148 *yuan* (Appendix). By contrast, the figures for Guanghan are very close; 1984 per capita net peasant incomes averaged 538 *yuan* while NVAIO per capita was 600 *yuan*. One reason for the disparity in the case of Shapingba is the high share of workers in total population. Data on peasant incomes obviously refer to the peasant population only—whereas NVAIO per capita figures refer to total NVAIO divided by *total* population. Thus the two figures will tend to converge only when the share of the peasant population in total population is high. Even so, it is still puzzling that NVAIO per capita is so low relative to peasant incomes, because that seems to imply that per capita urban incomes are low. The probable explanation is the impact of commuting. A high proportion of the net output generated by Shapingba's workers will accrue to Chongqing city proper, where many of these workers are employed, whilst the non-agricultural output per capita generated in Shapingba itself will tend to be low. However, the income derived from employment in central Chongqing will accrue to the urban population of Shapingba. Nevertheless, although NVAIO is a poor proxy for incomes in peri-urban locations like Shapingba, the overall impact on provincial measures of dispersion is slight. For most counties, commuting on the Shapingba scale simply does not occur.

A further test of the usefulness of NVAIO as a proxy for living standards is the extent to which per capita NVAIO correlates with per capita consumption. Very little information is available on spatial differentials in consumption for either 1939–43 or 1982. However, some that is available does at least suggest that NVAIO per capita is a reasonable proxy, as Table 5.2 demonstrates. To be sure, even after the omission of the mutton- and beef-eating prefectures of Garze and Aba, the correlation indicated in this table is less than exact, and certainly much less than one to one. However, one would hardly expect it to be so, given the different periods involved. On balance,

TABLE 5.2. *Pork Consumption and NVAIO by Prefecture, 1980s*

Prefecture[a]	Pork consumption per capita, 1980 (*jin*)	NVAIO per capita, 1985 (1980 *yuan*)
Wenjiang	40.8	441
Leshan	40.5	327
Ya'an	40.0	326
Baxian	34.5	290
Fuling	30.2	214
Neijiang	28.5	294
Wanxian	26.9	214
Nanchong	26.6	232
Daxian	26.5	260
Yibin	24.1	255
Mianyang	24.0	318
Liangshan	22.4	221
Correlation coefficient (Pearson): r = 0.71		

[a] Prefecture boundaries from *The Administrative Divisions of the People's Republic of China* (1980). I have renamed the prefecture entitled Yongchuan in this source Baxian to accord with usage in the rest of the book.

Sources: Pork—Fan and Zhuo (1981: 16); NVAIO—Appendix.

therefore, NVAIO per capita—whatever its other faults—does seem to be an adequate guide to spatial differences in consumption levels.

We must also recognize that the use of 1982 and 1939–43 data as proxies for 1931–6 and 1975–8 is not entirely satisfactory. Moreover, almost all Republican data are decidedly problematic in their coverage and quality, an issue discussed at length elsewhere (Bramall, 1989a).

However, there is no convincing evidence that these difficulties are such as to render futile an analysis of long-run trends in the spatial distribution of income. This is essentially because the estimates of dispersion discussed below are relatively insensitive to data changes. It is true that the relative standing of some counties and even prefectures can fluctuate wildly, depending upon which estimate of population one uses for the Republican period. There are relatively few such counties, however, and in every case their population is very small relative to the province as a whole. It is this low weight that must be given to counties inhabited by comparatively small numbers of ethnic minorities in any provincial analysis that guarantees the insensitivity of the provincial figure to fluctuation. Insensitivity is further ensured by the exclusion of much of the western Sichuan of the late 1970s from the comparison (because no acceptable data are available for the late 1930s).[2]

Spatial Income Differentials in 1939–1943

The overall degree of spatial inequality in Sichuan during 1939–43 is shown in Fig. 5 and the raw data collected in the Appendix. It was clearly substantial. If we exclude the county of Jinghua, for which population figures are very unreliable, the range is still around 9:1 between Mabian and Zhaohua (120 *yuan* per capita) and Yibin and Xuyong (14 *yuan*). Even if we ignore the figures for the first two and Mabian as implausibly high for counties with few transport links and poor agricultural conditions, the gulf between Yibin/Xuyong and Shifang is still immense. Moreover, it is probable that the range of differentials is understated by the absence of data on transport, commerce, and construction, value added per capita in all of which was positively correlated with NVAIO per capita at the county level (see Zhou, Hou, and Chen, 1946b for commerce).

Such per capita differentials at the level of the region (to which the

---

[2] The representativeness of the time periods is discussed later in this chapter.

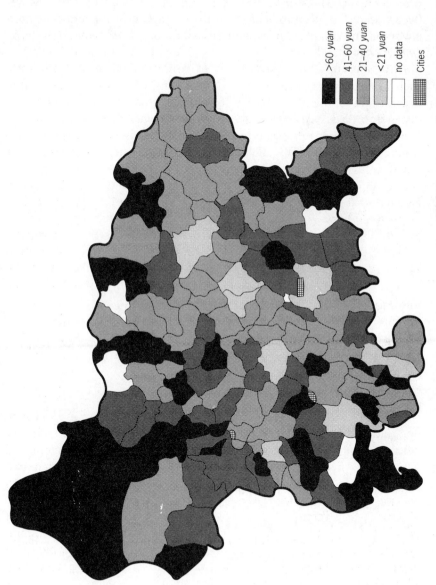

	>60 yuan
	41–60 yuan
	21–40 yuan
	<21 yuan
	no data
	Cities

FIG. 5. Net Industrial and Agricultural Output Value Per Capita by County in Sichuan, 1939–1943

nearest Sichuan equivalent is the prefecture) are by no means unique internationally, as Table 5.3 demonstrates. The pattern of spatial differentials existing in the Sichuan of the 1930s were evidently far from unusual. The province's coefficient of variation is very close to the average for Western Europe in 1977, a conclusion that is by no means intuitively obvious given the different development patterns experienced by the two. Moreover, although provincial differentials were far greater than those of Great Britain in the late 1970s, they

TABLE 5.3. *Spatial Differentials in Comparative Perspective*

	CV[a]	Type of CV	Unit	Admin. division
Sichuan (1939–43)	0.29	Unweighted	NVAIO p.c.[b]	Prefecture
Sichuan (1939–43)	0.21	Weighted	NVAIO p.c.	Prefecture
Malaysia (1970)	0.31	Unweighted	Income p.c.	State
Brazil (1950–9)	0.70	Weighted	Income p.c.	State
Colombia (1953)	0.54	Weighted	Income p.c.	Department
Philippines (1957)	0.56	Weighted	Family income	Region
India (1950–1)	0.28	Weighted	Income p.c.	State
GB (1812)	0.74	Unweighted	Income p.c.	Region
GB (1911–12)	0.62	Unweighted	Income p.c.	Region
UK (1977)	0.09	Weighted	GDP p.c.	Region
Portugal (1970)	0.37	Weighted	GDP p.c.	Region
W. Europe av. (1977)	0.22	Weighted	GDP p.c.	Region

[a] Coefficient of variation. The term 'weighted' here refers to population weighting of mean and standard deviation.
[b] Per capita.

Sources: Sichuan—calculated from Appendix; Malaysia—Anand (1983: 94–5); UK (1812, 1911–12)—C. H. Lee (1986: 131); Brazil, India, Colombia, Philippines—Williamson (1965: 167–9); 1977 and 1970 data—Nicol and Yuill (1982: 412). The UK and Portugal constitute the lower and upper ends of the range of coefficients of variations for W. Europe—defined to comprise France, West Germany, Italy, UK, Spain, Austria, Belgium, Finland, Greece, Ireland, Netherlands, Norway, Portugal, Sweden, and Switzerland.

compare favourably to those observed in the same country during the nineteenth century. Sichuan also comes well out of this comparison relative to other LDCs, notably Brazil and Colombia.

However, the degree of inequality is affected by the size of the unit under consideration (Williamson, 1965). One would expect to see rather greater regional inequality, *ceteris paribus*, in large rather than small countries. We should also remember that dispersion in general—though not in every case—is positively related to the number of administrative divisions used. Countries with few divisions benefit from an averaging out of spatial income differentials and vice versa. These two considerations make international comparisons like those in Table 5.3 problematic.

As far as the core/periphery distinction is concerned, there is little evidence to suggest that the Central Riverine Zone was exceptionally prosperous relative to the remainder of the province. It is true that there is evidence of relatively high living standards in both the area east of Chongqing and in Leshan prefecture. However, as has been noted, this is of little comfort to those who emphasize population density and transport to the exclusion of all else, because of the intimate connection between economic prosperity and Nationalist and warlord-led industrialization.

More importantly, the middle Basin west of Chongqing and around Luzhou seems relatively poor. Up to a point, this is explicable in terms of the closure of the Yangzi to trade after 1937 and the reorienta- tion of the province's trade on a north–south axis to conform with imports from Soviet Central Asia and Burma via Yunnan province. Even so, one would not have expected the Luzhou area to have been quite so far behind if its pre-1937 position had been akin to that implied by Skinner and Smith. Perhaps world depression, and growing Japanese competition during the mid-1930s, played a part, but this was probably more important in explaining the decline of the Santai region which was heavily dependent upon textile production.

Finally, the prosperity evident in Songpan and Fuling prefectures is not readily explicable in locational terms. These two are to be found on the periphery of the Basin (in the extreme north-west and south- east respectively) rather than at its core, as the Skinnerian approach would lead one to expect. To an analysis of these two we now turn.

Prosperity on the Periphery? Fuling and Songpan

One must not claim too much for the data on spatial differentials. Economic statistics for the Republican period are fraught with ambiguity, and one proceeds to analytical issues at one's peril. However, whether the deficiencies in per capita net output data are so great as to persuade one to abandon the attempt is much less certain.

Let us consider Songpan first. This prefecture had the highest NVAIO per capita in Sichuan in 1939–43 according to my estimates. Yet this does not seem plausible at first glance, mainly because of its economic geography. Both climate and topography were unfavourable. Its average elevation was in excess of 3,000 m. and, in the early 1940s, many parts of the prefecture were swamp, as the Red Army had discovered on marching through the area in 1935 (Salisbury, 1985). Furthermore, the prefecture did not enjoy the benefits of a navigable river or any roads worthy of the name.

One possible explanation for Songpan prefecture's prosperity is that the data from which NVAIO has been calculated are flawed. We know that NVAIO is sensitive to estimates of animal products, and hence to estimates of the size of the animal stock. It is not difficult to imagine the problems involved in obtaining reliable estimates of this stock, given the spatial dispersion of animals across very large areas, flock movements during the year, and the suspicion of the local ethnic-minority population towards Han Chinese enumerators. More-over, we know that throughout China, estimates of animal numbers provided the National Agricultural Research Bureau with a number of difficulties during the 1930s, and that the original method used for estimating animal numbers was changed in the middle of the decade. Nevertheless, as will become clear later in the chapter, the relative prosperity of many parts of north-western Sichuan was maintained in the 1980s. It is, of course, entirely possible that the enumeration problems of the 1930s continued to afflict investigators in the latter period, but it seems rather unlikely.

Moreover, it is important to recognize the advantages that the Songpan region enjoyed. For one thing, the average elevation is deceptive. Population centres were to be found in the lower-lying valleys, and here natural conditions were much more favourable, with about 300 frost-free days per annum; double cropping was therefore perfectly possible (Sun, 1960: 310). For another, the area enjoyed massive timber reserves, and the fast-flowing Min River allowed this to be floated downstream to Guan county and hence to Chengdu (Sun, 1960: 217, 218). Before dismissing the income estimate for heavily afforested Songpan prefecture as implausibly high, one does well to remember that timber production is *not even included* in the NVAIO per capita estimates given in the Appendix. Furthermore, the prefecture enjoyed the benefits to be reaped from its large herds of cattle of all types, for which abundant grazing was available on its vast grasslands. This feature distinguishes the Songpan area from both the highly cultivated arable areas of the Sichuan Basin (where almost all potential pasture land was given over to crops) and the arid mountains of north-west China (where water is so scarce that fodder is rarely available in any quantity) (Vermeer, 1988).

Most importantly of all, Songpan combined this wealth of natural resources with a very small population. In the early 1940s, its population density was less than 4 persons per square kilometre (on the basis of official population figures) compared to 220 and 355 persons in Mianyang and Wenjiang prefectures respectively. It was therefore seen to be a land of opportunity for Han settlers, and there was extensive in-migration in the half century before 1949. This would have been greater still but for intermittent conflict between the migrants and the indigenous, predominantly Tibetan, population. Resistance to perceived colonization was the norm, as one astute Western traveller discovered:

Along the lower waters of the Siao Ho [*the Wenchuan area*], all the Man-tze villages which have not been more or less destroyed—with the exception of a few which have been deserted, and are ready for occupation tomorrow, with the lands belonging to them, have been taken possession of by the Chinese, and evidently with much slaughter, for the number of graves is very great. . . . Many a blackened ruin of a once happy Man-tze hamlet stirs the traveller's wrath, and it is hardly less aggravating to find Chinese families comfortably living in the picturesque dwellings of the slaughtered or expatriated aborigines. (Bird, 1985: 378)

Even allowing for a certain bias (and Isabella Bird had been stoned by Han Chinese on the Chengdu plain), the picture is clear enough. It is, of course, true that the whole 'Tibetan question' remains hopelessly obscured up to the present by the respective claims and counter-claims of the Chinese and Tibetans. Nevertheless, this mutual antipathy served as a massive check upon migration and, as such, may have served to raise per capita incomes in the Songpan area.

There are, therefore, some grounds for accepting the economic data on Songpan at face value. Although it was a mountainous frontier district, its low population density and abundant grazing land make it at the very least a possibility that per capita incomes there were in excess of those in many other parts of the Sichuan basin.[3]

Rather more problematic is the case of Fuling prefecture, which

---

[3] Even if the Songpan data are wildly inaccurate, the conclusions reached on trends in the spatial distribution of income at the *provincial* level are virtually unaffected. The low sensitivity of estimates to the inclusion of this prefecture follows from its very small population and from the use of population-weighted measures of dispersion for estimation of the provincial aggregates.

enjoyed an NVAIO per capita on a par with that of Wenjiang prefecture's 48 *yuan*. Certainly some demand- and supply-side factors operated in Fuling's favour. In terms of geography, the western part of the prefecture is part of the Sichuan Basin rather than part of the periphery. The accompanying humid climate and absence of snow in the valleys were very conducive to grain production, and in consequence Fuling's share in NVAIO was the highest of any of Sichuan's prefectures. Further, the relative prosperity of the eastern portion may have been due to the gradual settlement of the Han in areas previously dominated by Miao and Tujia ethnic minorities in the same way as in the north-west. Additionally, wartime industrialization around Guiyang (in Guizhou province to the south) probably led to growing links between it and Chongqing. In the absence of a rail link, and given the cost of overland transportation, it was probably easier to ship goods from Chongqing via the Yangzi and Wu rivers to Pengshui, and then on by junk into northern Guizhou, than to transport them by road. The labour employed in this transport role had to be fed, and counties on the route therefore reaped the advantages of increasing demand.

By contrast, Luzhou prefecture to the west of Chongqing enjoyed no such advantage; the overland transport of goods to Guizhou was rendered doubly difficult by the relatively higher elevation of the part of Guizhou to the immediate south of this prefecture. On the demand side, grain production in the western part of the prefecture was undoubtedly given a stimulus by the proximity of Chongqing and the increased demand that resulted from its becoming the national capital. Furthermore, grain surpluses were undoubtedly shipped from Fuling and Fengdu to the Kuomintang capital in the early 1940s (see the map in Zhou, Hou, and Chen, 1946*a*). Finally, much of this prefecture was classified by Skinner (1964–5: 225) as being included in Sichuan's core, her Central Riverine Zone.

Yet none of this is really convincing. As far as demand is concerned, it is not clear why Fuling prefecture should have benefited more than the prefectures to the west of Chongqing on the Yangzi which were also included in Skinner's Central Riverine Zone; Fuling producers would have had to ship grain *upstream* to the great urban metropolis. Moreover, Fuling's supply-side advantages seem slight when compared to those enjoyed by Wenjiang, and yet both had the same NVAIO per capita. The latter benefited from its proximity to Chengdu city and the Dujiangyan irrigation system, but the former enjoyed few such advantages. The topography in the south-eastern corner of the province is much less favourable to farming. The terrain in general is more rugged than in the Sichuan Basin, with a maximum elevation of more than 2,000 metres and an average of more than 1,000 (Sun, 1960: 301). In addition, the export trade carried by the Wu (in tung oil) must have been adversely affected by the closure of the Yangzi, yet this is seemingly not reflected in the levels of NVAIO per capita. Finally, it is worth remarking that Fuling's relative standing in 1982 was far inferior to its position in the early 1940s, which suggest either that some remarkable change occurred after 1943 (a possibility discussed further in the next section when the 1982 data are considered) or that the 1939–43 data are inaccurate. None of this is proof that the figures for Fuling prefecture are inflated, but they do look suspiciously high.

Two other features of the pattern of spatial inequality in the early 1940s deserve a mention. The first is the relative prosperity of Wenjiang and Mianyang prefectures. Most of these counties were located on the Chengdu plain, and thus benefited from the Dujiangyan irrigation system radiating from Guan county. The Dujiangyan is one of China's oldest irrigation systems (dating from 250 BC) and it continued to distribute the waters of the Min River by canal over the Chengdu plain even in the troubled times of the 1930s and 1940s. In addition, the plain's extensive transport network and the proximity of the city of Chengdu and its urban markets encouraged the development of cash crops. Prominent amongst these activities was the level of Shifang's tobacco production, which contributed signally to that county's prosperity (an NVAIO per capita of 103 *yuan*).

It is noteworthy, however, that *modern* industrial development in this area was extremely limited in the 1940s despite the relative prosperity of the farming sector.[4] Limited transport modernization may well have played a key role here, for Skinner is undoubtedly correct to assert that its importance to the development process cannot be entirely discounted. Chengdu could be reached directly only by small junks via the Min River or overland using the fast deteriorating Imperial road network. As a result, and in the absence of railway links (though a good deal of work on the Chengdu–Chongqing railway had been completed by the mid-1940s), Chengdu enjoyed none of the benefits accruing to Chongqing before 1937 from its position on the Yangzi; these included ease of access both to foreign markets and, perhaps most importantly, to foreign technology. Interestingly, there appears to have been no attempt to develop a canal network linking

---

[4] Although it is important to recognize that the analysis of the Appendix necessarily does not include most household industry; data is unavailable for the most part, but it was undoubtedly of considerable importance in the Chengdu area.

Chengdu with Leshan and the lower Min River during either the Empire or the Republic. This presumably reflects engineering difficulties posed by the undulating nature of the Sichuan Basin and, after 1900, the belief that a canal would soon be rendered obsolete by the Chengdu–Chongqing railway.

A second notable feature is the existence of a number of pockets of prosperity in northern Sichuan despite widespread fighting and famine in the 1930s. Paradoxically, this instability *may* well have contributed to the area's prosperity in the early 1940s because, in the long term, the fall in population outweighed the reduction in cultivated area. This view gains indirect support from evidence on areas further to the east (Pingwu, Beichuan, and Jiangyou counties) through which Zhang Guotao's Fourth-Front Army had moved on its way to join Mao. This area was seen by the Kuomintang in the early 1940s as one that could be developed to raise agricultural output in the province. According to Chi (1939: 15), 'the reclamation area in northern Szechwan, in the two counties of Pingwu and Peichwan, is rich and fertile but its population was reduced by half and its fields made desolate by the internecine struggles in 1935'. This is reflected in the relatively high level of NVAIO per capita for Pingwu, and even in the 1950s there was perceived to be a manpower shortage in this area (Sun, 1960: 305). It is clear, however, that this picture of relative prosperity greatly overstates the position in the 1930s, which was distinctly bleak (see the discussion on the famine of the 1930s in Chapter 9).

Spatial Income Differentials in 1982

The pattern of differences in NVAIO per capita between counties in 1982 is evident in the data summarized in the Appendix and Fig. 6. A full analysis is postponed until the next section of this chapter, when these data are compared directly with those for the late Republican period. Nevertheless, a number of points about the general pattern of differentials in 1982 and trends in *inter-prefectural* inequalities between 1939–43 and 1982 are worth making at this stage.

In general, the extent of spatial inequalities in Sichuan during the 1980s seems to have differed little from those in other Chinese provinces (Table 5.4). That is unsurprising given that national policies were applied almost uniformly throughout China during the Maoist era. Even though Sichuan is larger than most Chinese provinces and therefore might be expected to show a greater income dispersion, the

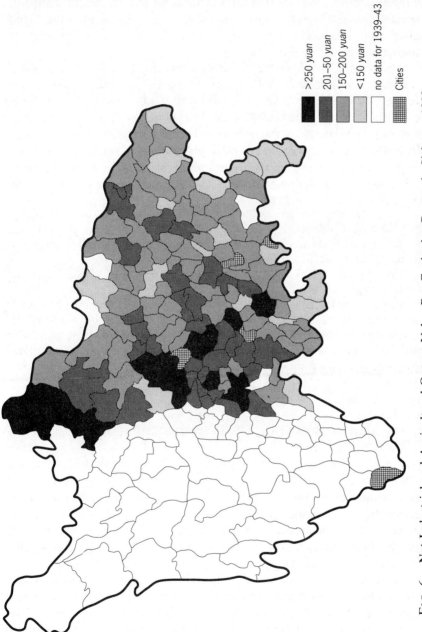

FIG. 6. Net Industrial and Agricultural Output Value Per Capita by County in Sichuan, 1982

TABLE 5.4.   *Inequalities within China's Provinces in the 1980s*[a]

	CV	Unit	Incomes per capita
Sichuan:			
1985	0.32 (w)[b]	NVAIO p.c.	287
1982	0.24 (w)	NVAIO p.c.	198
Anhui (1984)	0.23 (w)	net income p.c.	323
	0.27 (uw)[b]	net income p.c.	n.a.
Guizhou (1984)[c]	0.31 (w)	net income p.c.	261
Jilin (1985)	0.23 (w)	NDMP p.c.[d]	487

[a] These data are for counties only. The net income data are for peasants; others are for total county populations.

[b] (w) and (uw) indicate coefficients of variation weighted and unweighted by total county populations. All have been calculated from the raw data given in the sources listed above except for the unweighted coefficient for Anhui where Nolan's calculation is used.

[c] Income data for 20 of Guizhou's 73 counties are unavailable. The reason for this omission is not known, but it is doubtful that such counties constitute a random sample. It seems likely that income data collection was seldom undertaken in low-income counties because of the costs involved and for obvious propaganda reasons (Guizhou is one of China's poorest provinces, and the status of her poorest counties is rarely advertised).

[d] NDMP (net domestic material product—*guomin shouru*) includes commerce, construction, and transport sector value added.

Source: Sichuan—App. and Bramall (1989*b*: app. A8); Anhui—*Anhui jingji nianjian 1985*; Guizhou—*Guizhou sheng qing* (1986); Jilin—Jilin sheng renmin zhengfu bangongting (1987). Per capita net peasant incomes— ZGTJNJ (1985: 574).

very small size of the population in outlying areas ensures that their inclusion has little impact on the average degree of dispersion.

Substantial differentials in per capita incomes did nevertheless persist between locations in the early 1980s. The range about the provincial mean of 198 *yuan* was from 124 *yuan* (Huaying) to 542 *yuan* (Hongyuan). The distribution exhibits virtually no obvious tail, and even at the top end, per capita income exceeded 300 *yuan* in a mere seven counties. Shifang was the only county in eastern Sichuan with a per capita income of more than 400 *yuan*, and the gap between it and its neighbour Guanghan (470 to 329 *yuan*) was enormous in the context of the overall distribution. At the bottom end, there were 18 counties with per capita incomes of less than 150 *yuan*. The biggest concentration of these (four) was in Fuling prefecture in the south-western corner of the province; Fuling was also the poorest prefecture in the province. Unsurprisingly, all the poor counties were to be found outside the Sichuan Basin proper. The five prefectures without a poor county were all located in the centre of the Basin or on the Chengdu plain. This suggest that difficult physical geography was the principal cause of lingering spatial poverty in the province in the early 1980s.

In general, the correlation between prefectural rankings in the early 1980s and in the 1940s is rather imprecise (Table 5.5). However, it is interesting that there is much greater correlation between the rankings of 1985 and 1939–43 than there is between those of 1982 and 1939–43. Table 5.2 suggests that spatial inequalities were on the increase during the Dengist decade. The increase in the provincial coefficient of variation between 1982 and 1985 is significant, and there is little question that spatial inequalities increased even further during the late 1980s. These two trends suggest that the reforms of the 1980s, with their emphasis on removing constraints on the operation of the market, are leading to the re-establishment of the same pattern of inequality that characterized the late Republican period.

As far as the standing of the individual prefectures is concerned, the most remarkable feature of this table is the dramatic fall in the relative standings of Guangyuan and Fuling. In Guangyuan's case, it seems very likely that it is explained by 1982 being a very untypical year. It was ranked 14th in 1982 and yet by 1985 it had improved its ranking to 6th. Such an enormous change (and it was ranked 6th in 1939/43 as well) seems explicable only in terms of short-term harvest fluctuation.

The case of Fuling, whose ranking fell from 4th equal in 1939–43 to 16th in 1982 (and 15th in 1985) is rather more puzzling. Certainly its standing was not helped by the construction of a rail link between Chongqing and Guiyang, which made the Wu River much less im-portant as a major transport artery between Sichuan and Guizhou; but it is implausible to ascribe Fuling's precipitous decline to this alone because there is no positive counterpart: the growth in NVAIO per capita in the counties of Baxian prefecture south of the Yangzi is little different from that experienced in Fuling.

An alternative possibility is that the abolition of slavery in Sichuan's ethnic-minority areas in the 1950s, and its replacement by collective organizational forms, had a disastrous effect upon relative per capita output. As theories go, this at least has the merit of explaining

The Spatial Distribution

TABLE 5.5. *Prefectures Ranked by NVAIO Per Capita,*
1939–1943, 1982, and 1985[a]

Prefecture[b]	Rank[c]		
	1939–43	1982	1985
Wenjiang	4=	1	2
Neijiang	9	6	7
Baxian	14	10	8
Qionglai	8	4	5
Leshan	2	3	3=
Yibin	16	11	13
Luxian	12	7	9
Fuling	4=	16	15
Wanxian	13	15	16
Guang'an	10	14=	12
Nanchong	15	12	14
Santai	7	8	11
Mianyang	3	2	1
Guangyuan	6	14=	6
Daxian	11	9	10
Songpan	1	5	3=

[a] Spearman Rank Correlation Coefficients:
1939–43 and 1985: 0.66 and, excluding Fuling, 0.83.
1939–43 and 1982: 0.47 and, excluding Fuling, 0.61.
[b] Prefecture boundaries as of 1939–43. NVAIO in Chongqing, Chengdu, and Zigong cities proper excluded.
[c] 1 indicates the prefecture with the highest average NVAIO per capita, and so on.

Source: Appendix.

the relative decline of Songpan prefecture and Leshan prefecture's Mabian, Ebian, and Leibo counties, as well as that of Fuling prefecture. Moreover, the hypothesis is not *entirely* implausible. In the American context, the notion that the South's ante-bellum agricultural sector based upon slave labour outperformed the North's free labour, in terms of total factor productivity, dates from the late 1960s, was given general currency by the work of Fogel and Engerman (1974), and is now widely accepted by neoclassical cliometricians. However, it remains a subject of controversy. The difficulty is that the concept of total factor productivity in the aggregate is decidedly dubious in both theory and fact. Only if factors are paid their marginal products and capital can be measured using the current interest rate is this parable satisfactory. Yet these twin conditions will only be satisfied in conditions of perfect certainty and zero transaction costs (Desai, 1976). The difficulties in substantiating the 'slavery is efficient' hypothesis are rendered even greater by the absence of *any* previous work on the subject for Sichuan. Not surprisingly, the very notion is anathema to Chinese economists trained to accept the Marxian notion of a linear progression from slave via capitalist to socialist and communist modes of production. In sum, then, the case remains unproven.

Far more plausible is the idea that Fuling's growth performance was severely affected by the catastrophic famine of the early 1960s. As will be discussed in Chapter 9, Fuling was hit more severely than any other prefecture in terms of excess deaths, with Xiushan and Youyang counties registering a crude death rate almost double the (extremely high) provincial average for 1959 to 1961. It is possible that this could have reduced Fuling's growth rate in several ways. If excess deaths were heavily concentrated amongst the relatively skilled members of the population, the impact on the quality of the labour force would have been disastrous. Even if, as seems likely, excess mortality was concentrated amongst the young, the elderly, and the sick, it is likely that malnutrition would have severely impaired the productive capacity of the surviving able-bodied work-force. To this efficiency wage-style explanation of Fuling's relative decline may be added the hypothesis of a decline in 'productive enthusiasm'. If the famine was perceived by the ethnic-minority population to be, rightly or wrongly, a consequence of the extraction of 'excessive' amounts of grain, it does not seem likely that either levels or rates of growth of labour and capital productivity in the prefecture would have been as high after 1962 as they might have been. Why produce a surplus when it would simply be siphoned off to feed the Han population elsewhere in the province? Whether this was the true cause of Fuling's relative decline must, however, remain a matter for conjecture.

Literacy and Infant Mortality

The data collected during the 1982 population census also make it possible for us to consider the extent of differentials in broader measures of living standards such as literacy and infant mortality.

Considering the province as a whole (boundaries of 1939–43), the degree of dispersion of NVAIO per capita, illiteracy, and infant mortality is remarkably similar. The (weighted) coefficients of variation for 1982 are, respectively, 0.24, 0.20, and 0.24 (data from ZGRKTJNJ, 1988: 650–63). However, the degree of correlation at a county level is limited. The value of r for infant mortality and NVAIO per capita is a mere 0.13 for 1982. A few examples of counties in which capabilities diverge from NVAIO per capita figures are presented in Table 5.6.

The contrasting fates of Hongyuan and Xiushan here are remarkable. Hongyuan's NVAIO per capita was more than four times greater than that of Xiushan. Yet Xiushan's infant mortality rate was less than half that in Hongyuan, with a very considerably superior literacy rate as well. The comparison between Zoige and Youyang is similar. It is evident from this that high NVAIO per capita status was no guarantee that basic needs would be met. That is not surprising when one notes the geography of areas like Hongyuan, located high on the Himalayan plateau and therefore subject to high rates of infant mortality. One of the most interesting features of the pattern of infant mortality in Sichuan is that it is far greater in counties to be found on the Himalayan plateau, amongst which it is relatively insensitive to changes in either NVAIO per capita or per capita peasant income. If we consider the Sichuan of 1982, and thus take into account all rather than just a small part of western Sichuan, we find that the infant mortality rate was 100 or more in 20 counties, with the highest registered rate being 171 per 1,000 in Sertar county (ZGRKTJNJ, 1988: 650–63). More importantly, every one of these counties was to

TABLE 5.6. *Basic Needs and NVAIO Per Capita by County, 1982*

	NVAIO p.c. (*yuan*)	Infant mortality (per 1,000)	Illiteracy per 1,000
Hongyuan	542	108	47
Zoige	430	113	55
Youyang	136	41	38
Xiushan	130	40	36
Provincial average	198	43	32

Sources: NVAIO—Appendix; infant mortality and Illiteracy—ZGRKTJNJ (1988: 650–63).

be found in Aba, Garze, or Liangshan prefectures. Quite how far ethnic-minority customs and traditions contributed to this dreary litany of excess death is a moot point. As has already been seen, the records of Youyang and Xiushan are much better than those of western Sichuan, and the same is true of other parts of the Sichuan basin inhabited by substantial ethnic minority populations. It is doubtless unwise to generalize about ethnic minority practices, but all this evidence does suggest that the fight in western Sichuan has been to overcome the challenges faced in living at high altitude.

Long-Run Changes in the Spatial Distribution

It was suggested earlier that changes in the spatial distribution of income over time could be analysed using four different concepts of distribution—relative dispersion, absolute dispersion, relative poverty, and absolute poverty. We can now analyse how these various measures changed for rural Sichuan between the 1930s and the 1970s.

Relative Inequality

The approach most widely used in the development literature, though very rarely in the spatial context, is that of relative dispersion. This involves the use of mean-independent statistical measures to assess changes in the degree of difference in per capita incomes between spatial units over time. Three such measures are the coefficient of variation, the Gini coefficient, and the Theil entropy index. When these are computed from the data in the Appendix, the results are as shown in Table 5.7.

This table indicates an unambiguous reduction in the relative dispersion of county incomes between 1939–43 and 1982. The coefficient of variation fell by 52%, the Gini coefficient by 46%, and the Theil index by 67%. Even if one compares 1939–43 and 1985, the dispersion falls by 35%, 30% and 50% respectively. This change is even more striking in that the 1982 distribution Lorenz-dominates the 1939–43 distribution—every point on the 1982 Lorenz curve lies above every point on the 1939–43 curve. Invariably, Lorenz curves intersect when income distributions are compared, and therefore the result is ambiguous; but in the case of Sichuan over this time period, there is no such ambiguity: a reduction in inequality occurred across the entire income range.

These conclusions are not markedly affected by an explicit recogni-

TABLE 5.7. *The Relative Dispersion of Incomes by County,*
1939–1985

	CV[a]	Gini[b]	Theil[b]
1939–43[c]	0.49	0.24	0.09
1982	0.24	0.13	0.03
1985	0.32	0.17	0.05

[a] The coefficient of variation is the standard deviation divided by the mean. Here both mean and standard deviation are weighted using county populations.

[b] The Gini and Theil coefficients are calculated using the formulae given in Anand (1983: 311, 328).

[c] Provincial boundaries are those of 1939–43. Counties of 1982 and 1985 which fall outside these boundaries are excluded from the comparison.

Source: calculated from Appendix data.

tion that these estimates are not comparing like with like. The 1939–43 data are at 1939 prices, and are based on underestimates of both population and cultivated area, whilst the 1982 figures are at 1980 prices and are based upon reasonably accurate estimates of cultivated area and population. In addition, the use of 1939–43 official data implies either that opium cultivation was non-existent or that its share in net output was identical between counties, both of which are implausible. Little can be done about differences in opium production, but it is true that, if the estimates of 1939–43 NVAIO per capita are converted to 1980 prices, and if 'corrected' estimates of cultivated area and population are used (but see Bramall, 1989b: apps. A1, A9 for a fuller discussion), the relative position of those counties where the agricultural sector dominated improves. This is because agricultural production based on official data at 1939 prices underestimates true (i.e. based on corrected area data) production at 1980 prices by a considerable amount, whilst the use of 1980 prices to value industrial production has a relatively slight effect. Nevertheless, the overall impact of using 1980 prices and true cultivated area data is slight. For example, the coefficient of variation based upon data incorporating the corrections is 0.4906—virtually identical to the uncorrected coefficient of 0.4867.

A seemingly more serious problem is posed by the fact that our interest lies in what happened over the 1931–6 to 1975–8 period—not that of 1939–43 to 1982—because this is the most appropriate time-span for the comparison of aggregate rural living standards (Bramall, 1989*a*). A detailed analysis of growth rates of *GVAIO* per capita between 1982 and 1985 suggests the following trends (data are from the Appendix). First, the overall rate of growth over this period across all counties, in constant 1980 prices, averaged 47%. Secondly, poor counties, defined here as counties with a 1982 per capita GVAIO of less than 300 *yuan*, grew by only 30% over the same period, or by a good deal less than the mean. Thirdly, at the top end of the income scale, those counties with a 1982 per capita GVAIO of more than 600 *yuan* grew by around 43%, somewhat less than the mean growth rate but not excessively so. These findings suggest that middle-ranking counties closed part of the gap between themselves and rich counties during the early 1980s, and that the increase in the dispersion is accounted for by the failure of very poor counties to keep up with the mean growth rate. As the rate of economic growth accelerated during the 1980s, the poorest of Sichuan's counties were left behind. It is possible that spatial income differentials may have narrowed between 1978 and 1982; certainly the national evidence points in that direction.[5] However, there is some (limited) evidence for Sichuan that suggests a widening (see Table 5.9 below). Whatever the reality, the change was not large enough to alter the findings of Table 5.7. In addition, it was noted elsewhere (Bramall, 1989*b*) that the pattern of relative dispersion in 1939–43 differed somewhat with respect to the early 1930s, because of the impact of the closure of export markets and a degree of wartime industrialization in Leshan and Baxian prefectures; but, again, its impact upon the overall pattern of relative dispersion was not marked.

Accordingly, it is reasonable to conclude that the trend reduction in relative dispersion that occurred between 1939–43 and 1982 was little different from that occurring between 1931–6 and 1975–8.

Absolute Inequality

Assessing changes in the absolute dispersion is much more difficult. The data given in the Appendix for 1939–43 are based on uncorrected estimates of population and cultivated area; the resulting estimates diverge markedly from the true figure in each case (Bramall, 1989*a*).

---

[5] The unweighted coefficient of variation for per capita peasant incomes across *provinces* (excluding Qinghai and Tibet, for which there are no 1978 data) fell from 0.29 in 1978 to 0.28 in 1980 and to 0.25 in 1981. It rose steadily thereafter, to reach 0.40 by 1989. Calculated from data in LSTJ (1990).

Opium cultivation in 1939–43 has been ignored, and the 1939–43 data are in 1939 prices whilst those for 1982 and 1985 are at 1980 prices.

These problems matter little for the calculation of measures of relative dispersion, as has just been seen. Unfortunately, they cannot be ignored if one wishes to assess changes in *absolute* dispersion over time. One cannot reject the absolute-dispersion approach as an invalid way of assessing inequality simply because our data are not well suited to that purpose; and if one wants to assess absolute dispersion, there is no alternative but to correct the official data. It is meaningless to compare a 1985 mean per capita NVAIO of 286 *yuan* with a 1939–43 figure of 40 *yuan* unless they are calculated on the same basis. Accordingly, the data given in the Appendix have been corrected using the method outlined in an earlier work (Bramall, 1989*b*: app. A9). Estimates of the absolute dispersion of per capita NVAIO by county based upon these corrected data are summarized in Table 5.8.

The degree of absolute inequality of incomes between Sichuan's counties increased substantially between 1939–43 and 1985. Both range and variance were greater, and it seems probable that the 1939–43 range is something of an overestimate because of the un- reliability of the data on Jinghua county and the other predominantly ethnic-minority counties at the top end of the 1939–43 range. But when we compare 1982 and 1939–43, the picture is rather different. Although the 1982 mean is higher, the range and variance are both smaller, which suggests a significant narrowing of long-run spatial inequalities in the province.

Moreover, the use of 1982 data probably overstates the degree of absolute income inequality prevailing in the province in the late 1970s, because absolute measures of dispersion are not mean-independent

TABLE 5.8. *The Absolute Dispersion of Average Per Capita County Incomes, 1939–1985*[a]

	1939–43	1982	1985
Mean	142	198	286
Variance	4,880	2,312	8,262
Range	531	418	560

[a] Data are in 1980 *yuan*.

Source: Appendix; Bramall (1989*b*: app. A9).

and generally increase in line with the mean. Because mean per capita output, incomes, consumption, and capabilities unquestionably increased between 1978 and 1982, the absolute dispersion probably also increased. This observation gives rise to the possibility that the absolute dispersion in the late 1970s was *less* than in the 1939–43 period, and therefore that a 1939–43 to 1982 comparison seriously understates the true long-run reduction in absolute spatial inequality. We cannot be completely certain that this was not the case because the ideal data are unavailable. Nevertheless, the data presented in Table 5.9 suggest that the dispersion of incomes was indeed increasing between 1978 and 1982.

The locations used in this table represent the extremes within the province; Guanghan, Qionglai, and Xindu pioneered the post-1978 reforms and Shifang has long been a high-income 'model' county whilst, by contrast, Liangshan is the poorest prefecture in the province. It is therefore very significant that the gap between the richest counties and the provincial average in absolute terms was significantly bigger whilst simultaneously Liangshan fell further behind. Thus the absolute difference between Liangshan and Shifang increased from 125 *yuan* in 1978 to 301 *yuan* by 1982. If this sample is at all representative, it

TABLE 5.9. *Absolute Spatial Inequality in Sichuan, 1978–1982*

County	Rural income per capita (current *yuan*)		Relative to provincial average (current *yuan*)	
	1978	1982	1978	1982
Guanghan	178	373	+51	+117
Qionglai	144	319	+17	+63
Xindu	167	320	+40	+64
Shifang	196	451	+69	+195
Liangshan[a]	71	150	−56	−106
Sichuan	127	256		

[a] The Liangshan data are for Liangshan autonomous prefecture.

Sources: Sichuan—LSTJ (1990: 720). Guanghan, Qionglai, and Xindu—Chen (1985: 281). Liangshan—Yin (1986: 142) (the figure given above for 1982 is actually for 1983). Shifang—Nongcun xiaozu (1986: 11), *Shifang xian zhi* (1988: 9-7).

suggests powerfully that absolute inequality in the late Maoist period was even less than is implied by the use of the 1982 figures.

We also need to consider whether 1939–43 is a good proxy for 1931–6—not that there is any obvious alternative, given that the data on changes in the absolute dispersion between 1931–6 and 1939–43 are non-existent at the county or prefectrue level. An alternative, very rough, proxy method is to compare *provincial* mean per capita income in 1931–6 with that for 1939–43. As the variance is mean-dependent, an increase in mean provincial per capita income between the two periods would strongly suggest an increase in the absolute dispersion. The results of this comparison are shown in Table 5.10, which indicates that mean per capita output at the provincial level increased slightly between the mid-1930s and the early 1940s. This may seem rather a surprising result: was not China at war in the later period? That is true, and the Sichuan economy was undoubtedly disrupted as a consequence, but, on the other hand, Chongqing's status as Kuomintang capital brought some economic benefits. Moreover, there was nothing new about Sichuan's cities being bombed: Chengdu had been subjected to such spasmodic warlord attacks in the early 1930s. And the famine of 1937 may even have had a favourable medium-term effect, in that it reduced the province's population. Finally, the level of aggregate demand was higher in the early 1940s (at least if price inflation is used

TABLE 5.10. *Trends in Provincial Output Per Capita at 1978 Prices*[a]

	Total Output Value (*yuan*)	Population (no.)	Output value per capita (*yuan*)
1931–6	5,227,000,000	52,055,000	100
1939–43	4,825,900,000	46,302,774	104

[a] Commodities covered in 1939–43 are the same as in 1931–6. The same method of calculation is used, and value added and animal utilization rates are assumed to be identical. Total output value excludes services, commerce, and other 'non-material' sectors. The data for both periods are based upon official estimates of population and cultivated area.

Sources: 1931–6—Bramall (1989*a*: apps. A6 (output), A3 (population)). 1939–43—*The China Handbook, 1937–43*; *The China Handbook, 1939–45*; Zhou, Hou, and Chen, (1946*b*); opium and silk cocoon output assumed the same as in 1931–6; population from Sichuan sheng zhengfu tongjiju (1947: 57).

as an indicator), which probably stimulated production. In short, there is nothing implausible about such a growth trend over these years.

However, since the increase is a very small one, because the data are subject to considerable margins of error—the size of the wartime population is particularly open to doubt given the impact of migration and conscription—and because there was a boundary alteration in 1939, it is more sensible to conclude that there was very little change in provincial income per capita over this period. That does not mean that there were no changes in the spatial pattern of activity between the mid-1930s and the early 1940s; Leshan and Baxian prefectures were undoubtedly benefiting from wartime industrialization. Nevertheless, as has also been seen earlier, this spatial process was already under way in the early 1930s. This assessment, and the results of the table just considered on the overall trend, suggest that the use of data for 1939–43 as a proxy for absolute dispersion in 1931–6 is acceptable. We may therefore conclude with reasonable certainty that the absolute dispersion of per capita output at the spatial level *fell* between 1931–6 and 1975–8.

Relative and Absolute Poverty

We must also consider trends in the spatial dimension of poverty over the 1931–6 to 1975–8 period. These are measures of the relationship between poor counties and mean rural per capita output (relative poverty) and the number of counties in which per capita output fell below a constant-price poverty line (absolute poverty). Measurement is best undertaken by using the 1939–43 uncorrected data for relative-poverty measures (given the problems involved in correction) and the corrected data for the absolute-poverty measure. Changes in poverty, using a variety of criteria, are summarized in Table 5.11.

The sharp reduction in spatial poverty between 1939–43 and 1982 is evident from these figures. The two relative-poverty measures show that the share of the bottom 40% of the population in total NVAIO increased from 25 to 31 per cent, and that the percentage of population receiving less than 75% of mean NVAIO per capita fell by a very large 20 percentage points in the long run. The change in absolute poverty is equally striking. 29% of the population (27 counties) received an NVAIO per capita of less than 100 1980 *yuan* in 1939–43, but by 1982 not a single county fell into this category; the poorest county was Huaying, with an NVAIO per capita in 1982 of 124 *yuan*.

These results are not conclusive, however, because in principle the

TABLE 5.11. *Absolute and Relative Spatial Poverty in Sichuan, 1939–1982*

Poverty measure[a]	1939–43	1982
Income share of bottom 40% of population	24.8	31.4
No. of counties (% population) receiving less than 75% of mean provincial income	29 (30.9)	14 (10.3)
No. of counties (% population) with income per capita of less than 100 1980 *yuan*	27 (28.9)	0

[a] The first 2 indicators are measures of relative, and the 3rd a measure of absolute poverty.

Source: Appendix.

entire reduction in both relative and absolute poverty could have occurred between 1978 and 1982, making a comparison of 1982 with 1939–43 meaningless for our purposes. As it is known that real per capita output growth was rapid after 1978—certainly much more rapid than during 1957–78—this line of argument requires careful consideration.

As far as *relative* poverty is concerned, the trend between 1978 and 1982 is uncertain. However, Table 5.9 suggests that poor areas like Liangshan grew less quickly than the provincial norm and even less quickly than rich counties like Shifang and Guanghan. That implies that relative poverty may well have increased after the beginning of the reforms. After 1982, relative inequality increased (Table 5.7), and it seems likely that the same is true of relative poverty. There is no evidence for either period that the incomes of poor counties grew more quickly than the provincial mean.

Assessing changes in *absolute* poverty is even more of a problem. On the one hand, we know that poverty reduction was very rapid after 1978, when policy changes combined to raise the absolute income level of poor counties. Even before decollectivization, these included a 20% increase in average grain quota prices (and increases for other farm outputs) in 1979, the gradual removal of controls on non-grain farm production, and the increasing provision of 'appropriate' inputs, particularly transport equipment (such as trucks and hand-held tractors). Moreover, many academics have argued that decollectiviza-tion itself, by reducing average farm size, eliminated the diseconomies of farm production which had been a consequence of the enforced use by poor areas of a labour-intensive technique in the Maoist era.

On the other hand, we also know that some counties were still extremely poor in the late 1970s and into the early 1980s. For example, net per capita peasant income in Xiushan was a meagre 70 *yuan* in 1978—and fell to 48 *yuan* in the flood year of 1981 (Nongcun xiaozu, 1986). Net per capita peasant income in the very poor prefecture of Liangshan averaged a mere 71 *yuan* in 1978 (60 *yuan* in 1976) (Yin, 1986: 142). Many of the houses there still lacked windows, families shared their rooms with animals, and 15–20% of homes were incapable even of keeping out wind and rain as late as 1983 (p. 146). Although these figures are unsurprising in that they are broadly comparable with the degree of poverty in other areas of China, it is worth emphasizing how much lower incomes were at the end of the Maoist period compared to those prevailing in rich counties like Shifang, where net peasant incomes were approaching 200 *yuan* in 1978.

It is therefore extremely difficult to determine whether the marked fall in absolute spatial poverty evident between 1939–43 and 1982 was due to changes after, or before, the 1978 climacteric. The only way to resolve this question is by looking at direct evidence on the extent of real per capita growth in selected poor areas between the 1930s and the 1970s. Unfortunately, it is extremely difficult to formulate a conclusive answer to this question. The crucial obstacle here is the absence of data—on either real or nominal magnitudes—that are at all comparable in the long run; there are major doubts in the case of almost every county- or prefecture-level statistics about whether the year is representative and whether the boundaries are consistent. For example, a table in the provincial economic geography (SCJJDL, 1985) purports to estimate changes in GVAIO per capita measured in constant 1980 prices between 1952 and 1982 at the level of the prefecture. Sadly, analysis of population changes shows that growth rates differ so much as to be explicable only in terms of boundary changes or arithmetical errors; obviously this makes the per capita output data capable of various interpretations. This same table provides estimates of per capita GVAIO in the prefectures of western Sichuan—even though no population census was carried out there until 1964. There is the further difficulty that prefectures recovered at very different rates from the effects of civil war and 'liberation' in the early 1950s. As both occurred rather later in Sichuan than elsewhere in China in any case, 1952 is evidently not a very good base year for comparative purposes.

Yet there are limits to the extent to which problems of this kind can

The Spatial Distribution

TABLE 5.12.   *Growth of Real Per Capita NVAIO in Poor[a]*
Prefectures, 1952–1982[b]

Prefecture	1952	1982	% growth
Wanxian	112	177	+58
Luxian	86	263	+206
Yibin	106	187	+76
Neijiang	112	246	+120
Mianyang	115	221	+92
Nanchong	95	182	+92
Sichuan[c]	121	259	+114

[a] 'Poor' is defined as having a per capita NVAIO of less than the provincial average in 1952.

[b] Data are in constant 1980 *yuan*.

[c] The Sichuan figure is a weighted average and includes the large cities (not just their counties or semi-urban districts) of Chongqing, Chengdu, Dukou, and Zigong.

Source: SCJJDL (1985: 96).

mask true trends. This is particularly worth bearing in mind because the data just mentioned do show a significant increase in the real incomes per capita of poor prefectures. Excluding the prefectures of western Sichuan (which were not part of the province in 1939–43, and for which population figures are particularly unreliable), the performance of poor prefectures is summarized in Table 5.12.

These figures indicate that even the poorest performer—Wanxian—achieved a growth rate of more than 50% over this 30-year period, whilst Luxian grew by no less than 200%. In the case of Wanxian prefecture, suppose that we take into account the impact of the reforms undertaken after 1978, the possibility that recovery from the Civil War and the disruption caused by the land reform process was delayed until after 1952, and the benefits that Wanxian derived from international trade in the early 1930s which were lost by 1952. Then it is just possible that this means that there was no growth in per capita output between 1931–6 and 1975–8, and therefore that a conclusion based upon the observed growth of 50% between 1952 and 1982 would be invalid as a conclusion on growth over the years 1931–6 to 1975–8. But in the case of the other prefectures, the sheer magnitude of the observed real growth between 1952 and 1982 makes such a

TABLE 5.13. *Summary of Long-Run Spatial Trends*

Measure	1931–6 to 1975–8	1939–43 to 1982	Measure used
Relative inequality	Fall	Fall	Mean independent (CV; Gini; Theil)
Absolute inequality	Fall	Fall	Mean dependent (variance)
Relative poverty	Fall	Fall	Incomes of poor counties relative to the mean
Absolute poverty	Fall	Fall	Incomes of poor counties relative to a constant-price poverty line

conclusion unwarranted. Accordingly, it seems reasonable to draw the general conclusion that the number of absolutely poor counties was smaller in 1975–8 than it had been in 1931–6.

Spatial Trends in the Long Run: A Summary

The evidence discussed above is summarized in Table 5.13. Of the eight results shown in this table, not a single one strikes a discordant note. Of course, the field of Republican statistics remains one in which angels fear to tread, still less leaden-footed economic historians. So little is known, and so much of what is known is unreliable, that circumspection must need be the order of the day. Nevertheless, we may fairly safely conclude that spatial differentials in income at the level of the county narrowed between the early 1930s and the late 1970s. Relative and absolute measures of dispersion indicate a narrowing of inequalities; relative and absolute poverty measures indicate a reduction in poverty.

These conclusions are reinforced by the fact that the approach adopted in this study has two important strengths. First, it is a province-wide analysis and is not, therefore, vulnerable to the charge that it is spatially unrepresentative (which is *not* to say that one can draw *all-China* conclusions from it). It is thus more satisfactory than much of the qualitative work completed on China in the pre- and post-1949 periods. Secondly, whilst it is true that the measures of absolute poverty and dispersion depend upon a myriad of (sensitive) assumptions, the measures of *relative* dispersion and poverty are far more robust, precisely because they are mean-independent.

More generally, this chapter provides strikingly uniform evidence that the Maoist strategy of economic development was firmly egalitarian in its spatial consequences, at least in Sichuan. Spatial differentials had not been eliminated by 1978 but had been significantly reduced. There are many charges on which Maoism can be indicted before the jury of history, but growing spatial income inequality is not one of them.

6

An Analysis of Spatial Trends

The purpose of this chapter is to explain why the spatial distribution of income and capabilities became more equal between the Republican and late Maoist periods. It begins by discussing the role played by market forces in the form of migration and private capital flows between locations. The second half of the chapter concentrates on the role of the state and government policy in narrowing differentials.

Migration and Private Capital Flows

Corporate capital flows have often been seen in market economies as a key mechanism in the erosion of spatial income inequalities. This is because capital is alleged to be attracted to high-profit regions, and vice versa, but the hypothesis is not uncontroversial. Information on regional rates of profit may be imperfect. Moreover, a region characterized by a low level of real earnings may also be a region of low productivity. If this latter is the case, there may be no difference in profit rates—indeed, the poor (meaning low real earnings) region may also be a low-profit region—and hence no interregional capital flows. Accordingly, a precondition of private capital flows may be a pattern of economic development in the poor region which raises the rate of productivity more quickly than it raises real earnings. If real earnings are rising, regional disparities may well (it depends upon the relative performance of the rich region) decline *before* capital flows take place. Here the cause of convergence is to be found in the reasons for the poor region's economic development, not in market-determined movement of factors of production.

Such issues need not detain us, however, precisely because one would hardly expect these considerations to apply in a centrally planned economy such as China's after 1949. If there is one thing that is certain, it is that the free movement of capital between spatial units did not occur during the 1960s and 1970s. Indeed, the level and composition of investment undertaken even within the commune were strictly regulated; in particular, emphasis was placed on using retained surpluses to raise output rather than for research and development purposes. Instead, then, let us consider the role of labour migration.

Many economists have sought to explain changes in the pattern of spatial income differentials within countries and regions in terms of labour migration.[1] Part of the reason is that migration has been seen as acting both positively and negatively in terms of income inequalities.

The neoclassical assessment is in general optimistic. In a simple model, the migration of labour is determined by differences in real earnings. Economic development is characterized by accumulation and hence (assuming no labour-saving technical progress) rising demand for labour in regions which are growth poles. This will tend to put upward pressure on the equilibrium level of real earnings in the rich region. The labour force of a poor region receiving relatively low real earnings will be persuaded to migrate by the relatively higher real earnings on offer in a rich region. Invoking an assumption of diminishing returns to labour leads to the result that the transfer will depress average real earnings in the rich region and raise them in the poor region. In terms of a neoclassical model of the labour market, in-migration shifts the labour supply curve to the right in the rich region and hence depresses equilibrium real earnings. The converse applies in the poor region. Migration will continue until real earnings are equalized across regions.

Of course, few sophisticated neoclassical practitioners now state the theory in this simplistic fashion. That may not have been the case in the 1950s and early 1960s, when two-sector models based around an aggregate production function flourished. But in the 1980s, even the new classicals recognized that labour migration does not occur instantaneously and that there can be no claim that regional convergence is rapid. Moreover, in that the notion of regional convergence is tied up with models of general competitive equilibrium, it is quite plausible that a state of (general) disequilibrium may be stable. For example, if workers in the poor area are ill-informed about the level of real earnings in the rich area or the fixed costs of migration are very high, it is possible that migration will not take place, and therefore that earnings differentials will persist.

Nevertheless, many still take a positive view of the role of migration. According to Katzman (1977: 94), summarizing some of the Brazilian evidence:

---

[1] Although the bulk of this work has concentrated on the urban–rural dimension of migration—see e.g. Williamson (1988) for a survey.

From 1950 to 1960 . . . the rate of net immigration was directly related to state per capita income. . . . Furthermore during this period relative income gains were inversely related to the rate of net immigration: receiving states grew slower in per capita income, generating states grew faster. A similar pattern was visible between 1960 and 1970.

Moreover, many—including some market socialists—have suggested that income differentials between regions in Maoist China would have declined if migration had been encouraged. For Nolan (1988: 53):

The lack of labour mobility almost certainly had static efficiency costs, and probably inhibited the spread of ideas. It also enabled well-placed collectives to maintain their income, derived from superior location, undiminished through in-migration. It prevented peasants in poor areas improving their situation through migration and, perhaps, in turn improving the position of those left behind through remittances.

Many writers have, however, been far more pessimistic about the role of natural equilibrating mechanisms (Kaldor, 1970; Myrdal, 1957). According to the latter (p. 27):

the movements of labour, capital, goods and services do not by themselves counteract the natural tendency to regional inequality. By themselves, migration, capital movements and trade are rather the media through which the cumulative process evolves—upwards in the lucky regions and downwards in the unlucky ones. In general, if they have positive results for the former, their effects on the latter are negative.

This result is based upon several considerations. First, migration may be determined by non-economic factors, for example, the movement of Muslims and Hindus across the Indian subcontinent at the time of partition. It may therefore be the reverse of that implied by differentials in real earnings. Secondly, increasing rather than diminishing returns to labour may prevail, particularly external and agglomeration economies. Rich areas may therefore gain from in-migration whilst poor regions suffer from labour shortages. In terms of the labour market model, the demand-for-labour curve is horizontal or even upward-sloping. Nevertheless, the pattern of returns is difficult to identify, not least because it may vary over time. Friedmann (1966) argued that what he calls 'core regions' may suffer from energy shortages, transport bottle-necks, inefficient migrant absorption (leading to crime and unemployment), and housing shortages.

Finally, migrants often tend to be young and skilled, so that the poor region loses that section of its work-force which it can least afford to lose. Of course, remittances from successful migrants may facilitate development in poor regions, but this assumes a high level of remittance repatriation which is by no means certain, especially during the period when the migrant is trying to establish a new way of life. Conversely, an increased supply of skilled labour to a rich region may lead to an acceleration in its rate of technical progress (Boserup, 1981) and hence productivity growth. In terms of the model, shifts in the labour demand curve may not be independent of shifts in the labour supply curve. That is far from implausible if one recognizes that those who are skilled are much more likely to migrate, essentially because they are better informed of opportunities in rich regions.

In the light of considerations such as these, Friedmann has concluded (1966: 14, 18): 'The indisputable fact is that regional convergence will not automatically occur in the course of a nation's development history . . . On the whole, the unrestrained forces of a dynamic market economy appear to be working against a convergence of the center and periphery.'

However, migration does not seem to be a relevant consideration in the case of Maoist China because of the imposition of strict controls on both urban–rural and rural–rural labour migration. It is true that one has to be careful in areas such as this. For example, the conventional wisdom was that labour migration was negligible in late Tsarist Russia even after Emancipation until Olga Crisp proved the contrary. Nevertheless, a good deal of information is now available on Maoist migration patterns and, while it is indisputable that some migration did occur, its level seems slight. Jiangsu province, for example, experienced cumulative net out-migration of some 670,000 persons between 1954 and 1982 (Du, 1987: 82–3). Heilongjiang province, still in 1949 a frontier province where extensive land reclamation was possible, experienced a net inflow of fully 7.7 million persons between 1949 and 1982; the province's total 1982 population was 32.7 million (ZGRKNJ, 1985: 1069–72).

As far as Sichuan is concerned, we know that there was heavy in-migration during the eighteenth century from the provinces of south-eastern China that seemingly reflected overpopulation in the latter and the devastating impact of the Qing takeover on Sichuan's population (Smith, 1988). Far more interesting, of course, is the extent of migration within Sichuan during the 1930s when the costs of migration were high. The province's topography did not facilitate movement, the transport network was underdeveloped, and information on migration opportunities was imperfect. It is, therefore, perhaps, surprising that migration was as significant as it was. A survey of the place of origin of the inhabitants of a market town in Huayang county (adjacent to Chengdu city) revealed that only 89% were born in that town. Of the remainder, 6% came from the neighbouring counties of Renshou and Jianyang, and from Chengdu city itself. That leaves 5% coming from further afield (Treudley, 1971: t. vii). A more extensive 1933 survey by the NARB estimated that 6% of *families* abandoned their rural place of residence in that year (the national figures was 5%). Not surprisingly, the number of young men and women migrating was larger, affecting 11% of rural families (Y. Y. Zhang, 1957: iii. 886). Moreover, only 40% of the migration of entire households was 'distress' migration (in response to famine conditions) (p. 892). Of course, much of this migration (perhaps 60% of migrant families) was rural–urban, but this still leaves a substantial volume of rural–rural migration. Evidently, Sichuan's villages were far removed from being island communities.

Furthermore, economic factors seem to have played an important role in causing migration. The extent of 'distress' migration has already been noted and, more generally, it seems to have been the land-poor who were migrating. Some 77% of Sichuan's migrant families in 1935 operated farms of less than 10 *mu* in size (Y. Y. Zhang, 1957: iii. 887). However, only 47% of all farms fell into this category (X. M. Zhang, 1939: A24). As has been noted earlier, there was a considerable flow of Han settlers to the frontier regions of western Sichuan, particularly the Songpan plateau and the valleys of Liangshan prefecture. In the main, then, the pattern of migration during the 1930s seems to correspond fairly well with the neoclassical model. Of course, it was by no means extensive enough to bring about an *elimination* of per capita incomes, but then that is not the neo-classical claim.

Trends after 1949 are more difficult to establish. For the province as a whole, the level of net in-migration between 1954 and 1982 was a mere 491,000 (ZGRKNJ, 1985: 524). Of course, this may conceal important spatial effects. For example, there could have been major emigration from poor regions and massive immigration into rich regions, leaving a small net balance. For that reason, and because of the possibility of extensive *within-province* migration, we need to look at trends in more detail. Unfortunately, we are handicapped by limited information at a county level, although the publication of local records (*xian zhi*) is beginning to remedy this problem. It does appear, however, that the pre-1949 pattern of settlement in the frontier regions of western Sichuan continued, with the deliberate encouragement of the provincial government. In Songpan prefecture, the flow of migrants was large enough to allow the reclamation of much of the swamp land that confounded the Red Army in the 1930s (Salisbury, 1985). In Liangshan prefecture, state farms were established (mainly using prison labour) to open up the Anning valley for farming (Endicott, 1988). In Liangshan's Muli county, the total Han population in 1982 was slightly more than 30,000. Of these, almost 13,000, or 13% of the county's total population, had migrated after 1949 (*Muli Zangzu zizhixian gaikuang*, 1985: 43).

This last figure suggests heavy migration within the province after 1949. However, it is not clear how representative this is. Much of western Sichuan was a frontier region in the Maoist period, and in that context in-migration is not surprising. However, although it was a relatively simple matter to attract skilled workers to the new steel-producing complex at Panzhihua, it was much less easy to attract the farmers who were needed to supply the industrial work-force with food and other consumption goods. The fundamental obstacle was traditional Han antipathy to rural life in mountainous regions (partly because it involved a big change in diet) in which the bulk of the population were of ethnic stock. In the case of western Sichuan, the problem was compounded by the political instability of the region, the ingredients of this explosive cocktail being Tibetan nationalism and the imposition of land reform and collectivization by force in the 1950s. Even more importantly, the migration that did occur could not have been the factor responsible for the narrowing of spatial differentials in the long run because most of this area is excluded from the data used for the long-run comparison of 1939–43 and 1982 spatial distribution. Only a small number of counties on the Songpan plateau and in eastern Liangshan are included in the 1939–43 data.

As far as migration within the Sichuan *Basin* is concerned, almost nothing is known. The only data that are at all relevant on this issue are figures for population growth. The main trends at the prefectural level after 1939 are summarized in Table 6.1. However, it cannot be pretended that these are very helpful. We can only use long-run changes in population as a proxy for migration if it is assumed that natural rates of growth of population between regions were similar and if we can be sure that the pattern was not distorted by severe short-run shocks. The first assumption is probably quite reasonable. There were certainly big differences in natural growth rates between ethnic groups; the Han population grew at annual rate of 2.1% between 1964 and 1982, whereas the ethnic minority population grew at an annual rate of 4.2% (ZGRKNJ, 1985: 528). However, as the latter group were confined mainly to western Sichuan, this pattern is of little significance in explaining trends in the eastern part of the

TABLE 6.1. *NVAIO Per Capita and Trends in Population Density*

Prefecture[a]	Change in population density, 1939–82[b] (total % change)	NVAIO per capita, 1939–43 (1939 *yuan*)
Wenjiang	+82.5	48
Neijiang	+60.7	40
Baxian	+99.2	33
Qionglai	+76.5	41
Leshan	+104.8	63
Yibin	+89.6	29
Luxian	+114.8	34
Fuling	+109.3	48
Wanxian	+117.5	34
Guang'an	+84.7	38
Nanchong	+113.4	31
Santai	+84.9	42
Mianyang	+110.0	55
Guangyuan	+147.6	47
Daxian	+212.0	36
Mean (unweighted)	+107.2	41

[a] The counties of 1982 have been grouped into prefectures which approximate as closely as possible the prefectures of 1939–43 in terms of area. It is impossible to do this properly because of changes in county boundaries and therefore, if one compared changes in prefecture populations, the results would be very misleading. In order to reduce this distortion, population densities are used here on the grounds that changes in county boundaries would have a lesser effect upon prefecture densities than absolute prefecture populations. Even so, distortion cannot be eliminated; it is inevitable that some of the prefectures of 1982 have e.g. gained mountainous (= low density) areas and lost plain (= high density) areas compared to 1939–43. Partly because of such distortions, little causal relationship is evident from these data.

Songpan prefecture has been omitted because boundary changes since 1939–43 make it impossible even to make a rough comparison over the period in question. In any regression analysis, Daxian and Guangyuan would be obvious outliers.

[b] Population densities have been expressed in terms of persons/km^2, and the % figures cited above are for the entire 1939–43 to 1982 period.

Sources: Density—1939–43: area data from Zhou, Hou, and Chen (1946b) and population from the Appendix. 1982: census data given in ZSSWY (1984: 18–26). NVAIO p.c.—Appendix.

province. Within Han areas, there is some weak evidence that the natural growth rate was lower, and that a 'demographic transition' to a lower rate of population growth in the 1970s occurred earlier, in rich as opposed to poor counties. Thus natural growth rates in rich Shifang, Guanghan, and Mianzhu counties were below the provincial average in the 1970s (Lavely, 1984; Endicott, 1988; Lefebvre, 1979; Chang and Xin, 1981); but in general the differences are small and the timing of the 'demographic transition' very similar. Whether natural growth really did fall from around 3% in 1970 to around 0.5% by 1978, as the official data suggest, is very doubtful (it is a quite staggering change by international standards) but there do not appear to have been enormous spatial variations in the process. However, the fact remains that differences in population growth rates are a poor guide to the impact of migration because of the impact of short-run shocks—particularly the famine of the late 1950s and early 1960s. Those prefectures showing slow rates of population growth in the long run were almost certainly those hardest hit by that famine, an issue taken up in Chapter 9.

The limited micro-evidence that is available supports the contention that migration was of limited significance. In the case of Jingyan county (poor by provincial standards in 1982), out-migration seems to have peaked during the Great Leap Forward because of the devastating effect of the famine. Nevertheless, out-migration from the county was only 4,088 in 1959 and 1,962 in 1960 out of a total 1957 population of 305,215. Moreover, the cumulative impact seems to have been small. Between 1953 and 1985, total emigration was only 21,675, and even this partially reflects higher post-1978 migration (*Jingyan xian zhi*, 1990: 98). Of course, the migration of between 5% and 10% of the county's population over a 32-year period was by no means trivial, but it is hard to see flows of this order of magnitude as having had a significant effect on spatial income differentials. Perhaps Jingyan's 1982 level of NVAIO per capita would have been lower in the absence of such migration, but it is difficult to believe it would have had much effect. Even if one makes the (extreme) assumption that the 21,675 migrants had a marginal product of zero, the addition of them all to the county's 1982 population depresses NVAIO per capita by a mere 10 *yuan*.

In sum, the role played by endogenous forces in narrowing spatial income inequalities between Sichuan's counties in the decades after 1939 seems to have been slight although data limitations preclude a definitive conclusion. We turn now to the role played by the state.

Industrialization and the State

As a matter of arithmetic, convergence of NVAIO per capita between counties is a function of trends in industrial and in agricultural output per capita. Although the two are far from independent (industrial outputs can be agricultural inputs and vice versa), it is simpler to analyse the two separately. This section will therefore look at industrial output value and its impact on NVAIO in isolation, with the impact of industrialization on farming considered, for convenience, under agriculture in the next section.

The case adduced by Western economists for regional policy has always been that subsidies provide the means for financing industrial development. Within a market economy, indeed, some sort of pump-priming may be a necessary precondition for private-sector financial flows. Such transfers can also be seen as working towards convergence, in that they may be financed by taxation (or, in the case of a central government running a fiscal deficit, by means of money supply increases or the issue of debt) levied in the rich region. Such transfers have been an essential component in the regional development strategies employed in OECD countries and LDCs alike over the last quarter-century. These considerations are relevant because an important feature of the post-1949 Chinese economy has been financial transfers from central and provincial governments to finance the development of infrastructure, the purchase of consumer goods, and the growth of modern industry. Areas singled out included former revolutionary base areas, counties where ethnic-minority populations predominate, and, more generally, very poor locations. In addition, and perhaps more importantly in the context of Sichuan, state investment in 'Third Front' projects in relatively isolated parts of the province has been substantial. The area around Panzhihua (formerly Dukou) in Liangshan prefecture has been a major beneficiary.

However, the subsidization of poor regions is by no means universally applauded even within state socialist countries. Rather, it is often alleged that such subsidies crowd-out private-sector activity in the poor region. This is the essence of the argument proferred by Wang and Bai (1991) on the effect of subsidies in ethnic-minority areas of China, particularly Tibet. For them, subsidies have discouraged entrepreneurship and hence the development of native industry. They have also, it is alleged, been used to finance the inflow of consumer goods rather than the capital goods necessary for the development of a social and transport infrastructure. That proportion used for investment purposes has simply substituted for the mobilization of the large, indigenous 'savings surplus' which would otherwise have occurred. Their views are summarized as follow:

Funds and goods provided by the central government for backward regions in the course of more than three decades have not resulted in local productive capacity with which to develop the local economy. Of course, no one can deny that central government investment has brought tangible achievements such as the sealed roads, high-rises, motor vehicles, and factory chimneys, that have changed the face of backward regions. What needs to be stressed is that behind this picture of prosperity lie business losses which have been growing with each passing year, massive investment in the form of ever-increasing subsidies from the national treasury, and a situation in which one-third of the inhabitants of backward regions still live in dire poverty: in areas receiving more state aid, the rural population displays less entrepreneurial spirit. Precisely in this respect, by giving money the central authorities do an actual disservice to economic development in backward regions.   (Wang and Bai, 1991: 81–2)

This argument is not, however, very convincing. Running through an otherwise highly interesting and original analysis is a deep vein of racism superimposed upon the notion that poor people are intrinsically less enterprising than prosperous persons. Moreover, many of their conclusions are based upon the degree of entrepreneurship shown within a prefecture in Jiangxi province by in-migrants from rich out-side areas compared to native farmers. Unfortunately, this leads to an identification problem. Even assuming that entrepreneurship can be measured (itself a dubious proposition), is the superior performance of the outsiders due to their rich-province background (as Wang and Bai allege) or to their being migrants? It seems likely that migrant workers are inevitably more enterprising than non-migrants precisely because that is a necessary condition for being a migrant, and there-fore they are utterly unrepresentative of the 'population' from which they are drawn. Wang and Bai ignore this possibility.

More generally, Wang and Bai may well be correct in their con-clusion that there is inadequate indigenous investment in infrastucture and industry in regions such as Tibet; but fear of confiscation of business assets, arbitrary levies, and Han discrimination against ethnic minorities are arguably far more important constraints than any supposed lack of entrepreneurship. For example, the refusal of Tibetans to consume wheat instead of their traditional barley (*tsampa*) is condemned by Wang and Bai (ch. 6) as 'irrational' because the yield of the former is higher; but this neglects the symbolic importance of *tsampa*: its consumption represents a stand against sinification. A similar case is tourism. If Wang and Bai were correct in their hypothesis of entrepreneurial failure, one would expect to see that sector languishing along with the rest, but in fact it is (or was before 1987) highly profitable, precisely because Tibetans see it as a way of publicizing the problems of their country to the outside world. In short, one cannot help but conclude that the problems of Tibet and other supposedly 'backward' regions are as much political as economic or ethnic.

Furthermore, the crowding-out argument as devised by Wang and Bai is as unconvincing as that advanced in OECD economies when substantial excess capacity exists. Few Keynesians have denied that crowding-out occurs at full employment but that is a very different matter from accepting that it is a characteristic feature of economies suffering from widespread unemployment. Still, there is at least a *possibility* of little potential capacity in poor regions, and therefore the crowding-out argument does need at least some consideration in any assessment of the impact of capital flows.

Data on financial transfers to poor regions within Sichuan are very hard to come by except for ethnic-minority counties, and these are not relevant for our purposes because the 1939–43 data set excludes the main ethnic-minority areas of western Sichuan. However, we know that the principal long-run aim of subsidization was to develop industry, and therefore we can gauge its impact by looking at the extent of Maoist industrialization across Sichuan's counties. We have data on industrial output value by county for 1985, and they can be compared with the data for 1939–43 to determine the evolution of industry during the Maoist period. The extent of spatial differences in industrial development are summarized in Table 6.2.

It is evident from the coefficient of variation that differences in the degree of industrialization between prefectures were much greater in 1939–43 than it was in 1985. This reflects Maoist emphasis on rapid industrialization in areas where previously industry had been virtually non-existent. Particularly striking in this respect was the degree of industrialization achieved in Wenjiang, Mianyang, and Guangyuan by 1985 from extremely low levels in the early 1940s. This reflected the development of the entire Chengdu plain as an industrial base and, for Guangyuan, the exploitation of natural gas reserves. Of course, prefecture like Leshan, which had a strong industrial base before 1949, also benefited from Maoist industrial emphasis, as the increase in the prefecture's industry share from 31% to 56% indicates. However, the relatively rural prefectures benefited disproportionately because of their very low bases, and hence the coefficient of variation fell sharply.

TABLE 6.2.   *Spatial Inequalities in Industrialization*

Prefecture[b]	Share of industrial value added in NVAIO[a]	
	1939–43	1985
Leshan	31	56
Mianyang	3	48
Guangyuan	6	44
Wenjiang	2	42
Baxian	21	40
Yibin	22	38
Luxian	15	37
Guang' an	5	35
Qionglai	3	33
Neijiang	20	31
Fuling	11	28
Daxian	1	27
Songpan	neg.	27
Wanxian	16	26
Nanchong	4	25
Santai	10	21
Mean	10.63	34.88
SD	8.95	9.19
CV	0.84	0.26

[a] 1985 correlation coefficient for the share of industry in NVAIO and per capita NVAIO: $r = 0.62$

[b] Prefectures ranked by their 1985 industry share.

Source: Appendix.

The growth of *shedui qiye* (commune and brigade enterprises), it should be noted, contributed very little to this process of rural industrialization in the province before the 1980s. Although communes established industrial enterprises as early as the late 1950s, they only began to grow rapidly in the early 1970s, and even then their growth was most marked in areas where the prosperity of the farm sector was sufficient to allow communes to invest retained profits in establishing factories. Table 6.3 indicates their contribution to gross output value in 1976 for selected counties.

TABLE 6.3. *Output of Commune and Brigade Enterprises by County, 1976*

County	1976[a]		1982[a]	
	GVO[b] (million *yuan*)	Population[c] (million)	Per capita (*yuan*)	GVAIO per capita[d] (*yuan*)
Guanghan	10.59	0.471	22	759
Shifang	7.94	0.364	22	1,097
Youyang	1.47	0.584	3	226
Xiushan	2.10	0.452	5	234
Changshou	4.49	0.783	6	314
Guangyuan	4.50	0.746	6	317
Yunyang	4.30	1.046	4	234
Sichuan average	560.58	95.785	6	537

[a] 1976 output value data at 1970 constant prices, 1982 output value at 1980 constant prices.
[b] GVO is the gross output value of commune and brigade enterprises. It includes transport, commerce, etc. as well as industrial output.
[c] 1976 populations calculated using 1982 populations and the provincial population growth rate between 1976 and 1982.
[d] Provincial GVAIO per capita calculated from GVAO and GVIO data in LSTJ (1990: 704, 698).

Sources: Commune and brigade output—*Sichuan xiangzhen qiye shijian 1977–1986* (1988: 84, 91–6). Others—Appendix.

This table brings together a selection of very rich and very poor counties. By doing so, it shows that commune and brigade industry contributed very little to output value in any of those counties in 1976. Even in prosperous Shifang and Guanghan, the level of collective industrialization achieved by the late 1980s was a distant dream in the year of Mao's death, with collective enterprises contributing a mere 22 *yuan* to gross output value per capita. In so far as collective industries had been established at all in isolated and backward areas like Youyang and Xiushan by 1976, it is true that they were probably contributing to a more equal spatial distribution of industrial output; but for all that, their contribution was at best minor.

It is difficult to know by precisely how much a narrowing of differences in the extent of industrialization contributed to a narrowing of spatial income differentials. It is certain, however, that the relationship is imprecise. As Table 6.2 indicates, the correlation coefficient between per capita NVAIO and the industrial share is only 0.62. The coefficient has the correct sign, but it is not large. That, of course, is hardly surprising, given that NVAO exceeded NVIO in every prefecture except Leshan. Nevertheless, it is worth noting that the use of 1985 data may understate the impact of industry on income differentials before 1978. This is because the share of industry in NVAIO for the province as a whole actually fell from 46.6% in 1978 to 45.1% by 1985, largely as a result of the tremendous post-1978 growth in agricultural output.

Agricultural Modernization and Grain Production: Issues

A satisfactory explanation of convergence in spatial income inequalities must be based upon an explanation of convergence in agricultural output value because of its supreme importance in poor provinces such as Sichuan. Increases in agricultural output were a central part of the Maoist development strategy. The perceived threat posed by the USA precluded reliance on imports of consumption goods, and hence necessitated the adoption of an economic policy designed to ensure self-sufficiency; and the relative success of this type of strategy in the harsh environment of the CCP base area around Yan'an in the 1940s (Watson, 1984) provided evidence that it could succeed.

Nevertheless, the Maoist regime's freedom to achieve this aim was constrained by the simultaneous requirement to maintain the loyalty of the urban population and finance the development of a defence-oriented heavy industrial sector. If military expenditure were to be financed by monetary expansion, it was feared that inflation would be the consequence and that this would undermine the loyalty of the urban population just as it had in the mid- and late 1940s. With foreign borrowing an impossibility, the regime had no other recourse but to extract a savings surplus from the farm sector via taxation or via the manipulation of the intersectoral terms of trade. In the event, low state procurement prices and high prices for farm inputs supplied by the industrial sector were the principal instrument. As it turned out, and as was appreciated when this strategy of 'unequal exchange' was being formulated, the implications for farm sector growth were dire. Without adequate retained profits to finance investment in modern inputs, and with such inputs in any case severely rationed, how could per capita farm output be increased in the face of population growth so as to ensure self-sufficiency?

The basic Maoist answer was to subordinate agricultural policy to the production of grain, cotton, and other basic wage goods. At a national level this principle was given concrete expression in the setting of output targets for these crops. The policy was stressed in the Twelve-Year Plan for agricultural development drawn up in the 1950s, and 'Take grain as the key link' emerged as a slogan after 1966— although excessive emphasis was condemned by the National Planning Conference of 1970, where it was emphasized that grain production was merely the foundation of agricultural prosperity (Liu and Wu, 1986: 360–1). The Maoist strategy rested on three main pillars. First, all counties were to aim for self-sufficiency in grain and cotton production. For some, this would be an impossibility, although Mao went out of his way to point out that the experience of the Dazhai brigade showed that even poor mountainous areas could, via labour mobilization and productive enthusiasm, achieve self-sufficiency; 'Who says that a chicken feather can't fly up to heaven?' and 'The foolish old man who removed the mountains' were characteristically Maoist in tone and intent. Equally, strenuous attempts were made in peri-unban areas to raise production of wage goods.[2] Nevertheless, Maoist practice was less utopian, and for that reason a number of fertile areas throughout China were selected as commodity bases. In the case of grain, areas designated included Sunan, the Pearl River delta, the Jianghan and Chengdu plains, and the Dongting and Boyang Basins (Leeming, 1985: 159). To be so designated, areas had to demonstrate 'a fairly high per capita grain output, a fairly high commodity grain rate or else a large area of wasteland that can be brought under cultivation, or a very great potential to increase output of commodity grain.' (SAG, 1986: 61–3). These areas were thus required to produce a surplus that could be used to supply deficit areas. When these needs had been met, counties were then free to produce other cash crops and to diversify into industrial production.

Secondly, modern inputs were to be provided to the farm sector via the plan and via rural industry in so far as resource constraints permitted. Thus some state-owned industries producing farm inputs such as chemical fertilizers, plastics, simple tools, tractors, cement,

---

[2] For a discussion of the quest for food self-sufficiency in Shanghai, see Ash (1981).

and electricity were set up in rural areas, and the 'five small industries' set up by communes and brigades were to produce outputs that were in the main complementary to farm production. Even if a county did not have a state-owned factory within its boundaries, supplies of fertilizer, etc. would be provided from other localities via the planning mechanism.

Thirdly, especially during the winter slack period, underemployed labour was to be mobilized on an unprecedented scale to dig canals and reservoirs, to build dams and embankments, and to create a transport infrastructure. Perhaps even more importantly, labour mobilization would make possible a massive increase in the multiple cropping ratio. Much the same sort of strategy had been pursued for centuries by the Imperial government, and even the Republican era saw some attempts to mobilize labour for infrastructure construction. However, Maoist mobilization dwarfed previous efforts in its scale and the period of time over which it was sustained.

The adoption of this agrarian strategy had vast implications for patterns of spatial income inequality and rural poverty. A majority of economists have suggested that its impact was adverse. According to Lardy (1983: 186):

the data suggest that government policy contributed to the immiserization of a significant portion of the peasantry. Policies that encouraged or even compelled the pursuit of local self-sufficiency in food grains squeezed out the gains from specialized production based on local comparative advantage. Thus poverty in the late 1970s was widespread in some regions that historically had enjoyed a comparative advantage in cultivation of non-grain crops or derived a larger-than-average share of their income from animal husbandry.

Moreover, for Donnithorne (1967: 78–9):

it would seem probable that considerable differences in standards of living . . . between certain types of district must exist and have increased since the Great Leap. . . . The especially favoured districts would be those near cities and in areas designated as being of 'high and stable yield'. These areas have profited from priority for state and municipal investment funds and for agricultural machinery and fertilizers, as well as being the first to benefit from rural electrification. Better transport and proximity to urban markets means that peasants get better prices for free market sales, and also obtain many consumption goods at lower prices and in greater variety.

Yet none of this carries conviction. First, the imposition of quotas and the establishment of commodity grain bases might well have penalized rich counties. If we assume that their populations had a higher income elasticity of demand for non-basics and if, similarly, we assume that before 1949 they increasingly specialized in the production of cash crops and vegetables for urban consumption, the imposition of 'Take grain as the key link' would have severely constrained their income-earning possibilities because grain production was relatively less profitable. As Ash found in his study of peri-urban Shanghai (1981: 213):

The most fundamental problems have stemmed from the inability to reconcile a basic conflict of interest between the material self-advancement sought by the peasants and the broader economic objectives pursued by the planners. The contradiction between grain and vegetable production is an admirable illustration. If the aim is to seek all-round agricultural self-sufficiency in Shanghai, as long as normal yields can be maintained, it makes good sense to keep a fixed ratio between the various crop areas. However, from the peasants' point of view it has been more rational to substitute vegetables for grain.

By the same token, the hypothesis that the comparative advantage of poor areas lay outside grain production is unproven. Assuming zero transport costs, some counties in mountainous areas may have had a comparative advantage in planting hillsides with fruit, walnuts, and tung oil nut trees (Nolan, 1983a: 31–2). However, by definition, transport costs in mountainous areas were extremely high, and this undoubtedly militated against the exploitation of any notional comparative advantage; in some parts of south-western Sichuan up to 20% of labour days were absorbed in traditional transport (ZKCDY, 1980: 195). One can argue that this suggests a need for investment in transport infrastructure rather than the pursuit of self-sufficiency, but the returns on such investment would tend to be low even in the medium term. After all, the number of mountainous counties is a very small proportion of the whole, especially in terms of their share in total population.

In any case, the Lardy critique pays inadequate attention to the military dimension of the problem, for one can see how political and military considerations led to the single-minded emphasis on local self-sufficiency in grain production. To be sure, local self-sufficiency and national self-sufficiency do not go hand in hand. Even if China opted for the latter in the face of the American threat, she could have allowed regions to exploit their comparative advantage. For example, national grain production might have been concentrated in the Yangzi delta and other particularly fertile regions (the Chengdu plain, the Dongting lake area, and the Pearl River delta) whilst other less favoured areas produced relatively more animal products and cash crops. Grain deficit areas could have met their grain requirements by importing surpluses, and selective subsidies to grain-producing areas might have been used to ensure adequate surplus production (which almost certainly would not have occurred in a market economy).

In the circumstances of the 1960s and 1970s, however, the choices were less simple. As Walker has shown, high procurement levels in Sichuan in the 1950s designed to provide a surplus to feed deficit provinces and cities created a good deal of resentment, and it is arguably significant that in the aftermath of the Great Leap Forward Sichuan was never again a net grain exporter (Walker, 1984). More importantly, Mao and the leadership of the CCP were concerned about the impact of possible American air attacks on the transport infrastructure. The successful interdiction of transport networks would lead to widespread food shortages in deficit areas. Furthermore, the Yangzi delta was strategically vulnerable. If that area had been lost (as it had been to the Japanese in the Second World War), it would have been extremely difficult for the interior to have sustained protracted resistance. Accordingly, the only sensible strategy was to promote a pattern of grain production that relied as little as possible upon trade flows. As with the Third Front programme, the decline in the American threat after the late 1970s allowed the adoption of a strategy of grain production much closer to the ideal one of regional specialization.

As for the strategy of agricultural modernization, it is not difficult to see how this would have operated so as to narrow spatial differentials. To be sure, agricultural development necessarily involved raising levels of production in poor and rich counties alike. However, poor counties were able to raise per capita output levels more quickly because of the scope for catch-up via the adoption of the traditional technological package that was already proven in more advanced areas. This package was based upon organic fertilizers, animal power, and irrigation. It had been applied only on a limited basis in many of the poorest areas of China because rural insitutions were unable to mobilize labour on the scale required to surmount the formidable topographical obstacles. The potential of many areas was enormous if only dams, reservoirs, and terraces could be constructed. However, single villages were in no position either to mobilize sufficient labour or to solve the problems involved in co-operation with other villages to ensure a fair distribution of any resultant benefits. Irrigation systems on the scale of Sichuan's Dujiangyan were impossible in the absence of a strong state during the Republican period in areas where, in sharp contrast to the Chengdu plain, the geography was formidable.

Economic planning and collective organization lifted the horizons of poor areas. By means of the massive mobilization of labour, geographical obstacles to irrigation could be surmounted and multiple cropping would become possible. That would in turn make possible the adoption of the full traditional package, leading to a big increase in crop yields. Moreover, precisely because this package had already been introduced—in some areas for centuries—in rich localities, it was possible for poor counties to catch up at relatively low cost. New seed varieties had already been tried and proven, so that learning costs in backward areas were much reduced. In short, whilst the prosperous counties laboured to shift their production frontiers outwards and incurred high costs in the process, poor counties were able to move onto the production frontier via the spatial diffusion of the traditional technological package.

In addition, it seems that the benefits of the 'modern' or 'green revolution' package—chemical fertilizers, pesticides, mechanical irrigation, electrification, and even primitive mechanization—were widely dispersed. Many of the new chemical-fertilizer plants established in the 1950s and, in particular, after 1965 were set up in rich counties. However, in the main it seems that commodity grain and cotton bases were given priority. As we have seen, some of the bases were selected as much for their potential as for the levels of per capita output already reached; that tended to help the poorer echelon of counties. Moreover, precisely because the distribution of modern inputs was for the most part within the plan, all areas received a certain quota of these products. This contrasts sharply with the situation in more market-oriented economies, where retained profits are both a necessary precondition for the purchase of marketed goods and largest in those locations that have already reached a high level of income; in other words, a process of cumulative causation operates within market economies.

Finally, it may be that advanced areas were running up against decreasing returns to even the modern package by the late 1970s. Ash, for example, noted that yields were very high in the Shanghai area by the late 1970s, although on balance he still believed that there was scope for output increases:

It is instructive that grain yields in Shanghai are already a good deal higher than those achieved nationally by Japan. Indeed, they probably compare favourably with those achieved in the richest regions of that country . . .

Particularly important is likely to be the response to further increases in the application of chemical fertilizers. Availability of this input per hectare of arable land is already high in Shanghai. However, it is still far below that of Japan and there seems no reason to suppose that yields will not continue to rise as application is raised to still higher levels.   (Ash, 1981: 215–16)

Philip Huang has also shown that grain yields largely stagnated in Songjiang county (peri-urban Shanghai) during the 1980s at around 800 *jin* per *mu* (for rice). He does not suggest that further improvements are impossible, but notes that the yield plateau reflected the application of state-of-the-art technology prior to decollectivization (Huang, 1990: ch. 11).

   This suggests that there was considerable scope for catch-up for poor counties provided that they mobilized indigenous labour resources via collective farms to implement the traditional package fully, and provided that the state helped them to purchase the inputs that were an integral part of the modern package. Moreover, Huang's figures comparing Songjiang and the China average suggest that this was indeed happening. On average, rice yields in China as a whole averaged 62% of those for Songjiang for 1965–9. By 1975–9, the figure had climbed to 72%, and by 1980–4 it had reached 89% of Songjiang rice yields (calculated from Huang, 1990: 224). To be sure, per capita incomes have risen much more quickly in Songjiang in the 1980s but, as Huang rightly notes, this has been due to diversification into higher value-added types of economic activity—namely rural industry—not because of an agrarian revolution. It was the *combination* of agrarian development and constraints on diversification in rich counties that faciliated the process of spatial catch-up during the Maoist period.

   All in all, there is here a powerful theoretical argument that in principle explains how the narrowing of spatial income differentials between counties occurred in Sichuan between the Republican period and the Maoist twilight. We must now consider whether the evidence for the province supports this hypothesis.

Agricultural Modernization and Grain Production: Sichuan

We can conveniently look at the impact of Maoist agricultural policy by looking at trends in rich and poor counties separately. Our aim is to identify evidence which suggests that the rich counties were growing less quickly than they might have done and, conversely, for indications that poor counties were growing more quickly.

For rich counties, especially those located on the Chengdu plain, it is clear that the limits to traditional technology were being reached by the 1950s. There the traditional package of farm technology, combining extensive irrigation with heavy application of organic fertilizer, had been in place for centuries. Guan county's Dujiangyan irrigation system had been in operation since 250 BC, and Maoist mobilization of labour for irrigation purposes (labour accumulation) was hardly an innovation. Moreover, the scope for increasing the multiple-cropping index was limited in some areas. In Wenjiang prefecture, for instance, the index stood at 210% by 1957, and in Wenjiang, Pi, and Xindu counties it was even higher at 230–40% (Sun, 1960: 247 n.). These figures are very high for a traditional farming technology being operated in a non-tropical zone, and it is difficult to believe that they could have been easily increased. Indeed the average multiple-cropping index for the Chengdu plain was between 200% and 210% by 1977 (ZKCDY, 1980: 142) and had fallen to 190 by 1983 (Gan, 1986: 137–8) as attempts at triple cropping (two crops of rice as well as a winter crop) were abandoned.

The same arguments are echoed in the accounts of Western agricultural specialists before 1949, and those of Soviet specialists in Sichuan during the 1950s (such as Afanas' yeskiy), which suggest that diminishing returns were very much the norm. Brown and Li (1928: 70) thought that the only way out of the impasse was by means of rural industrialization or improvements in farm technology, including 'a) control of insect and plant diseases, b) improvements in seed type by selection and new varieties, c) increased productivity by means of artificial fertilizers'. Buck (1947: 4) took a very similar view:

Agricultural production can probably be increased 50 percent by the use of scientific knowledge to produce improved varieties of crops and animals, in controlling insects, in the use of more fertilizers and in other improved practices. It is the extreme density of population which, under present conditions, makes most of the farms an uneconomic sized unit.

However, there is no evidence that yields stagnated after the 1950s because of the gradual displacement of the old by increasingly new technology. More precisely, the process of technical change in Sichuan's farm sector can be divided into two periods: 1931–65 and the post-1965 period. In the first subperiod, decreasing returns probably were the norm in rich areas. It is true that the modernization of farming practice was already under way in the 1930s. New varieties of grain crops were introduced during the war, and experiments with fungicides were carried out. Indeed, even during the 1930s new varieties began to appear and agricultural research was begun. In Neijiang prefecture a sugar cane research station was established jointly by Sichuan University and the provincial Reconstruction Bureau. Three researchers were sent to America and they brought back (in 1937) a number of American and Indian sugar cane varieties. Some of these proved highly successful on experimental plots but inevitably, given peasant conservatism (entirely rational, as the technology was largely unproven in Sichuanese conditions) and the effects of war, rates of diffusion were slow (Wang and Huang, 1985). Accordingly, only *parts* of a 'modern' package were in place until at least the mid-1950s—hence the persistence of decreasing returns.

By the mid-1950s, however, the process of change had begun to accelerate. The new sugar cane varieties introduced before the war were widely planted by this time, and this had the effect of raising yields; Indian 290, for example, yielded on average 9,000 *jin* per *mu*, compared to the pre-war average of perhaps 5,000 (Wang and Huang, 1985: 179). According to Afanas' yeskiy (1960: 72), this cold-resistant variety accounted for more than half of sugar cane-sown area throughout the province by the late 1950s. A similar picture applies to grain crop varietal improvement, although the extent of diffusion seems to have been slow except in the case of corn (*SAG*, 1980: 41). Of course varietal improvement was not confined to rich areas. Neijiang, though the main sugar cane-producing prefecture, was by no means prosperous. Nevertheless, the incentive for change was much stronger on the Chengdu plain than elsewhere, in that rapid yield growth could only be achieved via technical progress. The process was facilitated by increased provision of modern inputs. Chengdu was being developed very quickly after 1949 as an industrial centre on a par with Chongqing, the acknowledged industrial capital of the entire south-western region of China. In consequence, a wide range of industrial inputs, including chemical fertilizer and, increasingly, farm machinery, became readily available to surrounding rural areas. In addition, the designation of the area as a grain base also brought industry-producing farm inputs to the Chengdu plain: by the late 1950s bone-meal and fertilizer plants had been established in Chengdu itself, and an ammonium sulphate plant with a capacity of 300,000 tons had been set up in Jintang county (Sun, 1960: 252). Rich areas benefited increasingly after 1965 as the growth of collective industry, an important product of which was chemical fertilizer, was far faster there than in poor areas. By the late 1970s the use of chemical fertilizer on the Chengdu plain was still considerably below Japan's position a decade earlier; but, given that it started from a very low base (Japanese agriculture was using almost 100 kg. of chemical fertilizer per hectare as early as the 1930s), it is evident that the counties of the Chengdu plain were catching up quickly.

Moreover, the experience of Shifang county in the 1980s shows that even this rich area had not yet reached the technological frontier in agricultural production (Table 6.4). Rice yields grew consistently after 1957, and accelerated dramatically after 1978. More startling is the trajectory of wheat. In 1952, wheat yields were barely one-third those of rice, yet by 1983 they were close to 80%; this reflects above all, the fact that the 'green revolution' (in China as elsewhere) was above all a wheat revolution. Thus, in Shifang, the latest high-yielding variety to be popularized (called *fanliu*) accounted for more than 80% of wheat-sown area by 1979 (*Shifang xian zhi*, 1988: 10–24). This general pattern of continual yield improvements is confirmed by Huang's figures for Songjiang county. Although it is true that the yields for 1986 and 1987 were unimpressive, taken as a whole the rice yield for 1985–7 stood at 795 *jin*, significantly higher than the 712 *jin* registered in 1980–4 and the 697 *jin* achieved between 1975 and 1979 (Huang, 1990: 224). There is no evidence of stagnation here, and this seems to reflect the continued scope that remained, even in the richest areas of China, for technology-based yield improvements in the late 1970s.

Nevertheless, rich counties were handicapped by the necessity of modernization because the process was so expensive, so that net agricultural output value grew quite slowly. According to Shifang's commune accounts, production costs as a share of gross income rose from 17.5% in 1965 to 25.1% by 1978 (*Shifang xian zhi*, 1988: 10–62).

TABLE 6.4. *Trends in Crop Yields in Shifang (*jin *per* mu)

	Rice	Wheat	Rape-seed	Tabacco
1952	471	165	90	154
1957	476	270	113	147
1965	476	228	171	170
1970	643	391	235	147
1978	628	498	316	214
1983	851	680	330	303

Source: *Shifang xian zhi* (1988: 9-7).

TABLE 6.5. *Material Production Costs in Jiangsu's Farm Sector*

	Input costs[a] in *yuan* per 100 *jin*		
	1965	1975	1979
Grain	4.14	5.27	4.92
Vegetable oil	9.76	10.23	11.65
Cash crops	20.76	27.05	28.54
AVERAGE[b]	4.15	5.88	6.18

[a] Production costs here exclude the cost of labour.

[b] The average here is for 32 different types of farm product.

Source: Zu (1985: 242).

The same seems to be true for Jiangsu, where the growing use of high-cost 'modern' inputs (chemical fertilizers, pesticides, and some machinery) led to increases in unit costs (Table 6.5). By contrast, poor counties which were much more reliant upon traditional technology did not face such rapid cost increases, and were therefore able to close the gap between themselves and their more prosperous neighbours.

Rich counties were further handicapped by state emphasis on the production of grain. To be sure, grain self-sufficiency was not pursued at all costs. For example, self-reliance is not inveighed against with the bile reserved for some of the other pre-1976 policies in the speeches and writings of Zhao Ziyang in the late 1970s, and it does not feature in the twelve-point programme for rural reform adopted by the provincial party congress in 1977. Indeed, there is much in these documents about the need to *accelerate* the growth of grain production along the lines adopted in Jiangsu's Suzhou prefecture in Zhao's analysis (Shambaugh, 1982). Moreover, self-sufficiency was manifestly not achieved in certain areas, notably the ethnic areas of western Sichuan. Aba autonomous prefecture imported 500,000 tonnes of grain from other parts of the province between 1953 and 1980 (*Aba Zangzu zizhizhou gaikuang*, 1985: 223) whilst 9 of Liangshan's counties imported 748 million *jin* between 1955 and 1980 (*Liangshan Yizu zizhizhou gaikuang*, 1985: 269). However, there is no evidence that animal husbandry and cash-crop production atrophied over the same period.

Nevertheless, the slogan 'Take grain as the key link' was more than empty rhetoric. As the evidence provided in the 1980 *Agricultural Geography of Sichuan* (*SAG*, 1986: 68) suggests:

Sichuan still does not produce an abundance of grain. In most villages, standards for commune members' grain rations are not high. Under these circumstances, as a result of the need to 'take grain as the key link' and to achieve self-sufficiency in grain or even to provide commodity grain in areas in which the growing of cash crops is concentrated . . . many communes and brigades do everything possible to look after grain crops, placing cash crops in a subordinate position.

Other evidence points in the same direction, notably the progress made in raising per capita grain production. For example, output of grain per head of rural population in Aba rose from 329 *jin* per annum in 1949 to 490 *jin* by 1976 (*Aba Zangzu zizhizhou gaikuang*, 1985: 222). Moreover, areas of the Sichuan Basin which before 1949 had been reliant upon 'imports' from other parts of the province became self-sufficient. Consider Baxian prefecture. In 1939–43, only 70% of demand for grain was met by indigenous production (Bramall, 1989b: apps. A2, A6). But by 1985, the corresponding figure was 98% or, excluding the districts of Chongqing, 114% (app. A8). Moreover, the Yangzi valley between Yibin and Changshou generated a substantial surplus, and the area became second in importance as a commodity grain base only to the Chengdu plain (app. A8; Leeming, 1985: 19–20, 159; *SAG*, 1986: 61–5).

In addition, the area sown to cash crops (although in those areas thought suitable for cotton production that crop was strongly en- couraged) was undoubtedly much lower in Sichuan by the late 1970s than it had been in the Republican period. In Shifang county's Lianglukou commune, the area sown to cash crops fell from around 17,000 *mu* in the 1950s to only 8,500 *mu* by 1979 (Endicott, 1988: 251). For the county *in toto*, tobacco-sown area fell from 96,690 *mu* in 1952—which gives an indication of the emphasis that would have been given to this product in a market economy—to 61,645 *mu* by 1978. Over the same period, the area sown to rape-seed fell from 70,337 to 56,215 *mu*, whilst grain-sown area *rose* from 547,810 to 583,830 *mu* (*Shifang xian zhi*, 1988: 9-7, 10–2, 28).

For the whole province, long-run trends are shown in Table 6.6. Even if opium is omitted from the 1930s data, the area sown to cash crops relative to grain was substantially lower in the late 1970s. More- over, even the removal of many of the restrictions on cash crop cultivation after 1978 did not restore the position of the 1930s. The cash crop share had crept up to 14%, equivalent to the official

TABLE 6.6.   *The Share of Cash Crops in Sown Area, 1931–1984*

	Share of cash crops in area sown to grain and cash crops (%)[a]	
	Official data	Revision 1[b]
1931–7[c]	14	26
1938–44[c]	14	—
1975–8	8	—
1982–4	10	—
1986–7	14	—

[a] The % is not the share of cash crops in total sown area because area sown to vegetables, fodder, melons, etc. is unavailable for 1931–7 and 1938–44, and this category has therefore been omitted from all periods.

[b] Revision 1 (see above) recognizes that official NARB data underestimated both sown and cultivated area because land sown to opium in the winter and non-opium crops during the summer was ignored. Classifying opium as a cash crop and allowing for the growing of peanuts, sesame, cotton, tobacco, and grains on this opium land in the summer produces the estimate of 26% as the cash crop share. As the impact of war on opium production is unclear (the Nationalist regime could not rely entirely on American largesse, and probably exported opium via Burma to some degree), no attempt has been made to compute a revised figure for 1938–44.

[c] The data for 1931–7 and 1938–44 collected by NARB omit information on a number of cash crops—hemp, ramie, and sugar cane amongst others. However, as a number of grain crops are also omitted (principally those grown on the Songpan plateau, e.g. buckwheat), it is unlikely that the 1931–7 and 1938–44 share of cash crops is understated.

Sources: 1931–7—*The China Handbook 1939–43*: 561–629, 1938–44— above, and *The China Handbook 1937–45*: 437–42, 1975–78—ZSSWY (1984: 135), 1982—*Zhongguo nongye nianjian 1983*: 36, 1983–4—CAY (1985: 114–15), 1986—ZGTJNJ (1987: 165), 1987—ZGTJNJ (1988: 243), 1988—ZGTJNJ (1989: 193).

Republican figure, by 1986–7, but this was still well below the true, poppy area-included, Republican figure. This was essentially because the area sown to grain crops remained carefully controlled during the 1980s. The need to raise cash crop output was recognized, but it was to be achieved by raising yields rather than by reducing grain sown area (Xie, 1984).

This policy hurt rich counties because of their pre-Revolution relative specialization in non-grain crops. If one correlates the share of grain production in NVAO with NVAO per capita at a prefectural level for 1939–43, the result is a correlation coefficient of −0.24, indicating a weak relationship but nevertheless one of the expected sign. This suggests that, as income increased, the demand for grain products fell and that for other farm products increased. Conversely, if the share of cash crop production in NVAO is correlated with NVAO per capita for data on Sichuan's prefectures in 1939–43, a positive coefficient of 0.48 is obtained. The correlation is not large in either case, and this may be because the pre-1937 pattern of specialization had already been significantly altered by wartime grain requirements that led to the imposition of a grain tax levied in kind, compulsory grain loans, and procurement quotas. This grain was used both to pay academic and administrative salaries and to feed Nationalist armies located inside and outside Sichuan. On the other hand, however, there were limits to the freedom of action of the Kuomintang. Cotton and sugar cane production were almost as important as grain, the former for clothing and the latter as a fuel substitute. Moreover, the writ of the Kuomintang did not extend far beyond Chongqing, and the need to build and maintain alliances with the warlord interests that had dominated the province before 1934 (which Chiang Kaishek had absorbed rather than eliminated) remained a critical constraint upon policy, especially as warlord wealth derived principally from opium production (Ch'i, 1982). Nevertheless, the general pattern is clear: a post-1949 policy emphasizing grain production at the expense of cash crops would have discriminated against rich counties and hence narrowed spatial differentials. Both rich and poor areas would have experienced reductions in the level and growth of incomes, but the reduction would have been much greater for rich than for poor. This interpretation receives support from a Chinese source discussing the situation in the late 1970s and showing that, despite Maoist policies, non-grain agricultural production still played a role in maintaining income differentials:

There are 22 counties where average per capita gross income per annum is 243 *yuan* which is 113 *yuan* higher than the provincial average and 157 *yuan* higher than the average in 33 low-income counties, the main differences being that income from non-grain crops was 61.4 *yuan* higher and that from forestry, fisheries, animal husbandry, and sideline occupations was 37 *yuan* higher. (Xie, 1984: 207).

TABLE 6.7.   *Procurement Prices in Sichuan, 1952–1978*

Crop	Procurement prices (*yuan* per *dan*)[a]			Price increase, 1952–78 (%)
	1952	1965	1978	
Wheat	5.61	11.00	13.00	+232
Rice (husked)	6.45	11.70	13.80	+214
Tobacco	34.70	72.00	72.00	+207
Rape-seed	9.20	22.33	28.00	+304
Ramie	46.30	80.50	94.00	+203
Sugar cane	0.76	1.50	1.73	+228

[a] These are procurement list prices.

Source: ZSSWY (1984: 710, 717, 719).

It therefore seems likely that, in the *absence* of Maoist policy, spatial income differentials would have been even greater.

None of this would have mattered but for the fact that cash crop and other types of agricultural activity, even with Maoist manipulation of the intersectoral terms of trade, were much more profitable than grain production. Over the whole 1952–78 period, price trends are as shown in Table 6.7. The interesting feature here is that procurement prices rose at a remarkably similar rate across crop types. This shows that no systematic attempt was made to bias prices in favour of grain and hence to enlist the price mechanism in support of the cause of planning. As Sicular has noted (1989: 247, 263):

Quantity planning in the form of targets and quotas was used as a substitute for or in conjunction with prices to guide resource allocation. . . . During this ten year period [1967–76] . . . pricing policy's primary objective was to maintain price stability, and only for a brief period was pricing used to influence resource allocation.

No data on material production costs by crop type are available for Sichuan, and therefore a precise comparison of value added in the 1970s is not possible. However, such materials are available for Jiangsu province, and these make a comparison of sorts possible (Table 6.8). The relatively higher profitability of cash crops—a consequence of Maoist policy in respect of both procurement and input prices—in both winter and summer is clear. The net output value of

TABLE 6.8.   *Value Added per* Mu *by Crop Type in Sichuan,
Late 1970s*

Crop	Yield[a] (*dan*)	Gross output[b] (*yuan*)	Prod. costs[c] (*yuan*)	Net output (*yuan*)
Winter crops:				
Wheat	2.86	37.18	14.24	22.94
Rape	1.59	44.52	17.63	26.89
Summer crops:				
Rice	6.11	58.05	29.39	28.66
Corn	3.79	36.01	15.27	20.74
Cotton	0.73	81.76	40.90	40.86
Tobacco	1.86	133.92	36.85	97.07

[a] Yields are 1977 averages per sown *mu* for the whole of Sichuan.

[b] Price data used to calculate gross output value are procurement list prices.

[c] Production costs (*chengben wuzhi*), excluding labour costs, are for Jiangsu province. These were originally expressed per 100 *jin* but have been converted into a cost per sown *mu* using the Sichuan yield data for 1978. It is not clear how far costs of production varied between Sichuan and Jiangsu (costs as a % of gross output value per unit area seem to have been very similar in the 1980s—*Zhongguo nongye nianjian 1986*: 332–42—but these are a poor guide to the 1970s given post-1978 relative price changes). The exceptions are wheat and cotton, for which 1976 cost data are available (C. N. Hu, 1982: 233). The cost of producing the former (including labour costs) seems to have differed little, but the cost of cotton production in Sichuan was slightly more than double that in Jiangsu. Accordingly, except for cotton, the Jiangsu production costs data have been used as proxies for those in Sichuan.

Sources: Jiangsu—Zu (1985: 242). Sichuan—prices: ZSSWY (1984: 719); yields: ibid. (141–4).

rape-seed was significantly higher than that for wheat during the winter, whilst there was an immense difference between net output value generated by rice and both cotton (despite its cost of production, which was 55% higher than the national average in 1976—H. Y. Hu, 1982: 233) and tobacco. That Shifang county's prosperity in the 1930s and in the 1980s was due in no small measure to tobacco production is also apparent from this table.

For many of Sichuan's rich counties, the effect of Maoist policies was to ensure that increases in gross output were not translated into large increases in income. Given the opportunity to choose in the 1980s, it is not surprising that many gradually (quantity controls remained strict) diversified away from grain production.

In poor counties meanwhile, strenuous efforts were made during the 1950s and much of the 1960s to raise yields and per capita output by the extension of the water and organic fertilizer-based traditional technological package. The most important precondition was to develop irrigation, and to this end the collective work-force was deployed as never before; in particular, the participation rate amongst women in labour accumulation was high. At its peak during the mid-1970s, perhaps 15 million workers were being mobilized, and the figure does not seem to have fallen below 10 million during the 1970s (*SAG*, 1986: 35). Mobilization on this scale in the counties located on the periphery of the Sichuan Basin was especially important because of the topographical difficulties. For example, in the counties located around the Yangzi Gorges, less than 10% of land had a slope of less than 10% (ZKCDY, 1980: 196). There was thus an enormous need to create terraces, to build canals, to fill ravines, and to create dams, and there are many examples of historically unprecedented engineering taking place:

In Fengjie county's Jiupan commune, the area of irrigated area was historically very small but in 1977 the labour of the masses was mobilized to build small-scale water conservancy and artificial irrigation facilities. Within a year, one reservoir had been extended and four new ones constructed in addition to four mountain tanks which amounted to an increase in water-holding capacity of more than 600,000 cubic metres . . .

Yonghong commune's Yonghong brigade in Qingchuan county . . . is located in an area which contains much steeply sloped mountainous land criss-crossed with ravines and experiences low air temperatures and frosts . . . in recent years, the brigade has tackled the problems of mountains, water, farmland, forestry, and roads in its high-altitude areas in a comprehensive way. It has constructed six long canals encircling the mountains, six large water tanks, more than 5,400 metres of dyke, reclaimed more than 300 *mu* from rivers using dykes, built more than 500 *mu* of terraced land on steep slopes, created farmland by filling in 70 *mu* of gullies, and in addition promoted tractor-ploughing throughout the entire brigade. Hand in hand with this transformation of conditions of agricultural production has gone a marked increase in grain output, and in 1973 the brigade achieved the target set out in the Twelve-Year Plan . . .   (ZKCDY, 1980: 198–9)

The investment in irrigation is not immediately apparent from the data. For the province as a whole, irrigated area was estimated at between 42 (Y. X. Peng, 1943: 51) and 48% (Zhou, Hou, and Chen, 1946*b*: 55) in the early 1940s. The percentage was put at 42% in 1977 (*SAG*, 1980: 101). However, this ignores the gradual reduction in *dongshuitian* (winter-flooded paddy) that occurred during the Maoist period. *Dongshuitian* was paddy-land left flooded during the winter and hence unavailable for double cropping; the purpose was to ensure that sufficient water was available for the spring planting of rice and, as Sichuan's winters are typically dry, the only way to guarantee supply was by winter storage. The construction of proper storage facilities and the associated canal network made the system increasingly unnecessary (except in mountainous areas prior to the gradual intro- duction of electrical pumping equipment), and hence the quality of irrigation gradually improved at the same time as more land was made available for winter cultivation. An example of the progress made comes from Jingyan county, a prosperous county in the late 1930s (but see below) although far behind counties like Shifang. *Dongshuitian* accounted for 90% of paddyland in 1952, but this figure had fallen to 80% by 1958 and 46% by 1978 (*Jingyan xian zhi*, 1990: 112). The position was similar in Suining county, where over 40,000 *mu* had traditionally been used during the winter for water storage. Thanks to the introduction of electrical irrigation, the land used for this purpose had fallen to a mere 400 *mu* by the mid-1960s (Ch'ai, 1964: 34). One of the great tragedies of the era of 'reform' in the 1980s has been the reversal of this trend such that, by 1985, the percentage of paddy given over to *dongshuitian* had risen again to 72% as the irrigation network suffered gross neglect. The same is true more generally throughout Sichuan, with *dongshuitian* accounting for some 50% of irrigated area in the central and eastern parts of the Sichuan basin and almost 70% in the southern part (Gan, 1986: 137).

The construction of water conservancy facilities was helped by state subsidies, especially to ethnic-minority areas. Although these areas were relatively prosperous in 1939–43, this had much to do with very low population densities and, given both their high natural growth rates and Han migration subsidies, were seen as essential to maintain per capita income and consumption levels. Youyang county con- structed 44 medium- and small-scale reservoirs, 425 mountain dykes, and 201 canals before 1983. In doing so, it was assisted by subsidies which accounted for no less than 45% of total county income between 1952 and 1957 (*Youyang Tujia Miaozu zizhixian gaikuang*, 1986: 82, 89). The same pattern was true for Aba autonomous prefecture; over the period 1951–80, her total expenditure was 1,033 million *yuan* compared to an income of 626 million, and the balance (39% of expenditure) was provided by state subsidies (*Aba Zangzu zizhizhou gaikuang*, 1985: 213).

It is, of course, easy to scoff at some of these accounts and some of these achievements. To be sure, some of the gains made during the Great Leap Forward were transitory. In Jingyan for instance, the reduction in *dongshuitian* to 61% of irrigated area by 1961 was not sustained, the figure rising to 90% by 1965. Nevertheless, a great deal was learned in the process which made it possible to surpass the achievements of the height of the Leap by the early 1970s. More generally, the diffusion of the traditional technological package made possible an unmistakable increase in yields. In Jingyan it made possible an increase in grain yields from around 230 *jin* per *mu* in the 1950s to around 330 *jin* by 1970 (*Jingyan xian zhi*, 1990: 173) and cotton yields rose from perhaps 15 *jin* in the 1950s to more than 30 *jin* by the late 1960s (p. 176). Jingyan is not precisely representative of poor counties, but there is no question that yields increased throughout the province well before agricultural modernization—in that county, a bare 4.2 *jin* of chemical fertilizers were being used per *mu* of cultivated land as late as 1965.

Nevertheless, there were necessarily limits to what could be achieved merely by the application of the traditional technological package in poor areas. Accordingly, and especially after the mid-1960s, a systematic programme of agricultural modernization was set in train. As a result, the use of modern inputs was far from trivial by the mid-1970s. Remarkably, and precisely because of subsidies, poor areas gained enormously from the process; for example, Aba prefecture received 5.33 million *yuan* between 1967 and 1978 in state subsidies for the explicit purpose of agricultural mechanization (*Aba Zangzu zizhizhou gaikuang*, 1985: 174). Of course rich counties received more in absolute terms; but, given the exhaustion of scope for further application of the traditional package on the Chengdu plain, that made perfect sense. Nevertheless, as Table 6.9 shows, poor areas were by no means ignored.

To be sure, some of these inputs were imported from other provinces, especially before 1965. We also know that their quality in many respects left a good deal to be desired. Nevertheless, this table does show just how advanced even very poor Chinese regions were by the late 1970s in their use of modern farm inputs. It indicates very clearly that one cannot simply assume that technical progress was non-existent, even in areas which were not receiving significant state subsidies. Moreover, although few reliable data are available for earlier periods, there is no question that the modern farm package was

TABLE 6.9. *Use of Modern Inputs by Location, 1977*

Zone	Chemical fertilizer used[a] (kg. per arable ha.)	Irrigated (% of arable area)	Tractor-ploughed (% of arable area)
Chengdu plain	294	76	33
Central basin	168	40	16
Southern basin	178	44	14
Eastern basin	133	38	8
Basin periphery	104	24	8
Liangshan	49	20	7
Anning valley	84	48	11
Western Sichuan	62	25	8
Far western Sichuan	16	21	26
All Sichuan	161	42	15
China (1983)	181	n.a.	n.a.
Japan (1983)	437	n.a.	n.a.
Taiwan (1976–9)	205	n.a.	n.a.
India (1983)	39	n.a.	n.a.

[a] Fertilizer figures are on an effective basis. Actual data for Sichuan have been converted to effective by dividing by 5.

Sources: Sichuan—*SAG*, 1980: 101. Taiwan—Barker, Herdt, and Rose (1985: 77) (per ha. of rice only). Others—World Bank (1986*b*: 190–1).

unheard of in poor counties in the 1930s. This makes the degree of modernization achieved by 1977 all the more significant.

The impact of farm modernization in the poorest counties of the province is even more apparent in a direct comparison of rich and poor counties for 1980 (Table 6.10); the first four counties in the table fall into the first category and the remainder were relatively poor. Of course, chemical-fertilizer use was much higher in counties like Guanghan and Wenjiang, but what is striking is that its application even in some of Sichuan's most impoverished counties like Leibo and Xiushan was significantly above the Indian average for the early 1980s. Moreover, electricity use was not confined to the rich counties on the Chengdu plain, although the growth of commune industry led to spiralling consumption levels (Guanghan being the obvious

TABLE 6.10.　*Farm Sector Modernization in Sichuan by 1980*[a]

	Electricity use (kWh per *mu*)	Chemical fertilizer used (kg. per ha.)	Effectively irrigated (% of arable area)
Wenjiang	20	329	100
Guanghan	48	282	98
Leshan	21	173	60
Shifang	14	278	85
Yunyang	8	181	25
Xiushan	7	80	32
Leibo	11	53	26
Wushan	9	176	6
Youyang	5	95	22
Guangyuan	13	84	28

[a] The area denominator here is cultivated area. Chemical fertilizer is here measured on a nutrient-weight basis. Land effectively irrigated was guaranteed water from canals and wells except in the most severe of droughts. Electricity used here is total rural use, and therefore includes power used for purely industrial purposes.

Source: Zhongguo guojia tongjiju (1989: 392–441).

example). Even in poor counties, electrical irrigation was relatively commonplace, and much agricultural processing was mechanized.

The Process of Spatial Convergence

The combined impact of the policies described above was to narrow differentials in per capita NVAO. This is particularly apparent in an intertemporal comparison of the dispersion of grain production. Take the dispersion by the agricultural zones specified in the 1980 Agricultural Geography. This approach divides the province into 9 units and gives data on grain production per capita in 1977; we can therefore directly compare the dispersion between zones in 1939–43, 1977, and 1985 by grouping counties using the zones of 1977. The resulting coefficients of variation are summarized in Table 6.11.

The fall in the coefficient of variation between 1939–43 and 1977 is significant, indicating that post-1949 policies led to considerable

TABLE 6.11. *Grain Production Per Capita in Sichuan*

Zone[a]	Grain production per capita[b]		
	1939–43	1977	1985
1 Chengdu plain	5.50	728	908
2 Central basin	4.32	636	824
3 Southern basin	3.31	577	775
4 Eastern basin	4.30	508	675
5 Basin periphery	5.76	602	683
Coefficient of variation	0.19	0.11	0.10

[a] Only 5 of the 9 zones of 1977 are included because of lack of data on the other 4 in 1939–43. It should also be noted that a number of the counties of Zone 5 are omitted from the estimates for 1939–43, again because of lack of data. These 8 counties (names of 1977) are Muchuan, Wulong, Wangcang, Qingchuan, Ya'an, Yingjing, Tianquan, and Lushan. There were 24 other counties in this zone.

[b] Units: 1939–43—*shi shi* per capita; 1977 and 1985—*jin* per capita. The coefficient of variation is in each case weighted by population.

The data are per head of total population. 1977 figures on per capita output are given in *SAG* (1986: 101) but these are for agricultural population only. Therefore, the figures given for the shares of each zone in provincial grain production and total population (p. 102) have been multiplied by provincial grain output (ZSSWY, 1984: 138) and total population (ZGRKNJ, 1985: 522) to calculate grain output per capita of total population.

Sources: Names of counties in each zone—ZKCDY (1980: 139). 1939–43 and 1985—Appendix. 1977—see n. *a*.

reduction in spatial inequalities in grain production. The continued fall in the coefficient of variation between 1977 and 1985 is somewhat surprising. It presumably implies that counties were switching from grain to cash crop production at the same rate, perhaps because the development of commune enterprises was perceived by the populations of the more affluent counties to offer a quicker route to yet more affluence than reverting to cash crop production.

This pattern of narrowing differentials in grain production is supported by a comparison of differentials at the *county* level between 1939–43 and 1985. This is undoubtedly preferable to zone-level analysis because it is much more disaggregated; substantial intra-zone

An Analysis of Spatial Trends

T ABLE 6.12.   *Dispersion of Per Capita Grain*
Production by County

	All counties	Excluding outliers[a]
1939–43	0.59	0.50
1985	0.23	n.a.

[a] Counties classified as outliers in 1939–43 are
Pujiang, Emei, Leibo, Mabian, Pingshan, Qingfu,
Xingwen, Naxi, Shizhu, Pengshui, Jiange,
Zhaohua, Pingwu, Nanjiang, Mao, and Jinghua.
See the discussion in the main text below.

Source: Appendix.

inequalities are masked by a high level of aggregation. The results are
shown in Table 6.12 for the 134 counties of the Sichuan of 1939–43.

In order to evaluate whether the fall in the coefficient of variation
reflected the inclusion in the 1939–43 data of counties where grain
production per capita seems unduly high, a number of counties were
designated outliers and excluded. The criterion for this was a per
capita annual grain output of more than 10 *shi shi* or around 1,300 *jin*.
Such levels of output are, arguably, suspiciously high; per capita
production did not reach that level in any of the province's counties in
1985. That does not necessarily mean that the data are simply 'wrong';
very high levels of grain production are certainly possible even in an
economy using traditional technology if cultivated area per capita is
also high and complementary inputs (draught animals and irrigation)
are available. But in any case, as the table amply demonstrates,
outlier exclusion has nothing more than a limited impact on the trend
decline in the coefficient of variation; this measure of dispersion still
falls by more than 50% between the two periods.

We can also look at the direct impact of the promotion of grain self-
sufficiency on spatial differences in NVAO. If it is true that grain
emphasis narrowed spatial differentials, we need to show that there
was a correlation between grain production and NVAO in Sichuan's
counties and prefectures. If that is so, it follows that a narrowing of
differentials in grain production will be accompanied by a narrowing
of differentials in NVAO, because then grain production is a *proxy*
for NVAO. Moreover, in principle there need not be a marked
correlation between the two. An increase in grain production might
simply lead to a reduction in, say, the output of cash crops as labour

power, working capital, and sown area is given over to grain production. On the other hand, there may be 'crowding in' if a part of the higher grain production is used as animal feed. Not only would increases in animal numbers add directly to NVAO, but also there would be linkage effects via the increased production of organic fertilizer and increased availability of motive power on cash crop production.

The extent of correlation between grain production and NVAO at the level of the prefecture at the beginning of the 1940s was high (Table 6.13). After 1949, and as a result of the policies to promote grain production adopted by the Maoist regime, the correlation became closer still, so that by the early 1980s agricultural output was overwhelmingly determined by the level of grain production. As a result, the spatial convergence in grain production led to the spatial convergence of NVAO.

A more graphic illustration of the process of convergence in farming is offered by a comparison of agricultural output trends in Shifang and Jingyan counties. Shifang, as has been noted on several occasions, was one of the most prosperous counties in the province, not least because of her location on the Chengdu plain. Jingyan, located in the south-western part of the Sichuan Basin near Leshan, was by contrast a poor county, although the data in the Appendix suggest quite the contrary. However, this was due to the special circumstance of relatively low population density, itself caused by famine conditions between 1936 and the mid-1940s which had the effect of reducing her population by some 30% (*Jingyan xian zhi*, 1990: 97). This period apart, Jingyan was poor in comparison with Shifang. GVAIO per capita in 1952 (current prices) was 216 *yuan* in

TABLE 6.13. *Correlation between Grain Production and NVAO*

	Correlation coefficient at prefectural level[a]
1939–43	0.73
1985	0.99

[a] These estimates exclude Songpan prefecture, for which the 1939–43 data are very poor.

Sources: 1939–43—Zhou, Hou, and Chen (1946*b*); Appendix. 1985—Appendix.

Shifang compared to 147 *yuan* in Jingyan, and per capita distributed income in 1965 was only 39 *yuan* in Jingyan compared to 88 *yuan* in Shifang (*Shifang xian zhi*, 1988: 9-7; *Jingyan xian zhi*, 1990: 155). Persistently lower yields were part of the problem, but so also was the impact of the Great Leap Forward; by 1962, NVAO was less than 50% of its 1957 value, whereas in Shifang it had fallen by only 30% (*Shifang xian zhi*, 1988: 9-7; *Jingyan xian zhi*, 1990: 141).

Nevertheless, the pace of industrialization in Jingyan did much to allow a narrowing of spatial differentials. The share of industry in GVAIO was virtually the same in Jingyan and Shifang in 1952, at 8% or 9%. Thereafter, until the early 1970s, Jingyan more than kept pace; by 1970, Jingyan's industry share was almost 20% compared to 17% in Shifang (*Shifang xian zhi*, 1988: 9-7; *Jingyan xian zhi*, 1990: 16–24, 99). Although the growth of commune industries gave Shifang an increasing advantage as the decade wore on (because they were financed out of farm sector profits and hence depended on agricultural prosperity), it is remarkable that a favourably located area like Shifang did not increase its lead in terms of living standards. It certainly would have done so in a market economy.

For all that, the gulf between Jingyan and Shifang was still large by 1969, and it seems that a decision was taken to narrow it by a pattern of investment that had as its objective the modernization of agriculture. In consequence, a consistent budget deficit was incurred during the 1970s, in sharp contrast to previous decades. The state subsidy that this implied was used in the main to finance investment and the development of agriculture. The key project was the construction of a nitrogen fertilizer plant on which 2.6 million *yuan* was spent in total during 1970 and 1971 (total within-budget county spending was only 4.1 million *yuan* in 1970 (*Jingyan xian zhi*, 1990: 385–91)). This was followed up by massive expenditure on the construction of three new reservoirs, Red Cliff, Red Star, and Mao Dam. The effect was to raise yields substantially during the 1970s, especially those for grain as irrigated area and chemical fertilizer use increased dramatically. This is evident in Table 6.14. As a result of farm sector modernization, the yield gap sharply narrowed. In 1965, and before the introduction of the 'green revolution' package in Jingyan, the ratio of grain yields in Shifang to Jingyan was 1.64 and it still stood at 1.56 in 1970. By 1978, however, the ratio had fallen to only 1.15. With the introduction of more *laissez-faire* policies after that date, the gap began to widen once more, and by 1983 the ratio stood at 1.40 (*Jingyan xian zhi*, 1990: 173; *Shifang xian zhi*, 1988: 10–20); it stood at 1.36 in 1988 (Zhongguo guojia tongjiju, 1990: 167).

TABLE 6.14. *Investment and Agricultural Performance in Jingyan*

	Jingyan county			Shifang county
	Fiscal deficit[a] (million *yuan*)	Fertilizer use[b] (*jin* per *mu*)	Grain yield[b] (*jin* per *mu*)	Grain yield[b] (*jin* per *mu*)
1952	+1.23	0.01	229	345
1957	+1.38	0.54	238	372
1962	+0.44	1.13	168	310
1965	+1.07	4.16	234	386
1970	−0.80	43.90	338	527
1978	−2.54	169.00	459	528

[a] A positive sign indicates a budgetary surplus. These figures are for within-budget items only. However, extra-budget expenditure was relatively small, amounting to only about a seventh of within-budget expenditure in 1978.

[b] Fertilizer use is per unit of cultivated area, whereas yields are per unit of sown area.

Sources: *Jingyan xian zhi* (1990: 173, 182, 383–92); *Shifang xian zhi* (1988: 10–20).

Agricultural Modernization and Spatial Convergence: A Summary

Maoist agricultural policy proved singularly effective in reducing spatial differentials in NVAO and hence contributing to a narrowing of differentials in NVAIO. Rich counties were handicapped to start with by the onset of severely diminishing returns to the traditional technological package of water and organic fertilizer. In that many of them were on or close to the production possibility frontier by the early 1950s, the cost of raising yields above the high levels already attained was heavy. To this burden was added the handicap of an agricultural policy that sought to impose the creation of significant grain surpluses. In that grain production was less profitable than that of vegetables, cash crops, and animal products, the prosperous counties on the Chengdu plain and elsewhere were unable to exploit their comparative advantage. Instead, a pattern of essentially alien production—at least by Republican standards—was forced upon them. The state did ease the burden somewhat by supplying modern inputs in increasing quantities as the Maoist period progressed, but even so, the growth rates they were able to achieve were far less than would have been possible in a market economy.

At the same time, poor counties were galvanized into a frenzy of activity in order to exploit the catch-up potential that existed. The collective made possible the mobilization of labour on a historically unprecedented scale for farmland construction and for the creation of water conservancy facilities. In this way, the traditional technological package was diffused extremely swiftly to counties on the fringes of the Sichuan basin. Moreover, 'Taking grain as the key link' in many cases simply reinforced their historic pattern of specialization. After 1965, as these counties in turn began to come up against the problem of diminishing returns, the state acted to modernize farm production by an increasingly liberal supply of chemical fertilizers, pumping equipment, and electricity.

The results of this process are clear. There was a marked convergence of grain yields and per capita grain production between locations over time and, as grain production was such an important component of agricultural output, a convergence too of NVAO per capita.

7

Poverty and Inequality in Sichuan's Villages in the 1930s

Our knowledge of the distribution of income within the confines of China's villages during the 1930s is slight. The only national study is due to Roll (1980) and is based upon the results collected by the National Land Commission. Some village surveys have survived and provided the foundation for recent work undertaken by, for example, Huang (1985) on north China and Vermeer (1988) on Shaanxi. Some provinces, including Shandong, Jiangsu, and Guangdong, have attracted the attention of Western researchers such as Myers (1970), Ash (1976), and Faure (1989).

However, the materials used in these studies are neither abundant nor the epitome of excellence. If anything, the situation is worse for Sichuan owing to the political turbulence that characterized life in the province during the late 1920s and early 1930s. As a result, the National Land Commission survey of 1934–5 (one of the best surveys of any aspect of the rural economy undertaken in the 1930s) did not encompass China's most populous province. The progressive bankruptcy that afflicted the fissiparous warlord regimes of Sichuan eventually forced them to acknowledge the suzerainty of Chiang Kaishek. With that suzerainty came an improvement in data collection. However, the lacunae were still numerous when the end of the Second World War saw the return to eastern China of the Nationalist government. Some extremely interesting surveys of *urban* incomes were carried out in Chengdu in 1937 and again in the early 1940s by the University of Nanjing's Department of Agricultural Economics, but there was no rural counterpart. Moreover, there is nothing on rural income distribution *per se* in any of the massive statistical compilations of the period, such as the seven-volume 1947 statistical yearbook or the equally weighty contributions of Lu (1936) and X. M. Zhang (1939).

One must not complain too much about this statistical dearth. Governments embroiled in the quest for political legitimacy or in the desperate struggle to dam the flood tide of Japanese imperialism have more pressing matters to engage their attention. Yet it does make Olympian pronouncements on socioeconomic relations in the Sichuanese countryside during the Republic a somewhat hazardous occupation. However, the importance of these issues involved are persuasive enough to convince this writer that the task is worth attempting.

We begin with a discussion of landownership. However, as discussed in Chapter 4, it is not enough to discuss land alone. Brandt (1989: 138) has made the issues here very clear:

The distribution of landownership greatly influences rural income distribution, especially when economic activity is not particularly diversified and households depend almost entirely on farming for income. Tenancy allows for slightly more equal access to land, but the fact remains that the richest households own the most land, the poorest are landless, and inequality has a high positive correlation with unequal land ownership. . . .

I believe that, rather than widening income differentials at the local level, accelerated commercialization in the Yangtse region (and other parts of China for that matter) probably helped to narrow them. By increasing the demand for labor both on and off the farm and by generating new off-farm opportunities, commercialization significantly decreased the influence that land distribution had on rural income distribution, perhaps even reducing inequality.

We therefore proceed from land to discuss the degree to which land-based income inequalities were modified by economies or diseconomies of scale, tenancy, taxation, interest rates, and wage income. We also consider the scope that existed for socioeconomic mobility.

Landownership

Land was the most important means of production in rural China during the 1930s, and therefore we should expect significant inequalities in landownership to be related to inequalities in income. It must be admitted that the data available to us on landownership are difficult to interpret (Feuerwerker, 1977; Huang, 1975; Esherick, 1981). Most of the standard materials exclude absentee landlords, and in some cases they omit the landlord class in its entirety. The same is frequently true of agricultural labourers. The level of statistical aggregation is also unsatisfactory. For example, the owner-tenant category cited by the National Agricultural Research Bureau (NARB) includes both those leasing large tracts of land and those renting mere morsels; quite why these two very distinct groups should be treated as identical is unclear.

Nevertheless, the data on Sichuan are such as to make the conclusion of stratification unavoidable. In comparative provincial perspective, some 55% of all rural households were classified as tenants in Sichuan for the period 1931–7. This compares to the national average of 30% and a figure for Shandong province of only 11% (Zhongguo guomin zhengfu zhujiju tongjiju, 1946: 6–7). These surveys were relatively large in scale; the 1934 one in Sichuan involved 306 crop reporters who visited 89 of the province's 148 counties (NARB, 1936: 11).

This general conclusion was not disputed by Buck. As Stross has pointed out, and as his own writings reveal, Buck was anything but susceptible to claims of endemic inequality in landownership in rural China.

Twenty years after he had first come to China . . . Buck still believed that China's rural problems could be reduced to the simple matter of matching production with population by increasing the one and reducing the other. Social tensions did not enter his field of view, except briefly. . . . Buck was blind to rural problems that were being discussed in his own time. And this blindness sometimes seemed to be almost wilful, in that he ignored problems simply because they did not fit into the models of ideal farm management or land utilization that he had brought with him from the United States. (Stross, 1986: 187)

It is therefore doubly significant that his land utilization survey showed that landownership was much more unequally distributed in Sichuan than was the China norm. Moreover, as Arrigo (1986: 280) has shown, Buck's statistical methods led to an underestimation of the true extent of inequality in landownership in the province because of his methods of aggregation:

According to Buck's summary, the largest farms were only three times the size of the average farm. In recalculation, the largest farms are shown to be six times the size of the average farms. According to Buck's summary for Szechwan (Sichuan), the top 10% of farms held about 24% of the land. By recalculation, the top 10% held 39% of the land.

The provincial data available on Sichuan from other sources confirm these broad conclusions. Two collections of data, the first for the 1930s and the second for the pre-Land Reform period, are summarized in Tables 7.1 and 7.2. Both sets of data present problems. Household shares by class are a poor guide to population shares by class because of differences in household size. The samples seem to overemphasize periurban and ethnic-minority areas. Many of the pre-Land Reform data were published at the height of the Great Leap Forward or in the midst of the 'slaveowners revolt' in western Sichuan

TABLE 7.1. *Landholdings of the Landlord Class by County,*
mid-1930s

County[a]	% of households	% of arable land
Jiang'an	7	63
Gusong	10	50
Chongqing city	2	96
Pi	7	78
Ya'an	12	68
Nanchuan	9	85
Qijiang	8	88
Pengshui	10	85
MEDIAN	9	82
Zigong	5	68

[a] Entries are for 1935 except for Zigong, which is for 1944.

The source for this table lists data on the household and arable land shares of landlords (*dizhu*), owner-cultivators (*zigengnong*), and owner-tenants (*banzigengnong*) for 30 counties in all. Only in the cases of those cited above do the % shares for both categories sum to 100. The other counties in the sample have therefore been excluded.

No indication is given as to whether the landlord category includes absentee landlords.

Sources: Lu (1936: 177–81); Sichuan sheng yinhang jingji yanjiusuo (1944: 382).

in the mid-1950s. Neither backcloth can have provided much of a spur to objective analysis. Moreover, there were undoubtedly areas in Sichuan where the extent of concentration was much less extreme. In a township in Li county, the share of landlords (including absentee) in cultivated land was only 15.3% in 1954 (ASL, 1985: 390–4). This was considerably larger than their share in population (only 5.1%) but it was still much less than the norm elsewhere in the province. A similar situation obtained in the mountainous part of Santai county, where a 1950 survey revealed that landlords accounted for 2.5% of the population and owned 16.4% of the arable land (Zhongyang nongyebu jihuasi, 1952: 287). This hardly shows that equality was the norm, but clearly the landlord class was rather less dominant than some CCP accounts have suggested.

Despite these qualifications, the evidence for Sichuan points over-

TABLE 7.2.   *Landownership by Class, before Land Reform*

Locations	Landlord share[a]		Poor-peasant share[b]	
	In popn.	In land	In popn.	In land
Chongqing city	14	86	34	1
Jiangjin	7	58	36	3
Xindu	5	44	60	7
Nanjiang	6	33	23	8
Tianquan	6	23	48	20
Jiangbei	12	29	22	1
Jingyan	7	38	51	23
Serxu[c]	2	34	74	13
Batang[c]	5	33	72	20
Youyang[c]	5	40	55	10
Gulin: Dongyuan	12	52	53	10
Zaihe	5	73	72	9
Junlian[c]	11	50	33	6
All Sichuan[d]	6	40	51	9

[a] In principle, class status was determined along the lines laid down nationally in 'Decisions concerning the differentiation of class status in the countryside' published in May 1948 by the Central Committee and revised in Aug. 1950 (Selden, 1979: 218–25). In practice, a degree of autonomy was given to the peasant associations responsible for the classification.

[b] It is not clear in most of the sources whether the poor-peasant category also includes landless labourers. It definitely does not in the cases of Jiangbei, Gulin, and Junlian, where the share of landless households is given separately. Treatment of temple land is similarly unclear except for Batang and Serxu, where it is given separately as 22% and 18% of total cultivated area. Arguably this should be added to the share of the landlord class in both cases.

[c] = % of households, not % of population.

[d] The all-Sichuan figures are medians.

Sources: Serxu—*Garze Zangzu zizhizhou gaikuang* (1986: 168). Batang—ibid. 168–9. Youyang—*Youyang Tujiazu Miaozu zizhixian gaikuang* (1986: 36). Gulin—*Sichuan sheng Miaozu Lisuzu Daizu Baizu Manzu shehui lishi diaocha* (1986: 73) (Zaihe village) and 74 (Dongyuan village). Junlian—ibid. 111. Jingyan—*Jingyan xian zhi* (1990: 146). Others—C. R. Li (1959: 120).

whelmingly to a conclusion of gross inequalities in landownership. It shows a degree of concentration substantially in excess of the national average, and one that was significant by the standards of other LDCs. It is true that one can find countries where the degree of concentration is higher. In Egypt in 1952, 0.4% of landowners allegedly owned 35% of cultivated land (Abdel-Fadil, 1975: 4–5) but few countries generally perceived to have highly unequal patterns of landownership appear more stratified than Sichuan. In India in 1960–1, the top 18% of rural households owned 62% of cultivated area (Balasubramanyam, 1984: 86). In Bangladesh in 1977, the top 10% of farms owned 49.6% of farm area (Alamgir and Ahmed, 1988: 19). Of course such international comparisons are fraught with difficulties; 'typical years' are an elusive concept, data are collected for politically motivated purposes, and the farm is not synonymous with the household. Nevertheless, the high degree of concentration of landownership in Sichuan compared to the national norm and many other countries seems to provide—for this province at least—an ample justification for the land reform that was imposed so bloodily in the early 1950s.

Economies of Scale

Inequalities in landownership are a poor guide to inequalities in rural incomes if large landowners were unable to take advantage of the massive farms that they owned. The existence, or otherwise, of economies of scale is, of course, a critical issue in this type of analysis, and it is not surprising that it has received much attention in the literature (see the 1981 survey of many of the issues by Abhijit Sen). Evaluation has been hampered by the difficulties involved in testing for the *pure* effects of scale (a comparison between a large managerial and a small family-run farm is meaningless). Moreover, explicit recognition of the importance of the level of farm technology, and therefore the conclusion that the relationship between yields and farm size cannot be discussed in purely *theoretical* terms, has been slow. Nevertheless, two general conclusions inform the literature.

The first of these is that large farms whose method of operation is labour-intensive will be subject to diseconomies. Only in a handful of areas like the Indian Punjab, where the full 'green revolution' package (of chemical fertilizers and pesticides, mechanical irrigation, high-yielding varieties, and tractorization) has been applied, have economies of scale been achieved. This general conclusion is not, however, clear-cut. Some have pointed to the poor performance of the Soviet collective farm during the Khrushchev years as evidence that a positive relation does not exist. Others, such as Francesca Bray (1986), have noted the technical difficulties caused by the aquatic environment inherent in the mechanization of rice-based agriculture. However, neither objection is particularly convincing. Poor Soviet performance can be explained either as a consequence of the organizational inadequacies of collective forms or as a result of the very poor quality of industrial inputs. The mechanization of rice-farming in Japan has not proved impossible, whilst the slow pace of mechanization in Taiwan since 1945 seems largely to reflect the nature of the land reform process, which imposed ceilings on landholdings, rather than the absence of increasing returns to farm size (Thorbecke, 1979). In any case, even in southern provinces of China such as Sichuan, non-rice cereal production was a significant proportion of provincial output in the 1930s.

The conventional wisdom on the issue of economies of scale is that, where mechanization is either technically impossible or financially prohibitive, diseconomies of scale swiftly make their presence felt on large farms (for a critique of this view, see Bramall, 1991). The main reason for this is that labour-intensive farming involves problems of supervision and control that increase faster than farm size (in sharp contrast to capital-intensive manufacturing processes). Farming involves a definite sequence of productive activities ranging from soil preparation to harvesting; only the last of these yields an easily identifiable final product. As a result, unless continuous supervision is provided or the labour force is self-motivated so that supervision is not needed, it is difficult to attribute the blame for a low yield to any particular one of the various production processes. For example, even if it is known that seeds were planted at the wrong depth, it is virtually impossible to determine if this played a more important role in determining yields than, say, poor weeding. There is the further difficulty that many aspects of the environment have a major impact upon yields and yet are outside the control of the farmer; this is very different from the factory case, where poor welding cannot easily be attributed to low rainfall. Finally, there is less scope for specialization in farming. The cycle of farm work necessitates that all rural workers carry out the same task simultaneously. It is simply impossible for a peasant to be a specialist seeder or harvester, in sharp contrast to the possibilities within Fordist manufacturing operations. The lack of variety in car assembly may produce a relatively higher degree of 'alienation', but it is not clear that the variety of farm operations is something that most manufacturing workers would wish to savour.

However, the second general conclusion on the pure effects of scale is that the relationship between yield and farm size appears to be non-linear (see Chattopadhyay and Rudra, 1976 for contemporary India). Although large farms are subject to diseconomies, those at the bottom end of the scale were able to benefit from economies of scale.

These twin conclusions both support and undermine the neoclassical 'defence' of relations of production in the countryside. On the one hand, large-scale farming in traditional agriculture does not yield the same economies of scale as manufacturing industry. The landlord might then be forced to lease out his land on terms that were relatively favourable to the tenant to avoid these diseconomies. On the other hand, the prevalence of economies of scale at the bottom end of the range meant that average costs per unit for peasant families operating units of a modest size were significantly lower than those faced by smallholders. This in turn implied considerable differentiation at any moment in time in the countryside. The tenant could only overcome this scale disadvantage if he were able to lease land from a landlord on favourable terms, an issue to which we turn later.

But what of the reality of Sichuan during the Republican period? Do the theoretical considerations mentioned above have any relevance to the province? The simple answer to this question is yes. According to Arrigo's (1986) interpretation of Buck's survey, the yield achieved on very large farms in Sichuan (farms averaging 68.3 *shi mu* in size) was 4,091 kg. of grain per hectare. By contrast, that achieved on large farms (averaging 23.7 *shi mu* in size) was considerably higher at 4,651 kg. (Arrigo, 1986: 351). On the face of it, this suggests that the extent of diseconomies of scale on estates which, in counties like Dayi, extended to 30,000 *shi mu* in some cases must have been severe.

In practice, no such diseconomies operated because such estates were never operated as single farms. Instead they were broken down into smaller units and leased out to tenants. Table 7.3 shows that the overwhelming majority of farms were less than 20 *mu* in size and that very few exceeded 60 *mu*. This pattern made average farm size in Sichuan somewhat smaller than the all-China norm (see *China Handbook 1937–43*: 609). By contrast, in each of the provinces of Ningxia, Chahar, and Suiyuan, more than 20% of farms exceeded 50 *shi mu* in size.

Some large farms do seem to have existed in the province in the 1930s. In Fuling county, 26 out of 74,376 farms exceeded 500 local *mu* according to a 1934 survey (X. M. Zhang, 1939: A25). But whether such estates were actually farmed is unknown. They may have been devoted to cattle-breeding or could have been deserted because

TABLE 7.3. *Average Farm Size in Sichuan, mid-1930s*[a]

Size (local *mu*)	Farm type (% of all farms)			
	All farms	Owner farms[b]	Owner-tenant farms	Tenant farms
<10	47	14	20	70
10–19	21	61	46	11
20–9	16	16	15	8
30–9	10	5	4	2
40–9	3	2	4	2
50–9	1	1	2	1
60+	2	1	2	3

[a] This results are derived from a survey conducted by the Bank of China (*Zhongguo yinhang*) covering 1,556 family farms at an unspecified date during the mid-1930s.

[b] Owner farms are those where all land was owned by the operator; similarly for the other categories.

Source: X. M. Zhang (1939: A24).

bandit activity made potential tenants reluctant to take on such farms. This may have been particularly true of land in mountainous areas, and certainly was the case in many parts of the East and West Mountains district close to Chongqing in the late 1930s (Hsiang, 1941: 450–1).

However, the central feature of farming during the 1930s in Sichuan was the prevalence of *economies* of scale on farms that were large by contemporary provincial standards. For whilst diseconomies may have set in at some point (perhaps beyond 20 *mu*), returns were assuredly increasing up to that level. The Arrigo recalculation of Buck's original yield data already mentioned shows that the yield achieved on small farms averaging 6.6 *shi mu* in size was 2,012 kg. of grain per hectare. Yet medium-sized farms (averaging 13.9 *shi mu* each) achieved a yield of 3,890 kg., and yield appears to have peaked for Buck's large farms (23.7 *shi mu*). As already noted, these achieved a yield figure of 4,651 kg. of grain (Arrigo, 1986: 351). Of course, such figures as these do not entirely settle the issue. Buck's sample was biased towards the more prosperous farms, and it is also possible that diseconomies of scale from larger-scale production were to be seen in rising costs per unit of land rather than in a tailing off in yields.

That having been said, there is little question that many farms in Sichuan during the 1930s were well below the optimum size. Tsui came to the same conclusion on the basis of a survey conducted in Huayang county (Tsui, 1944; 1946). Buck and Chen (1944) concluded likewise for the same area, and Buck himself reaffirmed his earlier conclusion in a 1947 paper: 'In China over 80 per cent of the farm units are below an economic-sized unit for farm operation. The most capable use of land is impossible in a farming system with so many uneconomic units' (p. 7).

In short, the situation prevailing in Sichuan during the 1930s seems to have been remarkably similar to that seen in many other traditional peasant economies. Beyond a certain size, which is impossible to define independent of the specification of land quality, growing conditions, and market access but which seems to have been in excess of 20 *shi mu*, diseconomies of scale set in. For the range that was relevant for the majority of farmers, however, economies of scale were the norm.

Tenancy

It has already been observed that the existence of diseconomies of scale ensured a considerable market in rented land. On the one hand, large landowners did not have the option of farming their holdings in large units because of the diseconomies of scale that this would involve. They therefore responded by dividing their holdings into smaller units and leasing them out to tenant or small-scale owner-farmers. The landowner can be seen here as maximizing his *potential* income (his actual income would depend upon the revenue-sharing arrangement he could impose on the tenant) by ensuring that farm size was optimal. Conversely, the tenant gained from the process, in that renting land enabled him to increase his holding to a more 'efficient' size and hence exploit any economies of scale that were available. As the landlord could only generate income if a peasant were willing to lease land from him, the presence of diseconomies went some way towards increasing the bargaining power of the putative tenant. Whether this supply of tenancies was enough to keep the 'price' low is the issue to be considered here.

For Mao, right was on the side of the poor peasantry who had been mercilessly exploited through the ages:

The most violent revolts and the most serious disorders have invariably occurred in places where the local tyrants, evil gentry and lawless landlords perpetrated the worst outrages. The peasants are clear-sighted. Who is bad and who is not, who is the worst and who is not quite so vicious, who deserves severe punishment and who deserves to be let off lightly—the peasants keep clear accounts, and very seldom has the punishment exceeded the crime. Secondly, a revolution is not a dinner party, or writing an essay, or painting a picture, or doing embroidery; it cannot be so refined, so leisurely and gentle, so temperate, kind, courteous, restrained and magnanimous. A revolution is an insurrection, an act of violence by which one class overthrows another.   (Mao, 1971: 29–30)

Tawney, no doctrinaire Marxist, was rather more restrained in his language. He did not welcome the prospect of revolution in the Chinese countryside but saw a certain inevitability in its coming:

The revolution of 1911 was a bourgeois affair. The revolution of the peasants has still to come. If their rulers continue to exploit them, or to permit them to be exploited, as remorselessly as hitherto, it is likely to be unpleasant. It will not, perhaps, be undeserved.   (1932: 74)

For the neoclassicals, as previously noted, this kind of assessment of landlord–tenant relations is misconceived. They point out that by no means all rural economies are characterized by land scarcity or by a population density that ensures a reserve army of tenants; the American case is often quoted as a counterexample. Accordingly, the relative scarcity of factors of production may induce a level of rent that is low by international standards. Furthermore, the ability of tenant farmers to rent land enables them to increase the size of their farm to an 'economic' level and thus raises income per unit of area. Tenancy, therefore, may well be a progressive institution which obviates the need for land purchase by small landowners. Moreover, when it comes to analysing 'real' situations, they argue that it is not enough to look at levels of rent alone. For example, a rent amounting to 50% of crop yield signifies, not exploitation, but either a situation in which the burden of risk lies heaviest upon the shoulders of the landlord or one where the owner is advancing fixed and variable capital inputs—such as equipment, draught animals, and seed—to the operator. In this last instance, rent is perceived to be in essence a legitimate return upon a risky investment by the landowning class in the tenant farmer.

Buck's writings constitute the classic denunciation of the Maoist case:

The Communist method of assuming all landlords to be crooks is unjust. The majority of the resident landlords have a character as good as that of the tenant [and therefore] their elimination is a backward step in social progress. (1947: 42)

There are certain evils in the tenancy system which should be eradicated. Farm leases are written largely from the standpoint of the obligations of the tenant, rather than in fairness to both the landlord and the tenant. . . . Observations indicate that in the hilly areas the payment of rent in the form of rice tends to cause a continued planting of rice on land where the water supply is unreliable, and where other crops might prove more profitable. (1943*a*: 12)

More recently, Ramon Myers has contributed a number of elegant restatements of the same view. For example:

Land and labour markets throughout the countryside appear to have been highly competitive. Land rents and rural wages fluctuated according to seasonal supply and demand. The number of landowners with land to lease and tenants seeking land to rent were usually so numerous that no single party could ever influence the general terms of rent agreed upon. Yet, it is possible that considerable economic power, enough to set rents above a competitive fair-share rent, sometimes accumulated in the hands of landowners. (1982: 45)

Sichuan provides additional evidence on this debate. Some general estimates of the incidence of rent are summarized in Table 7.4. These figures suggest that Sichuan's rents were higher than the national average in almost every category—the one exception being cash rents paid on dry land—and the difference between the levels of crop rent

TABLE 7.4. *Rents as a Share of Output in Sichuan and China, 1930s*[a]

	Irrigated land			Dry land		
	Crop[b]	Cash	Share	Crop	Cash	Share
Sichuan	65	20	58	51	9	48
All China	46	11	48	45	11	45

[a] The figures for each type of rent refer to the rent paid on the middle class of land (*zhong deng tian*. A detailed breakdown by land type for rents in 1931 is given in Lu (1936: 205–6).

[b] Crop rents were fixed rents paid in kind.

Source: Zhongguo guomin zhengfu zhujiju tongjiju (1946: 76–7).

on irrigated land is considerable. Inevitably such summary estimates are subject to qualification. Comparisons are always problematic when we know that survey methods were not rigorously standardized. Furthermore, harvest and exchange rate fluctuations make it difficult to select a truly representative year. Nevertheless, these figures receive a degree of confirmation from the microeconomic evidence available. These do not help us to compare Sichuan with other provinces, but at least they provide an indication as to whether tenancy was a desirable or undesirable state in the 1930s.

Some of the materials published after 1949, unsurprisingly perhaps, roundly condemn the whole system of tenancy. One account of sugar cane production by tenant farmers in Neijiang prefecture (Wang and Huang, 1985: 177–85) tells a grim story; a standard rent of 50% of output supplemented by a rent deposit amounting to a further 10% was onerous enough, but tenants were also forced to sell their unharvested crop prematurely in order to borrow the funds needed to buy essential inputs. A 1950 study of rents in Huayang found that they amounted to about 45% of crop income for middle peasants and 53% for poor peasants (Zhongyang nongyebu jihuasi, 1952: 298–301).[1]

Many accounts written before 1949 seem to share this view. Hsiang, in his study of the East and West Mountains District, concluded: 'Szechwan is a high tenancy region and absenteeism of the gentry [and] official and military combination is rampant. The existing rack-renting in kind leaves not enough grain for the peasants to eat' (1941: 459).

Lu Pingdeng's appraisal was also unfavourable. He emphasized the change in the relative bargaining position of landlord and tenant in the decades after the 1911 Revolution (for reasons that he does not explain—one plausible explanation might be that landownership was a very risky use of capital, given troop movements and the possibility of arbitrary confiscation). Landlords, he argues, took advantage of this shift by raising the level of rent deposits levied on tenants (Lu, 1936: 199). In counties located on the Chengdu plain, these had reached 7–8 *yuan* per *mu* by 1932 (pp. 199–200) or 60–70% of annual rent; in eastern Sichuan, the figure averaged 80% (p. 200). Rent deposits of this magnitude generally forced tenants to borrow the sum involved. According to Lu, only 14% of tenants were able to finance this deposit from their own capital. No less than 43% were forced to borrow the entire sum. The alleged improvement in the

---

[1] This is total rent as a % of crop income from *rented* land. The original data on total crop income is reduced to obtain the figures above in proportion to the share of owned in total farmed land.

relative bargaining strength of the landlord class also had a direct effect upon rents. In particular, supplements were levied on notionally fixed crop rents. In Xinfan county, the notional crop rent (*guzu*) per *mu* was 1 *shi* 7 *tou* to 1 *shi* 9 *tou* of rice, but the actual rent was in the range 2 *shi* to 2 *shi* and 12 *tou* (Lu, 1936: 207; copied in identical form in X. M. Zhang, 1939: M6). In nearby Peng county, rent on irrigated land was marked up from 1 *shi* and 7 *tou* to more than 2 *shi* (Lu, 1936: 207).[2]

It must, of course, be admitted that other evidence tends to lead to a more neoclassical conclusion. Notions of a rapacious landlord class are dispelled somewhat by evidence for the same county that if tenants were 'forced to bale water for irrigation using oxen or mules' (p. 207), it was recognized by the landlord that this increased costs for the tenant, and therefore the rent was marked down to its original level. Whether this was common only in Pengxian is unknown, although the crop rent system nominally involved the tenant paying a higher rent (than under cash or share crop tenancy) in return for which the landlord was supposed to provide all the means of production except labour (Buck, 1947: 27 n.).

Moreover, and predictably, the surveys carried out by the University of Nanjing's Department of Agriculture during its period in exile in Sichuan under Buck's direction generally reached optimistic conclusions. It is certainly important to recognize that data on rent are very difficult to interpret. For example, consider the level of average rents. According to the Land Law of 1930 (which was never implemented), 'land rent should not exceed 37.5% of the main produce of the land' (*China Handbook 1937–43*: 606).[3] This figure was undoubtedly exceeded at times during the 1930s, but not by as much as the figures above suggest, because almost all of these refer to rent as a percentage of the rice crop only. Buck was therefore able to conclude in a 1944 article, summarizing a survey conducted in Peng county, that the landlord 'actually takes 71% of the rice crop but the tenant has all the other farm receipts of winter crops and animal products for himself. There is no evidence, that on the average, the landlord is taking more than his fair share of farm receipts' (Buck and Pan, 1944: 339).

Barnett's study (1936) of an area of Baxian in the late 1940s found that a fixed rent of 60% of the theoretical productivity of cultivated

---

[2] These are local *shi* and *tou*. There were evidently more than 10 tou in a local *shi* in many areas.

[3] Here 'main product' means crop output as distinct from sideline acitivities or money raised by the sale of crop by-products, such as straw used for fuel and thatching.

land was by no means uncommon and that, in the case of share cropping, the landlord's share averaged in the range 50–80%; but he was also careful to point out that the figure refers only to the rice crop. Further, a survey of tenant farms conducted on the Chengdu plain in 1926 (Brown and Li, 1928: 62–4) put rents at around 45% of total tenant income (including food raised and consumed on the farm). This obviously exceeded the Land Law ideal, but not by as much as Communist accounts imply.

Moreover, rental levels during the early 1940s did accord with Buck's notion of a 'fair rent'—that is, the respective shares of land-lord and tenant in farm receipts should be in the same proportion as their shares in expenditure. In fact, some 31.8% of total receipts were received by landlords who also paid 31.9% of expenses (Buck, 1944). In this same survey, Buck concluded that tenant incomes (after rent) were lower than those of owners only because the real value of land taxation (discussed below) had fallen because of price inflation. He also identified some favourable aspects of the tenancy system. In the early 1940s, the average length of tenure on the farms surveyed was 10 years (Buck, 1943a: 13); in other words, leases were relatively long-term. Moreover, he also noted the practice of paying interest rates on rent deposits. In Pengxian, for example, an annual interest rate of about 17% was paid during 1942 (Buck and Shaw, 1943; Buck and Yien, 1943).

However, most of these surveys were conducted during the 1940s when even Chiang's regime began to realize that something had to be done to alleviate conditions in the countryside if the Communists were not to come to power. In consequence, it is unlikely that they give anything like a true guide to conditions in the areas sampled before 1937. More significantly, the problem with these apologetics is that they focus too much upon a very restrictive sample of counties. Peng county is close to Chengdu and Ba county close to Chongqing, the very sorts of area best suited to the 'reformist' package that Chiang's regime was promoting so assiduously to foreign observers in the 1940s. Elsewhere, conditions were altogether less favourable. Interest payments on rent deposits were a phenomenon confined to the Chengdu plain. Very large deposits were demanded without interest payments in areas such as Wanxian and Fuling. On the Chengdu plain itself, the interest rates on deposits fell from more than 4 *shi* per 100 silver taels before 1921 to 3.5–4 *shi* by the early 1930s. Even Buck admitted that the real interest declined between 1937 and 1942 (Buck and Yien, 1943: 107) although he neglected to emphasize the insig-nificance of a nominal rate of 17% per annum when compared to nominal rates on loans (in kind) which averaged 24% *per month* in the same year (p. 109). Further, Buck's argument that tenancy was often long-term is contradicted by other evidence. A NARB survey found that the average length of tenure in the province in 1938 was only 2.9 years (cited in Buck, 1947: 27).

Most seriously of all, any discussion of landlord–tenant relations is incomplete without a mention of the slavery that existed in many parts of the province. Nowhere was this more prevalent than in Liangshan prefecture. There a definite heirarchy existed. At the top were the Black Yi, or nobility, whose authority over the lower classes was absolute. Next came the White Yi, who appear to have been an independent farming class owning substantial amounts of property and slaves of their own. The third class were the Ajia, who were slaves in that they could be bought and sold by their Black and White Yi masters. They did at least enjoy some degree of economic independence in that they were allowed to own property (albeit subject to arbitrary confiscation). In that sense their position was superior to that of the Xiaxi, who were mere household slaves without economic independence of any kind. According to Chinese accounts, the life of this class was one of unmitigated horror. They were bought and sold at will, rarely had enough clothes to wear to be able to appear in public, and were not allowed to marry without permission. Some were periodically offered up as human sacrifices to the Gods.

The extent of slavery in ethnic-minority areas was considerable, and even in relatively non-stratified townships like Xinglong mentioned earlier, slavery persisted into the mid-1950s. Furthermore, the extent of slavery during the 1950s understates the pre-1949 position. In Xinglong, the pre-1949 peak slave number was 132 compared to 44 in 1949 (ASL, 1985: 394) and in western Sichuan in general slave-ownership was even more widespread. For example, of Liangshan autonomous prefecture's Yi population of 700,000, 5% were classified as slave-owners, 30% as farm labourers, and an incredible 65% as slaves who were bought and sold (Cheng, 1984: 208–9).

The inferior living standards of the slaves is evident from Table 7.5, which seems to confirm the often-stated point that the Xiaxi (and the Ajia to some extent) were forced to forage for the bulk of their diet because grain-consumption levels such as these are far below subsistence. In the main, they subsisted upon turnips (traditionally used as animal fodder in the Sichuan basin), husks, and wild herbs, vegetables, and grasses.

Materials on slavery need, of course, to be interpreted carefully. The investigations carried out by the Chinese were designed to serve

TABLE 7.5. *Incomes[a] by Caste in Liangshan, early 1950s*

Caste	Township			
	Chengnan	Buzi	Sanhouyida	Laligou
Black Yi[b]	2,164	2,618	1,914	4,697
White Yi	331	214	218	472
Ajia	96	66	33	203
Xiaxi	n.a.	10	28	69

[a] In *shi jin* of grain.
[b] A footnote to the original table indicates that this measure of income does not fully indicate the true level of Black Yi expenditure.
Source: LSL (1985: 5).

the purposes of propaganda rather than those of truth. Ethnic-minority people were to be shown as 'oppressed', 'longing for liberation', and as suitably grateful to their liberators for conferring upon them the inestimable benefits of Han civilization. Moreover, even if the accounts of the 1950s are taken at face value, one would not wish to pretend that slavery extended behind the province's ethnic-minority areas, the population of which accounted for perhaps 5% of the provincial total in the 1950s. Furthermore, some might wish to defend the slave mode of production on the grounds that slaves are fixed capital. Accordingly, there is no reason to expect a rational, profit-maximizing, slave-owner to mistreat his slaves; and therefore the incomes implied in this table understate the reality (for a famous argument along these line in the American ante-bellum context, see Fogel and Engerman, 1974).

The mere existence of slavery, however, and the unfreedom it involved, is a powerful indictment of relations of production in Sichuan during the Republican period, irrespective of the material conditions 'enjoyed' by the slaves. It is not convincing to suggest that slaves enjoyed satisfactory living standards or that the extent of slavery was so trivial as to be unworthy of our notice. The Han Chinese accounts may be exaggerated, but there is no reason to dispute their general conclusion. Moreover, anyone who is genuinely moved by the spectacle of inequality cannot ignore a situation in which no less than 5% of the population is condemned to a life of misery.

Similar sentiments apply to tenancy taken as a whole. It is quite plausible that CCP accounts exaggerate the misery suffered by the tenant and resolutely ignore any mitigating circumstances. However, there is nothing in the evidence reviewed above that persuades me that tenancy was anything other than a state to be avoided in Republican Sichuan. Rents were high and sundry miscellaneous levies an ever-present threat. Palliatives, such as the occasional payment of interest on rent deposits, were precisely that.

The underlying problem was the relative growth rates of population and cultivated area in the absence of a developmental state. Sichuan's population was growing at an unknown rate in the 1930s; as Skinner's recent work has emphasized (1987), the figures collected on the size of the province's population during the last century of the Empire are too unreliable to justify a statement any more precise than that. However, if the growth rate was in the order of 0.5% per annum, the usual estimate for China during the Republican period, that was still faster than the rate of growth of cultivated area. Data for this last are, if anything, even more unreliable than those on population (Bramall, 1989a). My own best guess puts the figure at around 115 million *mu*, close to the 1957 official Chinese estimate, but it is clear that no growth was taking place. Despite the enormous effort expended after 1949 to raise agricultural output by land reclamation and improvements in irrigation, cultivated area continued to fall. Gradually declining from its 1957 peak, by the early 1980s it stood at under 100 million *mu* (Liu, 1988: 29). By 1987 it had dropped further, to a mere 94.9 million (SCSHTJZL, 1989: 3). By the late 1930s, therefore, Sichuan's 'open frontier' had disappeared.

The result was an inexorable increase in the supply of potential tenants relative to cultivated land, and a corresponding increase in the bargaining power enjoyed by landlords. In the absence of remedial measures, such as rural industrialization to reduce tenant supply, rents tended to increase relative to the size of crop.

The only conclusion, therefore, is that offered by Tawney (1932: 69):

The theory that agitation is produced by agitators, not agitators by agitation, is among the western doctrines which certain circles in China have absorbed without difficulty. But no reference to communist propaganda is required to explain the no-rent campaigns and peasants' revolts which have taken place in parts of the country. It is surprising, indeed, that they have not been more frequent.

Taxation

The evidence reviewed in the last section is not decisive. Even if it is accepted that landlords levied exorbitant rents on tenants, it is possible that landlords gained little benefit from this if their rental income was taxed away and used by the state for military expenditure. As many of the armaments purchased by Sichuan's warlords emanated from either elsewhere in China or abroad, this expenditure constituted a net drain on provincial income.[4] In this instance, the impact of high but tax-induced rents on stratification might be negligible. Moreover, to the extent that taxation was the ultimate cause of poverty, the culprit was the state and not landlordism as such.

This argument plays an integral role in the analysis offered by neopopulist and neoclassical alike, as has been observed in Chapter 4. But the problem here is that the ultimate beneficiaries of high rents were not simply wasting their revenue in unproductive military expenditure but were using it to acquire land. Indeed, taxation can be seen as a device by means of which landowners were forced to sell land to the new warlord class. In the process, the tenant farmer's income was reduced to subsistence as the landlord desperately tried to pass on as much as possible of the tax burden.

The tax burden was not trivial, although it is extremely difficult to calculate. Two conflicting estimates are given in Table 7.6 for the province in the mid-1930s. The microlevel data almost uniformly supports the contention that the revised estimate is more accurate. One of the most important sources of revenue was the land tax. The traditional land tax (*zhengliang*) averaged 1.6 *yuan* per *liang* of land in 1914, but by the late 1920s and early 1930s, the rate was far above that level for two reasons.[5] First, the *zhengliang* was collected several times per annum (it seems to have varied between 3 and 14 times— Kuang, 1981; Lu, 1936: 477, 478–9, 484). Secondly, land tax surcharges were also levied. These also were collected more than once per year. Chinese accounts for this period show, for instance, that the land tax was collected well in advance of the date on which it was due. Zhang lists 28 counties in all of which, by 1930 and 1931, tax revenue had been collected a minimum of 5 years in advance. In 9 of them it had been collected 20 or more years in advance (Y. Y. Zhang, 1957: 40).

[4] Some of it was used to provide military employment for landless labourers, an issue to which I return later.
[5] The *liang* varied in size between locations; Gunde (1976: 26) gives a figure of 50 *shi mu* for Chongqing county's *liang*.

TABLE 7.6. *The Tax Burden in Sichuan during the 1930s*
(*millions of current* yuan)

	Rawski estimate[a]	Revised estimate[b]
Tax revenue	100	200
Provincial GDP[c]	5,010	2,053
Tax rate (%)[d]	2.0	9.7

[a] Rawski (1989) estimates provincial tax revenue from that of Liu Xiang's garrison area multiplied by the reciprocal of the garrison area's share in provincial troop strength. Provincial GDP is provincial GVAO multiplied by the national ratio of GDP to GVAO given in Liu and Yeh (1965). However, figures on relative troop strengths are too unreliable to be helpful, and an indication of this is that Rawski's estimate of provincial GDP is far too high. It implies that Sichuan's share in national GDP was 16.8%, which was *far* greater than the province's share in national income in the 1950s of 6.9%. It is implausible to suggest that the province's relative standing deteriorated by anything like this amount over a 20-year period.

[b] I have re-estimated the tax burden as follows. Liu Xiang's reported tax revenue in 1932 was 30,765 million *yuan* (X. M. Zhang, 1939: C18) and his garrison area covered 20 counties (Zhonggong Sichuan sheng wei dangshi gongzuo weiyuanhui, 1986: 5). That implies a per county tax revenue of 1.54 million *yuan*. There were 128 counties in Sichuan in that year, divided amongst 6 garrison areas (ibid. 5). That gives a total provincial tax revenue of 197 million *yuan*, which I have rounded to 200 million. Although per-county revenue in Liu's area benefited from his control of Chongqing, I doubt whether it was significantly higher than the provincial average. His area in south-east Sichuan included some very poor ethnic-minority counties, and did not include the fertile Chengdu plain, where revenue from opium tax collection must have been very high indeed. In any case, it should be noted that the figures cited for Liu are *budget* figures only. I suspect that true revenue was substantially higher.

[c] Provincial GDP is calculated as the Liu and Yeh (1965) national estimate for 1933 multiplied by the average provincial share in national net material product for 1952 to 1957. This latter is calculated as 6.87% from data in Zhongguo guojia tongjiju (1987: 341) and ZGTJNJ (1989: 29). This probably exaggerates provincial GDP in the 1930s. The province was larger in the 1950s, and probably increased its share in national GDP as a result of wartime growth and industrialization after 1949.

[d] Note that Ch'en (1985) has also suggested that Rawski underestimates the true tax burden. Ch'en's own calculations for a single county (Fuling) produce a tax rate of 12.8% which he rounds to 10% (ibid. 45–7).

In fairness to Rawski, these tax and GDP estimates are incredibly unreliable. And I do not at all disagree with his view that the *national* tax rate was in the order of 5% of GDP. However, Sichuan is not China, and my revised estimate of taxation for that province ties in much better with all the microaccounts suggesting extremely high tax burdens there in the early 1930s.

NARB estimates of land tax rates show a similar pattern. The 1931 land tax rate in Sichuan for paddy-land was 2.8%, slightly greater than the national figure of 2.1%. By 1934, the Sichuan rate had climbed to 4.2% as a result of rising land tax rates and falling land values; the national figure was 3.1% in the same year (NARB, 1936: 68).

In comparative international perspective, these rates seem very high. The Meiji land tax rate, which is often portrayed as being cripplingly high (it amounted to about 30% of income), was set at 4% in 1873 and subsequently revised downwards to 3% in 1877 (Smethurst, 1986: 49–51). Moreover, this was almost the only tax that Japan's peasants had to pay. By contrast, land taxes accounted for only 15% of Liu's revenue in 1932 (X. M. Zhang, 1939: C18). Opium was much more important, as is shown by the fact that the cultivation of poppies grew steadily during the 1920s and 1930s. This reflected the imposition of the 'lazy tax' which was levied on land irrespective of whether poppies were grown or not. When the harvest was good, opium taxes could usually be paid, but that was not so in poor years. The inevitable results were distress and resistance:

Opium is planted without let or hindrance as last year. Christians who don't plant are obliged to pay a 'lazy tax'. Owing to lack of rain, the opium crop was poor last winter and people had to sell their grain cattle and often even their land to pay the tax.   (Missionary report on western Sichuan in 1924–5, cited in Woodhead, 1926: 586)

farmers in four counties, Hongya, Kiakiang, Losan and K'ienwei [Hongya, Jiajiang, Leshan, and Qianwei respectively] simply served notice on the officials that they were not going to plant the drug and they have not done so. The officials had no alternative but to send them all to gaol or to chop off their heads and so far they have not resorted to such drastic action, but they have insisted that a certain number of lamps [*licensed opium dens*] be maintained in each township and are getting a good revenue from these. (Missionary report on central Sichuan, cited in Woodhead, 1931: 600)

A large proportion of tax revenue was being collected in Sichuan to finance military expenditure. But taxes were also being used to force traditional landowners to sell their land at low prices to the new warlord class. Some indication of their success in this regard—the growing concentration of cultivated land in warlord hands and the displacement of the Qing landlord—is summarized in Table 7.7.

Despite the considerable variation evident, it is clear that the traditional landlord class had largely been supplanted within a mere two decades of the 'Revolution' of 1911. Its inability to pass on or evade the burden of taxation is mirrored by the size of landholdings

TABLE 7.7.   *Percentage of Landlord-Owned Arable Land by Landlord Type, 1935*[a]

County	New landlords[b]	Old landlords
Chongqing	86	9
Dayi	125	neg.
Guan	77	23
Chongqing city	90	8
Wan	86	12
Yibin	78	16
Youyang	96	3
Ya'an	86	13
Jiangyou	95	5

[a] Some of these percentages do not sum to 100. Overestimation is probably a result of arithmetical error in the original, while underestimation is a consequence of the failure of the investigator to survey all landlord households in a given locality.

[b] The original data further disaggregate new landlords into warlords, bureaucrats, and others while the old landlords (those owning land at the end of the Qing) are differentiated by size of holding.

Source: X. M. Zhang (1939: A20–3) (also cited in Lu, 1936: 186–91).

that warlords were able to build up during the early 1930s. For example, the family of Liu Wencai, one of the leading provincial warlords, comprised 13 households. The three largest landowning households each owned more than 10,000 *mu*, their holdings being respectively 18,414, 15,935, and 15,488 *mu*; even the smallest land-owning household owned more than 2,000 *mu* (Cao, 1985: 280). More general evidence of the extent of warlord holdings is provided in Table 7.8.

With the average peasant household cultivating less than 10 *mu* (X. M. Zhang, 1939: A24) in Sichuan in the early 1930s, this table provides strong evidence of stratification. The fact that the burden of warlord taxation was borne by both traditional landlord and tenant in no sense overturns that conclusion. The existence of an extraordinarily powerful and wealthy warlord class in the countryside was sufficient to generate a degree of income inequality in Sichuan well in excess of the national average. There is, in short, no reason to alter Gunde's conclusion:

TABLE 7.8. *Landownership per Warlord Household, 1935*

County	Largest holding[a] (*mu*)	Average holding (*mu*)	% households[b]	% land
Chongqing	15,000	5,000	2.6	57
Dayi	30,000	3,046	2.9	66
Guan	5,000	3,000	0.7	21
Chongqing city	4,000	2,500	6.6	60
Wan	3,000	1,000	6.0	33
Yibin	2,000	800	4.0	20
Youyang	500	200	1.5	3
Ya'an	100	100	0.4	1
Jiangyou	200	100	0.6	10

[a] The data on holding size refer to the largest and average holdings of warlords only. The percentages represent the share of the warlord class in the landlord class as a whole—they are *not* percentages of total rural population or total *cultivated* land.

[b] Only in the cases of Guan, Wan, Ya'an, and Jiangyou counties are the *percentages* reliable. In the other cases, the land or population shares of the various strata within the warlord class sum to less than or more than 100, for reasons that are unexplained. It should also be remembered that the data on absolute holdings is almost certainly inaccurate because of the non-existence of land registration.

Source: X. M. Zhang (1939: A20–3).

During the second, third and fourth decades of this century, Sichuan province underwent a process of sweeping social change. A new class of landlords controlling large estates arose—a class made up of warlords in intimate association with ostensibly civilian bureaucrats, the two forming an elite which virtually monopolised political power and government authority. Under their rule, traditional society was deeply altered. The old landlord elite was destroyed, the numbers of small, free-owning peasants was steeply reduced, and tenancy increased in proportion.   (Gunde, 1976: 23)

Debt and Interest Rates

For many writers like Tawney, the income inequality implied by unequal landownership and high rents was compounded by the extent of indebtedness and the level of interest rates.

the indebtedness of Chinese farmers . . . is always extensive and sometimes crushing. The peasant's capital is tiny, and his income too small to enable him to save. Towards the end of the winter, when last year's grain is exhausted, he is often on the verge of starvation, and any unexpected emergency drives his head under water. . . . It is not the least of the evils of the present situation that, where capital could be used to the greatest general advantage, it hardly exists, and, where it exists, it cannot be used, or used to good purpose. Rural China is crying out for it, and, instead of being employed to finance agricultural improvement, it is diverted to speculation in land values in Shanghai. Interest rates as high as those charged to Chinese peasants are a crushing tax on agricultural progress. . . .   (Tawney, 1932: 58, 95)

It must be remembered that indebtedness by itself may be a sign of progress rather than stratification; borrowing by firms in OECD economies is so common as to be entirely unremarkable. Moreover, the term structure of borrowing is not as important as some authors suggest. Ideally, loans would be long-run and be taken out primarily to finance agricultural investment; but if distress—that is, short-run— loans were preventing famine, then one ought to see them as a progressive feature. The key issue is whether real interest rates were 'fair' given the degree of risk to which they were subject. As for the extent of peasant indebtedness in the 1930s, various estimates have been collected in Table 7.9 which suggest that some 50% of peasant households were debtors.

The literature on the impact of interest rates, like that on interest rates in developing countries in general, is divided into optimists and pessimists. Most Chinese accounts, in those written before 1949, fall into the latter category. Lu (1936) entitles one of his chapters 'Usury' (*gaolidai*), while Wang and Huang (1985: 183–4) argue that high interest rates, especially those payable on loans taken out to pay rent deposits, played an instrumental role in reducing debtor households to penury. The autobiographical account of the conditions that he found in northern Sichuan in November 1932 provided by Zhang Guotao, the leader of the Fourth-Front Army, is representative of most Communist accounts: 'The interest rate on loans was even more appalling. One hundred percent per annum was considered very light, because the common practice was to charge one hundred percent per month' (Chang, 1972: ii. 319).

Buck ranges himself with the optimists. The main source of loans was not the landlord class but the friends and relatives of farmers, and market interest rates were rarely usurious when adjusted for risk and price fluctuation. Low's contribution to Buck's *Land Utilisation* text (1937: 463–4) summarizes the optimist case as follows:

TABLE 7.9. *Percentage of Farm Households in Debt in Sichuan, 1930s*

Locality	Debtors	Year	Source[a]
Guang'an	73	1934	K. C. Lee (1939: 193–4)
Neijiang:			
Dongxing xiang	72	mid-1930s ⎱	Wang and Huang
Xifucheng xiang	76	mid-1930s ⎰	(1985: 183, 184)
Chongqing City[b]	7	1929	
Fuling[b]	62	1929	
Mianyang[b]	65	1930	X. M. Zhang
Neijiang[b]	31	1931–2	(1939: M25)
Daxian[b]	9	1931	
Suining[b]	22	1929	
Sichuan	66	mid-1930s	Lu (1936: 454)
Sichuan:			
Grain debtors[b]	46	1933	Hsu (1935: t. 41)
Cash debtors	56	1933	
Sichuan rice region	34	1931	Buck (1937: 462)
China:			
Grain debtors[b]	48	1933	Hsu (1935: t. 41)
Cash debtors	56	1933	
China	39	1929–33	Buck (1937: 462)

[a] Of these materials, the most reliable are those given in Hsu (1935) and Lu (1936). The former is from the NARB's crop report of 1933, which gathered information from 56 of Sichuan's counties, whilst the latter was based upon a survey of 1,556 farm households. However, the results of the other surveys do not differ to any great extent from these two. It is clear, and unsurprising, that spatial differences existed, and there is some evidence (weak, in view of the underlying data base) that indebtedness was increasing over time.

[b] Debt contracted in the form of grain.

The high rates of interest in general are due not only to the imperfect machinery for supplying credit and the degree of risk, but are also a result of the falling value of silver and the trend of prices upwards for many years prior to 1931. With rising prices a loan constantly diminished in the true value that it would buy. In the circumstances, the lenders demanded and the farmers paid fairly high rates of interest because the real value of the

Poverty and Inequality in the 1930s

principal was decreasing. This is not to say that the high rates were entirely justifiable. When the trend of prices began downwards in 1931–32, the burden of the interest rates, which had been adjusted to rising prices, became relatively much heavier.

It is true that some of the data assembled by Buck support his contention that the bulk of loans were provided by friends and relatives. His 1931 figures for Sichuan indicate a combined share for these two groups of 53% (Buck, 1937: 465) and 50% for 1941 (Buck, 1947: 18), but quite how 'friends and relatives' are defined is not clear. A friend is arguably anyone prepared to make a personal loan, and a 'relative' might also be a powerful member of the same lineage association, a merchant, or a landlord (and possibly all three). Moreover, the results of the NARB surveys of the early 1930s are at variance with Buck's results. The 1933 data show that only 20% of loans came from relatives, none from friends, and fully 50% from landlords (Hsu, 1935: t. 41). In the 1934 survey, the category 'personal loans' is broken down merely into loans from landlord, well-to-do farmers, and merchants; the 'relatives and friends' category is

TABLE 7.10.   *Mortgage[a] Interest Rates in Sichuan, mid-1930s*

County	Length of loan (months)	Nominal interest rates (%)
Huayang	12	30
Wan	18	36
Lu	12	30
Fushun	14	30
Hongya	8	30–40
Yibin	8	30
Ba	18	35
Jiang'an	10	40
Leshan	12	30
Yongchuan	12–14	40
Suining	8	35
Guanghan	12	30
Jiangbei	18	35
Chengdu	12	30

[a] Mortgage is a translation of *diantang*.

Source: Lu (1936: 449).

suppressed entirely. In all, personal loans accounted for 62.6% of all loans in that year (NARB, 1936: 70).

As for the level of interest rates themselves, many of the qualitative accounts suggest that these were often very high indeed. According to Huang and Wang (1985), periods of temporary grain shortage saw millet loans of 1 *dan* requiring a repayment of 4 *dan*, and monetary loans of 10 *yuan* requiring repayment in 4 instalments, each of 12 *yuan*.

However, the more systematic data available to us suggest a rather different picture. According to the 1934 NARB results, an interest rate of 20 to 30% applied to 33% of all loans and a rate of between 30 and 40% to 41% of loans. Only 4.7% of loans attracted a rate greater than 50%, compared to a national average of 13% (NARB, 1936: 71). More detailed county-level data for Sichuan point to the same conclusion (Table 7.10). An ideal answer to the question of whether these rates were 'too high' would require a properly specified theoretical framework along the lines suggested by Bhaduri and others but, in the absence of adequate microdata, we must content ourselves with a more qualitative discussion. Clearly, no discussion of interest rates can ignore the impact of risk, and this seems particularly relevant to Sichuan in the 1930s. Moreover, if ever a situation deserved to be described as uncertain rather than risky it was rural Sichuan in the 1930s.[6] These uncertainties related mainly to the political situation: which warlord would win the battle? Would his victorious troops loot? Would land be confiscated from landowners believed to have supported the losing side? Was there about to be a Communist incursion? If successful, would this involve land redistribution? How long would the military occupation last? When the usual risks of farm production were considered as well, such as the size of the harvest, price fluctuations, the death of or injury to a family member, it is unsurprising that interest rates were considerable during this period. The lender faced the ever-present prospect of having to write off the debts owed to him.

In addition, of course, we need to consider product prices because the true burden of debt is dependent upon the inflation rate. One would expect rapid price inflation to be associated with high interest rates because of the impact of the former on the real value of loans. Accordingly, we are interested in the level of real interest rates. The

[6] Where the terms have their Knightian meaning, viz., a situation involves risk if a probability can be assigned to an event taking place and uncertainty if a probability cannot. Keynes's favourite distinction was between throwing a die—risk—and the outbreak of a European war—uncertainty.

most obvious price to consider is that of (hulled) rice because it was the principal farm product; but wheat cannot be neglected, because many tenant farmers paid rents in rice and therefore sold rather more rice than wheat. For 1934, the year for which our nominal interest data are most plentiful, the rice price increased by 39% and that of wheat by 30% (Xu, 1983: 95; Buck and Hu, 1941: 119).

These price data suggest that interest rates of 30%–40% were not entirely illegitimate, given the general upward trend in prices. A farmer who borrowed at an interest rate of 35% in 1933 and repaid that loan in 1934 was evidently in a position to make such a repayment because rice and wheat prices had increased by 39% and 30% respectively in the interim. Over the long run, moreover, the farmer had also seen the rice price increase from an index of 40 in 1911 to over 180 by 1937. For the same reasons, however, short-term interest rate stickiness in response to price fluctuation was less legitimate, especially during the dramatic price falls of 1932 and 1933. That having been said, lender risk generally increases during a recession because of the greater likelihood of bankruptcy for borrowers. Accordingly, the prevalence of high interest rates during 1932 and 1933 can be given some sort of justification.

None of this analysis should be taken as meaning that interest rates were ideal from a *social* perspective. The case for government subsidization of credit in general (and the argument is applicable to Sichuan in the 1930s) is that the social rate of return on investment (in terms of employment, the multiplier effects on the suppliers of capital goods and the improvement in human capital when loans were used to purchase food) is generally higher than the private rate. Accordingly, a given market rate may be non-exploitative but still socially undesirable. Explicit recognition of this argument is provided by the promotion of (subsidized) rural credit co-operatives by the Kuomintang throughout China during the 1930s. The first Sichuan co-operative was founded in 1935 and by the end of that year 200 persons were co-operative members (Freyn 1941, 429); by May 1937, membership was still only 81,979 (X. M. Zhang, 1939: M26). It expanded much more rapidly after that, boasting over 1.2 million members in Sichuan by 1939 (Freyn, 1941: 429–30), and with this came a large increase in the percentage of loans from this relatively cheap source of finance.

It is, in sum, very difficult to find evidence which supports the hypothesis of usury in Republican Sichuan. This is not to deny that farmers were in debt, or that a significant proportion of their loans were contracted with landlords. It is not to deny that exploitative rates of interest were sometimes charged. There is unquestionably some basis in fact for such CCP claims. Yet when all that has been said, the fact remains that, when adjusted for uncertainty and the long-run trend increase in prices that began after the 1911 Revolution, interest rates in general were not unreasonable.

Rural Industry and Wages

The evidence on interest rates offers a few crumbs of comfort to those who believe that rural stratification was but one of many Communist myths. However, all that has been shown so far is that interest rates did not worsen the wide inequalities derived from unequal landowner-ship and onerous rents. To disprove the hypothesis of stratification, we need a mechanism that led to a *reduction* in original inequalities. A possible candidate here is the role played by the non-farm rural sector. Households did not derive their incomes entirely from farming in Republican Sichuan. Incomes also came from household handicraft industries, from the sale of wood and bamboo, and from wages paid on extra-farm employment. If these incomes accrued differentially in favour of land-poor, high-rent households, their impact might have been to mitigate the stratification already identified. This is certainly Brandt's view of the national economy (1989: 173–4):

Rising real wages, a growth in off-farm opportunities, and new nonagri-cultural sources of income all helped to reduce the role of landownership in income distribution. I believe the successively lower measures of inequality for landownership, cultivated area, and incomes reveal the equalizing tendencies these forces had between the 1890s and 1930s.

However, the evidence on the role of such non-farm occupations in the late 1920s suggests that too much faith in this equilibrating mech-anism is misplaced. To be sure, tenants gained more from these activities than did owner-farmers. According to Brown and Li (1928: 60), only 40% of owners and part-owners engaged in home industry compared to 79% of pure tenants; this is reflected in the relatively higher share of this category in total tenant income. However, to say more than that would be ill-advised. The combined income from handicrafts and off-farm employment of tenant farmers on the Chengdu plain amounted to only 12% of total income (Brown and Li, 1928: 66). The figure for the share of sidelines in GVAO for the province in the 1950s was not too different; for the period 1953–7, this category averaged 13.6% (SCJJNJ, 1986: 282).[7] The comparable share for pure owners was about 1.5%, though it should be noted that 10% of all pure owners received an outside income (mainly from rent) which tended to offset their comparatively smaller non-farm income from productive activities.

It seems reasonable to conclude from this that off-farm incomes may well have had an equalizing effect upon income differentials *within* the peasantry. A middle peasant owning a reasonable amount of land had no need to hire himself out as a farmworker or as an industrial employee; there was also less need for his family to be involved in cottage industry. These and other types of low-wage occupations were by contrast essential for the survival of the poor peasantry. However, it is very hard to see how sidelines eroded landlord–poor-peasant inequalities because, whilst poor peasants received low wages, the owners of capital enjoyed high profits. The growth of rural industry provided new opportunities for exploitation because it was the landlord class that also owned most rural industry, whether it was a paper mill, a textile factory, or a mine. Incomes received from the land in the form of rent and profits were supplemented by industrial profits. The growth of capitalism in the countryside therefore widened the income differential enjoyed by the landlord class, although it may have narrowed inequalities within the peasant class. Nevertheless, it is unlikely that even this latter would have persisted in the long run. As the experience of China since 1978 has shown, the benefits accruing from the growth of household industry have not been equally shared. Rather, the growth of privately owned household industry has led to a growing polarization in the countryside. A growing demand for wage labour may well have assisted the poor peasantry, but the profits so created have accrued to a small proportion of the rural population.

This analysis suggest that the impact of rural industrialization may have been most positive from a welfare point of view in that it has reduced *absolute poverty* by providing employment for landless labourers, rather than because it significantly reduced inequality. This has recently become an area of great controversy. The traditional neoclassical view has, for some time, started from the hypothesis that the Chinese economy was fully integrated into the world economy by

[7] A survey conducted in Huayang county in November 1950 produced the remarkable result that, for poor peasants, sideline income amounted to 44% of total income compared to only 13% for middle peasants. I suspect that this reflects an unusually high price for sideline output, itself a consequence of the shortages of such commodities that characterized the immediate post-Revolutionary period.

the early twentieth century. When the world economy prospered, China benefited, but during the 1930s, when demand for Chinese exports was depressed leading to an outflow of silver, and after 1937, when war with Japan vastly diminished China's ability to trade internationally because of the seizure of most Chinese ports, integration created enormous damage. In the absence of world depression, and the gradual drift into war against Japan, the growth of the first two decades of the century would have continued. This would have led to a gradual reduction in absolute poverty. According to Eastman (1988: 97, 98–9):

The forces playing on the peasants' standard of living in the 1930s was complex, and most evidence suggests that the net effect was very nearly catastrophic . . . most of the major surveys of conditions in China's villages were undertaken only in the 1930s and they, with only a few exceptions, accurately reported that the peasants were living in miserable poverty and that conditions had recently worsened. But viewing peasant life from the vantage point of the 1930s distorts the true picture of the peasants' living standards in the early years of the century. . . . Although rural life before the 1930s had by no means been cushy, the existing evidence argues against a continual decline in living conditions between the late nineteenth century and 1930.

Myers' interpretation (1972: 191) was for many years not dissimilar:

The process of commercialization in mainland China between 1890 and 1937 was interrupted severely only once—during the commercial and monetary deflation of 1930–33. The peasantry suffered greatly and there is every indication that for a time increased numbers of peasants lost their land and became tenant farmers in a given year. The catastrophic decline in farm prices hurt especially those already in debt and others who suffered poor harvests and had to borrow to buy grain.

This type of hypothesis certainly cannot be dismissed without some consideration, given the significance of 'shocks' in the 1930s. The Chinese economy was hit by the world depression and intense competition from Japanese textile products. An index of Chinese exports measured in volume terms fell from 156 in 1928 to 101 in 1932 and the terms of trade (here measured as import prices divided by export prices) worsened from 93 in 1929 to 143 in 1933 (in both cases, 1913 = 100; Feuerwerker, 1977: 100–1). It does not follow that this necessarily affected Sichuan significantly unless one can show that the province was integrated into the world economy; but it is clear that these adverse shifts in the international environment could have been important, and therefore the possibility cannot be ruled out by assumption.

However, recent work by new classical economists has suggested that the impact of depression on China, especially upon its interior provinces, has been much exaggerated, and therefore that the old neoclassical view is much too pessimistic. The essence of this revisionism is that the growth rate of per capita incomes attained during the inter-war years has been consistently underestimated, and that the reason the growth rate held up well during the 1930s was that monetary outflows in the form of silver were compensated for by domestic monetary expansion so that *total* money supply did not decline at all. As Rawski has argued (1989: 4–5, 177, 179):

The structure of China's economy makes it difficult to avoid the view that key economic forces originate in the domestic rather than the international sphere . . . Even in regions that specialized in producing tea, mulberry, cotton handicrafts, and other exports or import substitutes, the growth of foreign trade represented more an extension of historic economic patterns than an intrusion of totally new forces. . . . contemporary and retrospective accounts of the early 1930s as years of desperate crisis for China's economy contain large elements of exaggeration. . . . It is in highly commercial farming regions, and only in these areas, that the effect of the depression in China may be compared with the hardships experienced by both urban and rural residents in the major industrial nations . . . The continued expansion of China's money stock staved off deep and prolonged deflation and the associated reductions in output, employment, and real income despite the drain of metallic currency associated with the rising world price of silver.

Ramon Myers, previously an advocate of the traditional neoclassical interpretation, has even admitted that he was wrong (1989: 275):

I owe the greatest debt to Dr Loren Brandt, whose basic disagreements with my original approach and interpretation compelled me to retreat and agree with his general argument that China's economic growth continued through the 1930s and was not really affected by the Great Depression and the outflow of silver after 1934.

If true, this suggests a steady increase in the degree of rural industrialization and therefore a continued trend reduction in the extent of absolute rural poverty.

But is this interpretation correct? As I have argued elsewhere (Bramall, 1992), Brandt and Rawski are probably right to suggest that the world depression had little impact on the Chinese economy as a whole. However, this was *not* because of continued monetary growth but because the degree of integration (except in most of the treaty ports) was significantly less than they claim. The flaw in their analysis is that they overstate both the knowledge of economic agents and their ability to exploit notionally beneficial trading opportunities. Issues such as these are simply assumed away (by assumptions of perfect competion and zero transactions costs, to be precise) in the new classical models on which they rely. However, let us turn a blind eye to these theoretical absurdities and consider whether the Sichuan evidence supports the broad Rawski–Brandt claim.

In general, real earnings consisted of two main components: a cash wage and earnings in kind, in the form of food and lodging provided by the labourer's employer. The in-kind element amounted to 36 *yuan* for a labourer employed for a whole year in Sichuan in the early 1930s according to Buck (1937: 305). Buck's survey, being biased towards more prosperous localities, probably overstates the absolute figures involved, but it is nevertheless apparent that the in-kind element was considerably greater than the cash wage of 22 *yuan*. Moreover, biased or not, this estimate accords well with other available figures. Lu gives a figure of less than 20 *yuan* for the mid-1930s (Lu, 1936: 239) and the Farmers' Bank Survey puts its 1937 level at 23.5 *yuan* (Zhongguo nongmin yinhang, 1941: 731).

Our concern, however, is not with absolute magnitudes but with trends over time. For reasons that will become apparent, we need to distinguish between the food subsector of agriculture on the one hand and the cash crop/sideline subsector on the other. If we consider the food subsector first, the most important trend was the abrupt fall in product prices in the early 1930s. As Table 7.11 shows, food prices fell by around 50% in the province during the early 1930s and did not regain their 1931 levels until wartime.

Whether nominal earnings also fell is difficult to determine. On this vital subject, the only data available to us are for Su county (in Anhui) and Wujing (in Jiangsu) (Buck, 1943*b* and Hsu, 1935: 50–1, respectively). These show that farm wages lagged somewhat behind prices between 1911 and 1930. In the case of Su county, with 1910–14 = 100 for both wages and prices received by farmers, the 1930 price index was 206 and the wage index only 145, but this picture changed dramatically during the 1930s. Although farm prices fell sharply in the first part of the decade, money wages fell by a smaller amount—and therefore the real wage rose. If 1931 is taken as equal to 100 for both wages and prices, the index of wages in Su had fallen to 70 in the middle of 1934 whilst that of prices registered 42. In other words, real wages rose significantly.

This is of course by no means conclusive as an indicator of trends in Sichuan, but it does tally with Buck's assessment of national trends (1937: 319–20):

TABLE 7.11.   Retail Food Prices (yuan per shi shi) in Chengdu and Chongqing, 1928–1940

Year	Chengdu	Chongqing	
	Milled rice	Milled rice	Wheat
1928	n.a.	5.59	6.09
1929	n.a.	6.11	6.07
1930	n.a.	7.19	5.34
1931	13.75	11.85	7.74
1932	12.60	7.56	6.44
1933	8.60	5.36	4.31
1934	6.10	7.47	5.56
1935	6.85	n.a.	5.64
1936	11.20	n.a.	6.97
1937	11.85	11.40	7.70
1938	11.15	9.00	6.00
1939	12.35	9.90	7.50
1940	52.35	57.10	31.20

Sources: Chengdu—Zhongguo nongmin yinhang (1941: 507), Chongqing—Xu (1983: 95, 103).

During a period of falling commodity prices it is customary to hire less labour rather than to pay a lower rate of wages. During the period 1931–33, when prices received by farmers were falling, there was in most areas no corresponding fall in the wage rate of farm laborers.

We turn now to the question of employment. If we accept that real earnings increased (and assuming unchanged productivity and non-labour input costs), it follows that profits in the food-producing subsector fell. Farm producers could have responded to this in two ways—by reducing employment (and hence output) or by increasing their stocks of food. This choice would have been conditioned by expectations about future price trends; the latter strategy would only have made sense if there was an expectation of rising prices in the short term. It would certainly not if the fall in prices had been precipitated by a shift in the long-run demand-for-food function.

Of these two possible strategies, we cannot be certain as to which was followed. However, the hypothesis of unchanged output/employment combined with increased food stocks is at least plausible. For one thing, there is no evidence of a shift in the long run demand function. The province's population continued to grow, albeit rather slowly, and there is no evidence of any change in the share of total expenditure on foodstuffs. Furthermore, on the supply side, everything pointed to future shortages. 1931 and 1932 were both unusually good harvest years; in fact the 1932 level of rice output (184 million *shi dan*) was not attained again until 1949, by which time the province's population was considerably greater. In addition, after three relatively peaceful years, civil war erupted in the province during 1931, and any hopes of a subsequent return to stability were dashed by the arrival of Zhang's CCP forces in northern Sichuan. Both these supply-side factors must have been a spur to the hoarding of cereals in general and rice in particular, although a lack of adequate grain storage facilities operated as an offsetting factor. Thus it is possible that employment in the food subsector showed little, if any, change in response to declining product prices.

Trends within the cash crop/sideline sector are even less clear. There seems little question that those farms oriented towards export markets experienced sharp reductions in profits during this period; silk and tung oil are the most obvious examples. This was due to a combination of growing taxation on intraprovincial trade, world depression, and competition from Japan.

The impact of falling tung oil and silk prices on aggregate provincial employment and real earnings was probably unfavourable. Labouring households did not consume silk or tung oil in significant quantities, and therefore falling prices did not increase their real earnings in the same way as falling food prices. Moreover, there was less incentive for producers to accumulate stocks of these types of product. Trends in world markets were infinitely more difficult to predict than those in the provincial food market, the renewal of civil war made any form of commerical activity more risky, and, as products could not be consumed in the last resort by producers (again, unlike cereals), the safest strategy must have been to reduce money wages and/or reduce employment.

It is unlikely, however, that the living standards of labourers employed in the rural, non-cereal sector deteriorated sharply, because this assumption would have to ignore the expansion taking place in the defence sector. The massive increase under way in the late 1920s and early 1930s is evident from the growth of military expenditure in Liu Xiang's garrison area (Table 7.12). The seemingly inexorable rise in military expenditure, from less than 13 to close to 50 million *yuan*, is apparent. The short-lived increase in civilian expenditure in 1930

TABLE 7.12. *The Fiscal Deficit of Liu Xiang's 21st Army,*
1928–1933 (millions of current yuan)

	Expenditure[a]		Income	Deficit or surplus
	Military[b]	Total		
1928	12.7	14.1	12.0	−2.1
1929	16.9	18.6	19.1	+0.5
1930	22.3	25.7	30.2	+4.5
1931	26.6	30.3	26.1	−4.2
1932	34.2	37.4	32.0	−5.4
1933	47.9	51.9	46.4	−5.5

[a] Loan repayment and servicing is excluded from the expenditure totals.
[b] These data probably understate military expenditure (see Ch'en, 1985: 51–2).

Source: Xiao and Ma (1984: 296–7).

when Liu Xiang's programme of economic reconstruction was in full swing is also clear, as is its subsequent reversal (as a percentage in particular) with the renewal of armed conflict. But overall, whatever the inaccuracies of data such as these, there can be no doubting the growing importance of the defence sector as source of demand.

This programme of defence industrialization was impressive in its scope. For example, Liu Xiang granted tax relief to the Minsheng shipping company, which allowed it rapidly to displace other shipping companies on the lucrative Yangzi route. It was Liu who brought the first railway to Sichuan in the form of a short coal-carrying line north of Chongqing, which was itself a further result of Minsheng's tax-induced growth as it diversified into heavy industry. Other radical steps taken by Liu included the relocation of the city's cemetery to release scarce land for a new business centre, the establishment of a cement works, and increases in electricity-generating capacity (Kapp, 1973).

All this must have have gone some way towards negating the aggregate impact of growing unemployment in silk and tung oil sectors. The products of these industries could not easily be reoriented towards the military sector, but other industries (cotton, munitions, transport) and the cattle-rearing sector (providing horses for cavalry mounts and mules and oxen for draught purposes) must have expanded quickly. Whether such expansion was sufficient fully to absorb any labour released by the depressed export sector is difficult to gauge, given the imprecise nature of the statistics. According to figures cited by X. M. Zhang (1939: U2), the value of exports fell by no more than 7 million *yuan* between 1932 and 1934—which, being much less than military-expenditure increases, suggests that net aggregate demand was expanding. However, the number of omissions from the trade data (critically, opium exports and weapon imports) ensures that the precise macroeconomic dynamics of the province remain uncertain. In fact, given that opium was the usual resort of the warlord when arms were needed urgently, the value of provincial exports may have increased during these years. Moreover, even if the economy was characterized by excess demand, it does not necessarily follow that the supply response in the short term was strong enough quickly to absorb the newly unemployed.

That having been said, the degree of militarization of life in the province during the early 1930s was considerable. When CCP units, local militia, camp-followers, and defence-related industrial employment in the rural sector are added to the numbers deployed in the warlords' field armies, total employment in the military sector can hardly have been under 2 million. While much of this reflected the size of the pre-1930 military establishment, the renewal of conflict must have increased recruitment by both warlord and CCP forces. In the case of Zhang's Base Area, this undoubtedly did happen. His initial force numbered perhaps 5,000 in the autumn of 1932, but recruitment raised it to a peak of perhaps 80,000—despite casualties due to wounds and disease—which was no mean feat given that the population of his base area rarely exceeded 1 million persons.

Yet these policies, whilst they may have helped certain parts of the province to ward off the worst effects of the depression of the early 1930s, fell significantly short of producing an economic transformation. That was quickly apparent after the collapse of the garrison area system of 1934, which was the inevitable result of deficit-financing for largely military purposes on the scale attempted by Liu Xiang. The reassertion of central control for the first time since the dissolution of the Empire saw the end of industrialization. The Kuomintang did bring a number of grandiose schemes to Sichuan, but these were principally in the sphere of agriculture (for example, the establishment of a Provincial Reconstruction Bureau). In the absence of a developmental state, *laissez-faire* proved completely incapable of generating industrialization.

In sum, the impact of the macrodynamics of the 1930s on the poor peasantry of Sichuan was at best mildly positive. If real earnings rose in the food subsector and employment remained constant, if the growth of military employment compensated for the loss of employment in export industries, and if these two outweighed any increase in the effective incidence of taxation on landowning poor peasant households, then the extent of absolute poverty might have declined. However, there are many preconditions here, and the evidence to establish any of them with a degree of conviction is signally lacking. It is possible that the poor peasantry of Sichuan experienced an increase in their real income during the 1930s, and that the position of the labouring household may even have improved relative to that of the small landowner subject to land taxation. But we are talking of possibilities, not certainties.

Moreover, even if the fortunes of the poor did improve, such change was at the margin. There can be no pretence that their condition was *transformed* during the Republican period. This is evident from the microdata on consumption patterns at the bottom end of the consumption range. In Bazhong county in the early 1930s, the majority of peasants ate rice and wheat for only three months of the year. Coarse grains met their subsistence needs for the next five, but in the four months before the main harvest they were forced to eat increasing quantities of wild herbs (Lin, 1982: 485–6). In Maowen, 15% of the county's poor peasants were reliant upon aid (*Maowen Qiangzu zizhixian gaikuang*, 1985: 73) in the early 1950s, and 'During the first two years after Liberation, more than 580,000 *jin* of grain were supplied by the state to 4,131 households, or more than 40% of all *xian* [county] households' (p. 67). In Huayang, the poor peasant consumed on average no more than 279 *jin* of grain (*shimi*) and 3 *jin* of meat in a year, compared to 348 and 4 *jin* respectively by middle peasants (Zhongyang nongyebu jihuasi, 1952: 302). A study conducted by members of Jinling university in the same county in the mid-1940s estimated that the poorest person in Zhonghechang village consumed 2.5 *jin* of meat in a year (compared to 22.5 *jin* by the richest) (Treudley, 1971: 129). These figures are low even by post-1949 Chinese standards.[8]

In sum, the impact of growing non-farm rural incomes was probably to bring about a small reduction in the degree of absolute poverty in the countryside. In that sense, the warlords of Sichuan played a developmental role. Nevertheless, precisely because rural industrializa-

---

[8] The all-Sichuan rural average levels of meat and grain consumption in 1954 were put at 15 and 434 *jin* of unhusked grain respectively—ZSSWY (1984: 229).

tion was in its infancy and because the warlord-led growth of the early 1930s was not sustained, the effect of this process was marginal. The income differential between middle and poor peasantry may have narrowed somewhat, but there is no mechanism here to suggest that income inequalities in general were narrow by international standards at the end of the 1930s.

Socioeconomic Mobility

Finally, the mobility arguments outlined in Chapter 4 require consideration. These fall into two distinct categories, one general and the other specific. The former is in essence that, although inequalities exist at any one moment in time, in all competitive capitalist economies scope for socioeconomic mobility exist. A peasant in year 1 can thus become a landlord in, say, year 10 and therefore his status in year 1 is in no sense a true indication of the opportunities that confront him. Or, to borrow a notion from the macroeconomic literature on consumption functions, it is lifetime rather than current incomes that matter.

The difficulty inherent in this approach is that mobility was the privilege of the few, not the right of the many. Of course, there were some opportunities for mobility in Republican Sichuan. We have already seen that the landlords of the late Qing were displaced by the new warlords of the 1930s, and in some areas, the old Qing landlords were being replaced by the *peasantry* via the effects of CCP-induced land reform. For instance, in CCP base areas, and in sharp contrast to the trend in warlord-dominated areas, the concentration of landownership fell as the old elite was dispossessed. The most substantive CCP presence took the form of Zhang Guotao's Fourth-Front Army in northern Sichuan.[9] Zhang arrived in November 1932 and established his headquarters in Bazhong county. Although this area was abandoned in the spring of 1935, Zhang's presence in north-western Sichuan and eastern Xikang (the north-western part of modern Sichuan) persisted until the summer of 1936. He was joined in the Mougong area by Mao's battered forces *en route* from Jiangxi province to Yan'an in Shaanxi during the autumn of 1935, and by He Long and Xiao Ke's Second-Front Army in June 1936. There was therefore a CCP presence in much of the northern part of the province through-

[9] The dates and other data in this section are taken from Salisbury (1985), Chang (1972), and Zhonggong Sichuan sheng wei dangshi gongzuo weiyuanhui (1986).

out the early 1930s. These forces were more than a match for warlord forces, and were able to hold their own even when the warlords had been reinforced with Kuomintang units. Finally, Youyang and Xiushan counties in the extreme south-west of Sichuan were under He Long and Xiao Ke's control as part of the 'Four Corners' (of the provinces of Hubei, Hunan, Guizhou, and Sichuan) Base Area during the early 1930s until the area was abandoned in the autumn of 1935.

In Zhang's Sichuan–Shaanxi base area, land reform was undoubtedly carried out. It is certainly true that he was initially very reluctant to launch such a programme, largely on the grounds that he believed it 'premature' in such a 'backward' area (Chang, 1972; Ch'en, 1987: Salisbury, 1985). His initial programme even eschewed the establishment of a soviet, and substituted ceilings on rents and interest rates for land reform. However, Zhang's attitude did change when the Central Committee told him by radio that this was unacceptable. Under pressure from his colleagues to comply, he seems to have given way (Chang, 1972: 340). As a result, some redistribution of landlord property did take place. In Qingchuan county, some 10% of arable area was redistributed, and in Jiangyou the figure was 150,000 *mu* (Zhonggong Sichuan sheng wei dangshi gongzuo weiyuanhui, 1987: 330). However, we should not make too much of the impact of the CCP on land concentration within Sichuan in the 1930s. The base areas were not only relatively small and sparsely populated but also transitory. Even Bazhong, Zhang's capital, was not under continuous CCP control during the three-year life-span of the base area: it was occupied in January 1933, lost to Tian's forces in the spring, and regained during the late summer. From then on, the area was under continuous CCP government until December 1934 or January 1935, when it was abandoned as Zhang marched west to link up with Mao.

By contrast, there is very little evidence of *any* significant upward mobility on the part of the middle and poor peasants in warlord areas. This is clear from a consideration of the origins of both warlord and CCP leaders. Of Sichuan's five leading warlords in the early 1930s, the background of two is unknown. Of the other three, all seem to have come from landlord (albeit not particularly wealthy) families (Kapp, 1973: 25). As for the CCP, we have already noted that the poor and middle peasantry were the beneficiaries of land reform. But the leadership positions (even in the CCP, power led to an enhanced economic status) were filled by the relatively affluent. Of leading members of the CCP, Zhu De, later Commander-in-Chief of the Army, was born into a tenant family in Long county in Sichuan. However, the family does not seem to have been desperately poor;

thanks to an uncle, Zhu received an education (Smedley, 1956). Zhang Guotao, the Commander of the Fourth-Front Army operating in northern Sichuan in the 1930s, was born into a rich landlord family in Jiangxi province (Snow, 1972: 513). As for Deng Xiaoping, born in Guang'an county in Sichuan, his father commanded the local militia, and Deng himself received a secondary education before having the opportunity to study in France (Salisbury, 1985: 136).

This evidence is of course sparse. Very little biographical detail is available on the Sichuan warlords of the Republican era. Nevertheless, there is nothing in the above to suggest a wealth of opportunities for upward mobility on the part of poor peasants. Indeed, the share of the landlord stratum (old and new, or warlord, landlords combined) *may* even have been rising at the expense of middle and poor peasantry. There is therefore no good reason to see in socioeconomic mobility an instrument by which income differentials were significantly eroded.

Intralocal Income Distribution in the 1930s: A Summary

The evidence presented in this chapter that broadly supports the Maoist characterization of the Republican countryside is considerable. We have seen that the ownership of land, the key factor of production in a predominantly rural economy, was very unequal, and that Sichuan's warlord class had managed to acquire for itself a number of large estates by a combination of force and high taxation. It has been shown that the presence of diseconomies of scale beyond a certain point did not offset the advantages implicit in ownership because the majority of peasant farms were well below the optimum scale, and because large landowners were able to earn rental income from their estates. As rental contracts reflected the distribution of power in the countryside, and in the absence of any recourse to a quasi-independent judiciary, tenancy proved a lucrative activity for most landowners. Taxation did little of significance to equalize final incomes.

However, there were undoubtedly some forces acting in a more egalitarian fashion. Defence industrialization and military spending put upward pressure on real wages and provided employment opportunities outside the farm sector. The effects of world depression were localized precisely because the province was integrated neither into national nor international economies, and in any case offset by spiralling military spending by warlords and CCP alike. Interest rates were less oppressive than Tawney thought, and there was some scope for socioeconomic mobility for the poor. All these factors meant that inequalities in final incomes were smaller than they would otherwise have been, and that the pattern of stratification of a given year was by no means immutable. Moreover, even if warlord industrialization had little effect upon income inequality, it did at least serve to reduce absolute poverty amongst the landless and land-poor.

Nevertheless, and contrary to the writings of Brandt, Myers, and Rawski, one is struck by the weakness of these equilibrating mechanisms. Rural industry was in its infancy and hampered by a lack of basic infrastructure, political instability, and effective demand. Warlord spending acted at best as a palliative, and then only for a very short time. Moreover, the extra-economic power wielded by the provincial militarists enabled them to enjoy incomes well in excess of those that could have been commanded by mere landlords; it gave them abundant opportunities for the practice of both capitalist and feudal exploitation. Market-driven interest rates may not have been exploitative, but they were hardly designed to promote growth or provide social security; the need for subsidized lending by banks and credit co-operatives was pressing. Finally, the opportunities for upward mobility were few and far between.

Accordingly, the 'stylized facts' of provincial life during the 1930s seem much closer to the assessment given below than to the neoclassical vision:

Arbitrary increases in the burden of exploitative land rents imposed by landlords depressed peasant living standards and, by the day, the farm sector became progressively more depressed. This was particularly true during the years of warlord rule and its successive periods of civil war, which saw Sichuan's economic health increasingly deteriorate. Each warlord, in the garrison area under his control, conscripted and press-ganged people into service and simultaneously did his utmost to expropriate and plunder property. The warlords greatly increased the level of agricultural taxation, and this burden was passed on in the form of higher rents charged by landlords and despotic gentry to the poor peasants. Warlord taxes and levies on industrial production and commerce were increased in burden and widened in their coverage; these were passed on by commercial and industrial capitalists to consumers in the form of higher prices. In this way, year after year, the material and financial resources of the peasant massess were increasingly exhausted. (Zhonggong Sichuan sheng wei dangshi gongzuo weiyuanhui, 1986: 1)

This is not to say that Sichuan during the 1930s was typical of China. The fertility of the soil and abundant water resources—in contrast to much of northern China—made possible the existence of a parasitic class in the countryside, and Sichuan was quite unlike most of eastern China in being controlled by a group of warlords. These special factors did much to ensure that the Revolution of 1949 was particularly welcomed by the peasantry. The CCP at least offered them hope.

8

Poverty and Inequality in Sichuan's Villages in the 1970s

The National Pattern

The conventional wisdom on rural income distribution in China is easily stated. Before national data on rural inequality in the late 1970s were published, it was uncertain as to whether the narrow intra-collective differentials identified in a number of surveys conducted by Western social scientists after 1962 allowed one to conclude that *overall* rural income differentials were also narrow. This was reflected in the debate between Vermeer and others as to the importance of spatial differentials (Griffin and Saith, 1982; Vermeer, 1982; Griffin and Griffin, 1984).

The release of basic data on the rural income distribution did much to resolve these issues. As the figures collected in Table 8.1 demonstrate, the distribution of Chinese rural incomes was remarkably equal by international standards. Nevertheless, the overall distribution was much more unequal in the late 1970s than implied by *village* studies, thus confirming Vermeer's view that substantial spatial inequalities remained in the Chinese countryside. Other controversies were recognized as remaining largely unresolved. For example, the extent to which spatial differences in nominal income are a true indicator of differences in real income is uncertain because of possible regional and subregional price variations. Furthermore, the size of the urban–rural differential remains an issue of intense debate because of the difficulties involved in satisfactorily measuring the impact of urban subsidies. Yet if these were not merely questions of detail, they were not seen to have much bearing on the general parameters of rural inequality. The new conventional wisdom of the late 1980s is aptly summarized by Riskin (1987: 236):

We may conclude that China's rural income distribution in the 1970s was substantially more equal than that of other Asian low-income countries . . .

TABLE 8.1   *Rural Gini Coefficients for LDCs in the 1970s*[a]

Country	Year	Gini	Source
China	1979	0.31	World Bank (1983: 92)
	1978	0.22	Adelman and Sunding (1987: 448)
Taiwan	1978	0.29	Kuo, Fei, and Ranis (1981)
Pakistan	1971–2	0.33	Burki (1988: 77)
Bangladesh	1973–4	0.38	Alamgir, in Fields (1980: 88)
Thailand	1975–6	0.39 ⎱	World Bank (1983: 92)
Indonesia	1976	0.40 ⎰	
India	1968–9	0.43	Bhatty, in Fields (1980: 205)
Malaysia	1970	0.45	Anand (1983: 98)
Philippines	1971	0.46	ILO, in Fields (1980: 221)

[a] These data are not precisely comparable because of differences in the way income is defined and measured.

The wide rural inequalities that remained at the end of Mao's life were based upon differential access to fertile land, water, urban markets and industrial inputs.

Inequality in Collective-Distributed Incomes in Sichuan

The evidence on differentials in the incomes distributed by collectives in Sichuan in the late 1970s mirrors the national pattern. It is true that these data are fragmentary in nature and inconsistent in coverage. The materials that are readily available (Griffin, 1984; Lefebvre, 1979; Endicott, 1988; Nolan, 1983*b*) are drawn from different counties and cover different organizational units. Some give information on incomes by commune in a specified county. Others give household income within a given production team. Our interest is in the *totality* of within-county income distribution, sadly, a subject covered in none of these sources.

However, by putting together information from two sources (Lefebvre, 1979 and Nolan, 1983*b*), we can build up a view of the 'total picture' in the case of Guanghan county in 1977–8. It is not possible to do this for any other county. The results of this aggregation allow a meaningful assessment of income inequality if the Theil

TABLE 8.2.   *Collective-Income Differentials in Guanghan County,*
1977–1978

Level	Name of unit	Theil coefficient
Between households in same production team	Team 2 of Sanxing commune's Lixin brigade (1977)	0.039 (0.038)[a]
Between teams in same commune	Xiangyang commune (1978)	0.019
Between communes in same county	All of Guanghan's communes (1978)	0.006
All Guanghan[b]		0.064 (0.063)

[a] The figure in parenthesis is the Theil coefficient when aid allocated to poor households within a production team is added to distributed collective income.
[b] The Guanghan figure is simply the sum of the 3 Theil coefficients.
Sources: Team 2—Lefebvre (1979: t. 2). Xiangyang and all communes—Nolan (1983*b*).

coefficient is used for measurement purposes. This is because this particular measure can be decomposed *additively* into within-unit and between-unit components (one could alternatively use the variance of log-income). Calculated Theil coefficients for the various organizational units within Guanghan county are summarized in Table 8.2, which tells us that the extent of rural income inequality in Guanghan in the late 1970s was very small indeed.

One of the difficulties in concluding anything meaningful from this is a lack of data on other economies; most studies of income inequality use the Gini coefficient. Nevertheless, two examples can be given for comparative purposes. In the case of the rural areas of peninsular Malaysia in 1970, Anand (1983: 98) estimated the overall Theil coefficient to be 0.41 (not very different from the Gini—see Table 8.1), of which the within-location component was 86.3%. That implies a Theil for the average Malaysian state of 0.35. Malaysian rural income distribution was (and is) relatively unequal by Asian standards, and was vastly more unequal than that of Guanghan in 1977–8. However, a better comparison—Guanghan was far smaller in terms of area than a Malaysian state and therefore the range of geographical conditions was correspondingly smaller—is with Guanghan in 1983.

The Theil for the county is estimated as 0.15 (see Table 8.4) in that year, which is more than double our estimate for 1977–8.

The question, of course, is whether these data are useful as a guide to income differentials. Three distinct objections have been raised to these and figures like them. One is that they are taken from counties with high per capita incomes which in general enjoyed a more equal distribution about that mean than the provincial average. Therefore, data for a county such as Guanghan significantly understate true inequality. Another objection is that data on *collective* incomes understate inequality because they ignore the impact of incomes derived from private-sector activities. Finally, conventional accounts of income distribution in rural China completely ignore the corruption that was so widespread in the country by the time of Mao's death.

It is the contention in this chapter that none of these objections is sufficient to overturn the conclusion that Sichuan's villages enjoyed a very equal distribution of income by historical and international standards. However, objections such as these cannot be ignored. They need to be discussed and overturned. That is the purpose of the remainder of this chapter.

The Absence of Sample Bias

The case for spatial bias runs along the following lines. It is well known that the 1978 income surveys exhibit locational bias. The surveys were conducted in a period during which the collection of economic data was beginning anew after the emasculation of the State Statistical Bureau in the 1958–76 period. As a result, and especially given the purge of intellectuals that was carried out during the Cultural Revolution, there were severe shortages of trained personnel. This partially explains why the 1978 national survey was extremely small. It covered only 35,000 persons, almost trivial given the size of China's population, and there is little question that villages enjoying either unusually high average incomes or model status were overrepresented (Travers, 1982).

This resulted in measured income inequalities that understated true inequality for three reasons. For one thing, the model followed in the 1970s was that of the famous Dazhai brigade, in which a significant proportion of income was allocated according to political attitude and consciousness rather than according to work done. Thus those Sichuan villages that had earned the sobriquet of 'model' enjoyed a more equal income distribution than the norm. To earn a high number of work-points through expertise and effort on the one hand and to be politically 'red' on the other was almost a contradiction in terms; hence the Dazhai system narrowed, rather than reinforced, income inequalities. Secondly, because non-sampled areas were generally poor, they were forced to encourage the private sector much more than sampled areas. If one further assumes that private incomes were distributed more unequally than collective incomes, a greater role for the private sector in non-sampled localities implies that the sample understates true inequality. Finally, sampled areas—precisely because they were rich—enjoyed a more equal income distribution than non-sampled areas because their high productivity generated a greater 'surplus' for use in developing collective welfare programmes and in creating non-farm rural employment by setting up rural industry. This vastly increased the income-earning opportunities for poor households. Their members were healthier, and therefore they could participate in collective work rather than being mere dependants. Their education enabled them to take more skill-intensive and there-fore better-remunerated jobs. The creation of employment in the non-farm sector meant that a range of relatively undemanding (in the physical sense) jobs were available to the sick and disabled.

However, the evidence lends little support to these arguments. To be sure, the *counties* chosen were unrepresentative but there is nothing to suggest spatial bias in the choice of communes, brigades, and teams *within* counties. That certainly appears so in Guanghan's case. Per capita distributed income in Xiangyang commune was 110 *yuan* in 1978, which is in the middle of the range of commune incomes of 79 to 125 *yuan* (Nolan, 1983*b*). The corresponding figure for Lixin's team No. 2 was 120 *yuan*, again comfortably in the middle of the range for production teams in Guanghan county, which was 41 to 200 *yuan* in 1977 (Lefebvre, 1979: 28). Moreover, although the very low Theil coeficient suggests that inequality may have been understated, it is significant that only a few households in team No. 2 received aid—to be precise, 5 out of 62 (approximately 8%). This was con-siderably less than the percentage in Magaoqiao brigade in neighbour-ing Shifang county.[1] This implies that income distribution was more *unequal* in team No. 2 than in many others because the incomes of most of its households were related to work rather than need. In other words, these data may even *overstate* the true degree of inequality in rural Sichuan.

---

[1] 20% in 1975; this was a poor year in terms of yields but the aid percentage was little different in either 1980 or 1982—Endicott (1988: 233).

On the question of private-sector incomes (a subject discussed much more fully in the next section), the national evidence on the size of the private sector in poor as opposed to rich areas remains tentative.[2] Moreover, some writers have argued that the inequalities in distributed collective income reflected differences in the farm worker–dependent ratio between households, and therefore that the private sector tended to *reduce* income inequalities by utilizing the labour power of household members unable to participate in physically demanding farm work (Griffin and Griffin, 1984). Furthermore, there is no evidence that in Sichuan's case the private sector persisted in poor, rather than in rich, counties during the 1958–76 period. Indeed Shifang, the richest county in the province, flatly contradicts this in that contracting output to households was actually practised in the mid-1960s (Endicott, 1988: 125–6).

As far as the use of 'surplus' is concerned, the advantages enjoyed in principle by prosperous counties is apparent. For example, Shifang county was prosperous enough to be able to allocate 20,000 *yuan* for the construction of a new 20-bed hospital in Lianglukou commune in the late 1960s (Endicott, 1988: 157); that would have been inconceivable in a poor county. Such steps as these were reflected in longer life expectancy and higher literacy rates because, although households had to take out medical insurance and pay a fee for the education of their children, part of the cost was borne by the production team and often, if either was unable to pay, credit was granted. Moreover, the development of rural industry increased off-farm job opportunities, and thus provided employment for those who were not physically up to the demands of farm labour.

All this needs to be heavily qualified, however, because the central and provincial governments both played important roles in siphoning off a part of the surplus from rich counties and using it to finance welfare provision in poor counties. As a result, spatial inequalities in education and literacy were much less in late Maoist Sichuan than in other LDCs. Where they existed, they seem to have owed little to low levels of per capita output. This is demonstrated in Table 8.3.

It is noteworthy, though not surprising, that the relationship between NVAIO per capita and capabilities is very imprecise. It is more remarkable that the dispersion of capabilities between those counties at the top end of the income scale and those at the bottom—and

---

[2] For some evidence that household, rather than collective, production existed in poor areas after 1962, see Wang and Zhou (1985: 55–7). However, the degree of intra-village collusion against higher authority that this would imply seems implausible, I am grateful to Liu Minquan for this point.

TABLE 8.3. *Spatial Variation in Capabilities within Sichuan, 1983*

County	Crude death rate (per 1,000)	Infant mortality (per 1,000)	Illiteracy (%)	NVAIO per capita (*yuan*)
Guanghan	6.1	25	28.1	329
Shifang	6.4	36	31.5	470
Youyang	7.5	41	38.2	136
Xiushan	7.8	40	35.7	130
Wushan	7.1	59	41.5	141
Gulin	8.4	43	42.7	127
Mabian	7.8	49	54.6	165
Leibo	14.3	83	55.9	256

Source: ZGRKTJNJ (1988: 651–63) and Appendix.

located within the Sichuan Basin (i.e. those in the middle panel)—is not very great. Moreover, differences in capabilities between counties in the middle panel and those in the bottom one do not seem explicable in income terms. The key determinant of the very high infant mortality of the counties in Liangshan prefecture was geography. Located high on the Himalayan plateau and with water shortages a perennial problem away from the fertile Anning River valley, such counties unsurprisingly fared poorly in mortality terms. That their populations were comprised of predominantly ethnic minorities may also have been a contributory factor. As for literacy, it is not clear that it mattered much as a means towards the end of higher income. Literacy was hardly functionally necessary to be a high-productivity farm worker, and as the opportunities to use knowledge and skills in the private sector were strictly limited, it seems unlikely that it markedly affected lifetime earnings. For example, a 1984 survey of 2,035 households found that 'high-culture' (high was not defined precisely) households earned a net per capita income of 134 *yuan* in 1978 compared to the 126 *yuan* earned by 'low-culture' households (Nongcun xiaozu, 1986: 3), which suggests that the impact of education on incomes was slight.

Finally, it is not obvious that rural industrialization opened up a new vista of opportunity for low-income households. Non-farm employment opportunities in collective enterprises were still very

Poverty and Inequality in the 1970s

limited in Sichuan in the mid-1970s. Total employment was no more than 459,000 in 1975, and, although this had risen to 1.797 million by 1978 (ZSSWY, 1984: 169), it was still only a fraction of the labour-force employed in the farm sector. Of course, the importance of the collective-enterprise sector was relatively greater in the counties of the Sichuan Basin, and especially in counties located close to large cities (Gan, 1986: 214). Nevertheless, its significance was small even in counties like Guanghan. Its Sanxing commune (the most prosperous

TABLE 8.4. *Within-County Income Distribution in Sichuan, 1983*[a]

County	Theil[b]	Gini[c]	Net income per capita[d] (*yuan*)	Households (no.)
Shifang	0.141	0.253	508	253
Guanghan	0.153	0.258	446	274
Leshan	0.175	0.279	334	283
Jianyang	0.104	0.240	296	199
Wanyuan	0.163	0.265	281	205
Nanchuan	0.128	0.273	233	235
Nanjiang	0.086	0.219	225	182
Pengxi	0.092	0.234	207	200
Fushun	0.126	0.268	190	204
MEAN	0.130	0.254	302.2	2,035
SD[e]	0.030	0.019	103.8	
CV	0.231	0.075	0.343	

[a] The survey covered 6 production teams in each of the 9 counties, 2,035 households in all. It also covered 202 specialized households, but no information is available on their mean per capita income for each county.

[b] Overall Theil coefficient: 0.193.

[c] Overall Gini coefficient: 0.315.

[d] Mean per capita net incomes refer to household incomes (i.e. total household income divided by total household members) and are measured in current prices.

[e] SD: standard deviation; CV: coefficient of variation. Means, standard deviations, and coefficients of variation are all unweighted. The sample Gini and Theil coefficient (see notes *a* and *b*) include both spatial and within-county inequality.

Source: Nongcun yanjiuzu (1986: 488–515).

in the county) employed only 495 persons in its non-farm collective enterprises in 1978 out of a population of around 13,500 (Lefebvre, 1979).

Even more decisively, the evidence available to us on the distribution of per capita incomes from all sources for Sichuan during the 1980s refutes the hypothesis of spatial bias. The best of this material is a 1983 survey covering 2,035 households drawn from 9 counties. As the survey results are disaggregated by county, the spatial content (between county) of inequality can be eliminated entirely by averaging the results for each rather than estimating inequality for the sample as a whole.[3] The results are presented in Table 8.4. A superficial interpretation of this table is that income differentials, as measured by the Theil coefficient, varied substantially between counties. For example, the coefficient for Leshan is more than double that for Nanjiang. Further, the coefficients for both Leshan and Nanjiang differ substantially from the mean. However, the coefficient of variation for the Theil coefficients is not particularly high compared either to that for income levels or to some of those obtained in estimating spatial inequality in earlier chapters. Furthermore, if one measures differentials by means of the Gini coefficient, differences between county are much smaller. Thus the Gini for Leshan is only about 27% higher than that for Nanjiang. Moreover, the coefficient of variation for the Gini coefficients (0.075) is barely a third of that for the Theils. Further, to the extent that there are spatial variations, it is anything but obvious that they follow any consistent pattern. The degree of inequality in Shifang is little different from that in Fushun, even though there is a vast difference in mean per capita income. Mean per capita income is very similar in Nanchuan and Nanjiang, yet there is a significant difference in the degree of inequality.[4]

---

[3] This latter does not exclude the spatial dimension of inequality because it necessarily involves a comparison of poor households in a poor county with rich households in a rich county.

[4] The table also indicates that intralocal inequality was a more significant contributor to overall inequality than spatial inequality. This is clear if we compare the Theil coefficient given in notes *b* to the table (which measures total sample inequality, i.e. spatial and intralocal combined) and the mean Theil for the 9 counties, which suppresses all spatial inequality. The difference between the 2, 0.063, is the spatial component, which is obviously much smaller than the intralocal component of 0.130. Note that we cannot adopt the same procedure for the Gini coefficient because this cannot be disaggregated additively. It is, of course, worth remembering that the relative sizes of the spatial and intralocal components of inequality are sensitive to precisely how 'spatial' is defined. One might reasonably object to the procedure adopted here on the grounds that Chinese counties are very large and that inequality within counties had an important spatial dimension. It is thus arguable that the term 'spatial' ought to be applied to between-village inequality and 'intralocal' applied to within-village inequality. In short, this table *does not prove* that spatial inequality was less important than intralocal inequality in Sichuan in the early 1980s.

In sum, differences in income inequality between counties in the early 1980s were far smaller than one might expect given their very different locations. Moreover, to the extent that differences are significant between counties, there is no obvious indication of any systematic relationship between per capita income and inequality. It can therefore be concluded from this discussion of spatial bias in the late 1970s and in the early 1980s that there is no convincing evidence that intralocal inequality varied so much between locations that the choice of an apparently spatially unrepresentative sample severely distorts the true all-Sichuan picture. It is not at all clear, either in theory or from the evidence considered, that the extent of within-county inequality was greater in rich than in poor counties.

The Irrelevance of Private Incomes

A challenge to the hypothesis of a high degree of income equality within the villages of China and Sichuan during the late Maoist period comes from the existence of private incomes. By this is meant incomes generated outside the collective economy from household pursuits as varied as firewood collection, vegetable-growing, handicraft production, and the rearing of livestock and poultry. In principle, it is entirely possible than those households best able to profit from the collective sector were also best able, by inclination and by skills, to make money from household activities or sidelines, as they are usually called in the Chinese literature. In consequence, true rural income inequality could have been significantly greater than that resulting from differences in collective income considered in isolation.

This approach is based upon two assumptions. First, incomes from household sidelines were large enough significantly to affect the distribution of income. Secondly, the principal beneficiaries from sidelines were also the principal beneficiaries from collectively distributed incomes. I shall argue in this section that both assumptions are without foundation.

It is hard to believe that the significance of household sideline activities was great. The main reason for this is that government policy throughout the period 1965–76 was explicitly designed to prevent the re-emergence of income inequalities within the countryside. The very essence of Maoist policy was to 'cut off the tails of capitalism' in the countryside, and this is reflected in the very strict controls imposed upon the amount of land that households were allocated for their own private use. According to one Sichuanese

economist (Ni Wenze, cited in Nolan, 1983*b*), these accounted for
3–5% of arable area before 1980, when they increased to about 12%
(a maximum of 15% was permitted). However, according to Lin and
Gu (1985: 190), 1977–8 was the decisive period; during these years
the share of land occupied by private plots rose from 7 to 15%. This
latter chronology is in line with the promulgation of the 12 rules of
1977 under the direction of Zhao Ziyang, one of which guaranteed the
right of peasants to produce on private plots (Shambaugh, 1982). The
inconsistencies between these various accounts is probably explained
by differences between the maximum allowed and the figure in practice;
this latter was substantially less than the limit because of peasant fear
that an enthusiastic participation in sideline production might result in
their being singled out as 'capitalist roaders' in some future shift of
national and provincial policy. What certainly is clear is that the share
of private plots remained small even in the relatively liberal early
1980s; in Guanghan, they accounted for about 6% of all arable land in
1982 and for 6.9% in Xindu's Wugui village (Nolan, 1983*b*). This may
have reflected the relative strength of the collective sector, and hence
an absence of popular pressure for the creation of extensive private
plots, in relatively prosperous counties such as these; overall, the
figure cited by Ni may be more accurate. Nevertheless, if this was the
figure in the early 1980s, it must have been somewhat lower (probably
less than 10%) in the uncertain atmosphere of the late 1970s.

It is likely that the share of (*de facto*) private land in total cultivated
land understates the share of private income in total income. Value
added was probably higher in household activities such as pig-rearing
and vegetable-growing than in collective production, which was very
heavily orientated towards grain output. This is reflected in the survey
data for peasant incomes collected for the province in 1965 and 1978.
These show that the sideline share was about 30% of total net income
per capita in the province (SCTJNJ, 1985: 377). In some areas, it was
probably higher. In Qionglai county it stood at around 50% in 1978
(Chen, 1985: 281). However, it is important to realize that the choice
of years matters here. 1965 was in the middle of the relatively 'liberal'
period that immediately preceded the Cultural Revolution. By 1978,
the liberal policies which Zhao Ziyang had pioneered since becoming
provincial party secretary had been in force for perhaps two years. In
consequence, the data for 1965 and 1978 exaggerate the importance of
sideline incomes.

However, *even if* private incomes accounted for as much as 50% of
total income, it is not at all clear that this overturns the collective-
income-based conclusion that rural China's income distribution

was remarkably equal by world standards. Take team 2 of Sanxing commune's Lixin brigade in Guanghan county. In 1977, the highest per capita income within that team was 244 *yuan* and the lowest 36 *yuan*. Take these data at face value (which is unrealistic because the poor one-person household here was almost certainly in receipt of welfare payments). Make the extreme assumption that private income contributed half of the rich person's income and that the poor person received no private income at all. That still only has the effect of widening the range of incomes from 6.8 : 1 to 13.6 : 1. Of course, that constitutes an unequal distribution; but it is trivial when compared with the income range between landlord and peasants in other con- temporary LDCs, and trivial also when compared against the income differentials that had appeared in parts of China by the mid-1980s. In Zhejiang prefecture's Wenzhou municipality, where privately owned rural industry grew at an electrifying pace during the early 1980s, the income range was at least 3,000 to 1 (Bramall, 1990: 45). Further- more, according to a 1985 income survey in Sichuan covering 2,237 households across 9 counties, the range was 4644 *yuan* to 58 *yuan*, or about 80 to 1 (Nongcun yanjiuzu, 1986: 493). In short, the inclusion of sideline incomes does not alter the basic conclusion of modest within- village differentials.

The second assumption underlying the hypothesis of stratification induced by private incomes, that the rich benefited more than the poor, is also flawed. It is true that Walker's findings for Fujian and Yunnan provinces in the late 1950s show unambiguously that the share of private sector in total income was higher for middle and rich peasants than for the poor-peasant class. This was because 'the food producing and income earning assets . . . were highly concentrated into the hands of the middle peasants' (Walker, 1965: 38–9). How- ever, this was the very type of problem that the egalitarianism espoused during the Great Leap Forward and the Cultural Revolution was designed to eliminate. Pressure placed on middle and rich peasants to serve the collective interest during the Great Leap Forward and the Cultural Revolution, including asset confiscation and poor-peasant upward mobility, almost certainly led to a narrowing of inequalities in private asset-holding.

More importantly, other writers have argued that the inclusion of sideline income serves to *narrow* collective-income differentials even further. The rationale for this is that households receiving little income from collective work were often those with a high dependant– worker ratio. These dependants, while not able to work full-time on the collective, were nevertheless able to work part-time in sideline activities such as chicken-rearing, bamboo furniture-making, spinning and weaving, sericulture, and vegetable-growing. By comparison, households with a low dependency ratio were not able to supplement their collective income by very much, precisely because their members had very little spare time available. Households whose workers were employed in administrative positions at either the team or brigade level were even more disadvantaged because such work was extremely time-intensive. Indeed, in rural Guangdong, cadres were often chided by their wives for their neglect of household sidelines (Chan, Madsen, and Unger, 1984; Parish and Whyte, 1978). Griffin and Griffin therefore seem correct when they suggest (1984: 60): 'Contrary to what many believe, private sector activities have not resulted in greater inequality in the distribution of total household income and may well have helped to reduce inequality.'

This is supported by evidence that sideline income as a percentage of total income was higher for low-income groups than for those groups receiving high incomes in Sichuan before land reform. Data collected on Huayang county in 1950 immediately before rent reduction show that, for the poor-peasant class, sideline income (expressed in terms of *jin* of unhusked rice) contributed 44% of per capita total income. By contrast, sidelines provided only 13% of per capita income for middle peasants (although, as mentioned in the previous chapter, 1950 is not a very representative year). After rent reduction and the return of rent deposits, both the share and the absolute magnitude of sideline income fell for each group.[5] Even so, the poor-peasant sideline share in total income remained higher. A likely explanation for this is that, whilst middle peasants may have had more *opportunities* for sideline activities, the latter were a *necessity* for poor peasants if they were to raise their total income to subsistence.

This is, in any case, a very indirect approach to assessing the impact of household sideline income. A more direct route is to evaluate the rather sketchy material available on differentials in *total* per capita income in the late 1970s. Probably the best material is contained in a 1984 survey of 2,644 households drawn from 10 different villages, which sought to show how income inequalities between occupational types of household had changed over the 1978–84 period. Only

---

[5] The share of sideline in total income was 12.5% for poor peasants and 4.5% for middle peasants (Zhongyang nongyebu jihuasi, 1952: 300). In both cases, the windfall gain resulting from the return of rent deposits reduced the need to produce sideline products, and hence the 1950 share is not indicative of the figure in subsequent, pre-collectivization, years.

TABLE 8.5   *Net Per Capita Incomes*[a] *by Household Type,*
1978–1984

Household type[b]	1978		1984	
	Income per capita	Ratio	Income per capita	Ratio
Poor	78		92	
Specialized	162	2.1:1	1,155	12.6:1
Low education	126		353	
High education	134	1.1:1	422	1.2:1
Self-sufficient	126		356	
Commercial	155	1.2:1	1,297	3.6:1
Labour-poor	116		343	
Labour-rich	155	1.3:1	505	1.5:1

[a] Figures exclude borrowing, and are expressed in current *yuan*.

[b] Most of these household types are not defined. However, a 'labour-rich' household is almost certainly a household with a high worker–dependant ratio. 'Commercial' is explicitly defined as a household marketing more than 80% of its output, and 'self-sufficient' means that less than 30% was marketed. 'Specialized' is effectively a pseudonym for 'rich'. For example, of the 202 specialized households sampled in a 1983 survey (Nongcun yanjiuzu, 1986), only 3 had a per capita income of less than 200 *yuan* (the sample mean was 258 *yuan*) whilst 160 had an income of 500 *yuan* or more.

Source: Nongcun xiaozu (1986).

summary results are available for 1978, but these appear to show that inequalities between various types of household were small (Table 8.5).

Of course, some of the income definitions used for analyses such as these are dubious. Of course, the available data are fragmentary; we have hardly any data at all for the extremely interesting 1975–6 period. Of course, some households with high collective incomes may also have been able to profit from opportunities for private enterprise. However, all that notwithstanding, there is nothing in the evidence considered in this section to suggest that sideline incomes transformed narrow income differentials into rural stratification.

Rural Corruption

The final objection to the picture of relative rural income equality painted in the previous sections is that it takes no account of the corruption that is alleged to have been a pervasive feature of the rural landscape by the end of Mao's life. By this means, those inhabitants who were fortunate enough to be members of the rural bureaucracy—in Chinese terminology, rural cadres—were able to raise their true incomes to levels far in excess of their notional incomes. Their hold on the reins of power gave them a superior entitlement to the very limited range of high-quality consumption goods available within the planned economy. The only way to curtail such activity, it is frequently argued, is to dismantle the system of planning and to make the economy subject to the operation of market forces.

It cannot be denied that a substantial bureaucracy existed in rural China by the 1970s. These officials exercised effective day-to-day administrative, political, and legal control over the countryside. Of course, such functions had also been performed before 1949. The difference was that the size of this group had mushroomed as the degree of economic planning in the rural sector increased. By the 1970s, rural administration in a county was a multi-tiered affair, with cadres responsible at county, commune, production brigade, and production team levels for a variety of functions. The task, unlike in the 1930s, was no longer simply to maintain law and order. For farm production to be maintained, an incentive system based upon work-point allocation had to be devised, continually revised, and administered. Targets for the volume of grain and cash crops to be delivered to the state had to be met, and that, in turn, required close control over patterns of land use. Labour for water conservancy and other forms of farmland construction had to be mobilized and the remaining farm labour reallocated to ensure that the farm sector's performance did not suffer in their absence. Political education had to be maintained at a high level. Migration had to be carefully controlled. In addition, a variety of other bureaux existed within each county (Kueh, 1985). Inoculation, curative medicine and sanitation campaigns were controlled by a series of clinics and hospitals. A county-level planning authority existed. Most important of all were the finance and materials bureaux. The function of the first was to allocate loans and the function of the second was to allocate scarce capital inputs and consumer goods (produced in the urban sector and provided within the plan to the rural sector) between the county's various communes and brigades.

The size of the rural bureaucracy is difficult to determine with any precision, partly because many of those involved held more than one office. Within each production brigade, control was exercised by two committees, the management committee and the party committee. Quite a number of officials were members of both, although power essentially resided with the party. The officials involved were full-time and numbered about 15 in total. In addition, each production team was in turn controlled by a committee of part-time cadres (with 5–7 members), notionally elected by the production team's members but in practice needing to have their decisions approved by the brigade party committee. However, the number of persons who received work-points for their administrative work was larger still. In one of Shifang's county's teams, 24 persons fell into this category in the period immediately before decollectivization (Endicott, 1988: 137). Thus a production brigade of 2,000 persons divided into, say, 8 teams was run by some 60–70 cadres, and had up to 200 people employed in some form of administrative capacity. When one adds to this commune administrators and officials employed in county bureaux, it is evident that the rural bureaucracy was of considerable size by the late 1970s.

It was also corrupt in the sense of being willing to receive gifts and other emoluments in return for tangible favours and intangible goodwill. In part this reflected the existence of strong incentives for corrupt behaviour. It is true, of course, that many rural officials were strongly committed to the collective system when it was first established in the 1950s and were not motivated to any great extent by thoughts of *short-term* material gain. Their preoccupation genuinely was with 'serving the people'. All this is very clear from Western accounts of the early days of collectivization (Hinton, 1966; Crook and Crook, 1966; Chan, Madsen, and Unger, 1984). Although many of these writers were highly sympathetic to Maoist goals, there is no reason to believe that their accounts are pure fabrication. By the mid-1970s, however, the Maoist dream differed sharply from the reality. The process began during the Great Leap Forward, when many officials found themselves having to abuse their position in order to keep their family alive (Endicott, 1988: ch. 6). It gathered momentum during the 1960s as it became increasingly obvious that the bewildering changes in national economic policy reflected not economic but political considerations. Without any form of national 'leadership by example', and given that rural officials were forced to implement economic policies with which neither they nor the peasantry had any sympathy and which reduced their incomes—such as double cropping of rice in parts of Sichuan where the growing season was too short for it to be possible without abundant supplies of plastic sheeting for protection against frost damage—it is unsurprising that cadres sought to maintain (and increase) their living standard by other means. Moreover, there were obvious potential gains from corruption. Even in a relatively 'poor' economy such as China's, one's living standard could always be raised by consuming a higher quality of grain (i.e. white rice), a wider range of vegetables, or a superior brand of cigarettes. The productivity of a household's private plot could be increased by access to chemical fertilizers, pesticides, better seeds, and tools. Furthermore, an increasing range of consumer durables were becoming available by the late 1970s. By 1978, one in 20 of Sichuan's rural households owned a bicycle and a radio, whilst one in 14 owned a wrist-watch (ZSSWY, 1984: 229). Naturally, there was strong competition between households to acquire them.

In addition to these incentives to be corrupt, there were also considerable opportunities to engage in such practices. Consumption of durables in particular was conditional upon having both sufficient income and access rights because of the operation of rationing; neither by itself was sufficient. In both respects, officials were at an advantage. They could supplement their income by embezzlement or by compelling peasants to provide them with gifts to ensure they were not discriminated against in the allocation of land, work-points, and capital inputs. Further, in that the cadre both made and executed the law over a wide sphere of activities, the peasant ran the risk of imprisonment or even death if he or she did not conform to cadre-imposed norms. Moreover, officials undoubtedly had superior access to a vast range of goods that were allocated via the plan. Some of this was direct, as in the case of granary warehousemen or persons employed in the health clinics or hospital. However, it was also indirect. In particular, officials could bribe other officials (and even urban cadres). For example, a household might be allocated the right to a coveted job in a rural factory, or the right to purchase a bicycle, in return for some form of reciprocal favour.

The direct evidence on the existence of corruption is firm. In the case of Shifang county, it is evident that the rewards from corruption were seen to exceed the probable costs of being caught. Endicott (1988: ch. 9) notes that 5 out of 7 team-leaders in Magaoqiao brigade did not 'pass the gate', i.e. were not acquitted of charges of corruption during the big 'For Clean-Ups Campaign' in the mid-1960s. Their 'crimes' related mainly to the embezzlement of cash and grain, dining at the expense of the production team, and deducting work-points from their enemies. For example, one was accused of embezzling 276 *yuan* in cash (as well as some grain), a figure representing about three years' income for the average team member. Sometimes the figures involved were even larger. During 1966–7, one member of a rebel Red Guard faction stole 20,000 *yuan*, a staggering sum by Chinese standards.

Corruption took other, less blatant forms. One common phenomenon in Shifang was the use of connections to ensure a coveted position of employment in a rural factory and thus escape the squalor of working in the fields. According to an account cited by Endicott (1988: 91):

These enterprises were the gateway to privilege in the villages, many people wanted to use personal connections to squeeze in by the back door . . . [and the post-1982 system of selection was] different from the vulgar organisational afflictions of the past—getting somewhere by exchanging flattery and favours.

This evidence for Shifang is corroborated by materials collected in various parts of China, ranging from Guangdong (Unger, 1984; Chan, Madsen, and Unger, 1984; Mosher, 1982) to Shanxi (Hinton, 1983). Hinton's account is particularly significant because the location is much more typical of China than Guangdong, where the close links between the province and Hong Kong made corruption a very lucrative activity. It is also significant because one can hardly accuse Hinton of being unsympathetic to Maoist ideals. That he provides the following evidence (1983: 677) of corrupt activities suggest that Western materials as a whole on this subject are reliable: 'From 1967 to 1971 . . . at least two people misappropriated more than 1,000 *yuan* apiece while more than a dozen others made off with amounts that varied from 100 to more than 500 *yuan*.' This is further reinforced by evidence of obvious peasant resentment by the 1970s over the degree of corruption: 'To the young people's irritation, the best jobs increasingly were going to the relatives of village leaders; in practice, the "back door" of cadre privilege had begun displacing the class line' (Unger, 1984: 138).

For all that, it seems unlikely that the impact of corruption in rural Sichuan was such as to nullify the high degree of income equality brought about under collective farming. For one thing, there were countervailing forces in the countryside. In particular, the position of the cadre was by no means invulnerable. Production team committees were elected by production team members and were therefore accountable, and village (brigade-level) cadres were also subject to periodic assessment. As the accounts of Endicott (1988) and Chan, Madsen, and Unger (1984) make clear, cadres were often dismissed, had their possessions confiscated, were severely criticized, or even driven to suicide in the periodic 'clean-up' campaigns directed from above that were a feature of the 1960s and 1970s. Cadres could retain their positions for life, but in practice only succeeded in doing so if their peculations were limited.

Secondly, many peasants were tolerant in practice to what were by Western standards obviously corrupt practices. Official corruption was a feature of life under the Empire and the short-lived Republic, and was largely free of the stigma attached to it in modern Western democracies. Accordingly, some rural corruption was probably acceptable to the majority of the population during the People's Republic, though perhaps not during the early 1950s. The essential point here is that peasants were well aware that being a cadre was a very time-consuming occupation. That meant that cadres were unable to earn as many work-points on the collective farm as other farm workers. Moreover, their opportunities to engage in private activities in the household were extremely limited, and for the loss of this, unlike working on the collective farm, there was no compensatory payment of work-points. Accordingly, a degree of corruption was seen as legitimate compensation for the opportunity costs involved in being a cadre.

But villagers . . . expected cadres to profit financially from their posts by taking small gifts for doing modest favors, by using their official positions to gain access to scarce goods like building materials for one's house, and even by juggling account books to appropriate some public funds. As one of our peasant interviewees said: Of course cadres will use their position to gain some material advantage; if they couldn't do so, what would be the point in becoming a cadre? (Madsen, 1984: 76)

One might argue that the effect of corruption was to *narrow* inequalities in the countryside. In its absence, the collective system would have created a considerable body of overworked and underfunded officials at the bottom of the income scale. However, that is perhaps going too far. The legitimacy of a modicum of corrupt practice undoubtedly gave some of the more unscrupulous cadres opportunities substantially to increase their incomes. Nevertheless, it is hard to believe that it makes sense to talk of the emergence of a new rural élite in Sichuan by the late 1970s. Cadres may have eaten white rice more often and owned rather more bicycles, radios, and fans than the peasant norm, but we are hardly talking about the possession of opulent houses and motor vehicles, or even frequent foreign travel. Doubtless cadres in *urban* China had such opportunities, and much of this was to become far more common in rural China in the 1980s. For the previous decade, however, the perks enjoyed via corruption in rural Sichuan were modest.

The 1930s and 1970s Compared

Rural income inequalities in the province of Sichuan in the 1930s were enormous, stemming in essence from the very unequal ownership of land, the principal rural means of production. These inequalities were compounded by high levels of rent levied upon poor tenant farmers, themselves partly reflecting the penal rates of taxation introduced by the warlords in a vain attempt to finance their soaring military spending. Interest rates were not unreasonable, but they did nothing to eliminate initial land-based income inequalities. The same is true of non-farm sources of income.

These institutional features of the 1930s were swept aside by the Revolutionary settlement. The landholdings of the landlord class were expropriated and redistributed to the middle, poor, and landless peasantry. These small holdings were later amalgamated to form collective farms. These latter, necessarily involving collective ownership of other complementary means of production such as livestock, implements, and transport equipment, did much to eliminate the more extreme inequalities in income that remained after land reform (though progressive land taxation during the 1950s was operating towards the same end). Some inequalities remained by the 1970s, deriving mainly from differences in work-point earnings, but even these were offset by the impact of income from private land and the incomes in cash and kind to be garnered from the exploitation of the positions of power and responsibility abrogated by the cadre class.

That these residual inequalities were trivial by comparison with those that prevailed in the province in the 1930s is certain. Massive inequalities in landownership had been eliminated, and in a pre-industrial economy such as Sichuan's, this was decisive (in the rural sector at any rate) in removing the most glaring income differentials. Of course the data on which these conclusions are based are fragmentary and difficult to interpret. Of course it is impossible to delineate the precise parameters of income inequality in either period by the computation of village Gini coefficients. Of course there are many areas and issues on which we know little and would like to know more. Of course this justifies to some extent the Maoist socioeconomic development model, the horrors of which in terms of human rights we are only now beginning to understand. But we cannot be blind to the genuine achievements wrought in Sichuan after 1949. The lot of many of the poorest members of society was improved in almost every sense by means of a redistributive programme on a vast scale. The rural landscape did not merely change between the 1930s and the 1970s. It was transformed.

9

Famine

It has been alleged that up to 30 million excess deaths occurred during the Chinese famine of 1958–62 (Ashton *et al.*, 1984; Banister, 1984). For many, this single event is sufficient evidence of the folly of the Maoist strategy of economic development, and especially the Great Leap Forward.[1] 'Market forces' may not produce Utopia, but the absence of social engineering at least ensures the avoidance of large-scale famine. It is indeed ironic that governments committed to 'serving the people'—the Soviet Union under Stalin, Kampuchea under Pol Pot, and China under Mao—have presided over the worst famines of the century.

An indictment of the Maoist strategy on the basis of its famine record rests upon three pillars, all of which must be secure for the indictment to stand. First, it must be shown that the number of excess deaths was indeed large. Secondly, it must be demonstrated that the excess mortality was on a greater scale than during comparable periods of famine during the Republican period, for if the famine of 1958–62 had historical precedents, it suggests that the Maoist economic development strategy was guilty of a continued sin of omission rather than one of commission. Finally, it needs to be shown that the famine was caused by government policy rather than by some act of God. This issue of causality is taken up in the next chapter. The aim in this chapter is to discuss the first two issues in the context of Sichuan.

---

[1] The Great Leap Forward (I use the term to refer to the entire 1958–62 period) was an ambitious programme of growth launched by Mao in 1958. The intention was to transform China into an industrialized nation within 10–15 years. The main features of the Leap were the unbridled development of small-scale rural industry (especially iron and steel) and the establishment of large-scale rural communes in which material incentives were largely abolished; food, for example, was distributed largely according to need via communal canteens. It was hoped that the large-scale and unprecedented mobilization of women in the countryside would provide a labour force large enough both to maintain farm production and to develop rural industry. It is the current convention in both the West and in China to dismiss the Leap as a Utopian experiment, but it was arguably flawed more in execution than in conception. The link between the policies adopted during the Leap and the famine in Sichuan is explored in the next chapter. For a further discussion of the Leap, see Bachman (1991) and the brilliant study by MacFarquhar (1983).

Famines in Sichuan during the Republican Period

Sichuan's well-known sobriquet of 'Heavenly Garden' was massively inappropriate by the last decades of the Empire. According to von Richthofen (1903: 177):

the year 1871 . . . was the most disastrous in decades . . . I found the country people reduced to a state of great poverty and destitution. . . . Beggars thronged the gates of the large cities and were frequent along the roads. I passed many a corpse of persons who had died from starvation on the roadside and had been left to the ravens and dogs.

Such famines continued to occur during the Republic; for instance, Mallory (1926: 78–9) mentions a famine in 1925 caused by the removal of accumulated stores of grain and draught animals by troops from Guizhou province.

The greatest famine of the Republican period seems to have occurred in 1937. According to Kapp (1973: 129): 'In Peip'ei, the Min Sheng Company's model industrial community north of Chungking, women and children broke into the town and feasted on the bark and leaves of carefully nurtured ornamental trees.' Edgar Snow (1972: 117–18) mentions a survey by the provincial famine relief commission in which 30 million people were thought to be affected (Snow, 1972: 117–18) and a number of accounts of conditions in parts of northern Sichuan are given in Lu (1936) and Y. Y. Zhang (1957). This famine therefore deserves more detailed consideration, for if it really was on a scale comparable with that of the early 1960s, the charge that widespread starvation was a Maoist phenomenon is undermined.

Trends in per capita food consumption at the provincial level seem to confirm that nutrient availability was dangerously low (Table 9.1), with per capita consumption standing at no more than 2,000 Kcal per day. This is, of course, significantly above the figure based upon official data. Nevertheless, it still falls considerably below the World Bank's estimated subsistence level of 2,160 for China in 1979 and Piazza's figure of 2,100 for the 1950s (World Bank, 1983: 119; Piazza, 1986: 92). These estimates of food consumption in 1937 therefore appear consistent with the qualitative accounts of famine.

This conclusion is further reinforced by an examination of official population data. As noted elsewhere (Bramall, 1989a: app. A3), famine seems to offer an explanation for the fall in official estimates of provincial population between 1936 and 1940. A set of such official

TABLE 9.1. *Per Capita Food Consumption in Sichuan,*
1931–1936 and 1937 (Kcal per capita per day)

Commodity[a]	Average, 1931–6[b]	1937
Rice	1,325	678
Wheat	222	166
Corn	256	298
Gaoliang	70	87
Other grains	96	70
Sweet potatoes	54	99
Potatoes	neg.	neg.
Soyabeans	83	63
Broad beans	99	52
Field peas	71	38
Sugar	40	44
Vegetable oil	71	49
Peanuts	45	45
TOTAL	2,432	1,689

[a] Meat has been excluded. This contributed about 70 Kcal in 1931–6, but the slaughter rate in a famine year would have been higher. This is supported by a substantial fall in the provincial pig stock (the most important form of meat) from about 11.7 million head in 1935 to 8.2 million in 1937 (Xu, 1983: 299). Let us therefore assume that around 200 Kcal derived from this source in 1937. Adding another 100 Kcal for fruit and vegetables gives a revised 1937 total of almost 2,000 Kcal.

[b] The 1931–6 figure used here is Estimate E given in Bramall (1989a: 19). The 1937 figure uses the same methodology and sources.

population figures collected by the Ministry of the Interior is given in Table 9.2. Whilst the absolute magnitudes involved are open to doubt, the fact that all these data were collected by the same Ministry does suggest that the trend is reliable enough. This shows a massive fall after 1937 which coincides with the famine of that year. Taken together, this evidence on population, calorie consumption, and direct accounts was enough to convince this writer of the existence of a catastrophic famine in 1937 (see Bramall, 1989a). Food insecurity appeared to be a recurrent phenomenon in the province's history, seemingly unaffected by changes in regime.

TABLE 9.2. *Official Estimates of Population, 1935–1945 (millions)*

Year	Population[a]	Source
1935	52.06	Lu (1936: 77)
1936	52.71	Zhongguo guomin . . . tongjiju (1940: 24)
1937	52.09	Liu (1988: 59)
1938	46.35	
1939	46.40	
1940	46.70	
1941	46.44	
1942	45.83	Sichuan sheng zhengfu tongjiju (1947: 57)
1943	46.14	
1944	47.50	
1945	47.55	

[a] These data include urban population.

However, I now believe that this assessment is incorrect. For one thing, the estimates of calorific consumption given in Table 9.1 are actually quite high. It is, of course, extremely difficult to estimate a true subsistence line (Sukhatme, 1988). Requirements differ between persons and by sex, and also depend upon activity rates. For example, the requirement for a woman aged over 40 in rural Bangladesh in the mid-1970s was estimated to be less than 1,900 Kcal and falling with age to less than 1,400 if over 70. The requirement for males aged between 20 and 39 was, by contrast, more than 3,100 Kcal (Sen, 1988). Accordingly, a great deal of accurate information is needed before an average can be computed. Even so, it seems likely that the 1937 figure of about 2,000 Kcal for Sichuan was not much below subsistence. Certainly it does not seem compatible with the degree of starvation implied by official population data. Moreover, the shortfall in food availability during the 1930s was not sustained except for a relatively brief period. This is apparent when one considers the pattern of rice production, the key grain crop, over time (Table 9.3).

If one assumes that 'normal' production in the 1930s was about 7.8 million tonnes, it is evident that output fell below this level in 1936 and, to a greater extent, in 1937. However, it very quickly revived to its normal level in 1938. As for the later famine, if 'normal' 1950s production is assumed to have been 12 million tonnes, it is evident that output was below trend for a much longer period than in the

TABLE 9.3. *Production of Rice, 1931–1938 and 1956–1963*

Year[a]	Total output[b] (000 tonnes)	Year	Total output (000 tonnes)
1931	8,020	1956	13,165
1932	9,175	1957	12,560
1933	7,670	1958	12,095
1934	7,330	1959	8,220
1935	7,805	1960	6,320
1936	5,970	1961	5,765
1937	3,935	1962	7,640
1938	7,795	1963	9,125

[a] The data for the 1930s are based upon official estimates of sown area, and exclude glutinous rice (included in the 1956–63 data). Figures are for unprocessed rice in both periods.

[b] These figures are an inaccurate guide to relative per capita rice production in the 2 periods because the 1930s data are based upon official underestimates of sown area, and because population was considerably smaller.

Sources: 1931–8—Bramall (1989*a*: app. A5); 1956–63—SCJJNJ (1986: 283–4).

1930s. Even during the post-Leap recovery period in the early 1960s, production recovered slowly, and the 1956 level was regained only in 1966. In sum, the maximum peak-to-trough variation is very similar in both periods, but the shortfall lasted for far longer in the later period. It was the sustained nature of the fall in output during the Leap, and the fact that it began from a relatively lower per capita base, that seems to explain why mortality was so much higher.

Some other evidence also casts doubt upon the hypothesis of generalized famine in 1937. The price of wheat in Chongqing in 1937 was some 40% higher than it had been in 1935, while the rice price almost doubled in Chengdu over the same period. However, these seem relatively small increases if the province was indeed affected by a massive famine. For instance, in the Great Bengali Famine of the early 1940s, wholesale rice prices increased by a factor of at least four (Sen, 1981: 54–55). It is, of course, true that famine can occur without prices being high if most food production is for subsistence rather than for market sales. Nevertheless, these Sichuan price data give pause for thought.

286 *Famine*

In addition, the reliability of the Ministry of the Interior's population data is anything but self-evident. We have alternative estimates made by the Provincial Reconstruction Bureau that was established following the assertion of Kuomintang authority in the province in the mid-1930s. As already noted, the Ministry estimated provincial population as being 52.06 million in 1935 and 52.71 million in 1936. Its estimates for the 1940s show a marked decrease. Now, initial work in the statistical arena by the Reconstruction Bureau was hampered by lack of experience, but it is probable that by 1936–7 the Bureau was beginning to operate with a degree of success. There is, therefore, no reason to reject out of hand its population estimates for 1936 and 1937 of 47.99 and 49.3 million (Lu, 1936: 77; X. M. Zhang, 1939: B6). A further estimate for 1942 by the Bureau put the population at 47.22 million (Zhou, Hou, and Chen, 1946*b*: 49). If we accept the Bureau's data, the case for a famine in 1936–7 is seriously weakened, especially because a part of the modest fall in the Bureau's estimates of population between 1936 and 1942 can be explained by a 1939 boundary change whereby the province lost 1.3 million people to Xikang province.

However, the most decisive piece of evidence against a 1937 province-wide famine is the age composition of the population as revealed in the 1953 census, the results of which for Sichuan are now

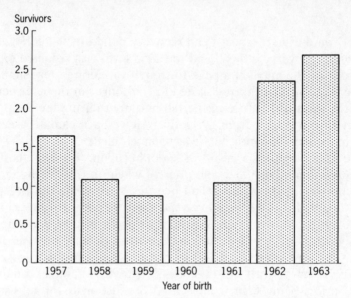

Fig. 7a. Famine Survivors from the Leap in Sichuan: Survivors by Year of Birth in Millions, 1982 Census. Source: SCJJNJ (1986: 272)

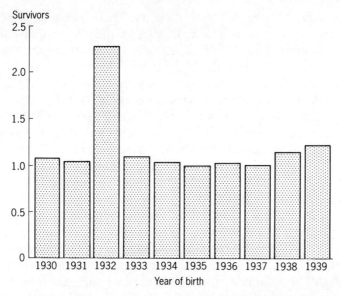

FIG. 7b.   Famine Survivors from the 1930s in Sichuan: Survivors by Year of
Birth in Millions, 1953 Census. Source: SCJJNJ (1986: 272)

available. This enables one to draw a population 'pyramid' indicating
the year of birth of the 1953 population. This graph is shown as Fig.
7*b*, alongside the results of the 1982 census (Fig. 7*a*) which indicates
the impact of the Great Leap Forward. If there had been a famine in
1937, one would expect the number of 'survivors' revealed in the
Census for that year to have been significantly lower than for either
preceding or subsequent years. Yet the graph reveals no such pattern.
It shows instead the enormous magnitude of the famine of the early
1960s.

Of course, one can very reasonably argue that the 1953 census left
a great deal to be desired, especially in its enumeration of ethnic
minorities. Indeed, it is difficult to explain the enormous number of
survivors discovered in the 1953 census for 1932–3 except as an
aberration.[2] But it strains belief to argue that the 1953 census was
so inaccurate that every trace of the 1937 famine was obliterated.
Accordingly, one can only explain the results of the 1953 census in
one way: the famine of 1937 did not happen on anything like the scale
suggested in my earlier monograph.

[2] It is possible that many persons reported themselves as born in 1932–3 to avoid any
doubt as to their eligibility to vote in post-1952 national 'elections'. The age qualification
was 18 years, and therefore stating one's age as 20 removed any doubt.

To be sure, 1937 was no year of plenty. There was no province-wide famine, but there was an intense localized famine in northern Sichuan, the area to which most of the available evidence relates. Its proximate cause was warfare during the early 1930s. This began with the arrival of Zhang Guotao's Fourth-Front army in November 1932, and the establishment of a CCP base area centred on Bazhong. The scale of military activity increased as Kuomintang and Mao's CCP forces were drawn into the conflict, and the outcome was without question a decline in food availability for the civilian population. This was due to the combined effects of crop confiscation, damage to crops and farm capital, and the conscription of farm labour, as well as increased demand for food because of higher activity rates.

In addition, climatic conditions were adverse. Measured rainfall in Chongqing was unusually low at 754 mm. in 1936, compared to an 1891–1936 average of 1,089 mm. (Zhongguo guomin zhengfu zhujiju tongjiju, 1940: 17) and northern Sichuan was particularly hard hit by drought. By contrast, the Chengdu plain suffered from flooding. 1,523 mm. of rain fell in 1936 and 1,821 mm. in 1937 (p. 18) compared to a 1951–80 average for the provincial capital of only 947 mm. (ZGTJNJ, 1987: 17).

Three further factors turned the food shortfall into famine. One was the inadequacy of the transport network. In an economy with a well-developed infrastructure, famine is much less likely than in an economy where the converse is true. For one thing, the government can transfer grain from surplus to deficit areas, as has happened in India since 1947. Alternatively, higher food prices in the deficit region may make it profitable for the private sector to supply food from surplus regions where profitability is lower. In Republican Sichuan, however, transport infrastructure was woefully underdeveloped. To start with, interprovincial transportation was difficult. The notorious Gorges of the Yangzi river were traversable by powered craft by the 1930s, and therefore the situation was somewhat better than in the 1870s, when von Richthofen saw grain imports by this route as an impossibility. Even so, the Yangzi route remained dangerous, and drought conditions in eastern Sichuan, by lowering the water level, did nothing to make the passage any easier. Had the province been linked to the rest of China by railway, this problem would have been infinitely less daunting. In addition, intraprovincial transportation presented a number of problems. Only two railways existed in the Sichuan of 1937; both were very short coal-carrying lines near Chongqing. Furthermore, northern Sichuan was not accessible by river to anything except small junks.

An additional reason for the outbreak of famine was that neither Kuomintang nor private suppliers had much to gain from famine relief. The potential private supplier saw only an area full of troops in which the expectation of confiscation of grain was higher than the expectation of profit. If profits were to be made, it was by selling to the army itself. Conversely, the Kuomintang's priority was to feed its armies; if the peasantry were reduced to starvation as a result, the price was small relative to the perceived advantages to be garnered from liquidating the CCP.

Thirdly, grain reserves were inadequate. During the Republican period, peasants throughout Sichuan enjoyed entitlements to granary contents in time of famine. However, these entitlements proved notional rather than real, because this stored grain was frequently confiscated by the military (Lu, 1936: 548–50). Moreover, even if peasants had received their full entitlements, famine would still have been unavoidable because of the limited capacity of the granaries. Very few had a capacity of more than 10,000 *shi* of grain. The size of the *shi* varied between locations, but in Baxian, for example, it comprised 400 lb. A 10,000-*shi* granary would therefore be hard put to support even 10,000 people for a year. In any case, these granaries were very rarely full (Lu, 1936: 548–50); only the Imperial government had assigned a high priority to this and, even so, was unable to prevent famines such as that of 1872–3.

This combination of factors led inexorably to starvation in northern Sichuan in 1937. The words of contemporary observers indicate its magnitude:

This year, the trees have been completely stripped of their bark, all available straw has been eaten, and so the peasants are turning to corpses. It has been heard that a *jin* of dead human flesh can be bought for 500 *jiao* and a *jin* of live flesh (*hourou*) for 1,200 *jiao*. . . . In each of Fuling, Cangxi, Tongjiang, Nanjiang, and Bazhong counties, 500 or 600 persons are dying every day. . . . on the opposite bank of the river from Zhong county, more than 10,800 bodies have already been buried as well as countless numbers of children. Every day, 500–600 bodies are being found on the Chengdu–Chongqing road. (Y. Y. Zhang, 1957: 805–6)

In Shifang county, on the edge of the war zone and where flooding had taken place in 1937, infant mortality rose from its Republican average of 200–50 deaths per 1,000 live births to 400 deaths, equivalent to the level reached during the Great Leap Forward (Lavely, 1984: 369). By way of comparison, the county's infant mortality rate was only 36 per 1,000 in 1981 according to the 1982 census returns (ZGRKTJNJ, 1988: 657).

There is little mention in any of these accounts of famine in southern Sichuan. Indeed, Peck, a knowledgeable Western observer, lived in the province for four months and yet saw no evidence of famine (Peck, 1941). He argued that this was because (despite the drought of which he was aware) he lived in the cities, could not distinguish famine victims from the ordinary poor, and only travelled in the countryside alongside water-courses. However, it is difficult to believe that he would not have noticed excess deaths if the famine had been province-wide; significantly, he had not visited northern Sichuan. Evidence for Jingyan county indicates a population decline of some 4,000 people between 1936 and 1937, whereas population fell by 30,000 between 1937 and 1944 (some 15%). This was due, according to the county records, to conscription (which claimed 11,584 people), famine, and attempts to avoid forced labour (*Jingyan xian zhi*, 1990: 97).

The hypothesis that there was no famine in the southern part of the province is supported by data on the spatial pattern of food prices. These were already high in northern Sichuan in early 1936, as indicated in Table 9.4. The spatial dualism evident in this table—one region heavily hit by famine and the others hardly at all—is consistent with the underdeveloped transport network and lack of political will noted earlier.

TABLE 9.4. *Retail Prices of Milled Rice and Corn by Region, January–June 1936*

Location	Milled rice (*yuan* per *shi*)	Corn (*yuan* per *shi*)	Sample size (no. of counties)
Jiange	3.18	3.60	1
Cangxi	4.34	3.93	1
Guangyuan	4.93	4.12	1
Lifan	4.50	2.82	1
Songpan	14.93	7.05	1
Average	6.38	4.30	5
Median	4.50	3.93	5
Chengdu plain average	2.24	1.74	12
Centre and south-west average	2.41	1.96	12
North-east average	2.66	1.84	6

Source: X. M. Zhang (1939: V4–32).

The threat of famine was ever-present in Sichuan during the late Imperial and Republican periods. Nevertheless, there is no evidence to suggest a loss of life on the scale that will be outlined over the next few pages.

The Great Leap Forward and the National Famine

Before the 1980s, there was no firm evidence that China had suffered from a famine of unprecedented proportions. There were a few refugee stories, but in general the view of most Western academics was sceptical. Selden's view (1979: 96, 97) was not untypical:

Beginning in 1960, food shortages resulted in serious malnutrition and starvation in some areas. The three-year food shortage was extremely severe. Yet in contrast with comparable natural disasters which in the first half of the twentieth century sent millions of Chinese to their graves and wreaked havoc on the economy, communal institutions and the supporting role of the state made it possible to minimise the damage . . . despite severe food shortages, partially alleviated by foreign grain purchases, few died . . .

It would be unfair to criticize Selden and others for reaching that conclusion; one does not rush into print with stories of 30 million dead without good evidence. However, following the publication of the results of the 1982 population census and a historical series of death rate data by China's State Statistical Bureau, it was apparent that the true dimensions of the famine were indeed of this order of magnitude.

Accounts of the tragedy at a local level convey a sense of the horrors of these years most vividly. In Anhui, for instance, the mortality crisis was particularly acute:

For the county [*Fengyang*] as a whole, 2,404 households, or 3.4% of the total, perished. In 27 villages, death wiped out everybody. All 12 members of the family of Wang Huanye, the principal of the county experimental primary school, perished. In the Beishan production team . . . 30 of 34 members of commune member Cao Yile's family died. . . . When people are extremely hungry, they are capable of anything. When a relative saw some people go to the grave pit and cut the calves from the legs of the dead to eat, she went too. At first, she was a little frightened, but later on she became used to it. . . . (Wang, 1988: 13)

That having been said, Fengyang has been used as a demonstration county in the 1980s to illustrate the success of private farming (Hinton, 1991). It may therefore be that the failures of the Maoist period have been deliberately exaggerated. The macroeconomic data on the famine are perhaps more telling. Some provinces like Jilin and Jiangsu fared much better than the national average, even though excess mortality did occur; for others, such as Anhui, Gansu, and Guizhou, the dying went on for half a decade. The 1960 figure for Anhui (Table 9.5) is particularly striking; in that year, over 11% ('normal' plus excess deaths) of her population perished. This province registered the highest crude death rate for a single year during the Leap (although the difference between the death rates in 1960 and in 1959 and 1961 seems suspicious; even large-scale grain imports could surely not have brought about such a rapid turnaround). The figure for famine intensity in Sichuan, to which we will return, shows that the province was the worst hit of all, with an index more than double the national average.

This picture of massive excess mortality has been painted several times in the literature (Riskin, 1987: Ashton *et al.*, 1984; Kane, 1988) during the 1980s, and a detailed provincial study has been carried out by Peng Xizhe (1987). The basic data come from official publications, and there has been no attempt by the Chinese authorities to disguise what happened. Various estimates of the scale of excess mortality have been made, with the highest being 30 million (Ashton *et al.*, 1984: 619). Judith Banister reached the same conclusion (1987: 85): 'The computer reconstruction of China's population trends utilized in this book which assumes under-reporting of deaths in 1957 as well as in all the famine years, results in an estimated 30 million excess deaths during 1958–61.'

Estimates such as these astound the Western imagination. It is therefore reasonable to ask whether they are plausible before passing on to discuss the events in Sichuan during these fateful years. Whilst Deng Xiaoping was involved in the collective decision to initiate the Leap, the present leadership does have a clear vested interest in making the events of the Maoist period seem as black as possible, in order to emphasize by contrast the achievements of the post-1978 Dengist development strategy.

The estimate made by Ashton *et al.* derives from two assumptions. The first is that, in the absence of famine, fertility would have fallen to its actual 1958–62 level, whilst mortality between 1957–8 and 1961–2 is calculated by extrapolation between those years. This assumption reduces the number of births in the hypothetical no-crisis period and therefore the number of deaths. In consequence, Ashton *et al.* arrive at a very low estimate of 'normal' deaths. For example, their figure for 'normal' deaths in 1960–1 is 9.5 million compared to

TABLE 9.5. *The Great Leap Famine in the Provinces*

Province[a]	Crude death rates per 1,000					Average	Intensity
	1957	1958	1959	1960	1961	1958–61	1958–61/1957
Sichuan	12.1	25.2	47.0	54.0	29.4	38.9	3.2
Anhui	9.1	12.3	16.7	68.6	8.1	26.4	2.9
Guizhou	8.8	13.7	16.2	45.4	17.7	23.3	2.6
Gansu	11.3	21.1	17.4	41.3	11.5	22.8	2.0
Qinghai	10.4	13.0	16.6	40.7	11.7	20.5	2.0
Hunan	10.4	11.7	13.0	29.4	17.5	17.9	1.7
Henan	11.8	12.7	14.1	39.6	10.2	19.2	1.6
Guangxi	12.4	11.7	17.5	29.5	19.5	19.6	1.6
Shandong	12.1	12.8	18.2	23.6	18.4	18.3	1.5
Hubei	9.6	9.6	14.5	21.2	9.1	13.6	1.4
Guangdong	8.4	9.2	11.1	15.2	10.8	11.6	1.4
Jiangsu	10.3	9.4	14.6	18.4	13.4	14.0	1.4
Fujian	7.9	7.5	7.9	15.3	11.9	10.7	1.3
Liaoning	9.4	8.8	11.8	11.5	17.5	12.4	1.3
Ningxia	11.1	15.0	15.8	13.9	10.7	13.9	1.2
Jilin	9.1	9.1	13.4	10.1	12.0	11.2	1.2
Yunnan	16.3	21.6	18.0	26.3	11.8	19.4	1.2
Hebei	11.3	10.9	12.3	15.8	13.6	13.2	1.2
Beijing	8.2	8.1	9.7	9.1	10.8	9.4	1.1
Shanghai	6.0	5.9	6.9	6.8	7.7	6.8	1.1
Jiangxi	11.5	11.3	13.0	16.1	11.5	13.0	1.1
Zhejiang	9.3	9.2	10.8	11.9	9.8	10.4	1.1
Shaanxi	10.3	11.0	12.7	12.3	8.8	11.2	1.1
Xinjiang	14.0	13.0	18.8	15.7	11.7	14.8	1.1
Heil'jiang	10.5	9.2	12.8	10.6	11.1	10.9	1.0
Tianjin	9.4	8.7	9.9	10.3	9.9	9.7	1.0
Shanxi	12.7	11.7	12.8	14.2	12.2	12.7	1.0
Nei Meng	10.5	7.9	11.0	9.4	8.8	9.3	0.9
NATIONAL	10.8	12.0	14.6	25.4	14.2	16.6	1.5

[a] Provinces are ranked here by the intensity of their famine. The measure chosen here for intensity is the average crude death rate for 1958–61 divided by the crude death rate for 1957, the last non-famine year. The Sichuan measure of 3.2 thus indicates that the crude death rate during the famine was on average 3.2 times the pre-crisis figure.

Sources: LSTJ (1990: *passim*); ZGTJNJ (1989: 88).

the last pre-famine year (1956–7) figure of 12.1 million—and the actual 1960–1 death toll of 19.2 million (ibid. 618–19). The justification for the fertility assumption is that 'if we had assumed steady fertility in the no-crisis case, excess deaths under age 10 would have been lower, but the difference represents persons in the no-crisis case who were never actually born' (Ashton *et al.*, 1984: 620). The second assumption is that the number of actual deaths is under-reported by the official Chinese population registration system. Ashton *et al.* reach the following conclusion on this question by the use of the data obtained in the 1982 Population Census and the 1982 Fertility Survey: 'the registration completeness of deaths under 10 was 30 percent while that for deaths over 10 was 80.5' (p. 640). These two assumptions have the effect of reducing the number of 'normal' deaths and raising the number of actual deaths, thus producing a very large figure for the difference, the number of excess deaths.

Of these two, the first has been heavily criticized by Riskin (1987: 146) as leading to a figure for 'normal' deaths that is 'unrealistically low'. He undoubtedly has a point because, although Ashton *et al.* argue that a higher fertility figure would lead to the inclusion of deaths of persons never actually born in 'normal' deaths, the very essence of counterfactual analysis is to consider events that never actually happened. However, in the absence of a crisis, the trend fall in mortality achieved during the 1950s might have continued into the early 1960s; fertility rates might also have fallen if one argues that the very high actual fertility rate in the mid- and late 1960s was simply a response to the demographic loss during 1958–62. In other words, a fall in the number of 'normal' deaths during 1958–62 is by no means as implausible an assumption as Riskin suggests.

If the first assumption by Ashton *et al.* seems fairly robust, so too does the second. This is because the 1982 census and the retrospective fertility survey of the same year provide reliable data both on 'survivors' by year of birth and on the number of children ever born to each mother which can be used to correct data on registered deaths. Indeed, other Western demographers have come to the same conclusions on the under-reporting of mortality, especially infant mortality:

Infant mortality has been the hardest component of mortality to measure in China. The registration of infant deaths is so incomplete that infant mortality rates officially reported from this system . . . are substantially lower than the true rates. (Banister, 1984: 251–2)

The impact of this correction is shown in Table 9.6.

In sum, there is no good reason to reject Ashton *et al.*'s estimate of

TABLE 9.6. *Estimates of Crude Death Rates (per 1,000) in China, 1957–1963*

Year	Officially registered	Banister	Ashton *et al.*
1957	10.8	18.1	
1958	12.0	20.7	19.1 (1957–8)
1959	14.6	22.1	24.4 (1958–9)
1960	25.4	44.6	32.8 (1959–60)
1961	14.2	23.0	29.5 (1960–1)
1962	10.0	14.0	21.2 (1961–2)
1963	10.0	13.8	15.1 (1962–3)

Sources: Official: ZGTJNJ (1987: 90). These registration data have not been reworked despite the evidence of under-reporting found in the 1982 census and fertility survey. Compare e.g. the 1957 crude death rate given in ZGTJNJ (1981) with the above—the two are identical. *Other sources*: Banister (1984: 254); Ashton *et al.* (1984: 618).

excess mortality of 30 million. The precise figure is a matter for debate, but it is far from obvious that the Riskin figure of 17 million is more plausible, because of its reliance on official mortality data. If this conclusion holds good at a provincial level (it is likely that mortality reporting varied widely between provinces), it may be that the data cited in Table 9.5 actually *understate* true mortality in Anhui.

The Famine in Sichuan

As for Sichuan, it has already been seen that no other province was as badly affected by the famine in either relative or in absolute terms. The evolution of the province's demography relative to the national norm is provided in more detail in Table 9.7.

The relative intensity of the Sichuan famine is now clear. The province's population began to fall in 1958 whilst nationally it continued to grow in that year and in 1959. Moreover, the national population never fell below its 1955 level, whereas Sichuan's population was lower than it had been in 1955 even in 1963. By 1963, China's population was 14% higher than in 1955, whilst in Sichuan it was more than 1% lower. These differences in demographic trajectory reflect, in the main, differences in the crude death rate. Sichuan's birth rate was significantly below the national average, but the dif-

TABLE 9.7. *Demographic Trends in Sichuan and China, 1955–1964*

	Population (millions)		Crude birth rate (per 1,000)		Crude death rate (per 1,000)	
	China[a]	Sichuan	China	Sichuan	China	Sichuan
1955	614.65	67.91	32.6	28.4	12.3	9.2
1956	628.28	69.45	31.9	28.5	11.4	10.4
1957	646.53	70.81	34.0	29.2	10.8	12.1
1958	659.94	70.78	29.2	24.0	12.0	25.2
1959	672.07	68.97	24.8	16.7	14.6	47.0
1960	662.07	66.20	20.9	11.7	25.4	54.0
1961	658.59	64.59	18.0	11.8	14.2	29.4
1962	672.95	64.86	37.0	28.0	10.0	14.6
1963	691.72	66.96	43.4	50.1	10.0	12.8
1964	704.99	68.98	39.1	46.9	11.5	13.9

[a] 'China' is defined as China less Sichuan for the population figures. However, the crude birth and death rate data for China do not exclude Sichuan.

Sources: China—ZGTJNJ (1989: 87–8); Sichuan—ZGRKNJ (1985: 522–3).

ference in mortality rates was more apparent. In 1959 in particular, the province's crude death rate was more than three times the national average.

For the reasons already discussed, these data probably underestimate true mortality trends. I have therefore attempted to adjust the Sichuan figures for under-reporting of deaths using a variety of assumptions. Four resultant estimates of excess mortality in the province during the Leap are summarized in Table 9.8. There is no reason to doubt the scale of the demographic catastrophe that engulfed Sichuan during these years, at least in the sense that virtually all the county-level data show a sharp increase in mortality in the early 1960s (as will be discussed in the next section). The data on the age composition of the population as revealed in the 1982 population census are equally consistent (see Fig. 7a). Although it may be that differences in official crude death rates across provinces are a partial reflection of different degrees of under-reporting rather than of differences in true death rates, Sichuan's experience cannot be explained entirely in this fashion because under-reporting is not one of the problems that affected the

TABLE 9.8. *True Excess Mortality in Sichuan: Some Alternative Estimates*

Estimate	Excess deaths (no.)
A	8,144,831
B	9,050,062
C	8,869,880
D	14,782,115

Notes:

1. Assumptions underlying these estimates (in each case, the population data to which death rates are applied *include* net migration):

(*a*) Official data on actual deaths and a counterfactual in which both the crude birth rate (CBR) and crude death rate (CDR) are assumed to have remained at their 1953–7 Sichuan average of 28.6 and 9.9 per 1,000 respectively.

(*b*) Official data on actual deaths and a counterfactual in which it is assumed that the CBR falls to 20 and the CDR falls to 8 per 1,000 during 1958–63. This counterfactual effectively assumes that per capita incomes continued to rise, leading to both falling fertility and falling mortality.

(*c*) Official data on actual deaths and a counterfactual in which it is assumed that the CBR rises to 40 and the CDR falls to 8 per 1,000. This counterfactual assumes that higher per capita incomes led to falling mortality but to *rising* fertility (in contrast to case (*b*) above).

(*d*) The same counterfactual as in (*b*) is used, but it is assumed that official data understate true mortality. Estimates of actual deaths and 'normal' (or counterfactual) deaths for each year are in both cases multiplied by the ratio of the number of true deaths *nationally* (as estimated by Banister) to the number of deaths officially reported nationally. This involves increasing both actual and 'normal' deaths by a factor of between 1.4 and 1.75 depending on the year; the official figures understated true mortality by a different amount each year. The result is that the number of excess deaths increases very significantly. Note that the Banister approach accepts official estimates of total population but revises both fertility and mortality upwards. Note also that under-reporting *may* have been much less of a problem in Sichuan than in China as a whole.

2. Migration is estimated as the difference between the change in total provincial population and the natural growth rate given for each year. This figure, of course, takes no account of intra-provincial movements.

3. These calculations show that estimates of excess death are far more sensitive to revisions of death rates due to official under-reporting than to different estimates of 'normal' population. It does not greatly matter whether one assumes a crude birth rate of 20, 28.6, or 40 per 1,000 for the counterfactual, basically because the counterfactual death rate is very low; the number of counterfactual deaths is far more sensitive to changes in the death rate than to changes in the size of the population to which it is applied.

4. Sources: Sichuan data—ZGRKNJ (1985: 522–3). Banister national crude death rate—Banister (1984: 254). Official national crude death rate—ZGTJNJ (1987: 90).

1982 population census. The age composition of survivors established in this census shows the greater dearth of survivors in Sichuan for the years of the Leap than nationally.[3]

On the basis of all the evidence available to us, it therefore seems right to conclude that there was an unprecedented demographic catastrophe in Sichuan in the late 1950s and early 1960s. The number of excess deaths in the province was higher than anywhere else in China because the province entered the famine years with a bigger absolute population; therefore, the degree of excess mortality, between 8 million and 15 million, is quite staggering. This single Chinese province suffered a disaster of such a magnitude as to make most other modern famines, whether in China, the Soviet Union, India, or Africa, seem insignificant. Only the events in Kampuchea during the 1970s appear comparable in terms of severity, although the materials available to us on this are very unreliable.[4] Sichuan's famine was also the most intense, in that the increase in her death rate above the 1957 base level was greater than in any other province. Moreover, the estimates of excess deaths in Sichuan are conservative in that they are restricted to a relatively short time-span. They take no account of deaths in later years that were in part a long-run consequence of malnutrition during the Leap. Nor do they take into account the way malnutrition amongst child-bearing women during the Leap affected the life expectancy of their children. Whichever way one looks at it, this was disaster on a cataclysmic scale.

Variations in Mortality within Sichuan

There are several interesting features of the mortality crisis in Sichuan during the Leap. For one thing, there is no evidence that rich rural areas escaped the impact of the famine. In prosperous Shifang county, mortality was extremely high. Endicott is reluctant to speculate on the

---

[3] e.g. one can calculate the coefficient of variation for the number of 1982 survivors born between 1956–7 and 1964–5 for Sichuan and China. If the hypothesis of a more severe famine in Sichuan is correct, one would expect to find a much greater peak to trough variation—reflecting high mortality and low fertility during the trough as well as higher fertility post-trough, reflecting births postponed—than nationally. This is precisely what one does find. The coefficient of variation for Sichuan was 0.452 while for China it was only 0.285 (calculated from data on the 1982 census given in SCJJNJ, 1986: 272 and ZGRKNJ, 1985: 604).

[4] Kampuchea's total population is said to have fallen—fewer births, more deaths—by about 30% under the Khmer Rouge, compared to 10% for Sichuan during the Leap. See Shawcross (1985: 331). Becker puts the number of deaths caused by the revolution at about 2 million (1986: 20, 449).

precise details but concludes (1988: 56) that 'it was a tragedy of major proportions'. His data in fact show that the population of Lianglukou commune fell from 18,500 in 1957 to 15,500 in 1960 (p. 228), although this was in part due to out-migration and labour transfers. According to Lavely (1984: 369), infant mortality increased to 400 per 1,000 live births in Shifang's Nanquan commune, which was well in excess of Banister's estimate (1984: 254) of the true peak national figure of 284 in 1960. Furthermore, the crude birth rate was significantly higher in the immediate aftermath of the famine in Shifang at 5.7% (Lin and Zhou, 1981: 160) than the provincial average of 5% (ZGRKNJ, 1985: 523). This differential probably reflects a more severe famine, and hence greater birth postponement, in Shifang than in Sichuan as a whole, a remarkable finding given that the county was one of the most prosperous in the entire province. All this is confirmed by recently released mortality data on the entire county, which shows the crude death rate rising from 9.3 per 1,000 in 1957 to 58.3 in 1959 and a staggering 69 per 1,000 by 1960 (*Shifang xian zhi*, 1988: 4–11). This was some 15 points higher than the provincial average, and the famine intensity index (see Table 9.5) was an incredible 4.9, well above the provincial average of 3.2 and more than three times the national figure. Note also that the mortality peaks achieved in Shifang do not appear to have been desperately unusual by Sichuan standards. Further to the south in Jingyan county, a peak crude death rate of 67.7 was recorded in 1960 (*Jingyan xian zhi*, 1990: 99).

Secondly, and unsurprisingly, the limited data available suggest that urban death rates were lower than those in rural areas. Whatever else the Leap achieved, it did not eliminate this urban–rural differential. In Chongqing municipality, the peak death rate occurred in 1960 at 34.8 deaths per 1,000 (*Chongqing nianjian*, 1987: 330), compared to the provincial average of the 54.0 in the same year (Table 9.7). As the provincial figure includes urban areas whilst the Chongqing figure also includes the counties administered by the Chongqing municipality, this substantially understates the true urban–rural differential. This is clear if one looks at mortality trends in Neijiang city proper, which itself is in no sense comparable to the great cities of Chengdu, Chongqing, and Zigong. In Neijiang, the death rate peaked at 26.2 per 1,000 in 1960 (*Neijiang shi zhi*, 1987: 94) or less than half the provincial average. Indeed, that city's population continued to rise at a time when the province's population was falling. Only after 1960 did rising mortality begin to make inroads into Neijiang's population.

By contrast, the impact on ethnic minorities is rather surprising. It is true that the level of mortality suffered by the Tujia and Miao ethnic minorities in south-eastern Sichuan was shockingly high. The crude death rate in Youyang and Xiushan counties averaged 81.4 per 1,000 (Liu, 1988: 322) during 1959–61 compared to a provincial figure of 43.5 which, as has already been seen, was itself far above the national average. But the death rate amongst the ethnic minority population in western Sichuan was considerably below the provincial average. For the period 1959–61, the crude death rate was 38.6 per 1,000 for the Yi minority living in south-western Sichuan and only 11.2 for ethnic Tibetans living in Sichuan (Liu, 1988: 322). In Garze county, high on the Himalayan plateau, the crude death rate fell from 11 per 1,000 in 1957 to a mere 4 per 1,000 in 1961 (Zhongguo renkou xuehui, n.d.: 285).

One can think of reasons why mortality might have been lower in western Sichuan compared to the provincial average. For example, there is no evidence that Tibet suffered any demographic crisis during the Leap, and therefore food might have been shipped into Aba and Garze prefectures from the west. An alternative explanation is that communes were not established in these areas until the 1960s. Land reform was not completed in most parts of western Sichuan until 1957; and, although cooperatives were established at a remarkable pace, the region was far behind eastern Sichuan and this may have saved it from the fate of the latter.

Nevertheless, these mortality figures remain incredibly low and the explanation offered rather strained. It is true that there are roads linking western Sichuan to Tibet, but these are extremely dangerous, and the notion of effective famine relief by this means is frankly implausible, even supposing that Tibet had a grain surplus that it was prepared to disgorge for Sichuan's use. Moreover, the disruption caused by collectivization in western Sichuan could hardly have been less than that caused by the introduction of communes in the east. The pace of collectivization during 1958 was frantic, and the so-called democratic reforms of the mid-1960s had been enough to trigger off full-scale rebellion; it seems unlikely, therefore, that collectives were greeted with enthusiasm.[5] Most decisive of all, however, are the data collected in the 1982 census (ZGRKTJNJ, 1988: 658–61). These show that the crude death rate exceeded 11 per 1,000—that is, the alleged 1959–61 average—in 16 of the 31 counties in Garze and Aba prefectures as late as 1981. As it is most implausible that the death rate rose between the late 1950s and early 1980s, the only conclusion is that the mortality estimates provided for ethnic Tibetans in 1959–61 are fabricated.

[5] These issues are discussed at rather greater length in ch. 10.

The only systematic figures we have on spatial variations in the impact of the famine come from the same census source. This shows the age structure of the population in 1982 by prefecture. We can therefore compare the number of 'survivors' in the cohort aged between 20 and 24 in 1982 (i.e. those born between 1958 and 1962) as a percentage of the total 1982 population with the same percentage for the cohort aged 25 to 29 (those born between 1953 and 1957). A large fall in the percentage of 'survivors' indicates a particularly intense famine and vice versa (Table 9.9).

TABLE 9.9.　*The Spatial Impact of the 1958–1962 Sichuan Famine*

Prefecture	Survivors as % of 1982 population by year of birth		% change in cohort share
	1953–7	1958–62	
Chengdu	10.17	6.50	−36
Chongqing	10.94	6.72	−39
Zigong	10.17	5.14	−50
Dukou	8.14	5.68	−30
Yongchuan	9.87	5.28	−47
Wanxian	8.89	5.08	−43
Fuling	7.99	3.93	−51
Neijiang	9.02	4.65	−48
Yibin	9.63	5.25	−45
Leshan	9.04	4.64	−49
Wenjiang	10.13	5.07	−50
Mianyang	9.03	5.79	−36
Nanchong	9.22	5.15	−44
Daxian	8.56	4.97	−42
Ya'an	8.95	4.60	−49
Aba	7.39	6.04	−18
Garze	7.44	6.17	−17
Liangshan	7.05	5.06	−28
All Sichuan	9.20	5.24	−43
All China	9.22	7.41	−20

Sources: Sichuan's prefectures—Liu (1988: 230). All Sichuan—ZGRKNJ (1985: 766). All China—ibid. 604.

Several aspects of this table are interesting. For example, although spatial variation is evident, the experience is uniform in the sense that no prefecture was unaffected by the famine. Moreover, neither high-income status nor favourable economic geography did anything to diminish the impact of food shortages. It is particularly noteworthy that prosperous prefectures like Leshan and Wenjiang were amongst the worst hit; the general experience of the latter is supported by the evidence on one of its counties (Shifang) that has already been considered (although, paradoxically, Mianyang prefecture as a whole seems to have been much less badly affected). One might have expected a rich and relatively developed prefecture to possess a surplus above subsistence consumption that could have been traded in exchange for grain, and a transport infrastructure that would have made such trade possible, but plainly this did not happen. It is difficult to believe that this was due to transportation problems, although many otherwise rich counties were still inaccessible except by means of a rather primitive road network. The most plausible explanation is, of course, that prefectures were restricted in their freedom to engage in such market-oriented transactions.

Moreover, and on a related theme, there is little in the table to suggest that the provincial government played a key role in shipping grain from relatively well-off to relatively badly-off areas; such movements would tend to reduce spatial disparities in famine deaths. This policy lacuna can be explained in two ways. Suppose that, as seems likely, all parts of the province were badly hit. Accordingly, although there may have been a net saving of lives if grain had been moved from a moderately affected to a hard-hit area, if this shipment was perceived as likely to cause some additional deaths in the exporting area it would have been fiercely resisted, and such a measure would therefore have been impracticable. It should be said, however, that there is no evidence to support this contention. Indeed, one particular problem with it is that Sichuan continued to export grain to the USSR during the Leap, and yet there is no evidence of resistance to procurements. An alternative explanation is that we are wrong in assuming that the provincial government had a free hand in directing the allocation of grain. The period of the Leap was characterized by the over-statement of output by huge margins (Endicott, 1988; Goodman, 1986). If the provincial government believed the figures that it was being given by lower-level administrative units, it would have seen no cause to act. In any case, Sichuan's Party committee would have been vulnerable to criticism from the Central Committee (and particularly Mao) if it had actively promoted famine relief—whether justified or not—given that there was probably no national perception of crisis until it was too late. Whether the provincial Party committee was constrained by either of these considerations is not clear, but it is a possibility.

It is also worth noting that these data on age composition do lend some support to the idea of low mortality rates amongst those ethnic minorities living in western Sichuan. The very high mortality rates observed amongst Tujia and Miao minorities are captured in the experience of Fuling prefectures, whilst the low death rate amongst ethnic Tibetans is seemingly revealed in the Garze and Aba survivor ratios.[6]

In spite of all these interesting conjectures, the fact remains that they remain little more than guesses about spatial variations in mortality. There is no reason for supposing that the census results in Table 9.9 have been fabricated. However, all that table provides is a percentage figure for 'survivors'. That may not be a true indication of the spatial intensity of famine because, in some areas, the lower percentage may reflect greater birth postponement rather than high infant mortality (clearly, postponement is a famine 'cost', but presumably it is less important a cost than mortality). Moreover, as has been mentioned, 'survivor' percentages are sensitive to differences in migration rates between prefectures.

The Sichuan Famine in Historical Perspective

The evidence considered in this chapter indicates that the famine experienced in Sichuan between 1958 and 1962 was unique in both historical and comparative respects. There were famines in the province during the last decades of the Empire and throughout the Republican period, most noticeably in 1937. But severe though that famine was, the scale of excess mortality pales into insignificance alongside the catastrophe of the Leap, during which between 8 million and 15 million of the province's population met a premature death. Moreover, the Sichuan famine eclipsed in scale the famines that occurred during the same period elsewhere in China. Amongst the ethnic minority living in the south-eastern corner of the province, the crude death rate averaged over 80 per 1,000 during 1959–61. This was far in excess of the provincial average, and even exceeded Anhui's

[6] This may simply reflect greater in-migration by those born between 1958 and 1962 elsewhere in the province. Such persons would include the occupants of prison, labour, and military camps, which would be populated disproportionately by persons in this age group.

1960 mortality rate of 69 per 1,000. Moreover, the excess mortality crisis in Sichuan lasted much longer than in any other province, because it started much earlier and because mortality rates of over 40 per 1,000 were maintained throughout the 1959–61 period, in sharp contrast to the situations in Gansu and Anhui. We are fortunate that few eyewitness accounts of these horrors have survived.

10

Food Availability Decline and Institutional Change

The intensity of the famine in Sichuan does not of itself constitute an indictment of the Maoist development strategy. For that to be so, we need to establish a causal link between economic policy and the outcome. That is one purpose of this chapter. However, the Sichuan famine is also interesting in that it serves as an additional test of the bold hypothesis put forward by Amartya Sen that catastrophes of this sort are frequently caused, at least in part, by distributional factors rather than merely a decline in per capita food availability: 'starvation . . . is a function of entitlements and not of food availability as such. Indeed, some of the worst famines have taken place with no significant decline in food availability per head' (Sen, 1981: 7).

A recent article by the same author has looked at the Chinese famine in more detail (see also Dreze and Sen, 1989). There Sen has argued that the fall in food output associated with the Leap *need not* have led inexorably to famine. That it did so reflected the absence of critical freedom and contact with the outside world:

There was, of course, a very remarkable drop in food output per head after the Great Leap Forward (though not much more than in some parts of India in different years, e.g., in Maharashtra in 1973), but there was no major revision of economic policy, no alert anti-famine relief operation, and not even an official recognition of the existence of famine for a number of years. . . . this failure is certainly one connected closely with the absence of a relatively free press and the absence of opposition parties free to criticize and chastise the government in power. (Sen, 1989: 775–6)

If true, this diagnosis has important implications for government policy. In particular, it suggests that the goal of development would be better served if governments paid less attention to growth maximization and more both to distributional questions and to the establishment of genuine democracy.

The Food Supply Crisis of 1958?

The Sichuan famine began in 1958, with the crude death rate more than double its level in 1957 according to official population data. All the available sub-provincial data confirm this conclusion. In Chongqing municipality, for example, the crude death rate increased from 12.1 to 20.4 between 1957 and 1958 (*Chongqing nianjian*, 1987: 330). In Neijiang city proper, the rate increased from 8.6 to 16.1 per 1,000 over the same period (*Neijiang shi zhi*, 1987: 94). Data collected on Shifang county exhibit a similar trend; the 1958 rate was 23.1 per 1,000 compared to only 9.3 per 1,000 in 1957 (*Shifang xian zhi*, 1988: 4–5).

Peng, in his study of provincial trends during the Leap, concluded (1987: 662) that this increase could not be accounted for by a decline in food availability:

Massive excess deaths reportedly occurred in Sichuan Province in 1958. Provincial vital statistics show that the crude death rate rose from 12.07 in 1957 to 25.17 in 1958. The number of registered deaths was about 0.85 million in 1957, but the figure rose to 1.8 million in 1958. Available data suggest that a bumper harvest in 1958 actually increased per capita grain availability for both agricultural and nonagricultural populations. The provincial average may conceal some local shortages and famines, but such large excess mortality seems out of line with grain data. The cause of the sudden increase in mortality, whether spurious or grounded in unrecorded abnormal conditions, remains unknown.

To be sure, there were local shortages. In Shifang county on the Chengdu plain, total grain production was 8% higher in 1958 than in 1957 (*Shifang xian zhi*, 1988: 10–20). However, this conceals the fact that production in 1957 was well below the level achieved in 1956; thus per capita output stood at 761 and 763 *jin* in 1957 and 1958 respectively, compared to 900 *jin* in 1956 and an average of 845 *jin* for 1952–6 (pp. 4–5). One does well to interpret these figures carefully, however, because output fell as low as 629 *jin* per capita in 1968— much *lower* than the trough of the Great Leap Forward—and the crude death rate fell in the same year. On balance, then, this evidence suggests that there may be something in Sen's contention that distributional changes can play a more important role in precipitating famines than is generally thought. This is reinforced by my own calculations of grain supply per capita in Sichuan's urban and rural areas (Table 10.1).

Moreover, there is no convincing evidence of a decline in the supply

TABLE 10.1. *Grain Availability in Sichuan, 1955–1964*
(Jin *Per Capita of Unprocessed Grain)*[a]

	Farmers[b]	Non-farmers[c]
1955	493	546
1956	535	589
1957	499	575
1958	542	715
1959	341	737
1960	351	635
1961	333	545
1962	411	552
1963	471	552
1964	493	588

[a] The population denominators used are end-year estimates for the farm and non-farm populations respectively. These definitions differ somewhat from the rural/urban distinction that is also used by the Chinese: e.g. in 1958 Sichuan's farm population was 61.14 million and her rural population was 61.50 million. This reflects the presence of workers employed in state enterprises in the countryside.

These estimates are *not* figures for human consumption. Some of the grain available was used for seed, for animal feed, for industrial purposes, or for reserves, and some was lost in transit or storage. Changes in non-human consumption of grain may have played a role in causing the increase in mortality, as will be seen below.

[b] The farmer estimate is total output less net procurements (where the last term is gross procurements less rural resales) divided by farm population. Original data on procurements are in terms of trade grain (*maoyiliang*) or semi-processed grain. These have been converted back into unprocessed grain (*yuanliang*) to make them compatible with the output data which are cited in unprocessed units.

[c] The non-farmer figure is the grain *ration*. Some workers may have supplemented this by growing grain on small plots.

Sources: Population—SCSHTJZL (1989: 29–30). Non-farm rations— ZSSWY (1984: 566). Procurement data—ibid. 559–66. Grain output—ibid. 138.

of other foodstuffs. It is true that rice output (total and per capita) was lower in 1958 than in 1957, and the same is true of vegetable oil production. However, the number of pigs per head of population seems to have increased slightly, and the decline in rice production was offset by increased output of wheat and sweet potatoes. In aggregate, the gross values of crop production and animal husbandry at 1957 constant prices increased somewhat between 1957 and 1958 (SCJJNJ, 1986: 281–5). Moreover, national income-based estimates of consumption show an increase in real terms of 1.2% for farmers and 16.4% for non-farmers in 1958 (Zhongguo guojia tongjiju, 1987: 345).

Whether these data on farm output are credible, however, is another matter. Everything that we know happened in China during this period, such as the collapse of the system of statistical collection and the exaggerated claims of the early stages of the Leap, suggests that they are not to be taken too seriously. The output claims made in Anhui's Fengyang county are typical of the exaggeration that was commonplace during these years:

Gross output of grain was 150 million *jin* but 405 million *jin* was reported to higher authorities. . . . The actual area sown to flue-cured tobacco was 57,388 *mu*, but the amount reported to higher authorities was 137,400, or more than double. The actual number of hogs produced was 43,000 head but 166,000 head were reported to higher authorities . . .   (Wang, 1988: 11)

Endicott's research for Shifang in Sichuan suggests similar practices there. It was commonplace, for instance, for two account-books to be kept, one true and one false (Endicott, 1988: 59). Yet there is no question that the figures for the Leap published since 1978 have been much revised compared to the original official figures. The first estimate made for grain production in the province in 1958 was 90,000 million *jin*, but this was revised downwards to 64,600 million in September 1959 (Goodman, 1986: 98). By the 1980s, this had been reduced still further. The figures cited since 1978 have settled on 44,910 million *jin* as the true figure (ZSSWY, 1984: 138; SCJJNJ, 1986: 283). Moreover, the very fact that a true book of accounts was kept during the Leap suggests that these revised data may indeed be close to the truth. The only conclusion is, therefore, that the hypothesis that per capita grain availability fell during 1958 is not proven. In the absence of any tangible evidence to the contrary, we must accept the view that the increase in the death rate was not due to any decline in average food availability.

However, that is not the same is concluding that the onset of famine can be explained in distributional terms. For such a claim to be convincing, we need to show how and why the distribution of available foodstuffs might have altered to produce such a result. We also need to consider other non-food explanations for the increase in mortality.

Shifts in the Distribution of Food Supplies: The Crisis of 1958

An explanation that relies neither on a food availability decline (FAD) nor upon a shift in entitlements relates to events in western Sichuan during this period. We know that land reform, or what the Chinese called 'democratic reform' (*minzhu gaige*), began in the ethnic-minority areas of the province after 1956. It has been alleged that this triggered off a full-scale rebellion which in turn forced the Chinese to send in troops. In the subsequent fighting, and the bloody suppression of (predominantly Tibetan) resistance that followed, very high excess mortality occurred:

the PLA . . . counter-attacked with a full fourteen divisions—over 150,000 troops. By mid-1957, a ruthless pattern of attack and reprisal developed, turning much of Kham into a wasteland. From their fields in Kanze and Chengdu, waves of Ilyushin-28 bombers flew sorties across Kham, while huge mechanized columns moved overland shelling into rubble scores of villages. . . . by some accounts the Chinese lost 40,000 soldiers between 1956 and 1958. . . . their campaign . . . let loose a series of atrocities unparalleled in Tibet's history. The obliteration of entire villages was compounded by hundreds of public executions . . .   (Avedon, 1984: 47–8)

There is no reason to doubt that fighting did occur in western Sichuan during 1958. So much is admitted in Grunfeld's dispassionate (and, if anything, pro-Chinese) assessment of these events (1987: 128–9). Chinese accounts mention the killing of landlords and headmen during 1954–6 and during the subsequent *si fan* (the four overturns) campaign (GSL, 1985: 158, 163). If this triggered opposition, then the very rapid transition to collectivization during 1957 and 1958 (ASL, 1985: 147; GSL, 1985: 172–3) must have provoked revolt. Even in Han areas in eastern Sichuan (and eastern China), where the pace was much more gradual and where one would have expected more sympathy for Maoist objectives, there was considerable opposition.

Nevertheless, the events in western Sichuan cannot by themselves explain the 1958 mortality crisis. The increase in the crude death rate for the province *in toto* between 1957 and 1958 implies a total increase in deaths of about 800,000. That is a very large number to have been killed in a rebellion and subsequent atrocities, especially given that the total population of the three autonomous prefectures of western Sichuan (Aba, Garze, and Liangshan) numbered only about 1.5 million at the 1964 census.[1] A second problem is that sub-provincial evidence for the Sichuan basin in areas such as Chongqing, Shifang, Neijiang, and Jingyan also indicates a mortality increase in 1958. The mortality, then, was very much a provincial rather than a localized phenomenon.

A distributional hypothesis therefore seems to offer a more promising explanation, and this becomes even clearer when the issues are addressed in more detail. One such detail is that in 1958, the year in which the Leap was launched, a big increase in the urban population occurred as a result of migration, itself precipitated by an accelerated pace of urban industrialization and the removal of many migration controls. Thus between 1957 and 1958, the non-farm population increased by almost 11% whilst the farm population fell by about 0.5% (SCSHTJNJ, 1989: 29–30). In Shifang county the rural population fell from 88% of the total in 1957 to only 76% in 1958 (*Shifang xian zhi*, 1988: 4–11). In addition, many *ad hoc* brigades of volunteers were formed to carry out mineral prospecting and to create dams, embankments, and reservoirs in inaccessible mountain areas. All this had serious implications for guaranteeing food supplies, because it necessarily meant that much more grain had to be transported from grain-producing to grain-consuming areas. This reduced effective grain supply because of in-transit waste and the higher consumption demands of the workers involved in grain haulage (the absence of machinery made this very much a manual operation).

Even more importantly, this vast increase in the scale of the urban population was associated with the collapse of effective planning. The statistical system broke down after 1958 because of the decentralization of decision-making and the pressures placed on all levels of government to exaggerate output. There were also massive administrative changes. The most important was the establishment of the commune; these were formed by amalgamating co-operatives into *lianshe* (federated co-operatives) and thence into larger *dashe* which were communes in all but name (Goodman, 1986: 144–5). This process was completed in its entirety during the summer of 1958; by September, 177,259 higher-stage co-operatives had become 5,096 communes

[1] However, it is not impossible. There is a great tendency to disbelieve the stories told by refugees of atrocities, but we perhaps do well to remember that they are sometimes true. Those who escaped to Hong Kong after 1962 if anything understated the scale of the famine induced by the Great Leap Forward. Certainly, as was mentioned in the previous chapter, few Western academics took them seriously, even though post-1978 data have vindicated their story.

(ZSSWY, 1984: 207–8). At the same time, county boundaries changed in many cases. Sichuan had 208 county-level administrative units in 1957 (SCSHTJZL, 1989: 11). Fifteen of these were affected in 1958 by boundary changes or changes in the prefecture under whose control they were placed (Pu, 1986: 550–86).

In such circumstances, it is unlikely that the provincial government had reliable data on population size by location. The breakdown of the system of statistical reporting would not have mattered *per se* in the absence of migration and boundary changes; populations could have been estimated in its absence from historical data and trends. However, the combination of a breakdown in statistical collection, migration, and boundary changes was devastating. It must have been virtually impossible to fix tax and procurement quotas, and to ensure that adequate grain reached all these areas, especially given the demands this placed on an inadequate transport system. It is difficult to see how the result could have been anything except local food surpluses and shortages. The situation was one of endemic uncertainty, and we can therefore safely rule out the possibility that the spatial distribution of grain was 'correct'.

In addition, it is unrealistic to judge the adequacy of food availability without reference to its demand. It is, of course, tempting to assume that grain demand remained constant during this period, yet there is no good reason for making any such assumption. The defining characteristic of these years in both Sichuan and China was the economic optimism radiated by government. Peasants were positively encouraged to believe that the economic problem was essentially solved. The upshot must have been a big increase in the demand for fine grains such as wheat and rice, a tendency to waste coarse grains such as sweet potatoes—why eat this when rice was supposedly available in abundance?—and greater use of grain for both seed and feed purposes. Moreover, this was a period of rapid industrial expansion, not least of the food processing industry. For example, the volume of grain (*maoyiliang*) used for industrial purposes and as an urban feedstuff increased from 371 million *jin* in 1957 to 843 million *jin* in 1958, an increase of 127%. Total urban grain use increased by only 47% over the same period (ZSSWY, 1984: 566).

At least as significant from a demand-side perspective was the enormous increase in activity rates in the province during 1958, particularly in the countryside. Many more women were mobilized to work full-time in the labour force, and the traditional winter slack season was effectively abolished; instead, the labour force was mobilized to establish rural iron and steel industries and for water conservancy projects. The scale of the Leap in 1958 was staggering. A provincial iron and steel office was established in 1958, and this presided over an increase in iron production from 280,000 tonnes in 1957 to 580,000 in 1958. In Shifang county the target for iron production for 1959 was set at 5,000 tonnes compared to a 1958 target of only 1,100 tonnes. More remarkably, actual output increased from 385 tonnes in 1958 to 2,786 tonnes in 1959; although this fell well below the target, it still amounted to an impressive increase (*Shifang xian zhi*, 1988: 9–3). During 1958, provincial production of all types of steel rose from 720,000 to 950,000 tonnes (SCJJNJ, 1986: 293) and the number of iron- and steel-making plants (even excluding small-scale rural enterprises) rose from 139 to 689 (ZSSWY, 1984: 377–8). This increase in turn required an enormous effort to raise energy production, and a big increase was indeed achieved. Coal output increased from 7.7 million tonnes in 1957 to 20.3 million the following year (ZSSWY, 1984: 272) and that of timber from 1.5 million square metres to 2.7 million (SCJJNJ, 1986: 294). Industrial expansion at this speed in turn required an enormous investment in construction. Real net expenditure in the construction sector increased by 179% in 1958, and its share in net material product rose from 3.5 to 8.9% (Zhongguo guojia tongjiju, 1987: 342–3) and investment in factory floor space, which was running at about 500,000 square metres in 1957, increased more than fivefold to 2.6 million in 1958 (Gao, 1987: 301).

It is easy to assume that an increase in the number of hours of labour time supplied is unambiguously good because such labour must be fed whether active or not; it therefore makes sense to mobilize it for productive purposes. Unfortunately, this treatment ignores the impact of higher activity rates on calorific demand. This is far from trivial. A WHO/FAO study assumed that a 'very active' member of the population requires 17% more food than a 'moderately active' person (World Bank, 1983: iii. 119). Whilst the figure itself is, of course, a matter for debate, there can be no question that a sedentary person requires far fewer calories than one involved all day in manual labour. The higher death rate in 1958 was probably due to some extent to the impact of markedly higher activity rates—there is no other way of describing the first year of the Leap—combined with virtual stagnation in per capita food availability.

Of course, much of this non-FAD explanation for the increase in provincial mortality during 1958 is speculative. It would be better if more hard microlevel evidence were available to support these macroconclusions. Nevertheless, a Sen-type explanation of the Sichuan famine of 1958 is not unconvincing. Indeed, it is reinforced by the fact of a supply-side crisis in the province in 1956–7, when the pace of industrialization and institutional transformation in the countryside was far slower than in 1958. In part this crisis was caused by over-emphasis on grain production, which led to shortage of other key inputs. However, there was also a severe transport crisis, which precipitated a series of emergency measures:

During the second half of 1956 and the beginning of 1957 Sichuan's leaders explicitly admitted that in general supply did not meet demand . . . despite improvements in the province's transport and distribution system, there was still in 1956, as Li Dazhang [*the provincial governor*] put it, 'a contradiction between the amount of material resources and the province's transport capacity'. . . . Within the province, measures were . . . taken to alleviate the situation. In industry, enterprises which had hoarded material resources (in response to shortages) were encouraged to make their surplus stock available in a series of mutually helpful reallocation meetings. An attempt was made to make the transport system more efficient, both by the provision and by the more efficient utilization of vehicles. A two-shift system was introduced and routes were adjusted so that vehicles should not return empty after delivery. Finally, a campaign was started to use 'the popular forms of transport—oxen, pack-horses, carts—as one way of making up the deficiencies and solving the problems of transport capacity'; and surplus labour was encouraged to participate in short-distance transportation. (Goodman, 1986: 50–1)

If this was the situation in 1956–7, when the growth rate was slow and provincial co-ordination relatively successful, the likelihood of chaos amidst the decentralization of the Great Leap Forward seems high.

The Food Availability Decline after 1958

The most important issue in identifying the causes of the intensity of the Sichuan famine during the late 1950s and early 1960s is to explain why it was so much more severe than the famines that happened simultaneously in other parts of China. Of course, Sichuan is interesting in its own right, but the identification of the unique combination of factors which were present in the province's case is even more important. For example, was the Sichuan disaster primarily a distributional phenomenon as it was in 1958? Or was the food availability decline more severe in the province's case than nationally? If so, why was the decline in food supply so catastrophic? Was the province more 'Maoist' than the national norm, or was the share of accumulation in NDMP higher?

314   *Food Availability Decline*

One thing that we may be sure of is that the decline in output was more pronounced in Sichuan than it was nationally (Table 10.2). That this unrelievedly bleak picture was in such striking contrast to the expectations voiced by the Politburo before the Leap etched the failure in even sharper perspective than these figures taken in isolation. The only real pre-Leap question for Mao was how long it would take for China to catch up with Britain. By 1962, the issue of whether China could catch up at all in less than, say, a century was no longer seriously discussed. The more pessimistic appraisals offered by Chen Yun, Sun Yefang, and others had been dismissed almost out of hand by Mao in his assessment of the co-operative movement. His talk was of growth aping the flight of Soviet satellites and the ease with which chicken feathers could reach the heavens. One only needed to dare to think and to do; the rest, for the new socialist man, was easy:

The reason the well-to-do peasants dared trot out such moth-eaten proverbs as 'chicken feathers can't fly up to heaven' was because . . . the Party had not yet pointed out why, in the era of socialism, the ancient truism . . . is no longer true.

The poor want to remake their lives. The old system is dying. A new system is being born. Chicken feathers really are flying up to heaven. In the

TABLE 10.2. *The Collapse of Output*[a]

	NDMP		NVAO		NVIO	
	China	Sichuan	China	Sichuan	China	Sichuan
1957	105[b]	111	103	110	112	114
1958	128	127	103	110	175	143
1959	138	121	86	84	229	185
1960	136	108	72	56	247	212
1961	96	74	73	55	144	108
1962	89	76	76	75	122	89
1963	99	85	85	83	137	104

[a] Output value indices, comparable prices: 1956 = 100. Output at comparable prices here is a linked series of output at 1957 and 1970 constant prices.

[b] In view of the unreliability of the data, it seems pointless to quote indices to even 1 decimal point.

Sources: Population—ZGRKNJ (1985: 522); ZGTJNJ (1989: 87). Output— Zhongguo guojia tongjiju (1987: 343); ZGTJNJ (1989: 30).

Soviet Union they have already got there. In China they've started their flight. Chicken feathers are going to soar up all over the world. (Mao, 1957: 138)

To be sure, the growth of industrial output in Sichuan was initially impressive, its value climbing to more than double the 1956 level by 1960. However, the decline thereafter was equally dramatic, with a fall in output of almost 50% in 1961 alone. Moreover, much of the initial increase in industrial output was probably spurious. It is difficult to believe that, in a market economy, the price of the poor-quality iron and steel products would have been anything but extremely low. In agriculture, the picture was rather different but equally uninspiring. There were not even gains during the initial stages of the Leap, and output value fell to a low point of barely half its 1956 level. With population falling quickly but at a much slower rate than output in either farm or industrial sectors, per capita output also plummeted.

The evidence on output trends in various parts of Sichuan during the Leap confirm this macro-assessment. In urban Neijiang, agricultural output value fell from its pre-Leap peak of 13.9 million *yuan* to 7.7 million by 1961 (*Neijiang shi zhi*, 1987: 287). In Ziyang county, the fall was equally dramatic. At 1980 constant prices, GVAO stood at 45.8 million *yuan* in 1961, compared to 99.5 million in 1957 (Ziyang xian nongye quhua weiyuanhui, 1985). Over the same period, GVAO fell from 68.5 to 36.5 million *yuan* in Qionglai county (on the southern edge of the Chengdu plain) (*Sichuan sheng jingji yuce shiliji*, 1986: 169–71). In Shifang, GVAO was only 37.6 million *yuan* in 1961 compared to 57.9 million in 1957, whilst grain production in the same year stood at barely 67% of its level in 1958 (*Shifang xian zhi*, 1988: 10–13). Further south, in Jingyan county, grain output even in 1962 was only 54% of its level in 1957 (*Jingyan xian zhi*, 1990: 173). Even the massive effort devoted to coal production came to naught. In Hechuan county's Sanhui township, 572 workers were employed producing 23,174 tonnes of coal in 1951. Under the direction of the province's coal industry office established in 1958, employment and output rose rapidly. In that year, no fewer than 3,068 workers were employed producing 151,495 tonnes of coal, and output increased slightly until 1960. Unfortunately, this level could not be sustained: by 1965, the firm employed only 539 workers, and its output of coal had fallen back to a mere 46,024 tonnes (Du and Zhang, 1986: 201–3).

The national trend was in general similar to that in Sichuan (although the timing of the turning-points was slightly different). Output, especially in the industrial sector, grew very quickly at the beginning of the Leap, whereas agricultural output remained stagnant. After

1959 the output decline was marked, with industrial output halving in 1961. In the farm sector the collapse in output was less dramatic but equally apparent. Nevertheless, the national trough was much less deep than in the provincial case. The index of Sichuan's NVAO levelled out at 55, whereas the national minimum was 73. The comparative figures for the industrial sector show a provincial nadir of 89 compared to 122 nationally. In other words, we can reasonably conclude that the fall in output was more pronounced in Sichuan's case, and this immediately gives us a clue as to why the famine was more severe there.

Unsurprisingly, an output collapse of the magnitude of that occurring in the early 1960s led to a massive decline in food availability in both China and in Sichuan. Table 10.1 shows this shortfall very clearly. In terms of the province taken as a whole, grain output per capita dropped from 634 *jin* in 1958 to only 353 *jin* in 1961. Over the same period, vegetable oil production per capita fell from 10.5 to 5.0 *jin* and the number of pigs per capita from 0.37 to 0.17. The total number of pigs in the province, the principal source of meat, declined from 26 to 11 million during these years (SCJJNJ, 1986: 284–5).

To facilitate a comparison of trends in food availability, national and provincial data are presented in Table 10.3. The picture here is one of a decline in food availability per head during the Leap that was undoubtedly more severe in Sichuan than in China. The provincial trough occurred in 1961 at 1,354 Kcal per capita per day, an extremely low figure for a population heavily engaged in manual work. By comparison, the national low-water mark was 1,578 Kcal, almost 200 Kcal higher. Moreover, the provincial food availability decline was sustained for a much longer period. For four years in a row, Sichuan's calorie supply fell below 1,700 Kcal per capita on average, whereas for China the consumption level fell below that line in only a single year. The average shortfall (a notional subsistence line of 2,000 Kcal less actual consumption averaged over the 1957 to 1963 period) in Sichuan was 277 Kcal per day, more than three times the national figure of 88 Kcal. This is important, because it is a *sustained* collapse in food availability that often creates a very severe famine.

It is clear, therefore, that the decline in the supply of food was much more marked in Sichuan than nationally, and that this provides the immediate explanation of the relative severity of the province's famine after 1958. Distributional factors may also have played a part, but it is manifest that in the case of this famine the contribution of a decline in food availability was extremely important. The next stage in the analysis is to identify the underlying causes for this relatively severe provincial supply crisis.

TABLE 10.3.   *Food Availability during the Leap in Sichuan and China*

	Grain output per capita[a] (kg. per annum)		Calories consumed per capita[bc] (Kcal per day)	
	Sichuan	China	Sichuan	China
1957	309	308	1,955	2,217
1958	318	306	2,176	2,248
1959	226	255	1,641	1,854
1960	198	215	1,422	1,578
1961	176	223	1,354	1,763
1962	222	241	1,684	1,867
1963	256	249	1,827	1,857

[a] Grain output data refer to unprocessed grain. The figure given for 1957 is an average for 1956–7. *Source*: Peng (1987: 653).

[b] Calorie consumption data (from all types of food) on China are from Piazza (1986: 83). For Sichuan, they are calculated as follows: (1) Begin with the per capita calorie consumption data given for 1975–8 in Bramall (1989*a*). (2) Assume that the % of output used for seed, feed, and industrial production and 'lost' in the form of waste was the same during the Leap as it was in the late 1970s. (3) Adjust the 1975–8 data to allow for the lower output and lower population levels of the Leap. Output data are given in SCJJNJ (1986: 283–5) for the Leap. Trends in peanut and sugar cane output can be proxied by the trend in vegetable oil output. (4) Subtract from these gross data net provincial exports of grain. Data on these are available in ZSSWY (1984). (5) Assume that meat consumption was double that of 1975–8 for 1959–62 inclusive. This arbitrary assumption takes account of the definite increase in pig-slaughtering that took place in response to famine conditions. It adds at most 40 Kcal per capita per day to consumption. (6) Arbitrarily assume that no more than 100 Kcal per capita per day derived from vegetables, fruit, and famine foods (berries and the like).

[c] In making these estimates for calorie consumption we must recognize that the exercise is speculative in several respects, in that we know very little that is concrete for this period. Nevertheless, it is unlikely that a more careful analysis will markedly alter the general pattern.

Causes of the Food Availability Decline

It is a great strength of Sen's work on famine that he asks the right questions. In the case of the Sichuan famine, these centre on the reasons for the food availability decline and, at least as importantly, the question of whether that by itself made famine inevitable. Much of Sen's work suggests that this need not be so if the state is prepared to play an enlightened interventionist role, and therefore these issues deserve a careful examination. Initially, however, the causes of the FAD (food availability decline) will be considered.

As a matter of arithmetic, output is the product of sown area and yield per unit area, and this makes it easy to identify the proximate causes of the output decline, for although there is still a dearth of information, it is clear that both sown area and yields fell after 1958. The fall in grain-sown area seems to have been particularly marked; for the entire province, grain-sown area in 1962, despite strenuous attempts to increase it in response to famine deaths, was still only 142 million *mu*, well below the 1957 area of 166 million. The area sown to cash and other crops in the same year was 17.7 million *mu*, again well down on the 1957 figure of 26 million *mu* (ZSSWY, 1984: 135). In some parts of the province, the decline in grain-sown area seems to have been even more marked. In Jingyan county, for example, grain-sown area was 662,000 *mu* in 1962, or only about 77% of its 1957 level of 859,000 *mu*; cash crop-sown area over the same period fell even more dramatically, from 41,700 *mu* to a mere 14,037 *mu* (*Jingyan xian zhi*, 1990: 173, 176).

More systematic data are available for Shifang county (Table 10.4). These show that grain yields held up very well up to and during 1959,

TABLE 10.4. *Grain Output, Yield, and Area in Shifang during the Leap*

	Output (million *jin*)	Sown area (*mu*)	Yield (*jin* per sown *mu*)
1957	211.3	567,651	372
1958	228.5	586,646	389
1959	189.0	488,880	387
1960	185.1	509,899	363
1961	160.2	528,785	303
1962	165.6	534,015	310
1963	187.2	537,200	348

Source: *Shifang xian zhi* (1988: 10–20).

when the grain yield was 387 *jin* per *mu* compared to 408 in 1956 and 372 in 1957. Only in 1961 and 1962 did yields collapse. The decline in grain-sown area was particularly marked much earlier. Although it actually increased in 1958 compared to 1957, area fell by no less than 17% in 1959, from 587,000 *mu* in 1958 to 489,000 *mu* in the following year, and the figure was little higher in 1960. By contrast, the area sown to cash crops seems to have held up rather better. The oil crop-sown area in 1961 was only about 9% lower than in 1957, whereas the yield was some 25% lower; the 1960 yield was more than 40% below the level for 1959 (*Shifang xian zhi*, 1988: 10–28).

The *underlying* causes of the decline in yields and sown area are more difficult to identify. An enormous effort has already been put in by Maoist apologists to show that the primary culprit was nothing more sinister than the indifferent weather experienced throughout China during the Leap. According to Crook and Crook (1966: 87), for example, 'The climatic conditions in 1959 throughout China were the worst for decades. Those of 1960 proved to be the worst in over a century.'

Sichuan certainly was affected by poor weather. Comparing rainfall during May–September for Shifang and Guanghan counties during 1959, 1960, and 1961 (Endicott, 1988: 229) with the average for Chengdu for 1951–80 (ZGTJNJ, 1987: 16), it is evident that rainfall was at least 20% higher than normal. Alternatively, if one looks at the month of June, the normal volume of rainfall was 111 mm. Yet in 1959 and 1960 there was drought, with only 25 and 56 mm. of rainfall in the equivalent month. By contrast, fully 588 mm. fell in 1961. This degree of climatic variation must have had severe consequences for the summer harvest. In other parts of the province, rainfall was also abnormal. In Xichong county, rainfall in 1959 was lower than in any year between 1959 and 1980 (710 mm. compared to an average of 967 mm.) (*Xichong wenshi ziliao xuanji*, 1985: 4). In Youyang county, the 47-day drought of 1960 was the longest of the post-1949 period (*Youyang Tujiazu Miaozu zizhixian gaikuang* 1986: 11). In Jingyan, some 79,000 *mu* were affected by drought, of which 34,000 were classified as disastrously affected (i.e. yields were more than 30% below normal); this amounted to about 6% of cultivated area (*Jingyan xian zhi*, 1990: 78). Even so, it is difficult to believe that the severity of Sichuan's food availability decline can be explained in this fashion. For one thing, Endicott found that few of the villagers he talked to in Shifang were willing to attribute much blame to climate; none mentioned serious flooding during the Leap. Moreover, climatic conditions were also abnormal in many other parts of China, and yet the famine was most severe in Sichuan. For example, there was no famine in Yangyi commune in Hebei province despite poor weather (Crook and Crook, 1966: ch. 8).

In any case, leading members of the Party have been increasingly willing to admit the part played by 'other factors'. Even at the time, this much was recognized. The most celebrated example was at the meeting at Lushan in July and August of 1959 (the Lushan Plenum), when Peng Dehuai sent his famous letter to Mao:

It now seems that some projects for capital construction in 1958 were too hasty or excessive, with the result that a portion of capital was tied up and some essential projects were delayed. This is a drawback, and the basic cause for this is lack of experience. We had not understood this sufficiently, and when we understood it, it was too late. As a result, in 1959, instead of slowing down a bit and appropriately controlling the speed, the Great Leap Forward was pushed ahead.   (Peng, in Howe and Walker, 1989: 88–9)

Yet the novelty of Peng's intervention lay in the boldness with which he stated his opinion rather than in the analysis *per se*. Few at Lushan dissented from the view that mistakes had been made during the Leap, and indeed Mao had admitted as much in February 1959 (see Selden, 1979: 467). Like Peng, Mao also focused on the excessive level of accumulation that was taking place, especially in the country-side: 'a good many communes and counties have extracted too much capital accumulation from the production brigades and, moreover, the administrative expenditures of the communes include a great deal of waste' (Mao, Feb. 1959, cited in Selden, 1979: 472).

The economic logic underlying this critique, though not explicitly stated, is clear. If the share of investment in national income was raised, that of consumption had to fall as a matter of arithmetic, except in the unlikely event of the investment involving extremely short gestation periods and hence an almost immediate increase in consumer good production. Hence consumption levels were almost bound to fall initially in any investment drive, a consequence well recognized in models of growth in 'socialist' economies as different as those of Feldman and Kalecki. This is what seems to have happened during the Leap. The bulk of new accumulation went into the con-struction of new coal-mines, iron and steel plants, and into ambitious new water conservancy projects. Moreover, the production of coal, iron, and steel in itself constituted capital formation; none of these (coal was not used for domestic heating purposes except in the cities of north-eastern China) were consumption goods.

All this was seen by Mao and other economic planners, with some justification, as being a *sine qua non* for the modernization of the rural economy. In practice, however, the long-run benefits were slow to materialize. There is no question that a good deal of learning by doing did take place in the countryside which was to yield great benefits later on, when rural industrialization began again in the late 1960s and early 1970s. In that sense, the Leap did achieve something. However, the capital goods produced in the furnaces and mines that littered the countryside were generally of extremely low quality and were fit for very little. Moreover, in that most of the iron and steel products were simply domestic cooking utensils resmelted, the net addition to the capital stock was not as great as some accounts of the Leap imply. Far more serious, however, were the implications of this programme for the farm sector. The iron and steel that was produced was largely irrelevant to the needs of the farm sector, which required increased chemical fertilizers and higher-yielding varieties rather than premature mechanization if the yields of grain were to be increased more quickly than the rural population. Moreover, the programme involved not only negligible benefits but also unmistakable costs. The production of iron and steel is highly energy-intensive, and because many parts of China were neither blessed with coal deposits nor able to 'import' coal from elsewhere because of crippling transport shortages, such production tended to entail deforestation. The long-run implications of this were in turn severe. The very high run-off rates that deforestation engendered increased the vulnerability of large tracts of arable land to flooding. They also increased the silt content of river, streams, and reservoirs, which in turn much diminished the efficiency of hydroelectricity generation, sluices, and pumps.

A different way of looking at the implications of the Leap is in terms of intersectoral labour allocation. The key input in rural China in the 1950s was the labour force, and therefore sectoral output was essentially an increasing function of its labour inputs. China's planners were, of course, aware of this. They also recognized that an unbalanced growth strategy along the lines of the Leap would inevitably take productive labour away from direct farm activities for other purposes. If farm output was not to fall in the process, it was essential that the productivity of the remaining farm labour-force was increased significantly or that the participation rate of the farm population increased. In practice, even though much was talked about the ability of the newly liberated peasant to raise his productivity under the leadership of the Party, the planners' main hope for 'squaring the circle' was the mobilization of women. As in most agrarian societies, women were frequently employed in the fields during peak harvest periods in rural China, but the Maoists hoped that their all-year participation could be guaranteed by the communal provision of child-care facilities and canteens. If this could be achieved, it was perfectly possible to increase the share of capital formation in net material product without having to depress per capita consumption levels. Moreover, the decline in grain-sown area that occurred after 1958 reflected a belief that the grain problem had been solved (or, at least, would be very soon) by yield growth. Accordingly, there was less need to 'waste' labour in cropping land that was no longer necessary to ensure adequate grain supplies. In practice, however, matters were rather more complex. Even at the height of the labour mobilization campaign (1958–9) there were acute labour shortages because of the sheer scale of non-farm industrialization and construction. Moreover, the mobilization of women on the required scale could not be sustained in the long run because of opposition by both men and women to the *de facto* abolition of the family.

In the specific case of Sichuan, the scale of the accumulation campaign undertaken during the Leap is shown in Table 10.5. The absolute magnitudes involved are, of course, distinctly suspect. These data have all been reconstructed since 1978 on the basis of the highly unreliable materials collected during the Leap. Moreover, it is unclear to what extent labour accumulation in the countryside, especially the digging of new wells and canals and the building of roads, has been included in the accumulation figure. Nevertheless, the very swift increase in the accumulation share in the initial years, and its dramatic collapse in the early 1960s, does conform with everything that we know about events in the countryside during these years; and therefore the trends are instructive.

However, 'excessive accumulation' does not adequately explains why the food availability decline was so much greater in Sichuan than elsewhere in China, for it is obvious from Table 10.5 that the share was much higher nationally than in Sichuan. The national peak came at 44% in 1959, whereas in the province accumulation as a percentage of NDMP never exceeded 35%. Moreover, the decline in grain-sown area in Sichuan—which can be used as a proxy for the diversion of labour from the farm to the non-farm sector—does not appear to have been very different from the national pattern in the early stages of the Leap (Walker, 1984: 150–1).

In a sense, of course, this point may be spurious, in that a given accumulation share might have had more deleterious effects in Sichuan than nationally because the initial level of per capita consumption was lower in the province. If there was a bigger 'surplus above necessary

TABLE 10.5. *Accumulation in Sichuan and China, 1957–1963*

	Total accumulation[a] (million *yuan*)		Accumulation share (% of NDMP)	
	Sichuan	China	Sichuan	China
1957	1,263	23,300	18	25
1958	1,937	37,900	24	34
1959	3,043	55,800	35	44
1960	2,301	50,100	29	40
1961	72	19,500	1	19
1962	−528[b]	9,900	−8	10
1963	588	18,300	7	18

[a] Total accumulation (*jilei*) is in current prices. The accumulation share is the total value of accumulation as a % of the total value of NDMP (*guomin shouru*), both at current prices. This somewhat overstates the share of gross investment in GDP. E.g. the accumulation share in China in 1984 was 31.5% (ZGTJNJ, 1987: 59), whilst the World Bank (1986b: 188) estimated the investment share for that same year as being 30%.

[b] This negative figure presumably reflects depreciation. The animal stock figure for that year actually shows an increase compared to 1961.

Sources: Sichuan—SCJJNJ (1986: 30). China—ZGTJNJ (1987: 59).

consumption' in China than in Sichuan, the dramatic national fall from a relatively high base might have been more easily accommodated. There is some evidence to support this hypothesis. Per capita net material consumption, measured in current prices, in Sichuan stood at only 86 *yuan* in 1957 compared to 107 *yuan* in China (ZGTJNJ, 1989: 29, 36; Zhongguo guojia tongjiju, 1987: 337, 341). However, as food prices were lower in Sichuan than nationally, it is doubtful whether the current-price consumption comparison is a good guide to true relative consumption levels. Moreover, whilst average per capita calorie consumption was marginally higher nationally than in the province (Table 10.3, p. 317), the difference is not particularly striking given the margins of error associated with the calculations of these food-consumption figures.

In addition, we need to recognize that this was not the only period in Sichuan's post-1949 history during which the accumulation rate was high. The average rate for 1969–73 was 28.9%, compared to only

26.2% during 1957–60 (Zhongguo guojia tongjiju, 1987: 337). A greater proportion of the former was financed out of the national rather than the provincial budget, which would necessarily imply a relatively lower effective tax rate in 1969–73 than the accumulation figures imply. However, the difference (86% of fixed investment financed out of the national budget in 1957–60 compared to 92.6% in 1969–73—Gao, 1987: 415–16) is not so great as to indicate that the larger investment effort in the later period imposed a smaller 'burden' upon consumption than in the earlier period. The same comments apply to the *structure* of fixed investment. About 64% of fixed investment was in the heavy industrial sector during 1966–75, somewhat less than the 72% finding its way to that sector during 1958–62. Again, the difference in the order of magnitude is not so great as to be decisive. On balance, this suggests to me that the scale of accumulation in Sichuan during the Leap was not primarily responsible for the decline in food availability.

An alternative hypothesis is that the Sichuan food availability decline was primarily a consequence of the export of grain. In other words, per capita output was adequate but a large proportion of it was diverted from non-domestic consumption. This contains an element of truth, in that Sichuan did continue to export grain, mainly to the Soviet Union, even in the depths of the famine. But, as Table 10.6 demonstrates, there is no evidence that the post-1958 food availability decline was *precipitated* by a big sudden *increase* in net provincial grain exports.

Almost 10% of provincial grain output was being transferred to other provinces and other countries even in 1959–60, when the level of per capita was already low. Most of this grain was being used to pay off China's debts to the Soviet Union. In 1959, Sichuan exported almost 89 million *yuan* worth of goods to the Soviet Union, out of total exports to all countries valued at 92 million *yuan* (ZSSWY, 1984: 589, 591). The precise value of grain exports to the USSR is not known, but in that same year the total value of Sichuan's grain and vegetable oil exports was 55 million *yuan*. This fell sharply in 1960, but even then, grain and vegetable oil exports were valued at nearly 16 million *yuan* and total exports to the USSR were still 63 million *yuan*. However, it needs to be pointed out that net exports as a percentage of output were higher on average during 1956–7, and yet there was no significant food availability decline in those years. In short, grain exports did nothing to alleviate famine, but it is not clear that they were the direct cause of the food availability decline (the indirect implications of forcing producers to export grain for incen-

TABLE 10.6.   *The Share of Net Sichuan Grain Exports in Output,*
1954–1963

	Net grain exports[a] (billion *jin* of unprocessed grain)	Grain output (billion *jin* of unprocessed grain)	Export share (%)
1954	2.159	38.06	5.7
1955	4.064	39.21	10.4
1956	5.563	43.12	12.9
1957	7.497	42.61	17.6
1958	4.118	44.91	9.2
1959	4.278	31.64	13.5
1960	3.161	26.79	11.8
1961	0.561	23.10	2.4
1962	−0.537[b]	28.70	−1.8
1963	1.086	34.01	3.2

[a] Net exports are outflows to other provinces and abroad, less inflows. These are given in the original source in terms of trade grain (*maoyiliang*), but have been converted into unprocessed grain for the purposes of this table, using data on gross procurements given in both unprocessed and processed grain in ZSSWY (1984: 559, 561). The conversion ratio is different for every year, reflecting the changing composition of grain procurements.
[b] A minus sign denotes a net inflow.

Source: ZSSWY (1984: 138, 571).

tives needs some consideration—see below). We really want to know why *production* was falling in the first place in the late 1950s.

Famine and Institutional Change

This leaves us with institutional change as the most likely explanation of the decline in food availability in Sichuan during this period. The most important change in the rural sector during this period was the establishment of People's Communes after 1958 and, crucially, the renumeration systems operated within them. This immediately opens up the possibility that the restructuring of the incentive system that took place had adverse effects upon productive enthusiasm and therefore led to a marked decline in per capita output.

Even Mao, no advocate of gradualism, admitted that the transition from collectives to communes had not been a smooth one, and recognized the importance of material incentives in stimulating productivity:

Even now there are a good many people who still don't recognise that the system of ownership by the commune must go through a process of development. Within the commune there needs to be a process of transition from ownership by a small collective, the production brigade, to ownership by a large collective, the commune, and this process requires a period of several years before it can be completed . . . They mistake socialism for communism, they mistake distribution according to labour for distribution according to need . . . In many places they deny the law of value and deny the necessity for exchange at equal value. Thus, within the confines of the commune they carry out the levelling of the poor and the rich, and equal distribution. (Mao, February 1959, in Selden, 1979: 470)

The logic of this interpretation is that, if the process of egalitarianism went further, if the transition to communalization was faster, and if the retreat therefrom after 1959 was slower in Sichuan than elsewhere in China, the severity of famine in the province would have been relatively greater.

To some extent, however, this view of the commune is in error. Although the evidence is rather patchy, there seems no doubt from Western accounts of the Leap (Crook and Crook, 1966; Hinton, 1983; Endicott, 1988) that many peasants voluntarily entered communes, and that they were genuinely motivated by the vision of 'building socialism'. Notions of abnegation of self, and the rejection of materialism, were undoubtedly popular, not least because they were being propagated by a Party (and in particular a leader) which had enjoyed an unbroken series of political, military, and economic successes going back to the early 1930s. If many peasants remained uneasy about the process, some were nevertheless prepared to give the central leadership of the Party the benefit of the doubt. Accordingly, the existence or otherwise of material-incentive systems was largely irrelevant to the achievement of a high level of labour productivity in the short term in some parts of China.

On balance, however, not too much should be made of these examples. Mao, after all, was the foremost advocate of the commune, and the leader least inclined to pay much attention to any evidence to the contrary. Accordingly, the very fact that he was critical of the process suggests that the evidence of an adverse impact on labour productivity was too widespread to be ignored.

Sichuan was one such area, because there the transition to the commune was remarkably swift. This was in marked contrast to the pace of collectivization, which was much slower in the province than the national average. Communes were universal in rural Sichuan as early as September 1958 (Goodman, 1986: 144). Moreover, they were very 'advanced', i.e., egalitarian in their methods of distribution. From the start, the province's communes generally incorporated a wide range of non-farm activities, including communal eating, education and medical services, and nurseries (p. 149). In addition, household sideline activities were abolished at an early stage, and the production brigade rather than the team was the basic unit of account. All these features led Mao to designate Sichuan as one of the three 'Leftist provinces' in August 1959 (p. 96). Goodman summarized the province's radicalism thus (p. 158):

Early in 1959, Mao had advocated the production team as the base in the consolidation of the communes, yet Sichuan opted for the production brigade. Later on, Mao had advocated greater caution, yet Sichuan showed itself reluctant to retreat from the initial principles of the commune.

Sichuan's institutional radicalism owed much to the aspirations of Li Jingquan, the provincial party secretary, to Politburo rank. By outdoing Mao in his advocacy of the commune, Li hoped to prove his loyalty; and Peng Dehuai's criticism of Mao at the Lushan plenum allowed Li to demonstrate explicitly just that, in a counterattack of his own (Goodman, 1986: 150). In economic policy terms, Li's ambition led him to persist with the more Utopian elements of the Leap even after they had been abandoned elsewhere. Thus household sidelines, with the exception of pig-rearing, remained under commune control until 1963 (pp. 155–6). As for the basic unit of account: 'Sichuan appears to have promoted the production brigade as the basic level of ownership within the commune right up to the summer of 1962, long after other provinces had decentralised ownership to the production team' (p. 155).

Of course, the desire to avoid starvation acted as a powerful incentive mechanism after 1960, even though incomes remained dependent upon the productivity of other brigade members. In that sense, the continued use of the brigade and the unsatisfactory payments system was perhaps less important after 1960 than before. Nevertheless, it was hardly 'a wager on the strong'; even after that date, the incentive system was such as to discourage households with high potential productivity from producing more than a subsistence level. It certainly was not conducive to the production of a surplus above subsistence consumption.

This institutional explanation of a decline in food availability is accepted by a number of Western scholars. According to Vermeer (1988: 308), writing of the experience of Shaanxi province:

There is no indication, however, that at any time the Shaanxi provincial or local communist leaders tried to be in the vanguard of the collectivisation drive. . . . If one considers the sad fate—over one million dead of starvation— of the neighbouring province of Henan, which had been a trend-setter, Shaanxi had no reason to regret its cautiousness.

This type of explanation is probably the most convincing of those considered for Sichuan. Procurements, 'excessive accumulation', and bad weather all played some role, but only institutional radicalism seems to explain why food shortages were so much worse in Sichuan than in other provinces. In addition, different rates of communaliza- tion and differing degrees of egalitarianism within regions *may* provide an explanation for spatial differences *within* Sichuan in the impact of famine—though this is largely conjectural, in that no information is available on rates of institutional change within the province.

Nevertheless, it is important not to emphasize this type of institu- tional change at the expense of all else, for another feature of the rural scene during the 1950s was the severity of the procurements system. One of the more remarkable features of the early stages of the Leap is the gulf that opened up between per capita grain supply in the urban and rural sectors (Table 10.1). In 1955 and 1956, rural grain supply per capita was running at about 90% of the urban level. In 1958, however, it fell sharply to only 76%, reaching a nadir of only 46% in 1959. This reflected in the main a big increase in the size of per capita procurements for the urban sector. As Endicott (1988) points out in the case of Shifang county, the scale of these procure- ments owed much to rural yield exaggeration. Thus the post-1958 Sichuan famine was in part distributional in origin. The available supply of food grains (in particular) was badly allocated between rural and urban sectors, with the result that the latter suffered a definite decline in food supply per head. In 1959, for example, the urban ration was 737 *jin* whereas the rural supply was only 341 *jin*, and there can be no question that an improved distribution of grain would have reduced mortality in that year. The same applies for 1961 and 1962, when the urban ration remained some 200 *jin* higher than the rural ration, and these distributional trends are reflected in the urban–rural mortality differential.

The impact of this redistribution of grain from the rural to the urban sector on rural productivity was adverse. In 1958, when 'urban bias' first became particularly marked, rural grain supplies were in general still maintained above subsistence; as has already been seen, rural grain availability per head was higher in 1958 than it had been in 1957. Nevertheless, the extraction of a proportionately larger surplus in 1958 must have adversely affected productive enthusiasm in the Sichuan countryside, and this probably contributed significantly to lower rural output in 1959. After all, there was little peasant incentive to produce merely for the benefit of the urban economy. In 1959, the problem of low farm sector productivity continued. With 1959 output below its level in 1958 and with procurement levels remaining high, rural grain availability per capita was driven below subsistence. The onset of starvation—although it obviously provided a strong incentive to higher rural production—in turn had further adverse effects upon productivity, in that the farm labour force was increasingly unable in a physical sense to match the labour productivity levels of the mid-1950s; in other words, the real wage rate was well below its efficiency level. These difficulties were compounded for many areas by the fact that their *reported* levels of output were still more than adequate. Rural communities thus became victims of their own exaggeration.

In addition, the role that Sichuan was playing in the national economy also contributed to the crisis. As Walker (1984) has pointed out, the province was one of the very few providing net grain exports that could be used in other deficit provinces and municipalities during the 1960s. The province's role in this regard began immediately after the introduction of the procurement system in the early 1950s, and continued throughout the decade. On the face of it, and especially given Sichuan's reputation as the 'granary of heaven', it does not seem unreasonable that she should perform such a role; yet when one remembers that Sichuan was one of the poorest provinces in China, it seems to make much less sense. Why was it that this poverty-stricken region should have, almost single-handedly, to feed the urban population of the great eastern cities and pay off China's debts to the Soviet Union in the form of grain exports? If Sichuan had not been a net exporter throughout the 1950s, she would have had much more substantial grain reserves that could have been used to good effect during the Leap crisis. Thus, even though excessive procurements did not trigger the post-1957 crisis, famine was, at least in part, the legacy of the policies pursued in the previous decade. Moreover, in the same way that redistribution of grain from rural to urban sectors within Sichuan adversely affected rural productivity, so too grain exports from the province must have adversely affected peasant productivity.

A contribution to 'building socialism' was one thing; building it unaided was a different matter.

In sum, and whatever the reasons for Sichuan's role in the economic order of the 1950s, it seems very likely that changes in the basic rural institution and the introduction of a unified system of procurements had highly adverse effects upon incentives. The consequent decline in productive enthusiasm seems, of those explanations considered, the most plausible reason for the food availability decline that Sichuan suffered after 1958.

Did the Food Availability Decline Make Famine Inevitable?

In a market economy operating along federal lines, Sichuan's role as a net exporter might have enabled her to avoid the worst effects of famine, because the province's ability to purchase goods produced elsewhere in China would have increased in proportion to her grain exports. For example, net export revenue could have been added to reserves which could subsequently have been run down by the provincial government to import grain during the Leap crisis. As it was, Sichuan's grain exports were not unrequited transfers. The peasants were paid for grain handed over to the state, except for that relatively small element which constituted the agricultural tax. Moreover, the province did benefit from the Soviet equipment and technology that their grain was being used to purchase. Nevertheless, it would be hard to describe this pattern of trade as fair. Sichuan's share in Soviet imports and technology was infinitely less than her share in Chinese exports to the USSR. Moreover, the prices her peasants received from the sale of grain and other commodities to the state was well below the national average (Table 10.7).

Sichuan's 'entitlement' to a share in national product was seriously compromised by price discrimination of this sort. It is instructive that, in the aftermath of the famine, the price differentials were gradually eliminated. By 1965, the national procurement price averaged only 1.5% more than the provincial price, and by 1981 it was down to a mere 0.3%. All this was rather late for those of Sichuan's population who died in the famine, but it does suggest that the discrimination practised during the 1950s was recognized to be a mistake.

One can make too much of these entitlement failures, however: ultimately, the inability to prevent food shortages leading to famine

TABLE 10.7. *Procurement Prices, 1957 (list price in* yuan *per 100* jin)

	Sichuan	China	Price differential[a] (%)
Rice	5.40	6.18	−12.6
Wheat	6.51	8.93	−27.1
Corn	5.50	5.58	−1.4
Vegetable oil	14.09	15.94	−11.6
Hemp	39.23	55.89	−29.8
Ramie	56.69	65.64	−13.6
Tung oil	9.95	14.91	−33.3
Pigs	27.71	36.57	−24.2
Average	n.a.	n.a.	−11.1

[a] The average differential figure quoted is for all procured farm and sideline commodities, and not just those listed in the table.

Source: ZSSWY (1984: 718).

was rooted in a much more general constellation of factors. Even if Sichuan's entitlements had been greater, it is implausible that they could have been used to offset the decline in food supply. Precisely because centralized economic planning was the norm, the province could not easily trade either with other provinces or, indeed, with other countries in *laissez-faire* fashion. This is a clear problem that can arise under a relatively rigidly planned economy, where national planners are operating under conditions of endemic uncertainty. Under a market system, a discrete spatial unit can take remedial action of its own accord (provided it possesses an entitlement) to prevent a serious food shortage. But under central planning, it has no such operational autonomy; the successful operation of such a system is, therefore, critically contingent upon accurate and timely informational flows.

Unfortunately for Sichuan, Politburo ignorance was the norm throughout much of the Leap. The Leap saw the dismantling of the system of data collection and the decentralization of decision-making to local government, and was characterized by a genuine mood of optimism. In such circumstances, inaccurate data on production and deliberate over-reporting were inevitable, and this assuredly led to complacency at higher levels. Moreover, even assuming that the leadership did become aware of the magnitude of the problem by mid-1960, it must be admitted that there was no simple, short-run solution. Few, if any, of China's other provinces had a grain surplus that could be sent to Sichuan, and the notion of allowing international relief agencies to operate on a quasi-independent basis within China was anathema to Mao and at variance with the frequently articulated goal of self-reliance. Thus it was that not until the autumn of 1962 did Canadian wheat begin to arrive to ease the famine.

Even so, in retrospect the complacency evident in the middle of 1959 seems astonishing, especially when Mao himself had drawn attention to the failings of the commune as early as February 1959. He made a self-criticism to the Lushan plenum in July, and Peng Dehuai went to some lengths to bring the magnitude of the crisis home to the leadership (see e.g. Selden, 1979: 476–80). Yet Mao's self-criticism seems to have been little more than symbolic:

The majority of comrades need to strengthen their backbones. Why are they not all strong? Just because for a time there were too few vegetables, too few hair-grips, no soap, a lack of balance in the economy and tension in the market, everyone became tense.   (Mao, July 1959, cited in Selden, 1979: 480–1)

If Mao had sanctioned grain imports at an early stage, there is little doubt that the extent of famine mortality would have been much less. That so many were allowed to die prompts the question as to whether Sichuan was being deliberately punished by the national leadership. After all, Sichuan had acted as Kuomintang redoubt during the Second World War, and her population had not suffered the horrors of warfare and Japanese occupation. It is true that all organized resistance had been shattered by the Red Army well before 1952, when Chiang Kaishek's most influential sympathizers fled to Taiwan. Moreover, there was no 'nationality question', in contrast to the Ukraine, which suffered most severely during 'Stalin's famine' of the early 1930s. Well over 90% of the province's population was ethnically Han. Further, as Goodman has shown, there is no evidence that the province pursued a strategy of development at variance with national policy before 1958; provincial separatism atrophied after the demise of the warlords in the mid-1930s. Still, it is possible to make the case that Sichuan had contributed less to, and suffered less for, the Revolution and therefore that it was right that she should bear a more than disproportionate burden after 1949. It is remarkably unlikely (or is it that the imagination recoils from the possibility?) that the leadership saw the famine as a deliberate part of that punishment strategy; but their policy *vis-à-vis* grain procurements (if such it was—the evidence for this hypothesis is non-existent) made some sort of mortality crisis increasingly inevitable.

Conclusion

The Sichuan famine began with the distributional crisis of 1958. The precise causes of the increase in mortality that occurred during that year remain obscure, but it is evident that food availability decline played little part in it. Food supply per capita in 1958 was, at a provincial level, higher than in 1957, although some local shortages undoubtedly existed.

The famine conditions that existed in the province during 1959 and the first three years of the next decade were triggered by a collapse in farm sector production. This output decline was in turn due to a variety of factors, but the primary reason for the more severe decline experienced in Sichuan than elsewhere in China appears to have been institutional change. The commune, and the deleterious incentive effects that it embodied, was introduced far too quickly. The procurement system adversely affected peasant incentives in that a significant, and what was seen as an unjust, proportion of output was being exported to the Soviet Union at unfavourable prices. The marked increase in relative per capita grain supplies in urban areas, and the consequent widening of the urban–rural differential, also did nothing to encourage productive enthusiasm.

This food availability decline did not make the Sichuan famine inevitable. To be sure, the Politburo had limited information about its intensity because of the collapse of the planning system—which made it more difficult to launch a timely and effective relief operation. Nevertheless, one is struck by the paralysis exhibited by the Party leadership. Although the international situation was not conducive to trade in 1960, it was no more unfavourable in 1962, when imported wheat finally began to arrive. Action on similar lines two years earlier would undoubtedly have gone far to mitigate the famine's intensity.

Conclusion

The aim of this book has been to assess critically, and to extend, certain aspects of recent reassessments of Maoist economic development undertaken by Carl Riskin, Peter Nolan, and Mark Selden. The analysis here differs from these earlier works in that it makes an explicit comparison of living standards in the 1930s with those in the late 1970s, and because spatial aspects of income distribution have been analysed in detail; non-material aspects of the living standard have also received considerable attention. Even more importantly, I have tried to evaluate the degree to which Maoist economic development was constrained by the international environment. This evaluation has been conducted at the level of the province in the belief that a comparison of the national picture in the 1970s and the 1930s would be premature, given how little systematic macroeconomic work has been completed on the Republican period.

The Maoist record in terms of macroeconomic aggregates is patchy. Food consumption in terms of quantity and quality was lower in the late 1970s than it had been in the early 1930s, and consumption per capita in more general terms grew slowly. The rapid increases in consumption achieved during the 1980s constitute an indicator of underperformance. Nevertheless, there is a great danger in concluding from this that Maoist economic development in Sichuan was a failure. It is not reasonable to talk of chronic hunger in the province in the immediate aftermath of Mao's death; at worst, food consumption levels were adequate in the late 1970s. Moreover, industrial performance in the long run was impressive when compared with virtually all other developing countries; and, crucially, it was this industrial foundation that made possible many of the achievements of the Dengist years. Most significantly of all (and it is a point that bears repetition), the province's record in terms of capabilities was astonishing. The degree of literacy and average life expectancy were not merely improved but transformed in the years after 1949; none of this improvement depended upon increases in per capita consumption. As a result, China by the late 1970s was on a par with middle-income countries despite her low per capita income level. If one believes that capabilities are a better indicator of economic development than opulence, both China and Sichuan had developed a great deal by the time of Mao's death. That the World Bank chooses to place more emphasis on opulence is an entirely normative decision.

When Maoist economic development is placed in its wider international context, the record is still more impressive. Sichuan's economic development, like that of many parts of China, had been hampered by the political instability of the Republican period. China's refusal to acknowledge *pax Americana* after 1949 and conform to the dictates of Washington forced upon her a strategy of defence industrialization. The wisdom of her decision to develop an independent nuclear capability and to invest heavily in defence-oriented heavy industry was confirmed by American imperialism in Vietnam. However, the price was high. The diversion of national income from consumption to investment, and non-productive defence investment at that, inevitably slowed the growth of material living standards. None of this merits the term 'failure': consumption grew slowly in Maoist China primarily because of the American threat. The repeated attempts to blame Mao for all of China's ills are little more than special pleading by the American academic establishment. China could only have avoided this fate by surrendering her sovereignty.

Planning in the main did not fail after 1949 in Sichuan. When the American threat was slight (during the 1950s, thanks to the Sino–Soviet alliance) and when it receded after 1978, the Chinese economy grew remarkably quickly. It is certainly not coincidence that the restoration of diplomatic relations with the USA saw the beginning of the Dengist economic 'miracle'. After 1979, investment could be reoriented towards the civilian sector, and increments to national income could be consumed rather than invested. Moreover, it was the shift in the production possibility frontier that had been achieved during the Maoist years—creation of industrial capital, the building of transport infrastructure, the massive investment of labour time in water conservancy, and a better-educated work-force—that made possible that acceleration of growth. Further, it was not planning that failed during the Great Leap Forward but rather the absence of central economic direction. None of this is to suggest that micro-economic failures did not happen; the insistence on double rice-cropping in areas where the climate was mainfestly unsuitable is one notable example. However, there are examples of technological failure occurring under all manner of economic system. What matters is not isolated failures but the *net* impact of planning, and there is reason to conclude that the rate of technical progress achieved in the circumstances was impressive; the extent to which high-yielding varieties had been pioneered and diffused by the late 1970s is a particularly remarkable instance of success. There is a marked contrast between these achievements and the record of the Republican period when development was 'left to the market'. Development was non-existent until the province's warlords (albeit with military aims in mind) grasped the notion that the state could play a developmental role in the late 1920s. Performance lapsed again after 1935, when Chiang's corrupt and incompetent regime sought no more than to maximize American aid and minimize any expenditure that did not contribute to preparing for civil war with the CCP after the collapse of the Japanese Empire.

When one turns to the distribution of incomes and capabilities, the record of Sichuan is better still. In terms of the spatial distribution, it is undoubtedly true that spatial differentials remained by the late 1970s. Nevertheless, these were much smaller than in many other developing countries, and an unambiguous narrowing of differentials took place between the Republican and late Maoist periods, a conclusion that does not vary with the use of inequality or relative-poverty measures of income distribution. To dismiss these achievements by pointing to residual spatial inequalities in the late 1970s is a wilful failure to accept the reality of Maoist success. The fact remains that the achievements of the Maoist era, especially in terms of capabilities, were shared amongst a peasantry living in locations as diverse as the Chengdu plain, the hills of the Sichuan Basin, and the hills of the Himalayan plateau.

Economic planning played an instrumental role in this process. Modern state industry was established in the rural periphery for military purposes—the growth of the Panzhihua conurbation is the most obvious example—and to benefit poor areas. It would not have happened of its own accord within a market economy, and county governments would have been unable to marshal the necessary funds themselves; central financial support was critical. At the same time, Maoist emphasis on the achievement of local self-sufficiency in grain production and the creation of grain bases in fertile regions penalized rich counties by preventing them from diversifying into cash crop production, where rates of profit were higher. Some poor areas may have suffered as well, but in the main such localities, especially when densely populated, had traditionally emphasized grain production anyway; Maoist policy therefore merely reinforced an existing tradition. This policy may not have been the first best, but, in the face of threatened American interdiction of transport networks, it was less irrational than many have suggested. Perhaps most importantly for the erosion of spatial differentials, state emphasis on labour mobilization for the purpose of water conservancy allowed many backward areas to introduce for the first time the full traditional 'package' of water and organic fertilizer and thereby to exploit catch-up opportunities. By contrast, rich counties were already close to their production possibility frontier by the early 1950s, and were forced to invest heavily in the new 'green revolution' package to maintain yield growth. As the state deliberately avoided the exclusive concentration of modern inputs like chemical fertilizers, pesticides, and electricity in rich areas—the distribution of modern inputs was surprisingly equal in the late 1970s—rates of output growth in areas such as the Chengdu plain were relatively slow.

Within Sichuan's counties, Maoist policy was also remarkably effective in reducing income differentials. The popularity of land reform stemmed at least in part from hostility towards the inequalities that were evident in the countryside in the 1930s. Income distribution within the province's village communities was unequal by both international and Chinese standards, and, as was the case elsewhere in China, these inequalities derived in the first instance from unequal ownership of land and exploitative rents. Superimposed upon this in Sichuan was the use of both taxation and military force as instruments of warlord power. The resulting 'feudal exploitation' marked the province out from the national norm, as scores of surveys and reports commissioned during the period make clear. To be sure, there were mechanisms in the countryside that operated in a more egalitarian fashion. In parts of the province, some socioeconomic mobility was brought about by sporadic land reform even during the 1930s, and the rise of the warlord meant a decline in the economic and social position of the traditional gentry. Moreover, there is little evidence that interest rates were markedly unfair. Nevertheless, these mechanisms did little to improve the relative standing of the poor peasantry and neither, despite some recent attempts to show the contrary, did rural industrialization. Warlord-sponsored defence industrialization helped to reduce *absolute poverty* by increasing the demand for labour. However, this industrialization petered out after 1935; and, in any case, it probably led to a widening of income inequalities because industrial profits accrued to the warlord class. Much of the evidence on the growth of private industry in China during the 1980s points to a similar conclusion.

All this was changed after 1949. The elimination of the landlord class, collectivization of agriculture, and the suppression of private industry ensured that the distribution of income within Sichuan's villages was remarkably equal by international standards as it was throughout the whole of China. Rural sidelines seem to have helped bring about a further equalization of incomes within the peasantry, although their significance compared to that of the collective economy was slight. Corruption was ever-present in the countryside, as it had been under Imperial and Republican governments, and the growing reach of the state may have led to some increase as the rural administrative cadres became more numerous. Nevertheless, there is no evidence that this had other than a marginal effect upon the overall distribution of income.

Maoist economic development thus brought about in Sichuan a transformation in aggregate capabilites, a modest increase in per capita consumption, the laying of the foundations of future growth via industrialization and infrastructure construction, a massive reduction in spatial inequality, and put paid to the landlord and the rich peasant. That this was achieved in the face of a hostile world environment makes it all the more remarkable. Nevertheless, these achievements have to be set against the catastrophic famine of the early 1960s. Of course, severe famines like those of 1872–3 and 1936–7 were a normal characteristic of life in pre-modern Sichuan. However, they were small compared to the loss of life that came in the wake of the Great Leap Forward. The absolute level of excess mortality was in the order of 8 million, well in excess of the toll in any other Chinese province. The famine was also relatively more severe in Sichuan, as measured by the average crude death rate during the Leap compared to the 1957 rate. Anhui province seems to have recorded the highest rate for a single year, but that mortality peak was maintained for only a short period of time, in contrast to Sichuan.

When Sichuan's famine began in 1958, there is no evidence of any food availability decline; it seems rather that the maldistribution of grain (in particular) between rural and urban sectors was primarily responsible. In 1959 and beyond, there is no question that a severe decline in food availability occurred; its immediate causes were both a decline in grain yields and a decline in grain-sown area, although the latter seems to have been more important in the early stages. The underlying reason for Sichuan's relatively more severe famine seems to have been that communalization was more rapid and more advanced (in respect of the unit of account and the method of distribution within communes) than the national norm. Certainly there is no evidence that the relative intensity of the Sichuan mortality crisis can be explained by excess accumulation, grain exports, or bad weather.

Moreover, there is little doubt that the famine was avoidable. If the pace of communalization had been slower, if Sichuan had been allowed to accumulate grain reserves during the 1950s instead of experiencing state-imposed surplus transfers to deficit provinces and cities, or if the Politburo had sought to import grain at an earlier stage, the mortality crisis would have been much less severe, and might have been avoided entirely. That it was not marks the famine out as the worst failure of the Maoist era. Nevertheless, one can argue that the lesson had been learnt by the 1970s and that the likelihood of another such famine occurring was extremely remote. In that sense, although the price was heavy, Maoist economic development was without doubt successful in Sichuan. Without it, the 'miracle' of the 1980s would have been impossible.

Appendix

Net Output Value Per Capita, 1939–1943

This section of the Appendix summarizes the output and population data by county used to estimate the extent of spatial inequality in the province in the early 1940s. The precise method of calculation, and the sources used, is given in full in Bramall (1989*b*: appendix). The principal source of the output data is Zhou, Hou, and Chen (1946*b*).

The abbreviations used in the following table are as follows:

Cash   output value derived from production of cash crops
Food   output value derived from production of food crops
Animal   output value of animal products
Industrial output value of industrial products

These subtotals are summed to produce a figure for total net output value in every county ('Total'). Dividing this figure by the county populations produces an estimate of net output value per capita for each county ('Output p.c.').

The county data below are grouped by the prefectures of the early 1940s. Italicized county names indicate the name of the prefecture, main text, I have followed standard Chinese usage and identified Ba prefecture as Baxian prefecture; the same applies to Luxian, Wanxian, and Daxian prefectures.

Value data in million *yuan*: population in millions.

Xian	Food	Cash	Livestock	Industry	Total	Population	Output p.c.
Peng	9.95	2.63	3.12	0.18	15.88	0.36	44
Chongqing	11.58	4.08	2.88	0.34	18.87	0.38	49
Huayang	8.49	1.21	3.35	neg.	13.05	0.41	32
Guan	7.22	4.01	2.72	0.49	14.44	0.29	49
Xinjin	5.34	0.83	0.66	0.07	6.90	0.14	48
Shuangliu	3.80	0.95	1.28	neg.	6.03	0.15	40
Pi	3.47	4.23	1.86	neg.	9.56	0.18	55
Wenjiang	4.49	2.89	1.58	1.35	10.31	0.16	63
Xindu	3.21	5.24	1.19	neg.	9.64	0.15	63
Chongning	2.77	1.67	1.07	neg.	5.51	0.09	61
Xinfan	3.40	1.72	0.72	neg.	5.84	0.10	57
TOTAL	63.71	29.46	20.41	2.44	116.03	2.43	48
% SHARE	0.55	0.25	0.18	0.02			

Xian	Food	Cash	Livestock	Industry	Total	Population	Output p.c.
Renshou	10.88	6.14	4.64	1.12	22.77	0.90	25
Jianyang	12.17	5.59	6.50	4.66	28.94	0.86	34
Rong	10.68	5.92	4.49	1.02	22.12	0.49	45
Zizhong	14.81	3.37	5.27	14.16	37.61	0.68	56
Neijiang	11.81	2.24	2.70	8.71	25.46	0.58	44
Ziyang	8.24	1.17	2.83	1.75	13.99	0.54	26
Weiyuan	12.64	2.27	2.90	3.39	21.20	0.34	63
Jingyan	7.85	0.58	1.04	0.90	10.37	0.17	63
TOTAL	89.09	27.28	30.38	35.71	182.45	4.54	40
% SHARE	0.49	0.15	0.17	0.20			
Jiangjin	9.85	3.16	5.26	0.77	19.03	0.81	23
Ba	9.73	1.39	3.32	1.62	16.06	0.80	20
Hechuan	9.45	4.20	6.78	2.08	22.51	0.67	34
Jiangbei	11.69	1.51	3.14	9.43	25.77	0.52	49
Qijiang	2.87	0.47	4.44	12.60	20.38	0.38	54
Tongliang	7.57	0.45	2.37	2.29	12.69	0.41	31
Yongchuan	6.92	0.86	2.88	2.00	12.66	0.37	34
Rongchang	8.05	1.53	2.08	0.94	12.13	0.31	39
Bishan	7.99	0.46	1.72	2.26	12.42	0.31	41
Dazu	6.39	1.20	1.71	0.21	9.51	0.36	27
TOTAL	80.50	14.75	33.69	34.20	163.14	4.95	33
% SHARE	0.49	0.09	0.21	0.21			
Qionglai	14.43	1.85	2.01	0.21	18.49	0.35	53
Meishan	3.81	1.33	2.07	0.15	7.37	0.37	20
Dayi	10.03	1.84	1.94	0.05	13.86	0.24	59
Hongya	2.54	0.27	1.28	0.36	4.45	0.19	24
Pujiang	7.18	0.81	0.35	neg.	8.33	0.11	76
Pengshan	3.01	0.26	1.37	0.05	4.69	0.14	34
Jiajiang	2.61	0.69	0.96	1.55	5.81	0.16	37
Danleng	1.67	0.26	0.69	neg.	2.62	0.08	30
Mingshan	3.66	0.85	1.16	neg.	5.67	0.12	48
Qingshen	3.08	1.27	0.76	0.02	5.13	0.11	45
TOTAL	52.02	9.43	12.59	2.39	7.64	1.87	41
% SHARE	0.68	0.12	0.16	0.03			
Qianwei	4.12	0.77	3.34	15.94	24.17	0.53	45
Leshan	3.65	4.42	2.85	11.70	22.62	0.35	65
Pingshan	17.08	3.04	2.65	0.03	22.80	0.27	86
Emei	7.97	1.63	0.69	0.06	10.35	0.15	68
Leibo	2.14	0.24	neg.	neg.	2.38	0.02	97
Ebian	1.53	0.18	0.38	neg.	2.09	0.04	48
Mabian	3.26	0.55	0.20	neg.	4.01	0.03	120
TOTAL	39.75	10.84	10.09	27.73	88.42	1.40	63
% SHARE	0.45	0.12	0.11	0.31			

Xian	Food	Cash	Livestock	Industry	Total	Population	Output p.c.
Yibin	3.64	0.62	4.41	1.54	10.21	0.74	14
Nanxi	3.40	0.51	2.22	0.46	6.53	0.28	23
Jiang'an	4.81	0.94	1.42	0.10	7.26	0.23	32
Gao	1.99	0.51	0.94	0.31	3.75	0.17	22
Changning	5.88	0.79	1.84	0.02	8.53	0.22	39
Qingfu	10.67	1.24	0.73	0.20	12.84	0.17	76
Gong	2.21	0.25	0.77	0.10	3.34	0.15	23
Xingwen	4.04	0.43	0.43	neg.	4.90	0.07	71
Junlian	2.45	0.52	0.39	0.12	3.47	0.08	45
TOTAL	39.09	5.81	13.10	2.85	60.85	2.11	29
% SHARE	0.64	0.10	0.22	0.05			
Lu	14.75	2.23	5.48	1.38	23.84	0.97	25
Fushun	10.70	0.77	3.40	3.11	17.98	0.75	24
Xuyong	2.08	0.29	1.55	0.09	4.01	0.30	14
Hejiang	16.31	3.07	2.56	0.21	22.15	0.39	57
Longchang	14.06	1.14	1.84	2.39	19.43	0.32	62
Gulin	7.73	1.71	1.45	0.28	11.17	0.33	34
Gusong	3.04	0.64	0.55	0.02	4.24	0.10	42
Naxi	7.37	0.62	0.29	0.02	8.31	0.09	94
TOTAL	76.03	10.47	17.12	7.51	111.13	3.23	34
% SHARE	0.68	0.09	0.15	0.07			
Fuling	23.17	3.03	6.38	0.86	33.44	0.79	42
Youyang	17.13	3.07	1.51	0.01	21.72	0.50	43
Fengdu	14.64	1.54	2.44	0.05	18.68	0.49	38
Xiushan	14.98	2.31	1.37	neg.	18.66	0.34	55
Pengshui	17.61	2.37	1.17	0.68	21.82	0.28	77
Nanchuan	9.32	1.37	1.76	0.21	12.67	0.30	42
Qianjiang	3.15	0.45	0.87	neg.	4.48	0.14	33
Shizhu	11.23	1.39	1.10	0.02	13.74	0.19	73
TOTAL	111.24	15.53	16.60	1.83	145.20	3.04	48
% SHARE	0.77	0.11	0.11	0.01			
Wan	11.55	4.95	7.97	0.86	25.33	0.83	31
Fengjie	6.64	0.95	3.07	1.09	11.74	0.39	30
Kai	12.63	2.47	4.80	1.56	21.46	0.59	36
Yunyang	7.41	0.90	3.12	10.60	22.02	0.47	47
Zhong	7.68	1.09	3.63	0.22	12.62	0.45	28
Wuxi	1.51	0.16	1.35	2.71	5.74	0.16	36
Wushan	2.65	0.15	0.98	0.07	3.86	0.15	26
Chengkou	1.79	0.54	0.57	neg.	2.90	0.08	37
TOTAL	51.87	11.21	25.49	17.11	105.68	3.11	34
% SHARE	0.49	0.11	0.24	0.16			
Guang'an	5.71	0.62	3.12	1.49	10.94	0.65	17
Qu	10.52	1.24	3.80	0.86	16.42	0.73	22
Dazhu	8.11	1.10	2.63	0.68	12.52	0.43	29

Xian	Food	Cash	Livestock	Industry	Total	Population	Output p.c.
Liangshan	16.28	2.40	2.19	1.54	22.42	0.38	59
Changshou	23.52	2.76	1.71	0.51	28.51	0.33	87
Linshui	13.40	1.96	1.52	0.42	17.30	0.32	54
Dianjiang	6.73	1.01	0.87	0.03	8.63	0.20	43
TOTAL	84.26	11.10	15.85	5.54	116.74	3.04	38
% SHARE	0.72	0.10	0.14	0.05			
Nanchong	16.45	4.76	6.55	0.20	27.97	0.83	34
Yuechi	6.60	1.22	1.94	0.03	9.79	0.54	18
Nanbu	15.68	4.46	2.22	2.99	25.35	0.70	36
Wusheng	5.98	0.86	2.91	0.02	9.77	0.33	30
Yingshan	10.53	1.35	1.78	neg.	13.66	0.41	34
Peng'an	6.37	0.79	2.18	neg.	9.35	0.35	26
Yilong	2.89	1.81	1.77	neg.	6.47	0.30	22
Xichong	12.58	1.72	1.21	1.40	16.91	0.34	50
TOTAL	77.08	16.97	20.57	4.64	119.26	3.79	31
% SHARE	0.65	0.14	0.17	0.04			
Anyue	6.97	0.62	4.74	neg.	12.33	0.64	19
Santai	18.91	12.74	5.10	3.59	40.34	0.86	47
Zhongjiang	10.09	3.83	4.51	2.00	20.42	0.82	25
Suining	17.41	10.89	3.62	1.87	33.79	0.59	57
Pengxi	10.62	1.76	1.91	6.40	20.69	0.61	34
Tongnan	7.22	1.11	2.19	neg.	10.52	0.27	38
Shehong	19.45	10.73	5.70	2.98	38.86	0.44	88
Lezhi	9.85	1.81	1.81	3.48	16.94	0.42	41
Yanting	11.23	1.18	1.65	1.29	15.35	0.27	56
TOTAL	111.75	44.67	31.21	21.61	209.24	4.93	42
% SHARE	0.53	0.21	0.15	0.10			
Mianyang	16.93	1.28	3.34	2.20	23.75	0.38	62
An	8.36	1.92	1.59	0.03	11.91	0.20	59
Jintang	10.72	7.26	3.28	0.41	21.67	0.50	44
Mianzhu	10.21	5.50	2.96	0.17	18.84	0.27	70
Guanghan	7.10	1.64	2.01	0.23	10.99	0.26	42
Shifang	6.08	13.66	1.75	0.26	21.76	0.21	103
Deyang	5.33	2.18	1.75	0.39	9.65	0.20	49
Zitong	2.45	0.33	0.78	neg.	3.56	0.16	23
Luojiang	3.93	0.25	1.25	0.01	5.44	0.15	36
TOTAL	71.23	34.02	18.73	3.71	127.58	2.33	55
% SHARE	0.56	0.27	0.15	0.03			
Pingwu	3.76	0.62	0.80	0.01	5.19	0.09	60
Guangyuan	2.85	0.45	1.33	1.25	5.88	0.18	33
Jiange	18.05	1.35	1.17	neg.	20.58	0.26	79
Jiangyou	3.28	2.33	0.19	0.03	5.82	0.20	30
Langzhong	5.15	3.11	0.09	2.99	12.17	0.36	34
Cangxi	5.47	0.80	1.03	neg.	7.30	0.24	30

Xian	Food	Cash	Livestock	Industry	Total	Population	Output p.c.
Changming	2.72	0.31	0.87	neg.	3.91	0.11	35
Zhaohua	9.70	1.16	0.61	0.07	11.53	0.10	120
Beichuan	0.96	0.38	0.21	neg.	1.55	0.04	41
TOTAL	51.93	10.52	7.13	4.35	73.93	1.57	47
% SHARE	0.70	0.14	0.10	0.06			
Bazhong	14.85	3.68	3.19	neg.	21.72	0.50	43
Da	7.53	1.33	3.57	0.30	12.74	0.65	20
Xuanhan	7.09	1.62	2.67	neg.	11.38	0.44	26
Tongjiang	2.46	0.23	0.62	0.40	3.71	0.17	22
Wanyuan	8.04	1.15	0.96	0.25	10.40	0.15	70
Kaijiang	5.24	0.63	0.71	0.03	6.61	0.21	31
Nanjiang	13.37	1.77	0.63	neg.	15.77	0.16	82
TOTAL	58.58	10.41	12.36	0.98	82.34	2.29	36
% SHARE	0.71	0.13	0.15	0.01			
Lifan	0.34	0.03	0.20	neg.	0.57	0.02	24
Songpan	0.27	0.02	1.82	neg.	2.12	0.03	78
Mao	3.84	0.31	0.22	0.01	4.39	0.04	119
Jinghua	1.15	0.06	0.03	neg.	1.25	0.01	141
Wenchuan	0.64	0.10	0.17	neg.	0.90	0.02	41
Maogong	0.41	0.05	0.40	neg.	0.86	0.02	41
TOTAL	6.66	0.57	2.86	0.01	10.09	0.14	72
% SHARE	0.66	0.06	0.28	neg.			

Output and Capabilities by County in Sichuan, 1982

1. NVAIO per capita has been calculated in the table below from GVAIO per capita as follows:

$$\text{NVAIO}^{82} \text{ p.c.} = \text{GVAIO}^{82} \text{ p.c.} \quad (\text{NVAIO}^{85} \text{ p.c.}/\text{GVAIO}^{85} \text{ p.c.})$$

The superscript numerals indicate the year.

2. Prefecture boundaries are those of 1939–43. Counties falling outside the border of the Sichuan of 1939–43 are not included.

3. No data are given in ZGRKTJNJ (1988) on those districts of Sichuan's cities which were included within counties in the early 1940s. In that sense, the comparison between 1939–43 and 1982 is inexact.

4. Small cities are treated as for the 1985 data (see the next section of the Appendix). Note that, as for 1985, a direct comparison between counties over the 1939–43 to 1982 period is not possible because of boundary changes.

5. *Source*: ZGRKTJNJ (1988: 650–63).

6. Illiteracy rates are percentages, and are for the population aged 12 and over.

7. Infant mortality rates are deaths per 1,000 live births.

Xian	GVAIO p.c.	NVAIO p.c.	Population	Illiteracy	Infant mortality
Peng	537	256	692,336	27	35
Chongqing	546	271	577,259	22	46
Guan	642	283	490,678	21	33
Xinjin	491	223	256,186	21	56
Shuangliu	467	218	780,589	21	47
Pi	576	276	392,994	19	48
Wenjiang	660	308	241,962	21	40
Xindu	685	295	487,822	20	30
AVERAGE		262			
Renshou	355	205	1,378,180	31	51
Jianyang	482	251	1,290,344	28	47
Rong	399	210	817,686	30	39
Zizhong	432	225	1,137,429	30	33
Neijiang	613	268	1,129,229	27	30
Ziyang	531	254	921,763	29	36
Weiyuan	446	213	657,906	31	39
Jingyan	372	197	393,306	30	46
AVERAGE		231			
Jiangjin	382	181	1,374,293	26	37
Ba	425	189	1,178,277	19	24
Hechuan	435	218	1,405,315	30	35
Jiangbei	390	190	976,910	18	26
Qijiang	311	135	864,541	28	38
Tongliang	400	213	746,930	28	24
Yongchuan	453	225	924,301	25	39
Rongchang	331	149	700,315	28	37
Bishan	377	189	545,876	23	24
Dazu	348	185	776,690	33	39
AVERAGE		189			
Qionglai	538	245	584,096	21	32
Meishan	571	273	707,759	23	45
Dayi	526	253	445,962	23	42
Hongya	394	218	307,929	29	33
Pujiang	468	242	229,620	20	30
Pengshan	418	219	279,019	26	49
Jiajiang	365	190	324,242	23	44
Danleng	395	219	143,489	26	41
Mingshan	393	211	233,950	23	32
Qingshen	380	195	184,742	23	42
AVERAGE		236			

Xian	GVAIO p.c.	NVAIO p.c.	Population	Illiteracy	Infant mortality
Qianwei	413	207	520,746	31	33
Leshan	663	311	954,384	21	45
Pingshan	272	165	219,812	37	52
Emei	734	290	372,787	22	28
Leibo	256	146	185,379	56	83
Ebian	454	224	120,161	44	30
Mabian	271	165	148,781	55	49
AVERAGE		249			
Yibin	527	226	1,294,475	28	39
Nanxi	342	153	492,191	32	39
Jiang'an	258	135	436,980	28	35
Gao	266	152	465,466	35	34
Changning	286	162	369,120	35	49
Gong	413	187	311,428	34	45
Xingwen	278	152	138,100	37	48
Junlian	284	151	300,256	34	51
AVERAGE		179			
Lu	693	288	1,674,518	30	24
Fushun	354	193	1,045,260	33	38
Xuyong	273	149	737,685	33	33
Hejiang	326	187	783,324	33	41
Longchang	359	164	662,585	30	35
Gulin	229	127	674,898	43	43
Naxi	350	196	455,586	30	42
AVERAGE		203			
Fuling	400	182	961,622	28	39
Youyang	226	136	611,487	38	41
Fengdu	302	164	703,595	32	48
Xiushan	234	130	473,087	36	40
Pengshui	277	162	517,770	44	53
Nanchuan	393	187	600,353	26	43
Qianjiang	253	142	384,709	37	44
Shizhu	240	140	417,091	42	50
AVERAGE		159			
Wan	429	188	1,456,475	27	48
Fengjie	288	164	848,775	41	66
Kai	315	174	1,286,112	29	38
Yunyang	234	133	1,093,597	35	60
Zhong	275	161	903,528	32	55

Xian	GVAIO p.c.	NVAIO p.c.	Population	Illiteracy	Infant mortality
Wuxi	266	158	457,848	43	72
Wushan	246	141	496,419	42	59
Chengkou	273	165	215,431	46	66
AVERAGE		164			
Guang'an	271	150	1,049,714	33	44
Qu	333	178	1,175,199	37	40
Dazhu	468	234	928,461	34	44
Liangping	290	153	780,449	27	49
Changshou	314	128	819,332	23	31
Linshui	309	165	775,864	34	38
Dianjiang	310	171	767,545	35	49
Huaying	311	124	301,503	35	37
AVERAGE		167			
Nanchong	473	207	1,535,233	28	43
Yuechi	258	151	970,715	35	60
Nanbu	249	143	1,163,282	43	46
Wusheng	296	174	688,418	34	55
Yingshan	281	164	775,781	35	49
Peng'an	343	192	587,534	34	48
Yilong	255	154	844,810	42	64
Xichong	326	180	604,269	28	49
AVERAGE		171			
Anyue	328	197	1,324,758	36	40
Santai	351	189	1,340,553	34	63
Zhongjiang	327	188	1,297,840	36	53
Suining	445	222	1,139,341	33	37
Pengxi	376	212	1,089,032	33	43
Tongnan	319	180	772,951	34	42
Shehong	376	189	905,963	34	40
Lezhi	368	216	814,501	35	48
Yanting	325	183	593,243	31	52
AVERAGE		198			
Mianyang	594	232	776,162	34	40
An	399	216	454,992	37	42
Jintang	328	166	756,607	34	51
Mianzhu	626	307	473,431	39	36
Guanghan	759	329	493,292	28	25
Shifang	1,097	470	380,522	32	36
Deyang	592	239	685,900	31	27

Xian	GVAIO p.c.	NVAIO p.c.	Population	Illiteracy	Infant mortality
Zitong	368	214	381,906	37	45
AVERAGE		258			
Pingwu	320	158	184,718	43	42
Guangyuan	317	132	780,785	36	47
Jiange	282	169	582,301	37	58
Jiangyou	483	186	768,606	37	37
Langzhong	363	184	822,995	35	47
Cangxi	280	160	723,125	39	45
Beichuan	315	184	150,099	43	55
AVERAGE		167			
Bazhong	387	212	1,044,166	43	56
Da	519	236	1,400,498	27	49
Xuanhan	313	176	1,001,641	33	51
Tongjiang	259	155	598,113	39	38
Wanyuan	393	243	394,067	39	62
Kaijiang	274	149	473,197	34	62
Nanjiang	277	164	521,335	38	47
Pingchang	314	181	724,722	38	46
AVERAGE		195			
Li	393	213	42,262	37	50
Songpan	403	216	60,633	52	71
Maowen	368	196	79,208	51	46
Wenchuan	357	148	84,976	32	46
Xiaojin	345	205	68,345	42	78
Heishui	374	204	58,119	59	89
Nanping	349	176	49,430	52	46
Zoige	722	430	53,050	55	113
Hongyuan	927	542	27,029	47	108
AVERAGE		234			

Net Per Capita Output Values by County, 1985

This section of the Appendix summarizes county net output value data, both total and per capita, for 1985. The original data are of *gross* industrial and agricultural output value. These are converted into *net* output values as follows:

1. For agriculture: all-Sichuan NVAO for 1985 is available from the breakdown of NDMP (*guomin shouru*) given in SCTJNJ (1985). By dividing

this into all-Sichuan GVAO for the same year, an estimate of value added can be derived. This percentage, calculated to be 0.6835 per *yuan* of GVIO, is then applied to GVAO for each county to derive NVAO.

2. For industry: the same procedure as for agriculture is used. Calculated value added for industry is 0.3183 per *yuan* of GVIO.

This method is an approximation because it assumes that the structure of GVAO and GVIO is identical to the provincial average in each county. However, it is clearly preferable to considering gross output value data, which would bias the comparison towards counties with a high GVIO relative to GVAO.

Abbreviations

NVAO	net value of agricultural output (including rural industry)
NVIO	net value of industrial output (excluding rural industry)
NVAIO	sum of NVAO and NVIO
Grain	total grain output (*yuanliang*)
NVAIO p.c.	per capita NVAIO
Grain p.c.	grain output per capita
Q'jiang	Qingbaijiang (Chengdu)
Long'yi	Longquanyi (Chengdu)
Sh'qiao	Shuangqiao
Sh'ba	Shapingba
J'bei	Jiangbei
Nan'kuang	Nantongkuang
Xi'cheng	Xiangcheng county (Garze)

Units

NVAO, NVIO, and NVAIO	millions of 1980 *yuan*
Population	millions
Grain	million *jin*
NVAIO p.c.	1980 *yuan*
Grain p.c.	*jin*

Omissions

No data are included in SCTJNJ (1985) on Chengdu city proper, Chongqing city proper, including Dadukou district, Zigong city proper, and Dukou city, including Renhe district.

Treatment of small cities

Administrative units identified as *shi* (city), such as Deyang and Leshan, have been treated as county equivalents because most of their economic activity took place in the rural sector. They are not cities in the Western sense, or comparable to Chongqing, Chengdu, Zigong, or Dukou. An exception to this rule applies when a city and a county bear the same name; most of these cities are small in terms of population and therefore have been simply included within the county totals. Thus, for example, the data listed next to Nanchong are for Nanchong county (*xian*) and Nanchong city (*shi*) combined.

The districts of Chengdu and Chongqing

Although many of these are small, and therefore ought not to stand as *xian* equivalents, there is no satisfactory way of aggregating them. Their omission would distort comparisons with the 1939–43 period because all were then part of counties—for example, the three districts of Chengdu city formed the major part of the Huayang county of 1939–43.

Aggregation

Counties have been grouped by the districts of 1939–43 for convenience, except for Western Sichuan, where the 1985 autonomous prefecture boundaries are used.

Boundary changes

Output and population data for 1985 or 1982 cannot generally be compared directly with those for 1939–43 for individual counties, even where county names have remained unchanged. The difficulty is that of changing county boundaries; for example, the Qingfu county of 1939–43 seems to have been absorbed into Gao county at the end of the 1950s.

Source: SCTJNJ (1985: 72–109).

Xian	NVAO	NVIO	NVAIO	Grain prodn.	Population	NVAIO p.c.	Grain p.c.
Peng	169.82	103.52	273.34	610.21	0.70	389	869
Chongqing	148.39	72.98	221.37	678.22	0.59	376	1,152
Guan	111.88	102.23	214.11	423.67	0.50	424	840
Xinjin	54.15	42.71	96.86	242.25	0.26	371	927
Shuangliu	181.54	122.40	303.94	781.84	0.80	382	983
Pi	108.37	64.14	172.51	466.34	0.40	432	1,168
Wenjiang	59.47	40.27	99.74	277.43	0.25	399	1,110
Xindu	120.92	126.49	247.41	483.34	0.50	496	969
Jinniu	90.82	124.70	215.52	292.94	0.53	405	551

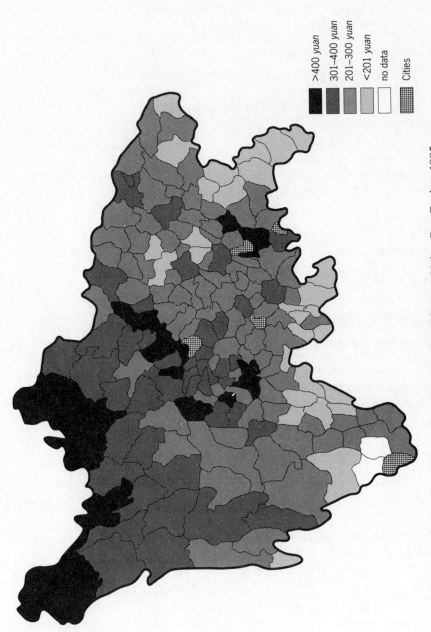

Fig. 8. Net Industrial and Agricultural Output Value Per Capita, 1985

Xian	NVAO	NVIO	NVAIO	Grain prodn.	Population	NVAIO p.c.	Grain p.c.
Q'jiang	66.98	32.91	99.89	303.34	0.36	279	846
Long'yi	89.85	31.84	121.69	353.78	0.35	344	1,001
TOTAL	1,202.19	864.19	2,066.38	4,913.36	5.24	394	937
Renshou	324.25	63.24	387.49	1,257.04	1.40	278	901
Jianyang	323.12	121.23	444.35	1,246.39	1.30	342	958
Rong	175.75	62.16	237.91	869.65	0.83	286	1,044
Zizhong	225.66	85.70	311.36	983.70	1.16	269	849
Neijiang	212.44	203.44	415.88	825.94	1.17	356	708
Ziyang	183.53	110.20	293.73	772.76	0.93	315	828
Weiyuan	125.56	73.62	199.18	580.00	0.67	297	864
Jingyan	82.66	28.34	111.00	358.64	0.40	280	903
TOTAL	1,652.97	747.93	2,400.90	6,894.12	7.86	306	878
Jiangjin	250.56	155.02	405.58	1,128.17	1.39	292	812
Ba	300.08	259.21	559.29	1,214.01	1.19	468	1,017
Hechuan	324.02	148.23	472.25	1,419.99	1.42	332	998
Jiangbei	171.89	93.54	265.43	743.40	0.99	269	753
Qijiang	137.25	139.91	277.16	722.28	0.88	315	821
Tongliang	160.66	52.49	213.15	713.11	0.76	282	943
Yongchuan	185.73	89.74	275.47	903.65	0.95	291	956
Rongchang	119.48	97.41	216.89	578.98	0.72	300	800
Bishan	96.88	44.55	141.43	453.92	0.56	254	817
Dazu	152.93	50.73	203.66	698.48	0.80	255	875
Sh'qiao	3.85	2.20	6.05	19.57	0.03	181	584
Sh'ba	16.19	62.04	78.23	6.79	0.53	148	13
J'bei qu	8.73	21.99	30.72	11.09	0.29	105	38
Nan'an	13.75	36.59	50.34	20.78	0.29	171	71
Jiulongpo	26.38	51.37	77.75	35.45	0.45	173	79
Nan'kuang	27.28	25.58	52.86	118.79	0.24	221	496
TOTAL	1,995.66	1,330.60	3,326.26	8,788.46	11.49	290	765
Qionglai	131.46	102.82	234.28	598.14	0.59	396	1,011
Meishan	162.42	97.22	259.64	707.00	0.72	362	986
Dayi	105.10	60.36	165.46	466.72	0.45	366	1,034
Hongya	69.69	17.79	87.48	267.39	0.31	280	857
Pujiang	59.18	23.00	82.18	237.35	0.24	349	1,008
Pengshan	59.09	21.69	80.78	281.02	0.28	284	988
Jiajiang	60.24	22.41	82.65	216.72	0.33	253	663
Danleng	36.20	9.22	45.42	142.90	0.15	311	977
Mingshan	49.21	15.31	64.52	219.26	0.24	270	916
Qingshen	40.93	16.37	57.30	147.15	0.19	305	784
TOTAL	773.52	386.19	1,159.71	3,283.65	3.49	332	940
Qianwei	101.92	47.92	149.84	395.66	0.53	281	741
Leshan	136.77	357.30	494.07	664.88	1.03	481	647

Xian	NVAO	NVIO	NVAIO	Grain prodn.	Population	NVAIO p.c.	Grain p.c.
Pingshan	37.93	4.94	42.87	120.32	0.23	189	529
Emei	59.70	105.09	164.79	230.30	0.39	428	598
Leibo	30.27	6.39	36.66	116.48	0.20	188	596
Ebian	21.63	10.81	32.44	76.22	0.12	262	616
Mabian	27.96	3.33	31.29	104.25	0.16	202	672
TOTAL	416.18	535.78	951.96	1,708.11	2.65	360	645
Yibin	222.57	218.50	441.07	883.50	1.52	291	583
Nanxi	52.53	44.17	96.70	222.33	0.36	268	616
Jiang'an	63.93	22.52	86.45	315.84	0.45	192	703
Gao	68.49	14.56	83.05	278.79	0.44	188	631
Changning	61.67	13.65	75.32	282.96	0.38	199	748
Gong	42.30	33.04	75.34	190.39	0.35	217	550
Xingwen	47.26	13.03	60.29	237.89	0.39	156	616
Junlian	45.32	15.01	60.33	184.63	0.31	193	590
TOTAL	604.07	374.48	978.55	2,596.33	4.19	234	620
Lu	283.97	363.32	647.29	1,264.11	1.71	379	741
Fushun	209.44	59.59	269.03	845.16	1.06	253	794
Xuyong	76.84	22.08	98.92	341.24	0.58	172	593
Hejiang	164.18	32.80	196.98	738.79	0.79	250	937
Longchang	97.29	75.05	172.34	420.53	0.68	254	619
Gulin	85.08	22.24	107.32	297.59	0.62	173	479
Naxi	99.44	24.21	123.65	372.42	0.46	267	804
TOTAL	1,016.24	599.29	1,615.53	4,279.84	5.90	274	726
Fuling	148.18	114.58	262.76	751.08	0.97	270	772
Youyang	92.63	12.57	105.20	411.90	0.64	166	649
Fengdu	110.23	32.28	142.51	468.97	0.72	198	652
Xiushan	74.85	18.29	93.14	309.26	0.49	189	627
Pengshui	84.18	14.19	98.37	311.54	0.53	184	583
Nanchuan	111.79	68.64	180.43	462.12	0.61	298	762
Qianjiang	63.83	15.01	78.84	227.16	0.40	195	563
Shizhu	64.51	11.23	75.74	282.98	0.43	177	660
TOTAL	750.20	286.79	1,036.99	3,225.01	4.79	216	673
Wan	211.62	203.87	415.49	686.04	1.48	281	464
Fengjie	145.22	30.31	175.53	547.19	0.87	202	630
Kai	225.43	58.91	284.34	882.27	1.31	218	675
Yunyang	153.10	33.27	186.37	628.40	1.12	166	561
Zhong	146.46	26.23	172.69	578.33	0.92	188	628
Wuxi	82.05	12.81	94.86	327.37	0.47	202	697
Wushan	83.62	16.83	100.45	374.26	0.51	196	730
Chengkou	39.23	4.97	44.20	142.95	0.22	201	651
TOTAL	1,086.73	387.20	1,473.93	4,166.81	6.90	214	604
Guang'an	163.54	42.19	205.73	801.01	1.06	195	758
Qu	186.79	58.36	245.15	807.57	1.19	205	677

Xian	NVAO	NVIO	NVAIO	Grain prodn.	Population	NVAIO p.c.	Grain p.c.
Dazhu	184.09	86.02	270.11	874.30	0.94	288	933
Liangping	125.78	44.09	169.87	548.76	0.79	215	694
Changshou	156.82	229.78	386.60	696.28	0.83	466	839
Linshui	123.03	39.06	162.09	622.96	0.79	206	792
Diangjiang	125.68	32.94	158.62	553.02	0.78	203	709
Huaying	36.02	57.84	93.86	165.12	0.31	299	527
TOTAL	1,101.75	590.28	1,692.03	5,069.02	6.69	253	758
Nanchong	240.85	234.47	475.32	1,026.49	1.58	301	650
Yuechi	165.22	28.27	193.49	795.25	0.99	196	806
Nanbu	196.70	38.79	235.49	779.07	1.18	199	658
Wusheng	131.14	21.26	152.40	572.58	0.70	217	816
Yingshan	151.53	26.52	178.05	640.09	0.79	224	806
Peng'an	120.90	28.71	149.61	428.46	0.60	248	711
Yilong	143.70	18.51	162.21	592.32	0.86	188	686
Xichong	124.60	32.69	157.29	425.35	0.62	255	691
TOTAL	1,274.64	429.22	1,703.86	5,259.61	7.33	233	718
Anyue	278.88	38.38	317.26	1,265.63	1.36	233	929
Santai	271.20	82.67	353.87	1,148.10	1.35	262	851
Zhongjiang	278.85	55.45	334.30	1,120.97	1.31	256	858
Suining	238.69	112.00	350.69	934.03	1.17	298	795
Pengxi	242.27	53.94	296.21	1,053.49	1.12	263	937
Tongnan	172.73	38.28	211.01	740.05	0.80	265	931
Shehong	179.30	81.24	260.54	668.31	0.91	286	733
Lezhi	190.48	31.58	222.06	735.99	0.82	271	899
Yanting	123.67	27.52	151.19	507.35	0.59	255	857
TOTAL	1,976.07	521.06	2,497.13	8,173.92	9.44	265	866
Mianyang	148.86	286.20	435.06	635.79	0.85	513	749
An	117.08	34.56	151.64	477.95	0.45	335	1,057
Jintang	144.03	63.78	207.81	678.24	0.77	272	886
Mianzhu	123.19	64.85	188.04	528.06	0.44	431	1,210
Guanghan	150.90	152.78	303.68	530.91	0.51	600	1,050
Shifang	124.18	133.70	257.88	350.15	0.39	665	903
Deyang	160.41	243.80	404.21	752.35	0.75	537	999
Zitong	93.07	16.71	109.78	373.72	0.37	301	1,023
TOTAL	1,061.72	996.38	2,058.10	4,327.17	4.51	456	958
Pingwu	39.01	19.80	58.81	140.37	0.17	339	809
Guangyuan	117.98	149.43	267.41	532.13	0.81	332	661
Jiange	116.61	16.62	133.23	518.40	0.59	228	886
Jiangyou	144.67	294.44	439.11	623.29	0.78	562	798
Langzhong	146.45	63.86	210.31	600.77	0.83	254	724
Cangxi	139.04	28.45	167.49	638.85	0.73	228	871
Beichuan	30.21	5.37	35.58	119.57	0.15	238	799
TOTAL	733.97	577.97	1,311.94	3,173.38	4.06	323	782

Xian	NVAO	NVIO	NVAIO	Grain prodn.	Population	NVAIO p.c.	Grain p.c.
Bazhong	243.12	67.19	310.31	981.01	1.05	295	932
Da	267.08	211.29	478.37	1,230.19	1.42	337	865
Xuanhan	188.93	42.49	231.42	724.26	1.02	226	709
Tongjiang	117.95	16.25	134.20	455.15	0.61	219	744
Wanyuan	102.17	56.29	158.46	329.75	0.47	338	704
Kaijiang	82.81	23.73	106.54	326.53	0.48	224	685
Nanjiang	109.71	16.79	126.50	424.86	0.53	239	804
Pingchang	150.09	28.23	178.32	591.85	0.74	241	801
TOTAL	1,261.86	462.26	1,724.12	5,063.60	6.32	273	801
Li	10.59	3.14	13.73	30.84	0.04	336	741
Songpan	16.49	5.27	21.76	50.18	0.06	350	807
Maowen	17.33	5.67	23.00	62.91	0.08	275	753
Wenchuan	15.09	19.25	34.34	57.85	0.09	395	666
Xiaojin	16.38	2.45	18.83	47.03	0.07	271	678
Heishui	14.14	3.97	18.11	47.54	0.06	316	828
Nanping	10.93	4.80	15.73	35.50	0.05	320	723
Zoige	23.64	3.48	27.12	15.12	0.06	491	274
Hongyuan	16.77	2.86	19.63	neg.	0.03	701	neg.
TOTAL	141.36	50.89	192.25	346.97	0.53	360	650

References

Chinese-Language Sources

Romanization is pinyin, even for pre-1949 publications. Books which have no obvious author/editor, or where the editing has been done by an *ad hoc* editorial group named after the book's title (e.g. Aba Zangzu zizhizhou gaikuang bianxiezu—Editorial Group for the Aba Autonomous Prefecture Survey) are cited by title only. Abbreviations for editors or titles are used only if the full form is very cumbersome or the reference is cited frequently.

Aba Zangzu zizhizhou gaikuang (A Survey of Aba Autonomous Prefecture's Tibetan People) (1985). Chengdu: Sichuan minzu chubanshe.

Anhui jingji nianjian 1985 (Anhui Economic Yearbook) (1985). Hefei (?): no publisher.

ASL (1985): *Sichuan sheng Aba zhou Zangzu shehui lishi diaocha* (An Investigation into the Social History of the Tibetan Minority Living in Sichuan's Aba Prefecture). Chengdu: Sichuan sheng shehui kexueyuan chubanshe.

CAO, D. M. (1985). 'Cong Liu Wencai jiazu de baofa kan Sichuan junfa de fengjianxing he lueduoxing' (The Feudal and Predatory Characteristics of Sichuan's Warlords Can Be Seen from the Newly Acquired Riches of Liu Wencai's Family), in Xinan junfa shi yanjiuhui (Research Conference on the History of the Warlords of South-West China) (ed.), *Xinan junfa shi yanjiu congkan* (A Collection of Essays on the Warlords of South-West China), 275-286. Kunming: Yunnan renmin chubanshe.

CAO, M. G. (ed.) (1988). *Zhongguo renkou: Jilin fence* (China's Population: Jilin volume). Beijing: Zhongguo caizheng jingji chubanshe.

CHANG, W., and XIN, H. (1981). 'Nongye baochan daozu hou jihua shengyu gongzuo ruhe kaizhan' (Improving Family Planning in the Aftermath of the Introduction of Contracting Responsibility to Work Groups in Agriculture), in Beijing jingji xueyuan renkou jingji yanjiusuo (Institute of Population Economics, Beijing College of Economics) (ed.), *Zhongguo renkou kexue lunji* (A Symposium on Chinese Population Science). Beijing: Zhongguo xueshi chubanshe.

CHEN, W. Y. (1985). 'Sichuan sheng Guanghan, Xindu, Qionglai san xian nongcun jingji tizhi gaige diaocha' (A Survey of Systemic Rural Reform in Sichuan's Guanghan, Xindu, and Qionglai Counties), in H. S. He (ed.), *Nongye jingji luncong* (Collected Essays on the Agricultural Economy), i. 278–82. Beijing: Nongye chubanshe.

CHENGDU SHI RENMIN ZHENGFU JINGJI YANJIU ZHONGXIN (Economic Research Centre of the People's Government of Chengdu Municipality) (ed.) (1987).

358   *References*

Chengdu jingji (The Economy of Chengdu). Chengdu: Xinan zhengjing daxue chubanshe.

CHENGDU SHI TONGJIJU (Chengdu Municipality Statistical Bureau) (ed.) (1985). *Chengdu shi xian qu jiben qingkuang tongji ziliao* (Basic Statistical Materials on Conditions in the Counties and Districts of Chengdu Municipality). Chengdu: no publisher.

Chongqing nianjian (Chongqing Yearbook) (1987). Chongqing: Kexue jishu wenxian chubanshe.

CUI, X. H., SHI, Z. K., FAN, G. Z., and XIONG, Z. Y. (1985). *Sichuan chengshi jingji* (Sichuan's Urban Economy). Chengdu: Sichuan kexue jishu chubanshe.

DA, F. Q. (1982). 'Cong shiji chufa fanrong minzu jingji' (Set Out From Reality to Create a Booming Economy in Ethnic Areas), in *Nongye jingji wenti* (Problems of Agricultural Economics), 10 (Oct.): 25–31.

DU, S. H., and ZHANG, X. J. (1986). *Jinxiandai Sichuan changzhen jingji zhi* (The Economic Records of Market Towns in Modern Sichuan). Chengdu: Sichuan sheng shehui kexue chubanshe.

DU, W. Z. (ed.) (1987). *Zhongguo renkou: Jiangsu fence* (China's Population: Jiangsu volume). Beijing: Zhongguo caizheng jingji chubanshe.

FAN, J. C., and ZHUO, Y. M. (1981). 'Dangqian shengzhu shengchan zhong de jige lilun he zhengce wenti' (Current Theoretical and Policy Issues Concerning Pig Production), in *Sichuan Daxue Xuebao* (Journal of Sichuan University, Social Science Edn.), 4: 11–17.

FU, Y. Z. (1983). 'Jiefang qian de Chongqing dianli gongsi' (Chongqing's Electrical Power Company Before Liberation), in *Chongqing gongshang shiliao* (Historical Materials on Industry and Commerce in Chongqing), ii. 179–98. Chongqing: Chongqing chubanshe.

GAN, S. L. (ed.) (1986). *Sichuan sheng nongye ziyuan yu quhua* (Sichuan's Agricultural Regions and Natural Resources), ii. Chengdu: Sichuan sheng shehui kexueyuan chubanshe.

GAN, Y. P., and YANG, L. F. (1984). 'Wo sheng xiaofeipin gongye mianlin de jueze' (Identifying the Obstacles that Sichuan's Consumer Goods Industry Faces), in Sichuan jihua jingji xuehui (Sichuan Institute of Economic Planning) (ed.), *Jihua jingji de lilun yu shijian* (The Theory and Practice of Planned Economy). Chongqing: Chongqing chubanshe.

GAO, Y. T. (ed.) (1987). *Dangdai Sichuan jiben jianshe* (Capital Construction in Modern Sichuan). Chengdu: Sichuan sheng shehui kexueyuan chubanshe.

Garze Zangzu zizhizhou gaikuang (A Survey of Garze Autonomous Prefecture's Tibetan People) (1986). Chengdu: Sichuan minzu chubanshe.

GSL (1985): *Sichuan sheng Garze zhou Zangzu shehui lishi diaocha* (An Investigation into the Social History of the Tibetan Minority Living in Sichuan's Garze Prefecture). Chengdu: Sichuan sheng shehui kexueyuan chubanshe.

GU, Z. C. (1985). 'Sichuan gongye jiegou de tedian yuji gaishan de tujing' (Peculiarities in Sichuan's Industrial Structure and Ways to Improve It), in Sichuan sheng shehui kexueyuan jingji yanjiusuo (Economic Research Institute of the Sichuan Academy of Social Sciences) (ed.), *Zhongguo shehuizhuyi jingji yanjiu* (Research on China's Socialist Economy). Chengdu: Sichuan sheng kexueyuan chubanshe.

Guizhou sheng qing (Conditions in Guizhou) (1986). Guiyang: Guizhou renmin chubanshe.

Hu, C. N. (1982). *Jiage xue* (Price Studies). Beijing: Zhongguo renmin daxue chubanshe.

Hu, H. Y. (ed.) (1987). *Zhongguo renkou: Shanghai fence* (China's Population: Shanghai volume). Beijing: Zhongguo caizheng jingji chubanshe.

Huang, X. L. (ed.) (1988). *Zhongguo renkou: Guangxi fence* (China's Population: Guangxi volume). Beijing: Zhongguo caizheng jingji chubanshe.

Jilin sheng renmin zhengfu bangongting (General Office of the People's Government of Jilin) (ed.) (1987). *Jilin sheng qing* (Conditions in Jilin). Changchun: Jilin renmin chubanshe.

Jingyan xian zhi (Records of Jingyan County) (1990). Chengdu: Sichuan renmin chubanshe.

Kuang, S. J. (1981). 'Sichuan junfa tongzhi xia de tianfu fujia he yuzheng' (Land Surtaxes and Pre-Collections of Land Taxes under the Rule of the Warlords in Sichuan'), in *Sichuan Daxue Xuebao* (Journal of Sichuan University, Social Science Edn.), 1: 79–85.

—— and Yang, S. R. (1985). 'Sichuan junfa yu yapian' (Sichuan Warlords and Opium), in Xinan junfa shi yanjiuhui (Research Conference on the History of the Warlords of South-West China) (ed.), *Xinan junfa shi yanjiu congkan* (A Collection of Essays on the Warlords of South-West China), 250–62. Kunming: Yunnan renmin chubanshe.

Li, C. R. (1959). *Zhonghua renmin gongheguo nongye shui shi* (An Outline History of Land Taxation in the People's Republic of China). Beijing: Caizheng chubanshe.

Li, S. P. (ed.) (1989). *Sichuan renkou shi* (A History of Sichuan's Population). Chengdu: Sichuan daxue chubanshe.

Liangshan Yizu zizhizhou gaikuang (A Survey of Liangshan Autonomous Prefecture's Yi People) (1985). Chengdu: Sichuan minzu chubanshe.

Lin, C. (ed.) (1982). *Chuan–Shaan geming genjudi lishi* (A History of the Sichuan–Shaanxi Revolutionary Base Area). Chengdu: Sichuan renmin chubanshe.

Liu, H. K. (ed.) (1988). *Zhongguo renkou: Sichuan fence* (China's Population: Sichuan volume). Beijing: Zhongguo caizheng jingji chubanshe.

Longchang wenshi ziliao xuanji (Selected Materials on the History and Literature of Longchang) (1986), vii. Longchang (Sichuan): no publisher.

LSL (1985): *Sichuan sheng Liangshan zhou Yizu shehui lishi diaocha* (An Investigation into the Social History of the Yi Minority Living in Sichuan's Liangshan Prefecture). Chengdu: Sichuan sheng shehui kexueyuan chubanshe.

LSTJ (1990): Zhongguo guojia tongjiju (State Statistical Bureau) (ed.),

Quanguo gesheng zizhiqu zhixiashi lishi tongji ziliao huibian (Collection of Historical Statistical Materials on China's Provinces, Autonomous Regions and Centrally Administered Cities). Beijing: Zhongguo tongji chubanshe.

LU, P. D. (1936). *Sichuan nongcun jingji* (Sichuan's Rural Economy). Shanghai: Commercial Press.

Maowen Qiangzu zizhixian gaikuang (A Survey of Maowen County's Qiang People) (1985). Chengdu: Sichuan renmin chubanshe.

Muli Zangzu zizhixian gaikuang (A Survey of Muli Autonomous County's Tibetan People) (1985). Chengdu: Sichuan minzu chubanshe.

Neijiang shi zhi (The Records of Neijiang City) (1987). Chengdu: Bashu shushe chubanshe.

NING, Z. C. (1983). 'Sichuan shuiniu chang de chuangli he yanbian' (The Foundation and Evolution of the Sichuan Cement Company), in *Chongqing Gongshang Shiliao* (Historical Materials on Industry and Commerce in Chongqing), ii. 166–78. Chongqing: Chongqing chubanshe.

NONGCUN XIAOZU: NONGCUN DIAOCHA LINGDAO XIAOZU BANGONGSHI (Office of the Party Rural Survey Group) (ed.) (1986). *Quanguo nongcun shehui jingji dianxing diaocha* (A National Typical Example Survey of the Rural Economy and Society), vii. Beijing: unpublished.

NONGCUN YANJIUZU: ZHONGGONG SICHUAN SHENG WEI NONGCUN JINGJI SHEHUI FAZHAN ZHANLUE YANJIUZU (Research Group for the CCP's Sichuan Committee on the Development Strategy for Rural Economy and Society) (ed.) (1986). *Sichuan nongcun jintian he mingtian* (Rural Sichuan Today and Tomorrow). Chengdu: Sichuan kexue jishu chubanshe.

NYJJWT (1986): 'Zhongguo nongcun shehui jingji dianxing diaocha qingkuang zonghe baogao' (Summary Report of a Typical Example Investigation of the Economic and Social Situation in Rural China), in *Nongye Jingji Wenti* (Issues in Agricultural Economics), 6: 4–13.

PENG, J. S., and CHEN, R. (1985). *Sichuan jingyan shi luncong* (Collected Essays on the History of Well Salt in Sichuan). Chengdu: Sichuan sheng shehui kexueyuan chubanshe.

PENG, Y. X. (1943). *Chuan sheng tianfu chengshi fudan yanjiu* (A Study of Land Taxation in Sichuan). Chongqing: Commercial Press.

PU, X. R. (ed.) (1986). *Sichuan zhengqu yange yu zhi di jin shi* (An Explanation of the Evolution of the Current Administrative Divisions of Sichuan). Chengdu: Sichuan renmin chubanshe.

SCJJDL (1985): *Sichuan sheng jingji dili* (An Economic Geography of Sichuan). Chengdu: Sichuan kexue jishu chubanshe.

SCJJNJ (1986): *Sichuan jingji nianjian 1986* (Sichuan Economic Yearbook). Chengdu: Sichuan kexue jishu chubanshe, 1987.

SCJJNJ (1987): *Sichuan jingji nianjian 1987* (Sichuan Economic Yearbook). Chengdu: Sichuan kexue jishu chubanshe, 1988.

SCSHTJZL (1989): SICHUAN SHENG TONGJIJU (ed.), *Sichuan shehui tongji ziliao* (Statistical Materials on Sichuan's Society). Beijing: Zhongguo tongji chubanshe.

SCTJNJ (1982): Sɪᴄʜᴜᴀɴ ᴛᴏɴɢᴊɪᴊᴜ (Sichuan Statistical Bureau) (ed.) (1982). *Sichuan tongji nianjian 1982* (Sichuan Statistical Yearbook). Chengdu: no publisher.

—— (1984). *Sichuan tongji nianjian 1984* (Sichuan Statistical Yearbook). Chengdu: no publisher.

—— (1986). *Sichuan tongji nianjian 1985* (Sichuan Statistical Yearbook). Chengdu: no publisher.

Shenbao nianjian (Shenbao Yearbook) (1933). Shanghai: Shenbao nianjian chubanshe.

Shifang xian zhi (The Records of Shifang County) (1988). Chengdu: Sichuan daxue chubanshe.

Sɪᴄʜᴜᴀɴ ɴᴏɴɢʏᴇ ɢᴀɪᴊɪɴsᴜᴏ ᴛᴏɴɢᴊɪsʜɪ (Statistical Office of the Sichuan Agricultural Reform Bureau) (1942). *Sichuan nongcun wujia zhishu* (Rural Price Indices for Sichuan). Chongqing.

Sichuan sheng jingji yuce shiliji (Some Illustrative Calculations for Sichuan's Economy) (1986). Chengdu: no publisher.

Sichuan sheng Miaozu Lisuzu Daizu Baizu Manzu shehui lishi diaocha (A Survey of the Social History of Sichuan Province's Miao, Lisu, Dai, Bai, and Manchu Ethnic Minorities) (1986). Chengdu: Sichuan shehui kexueyuan chubanshe.

Sɪᴄʜᴜᴀɴ sʜᴇɴɢ ʏɪɴʜᴀɴɢ ᴊɪɴɢᴊɪ ʏᴀɴᴊɪᴜsᴜᴏ (Economic Research Institute of the Bank of Sichuan) (ed.) (1944). *Sichuan jingji jikan* (Sichuan Economic Quarterly), 1(4).

Sɪᴄʜᴜᴀɴ sʜᴇɴɢ ᴢʜᴇɴɢғᴜ ᴛᴏɴɢᴊɪᴊᴜ (Statistical Bureau of the Sichuan Provincial Government) (ed.) (1947). *Sichuan sheng tongji nianjian* (Sichuan Province Statistical Yearbook), 7 vols. Chengdu: no publisher.

Sɪᴄʜᴜᴀɴ sʜᴇɴɢ Zʜᴏɴɢɢᴜᴏ ᴊɪɴɢᴊɪ sʜɪ xᴜᴇʜᴜɪ (Sichuan Institute of Chinese Economic History) (ed.) (1986). *Zhongguo jingji shi yanjiu luncong* (Essays on Research in Chinese Economic History). Chengdu: Sichuan daxue chubanshe.

Sichuan xiangzhen qiye shijian 1977–1986 (A Decade of Rural Industry in Sichuan) (1988). Chengdu: Sichuan renmin chubanshe.

Sichuan yuye jingji (Sichuan's Fishery Industry) (1985). Chengdu: Sichuan shehui kexueyuan chubanshe.

Sᴏɴɢ, N. G. (ed.) (1987). *Zhongguo renkou: Nei Menggu fence* (China's Population: Inner Mongolia volume). Beijing: Zhongguo caizheng jingji chubanshe.

Sᴏɴɢ, Z. X. (ed.) (1987). *Zhongguo renkou: Liaoning fence* (China's Population: Liaoning volume). Beijing: Zhongguo caizheng jingji chubanshe.

Wᴀɴɢ, D. W. (1985). 'Jiefang qian Neijiang jietangye gaikuang' (The State of Neijiang's Sugar Industry Before Liberation), in *Sichuan wenshi ziliao xuanji* (A Compilation of Reference Materials on Sichuan's History and Literature), xxxv. 185–94. Chengdu: Sichuan renmin chubanshe.

—— and Hᴜᴀɴɢ, J, L. (1985). 'Jiefang qian Neijiang ganzhe zhongzhi gaikuang' (A Survey of Sugar Cane Cultivation in Neijiang Before

Liberation), in *Sichuan wenshi ziliao xuanji* (A Compilation of Reference Materials on Sichuan's History and Literature), xxxv. 177–84. Chengdu: Sichuan renmin chubanshe.

WANG, M. H. (1985). *Xiaofei jingji gailun* (An Introduction to the Consumption Economy). Beijing: Zhongguo caizheng jingji chubanshe.

WANG, M. Y. (ed.) (1987). *Zhongguo renkou: Hebei fence* (China's Population: Hebei volume). Beijing: Zhongguo caizheng jingji chubanshe.

WEN, S. H. (1983). 'Chongqing zilai shuishi de xingjian he jingying' (The Foundation and Operation of the First Chongqing Water Company), in *Chongqing Gongshang Shiliao* (Historical Materials on Industry and Commerce in Chongqing), ii. 199–202. Chongqing: Chongqing chubanshe.

XIAO, B., and Ma, X. W. (1984). *Sichuan junfa hunzhan* (Tangled Warfare between Sichuan's Warlords). Chengdu: Sichuan sheng shehui kexueyuan chubanshe.

Xichong wenshi ziliao xuanji (Selected Materials on the History and Literature of Xichong County), iv. Nanchong: no publisher.

XIE, W. D. (1984). 'Dui Sichuan nongye fazhan zhanlue yi xie kanfa' (Some Thoughts on Sichuan's Agricultural Development Strategy), in Sichuan jihua jingji xuehui (Sichuan Institute for Economic Planning) (ed.), *Jihua jingji de lilun yu shijian* (The Theory and Practice of Economic Planning), 204–16, Chongqing: Chongqing chubanshe.

XIN, W. (1984). 'Guanyu wosheng jingji shehui fazhan zhanlue de jige wenti' (Some Questions Concerning Sichuan's Economic and Social Development Strategy), in Sichuan jihua jingji xuehui (Sichuan Institute for Economic Planning) (ed.), *Jihua jingji de lilun yu shijian* (The Theory and Practice of Economic Planning). Chongqing: Chongqing chubanshe.

XU, D. F. (ed.) (1983). *Zhongguo jindai nongye shengchan yu maoyi tongji ziliao* (Statistical Materials on Agricultural Production and Trade in Modern China). Shanghai: Shanghai renmin chubanshe.

YIN, C. Y. (1986). 'Dui Liangshan shehui jingji fazhan wenti de zai renshi' (Some Further Insights into the Problems of Economic and Social Development in Liangshan), in Zhongjue minzu xueyuan shaoshu minzu jingji yanjiusuo (The Ethnic Minority Economic Research Institute of the Central Nationalities School) (ed.), *Xibu minzu diqu jingji kaifa tansuo* (An Exploration into the Economic Development of Ethnic Minority Regions in Western China), 126–74. Beijing: Zhongjue minzu xueyuan chubanshe.

Youyang Tujiazu Miaozu zizhixian gaikuang (A Survey of Youyang County's Tujia and Miao Peoples) (1986). Chengdu: Sichuan minzu chubanshe.

YOUZHENG ZONGJU (Head Office of the Postal Service) (1937). *Zhongguo tongyou difang wusheng zhi* (A Record of Wholesale Prices in China's Postal Districts), 2 vols. Shanghai: Huashi chubanshe.

ZGGY (1985): ZHONGGUO GUOJIA TONGJIJU (ed.) (1985). *Zhongguo gongye jingji tongji ziliao* (Statistical Materials on China's Industrial Economy). Beijing: Zhongguo tongji chubanshe.

ZGRKNJ (1985): SHEHUI KEXUEYUAN RENKOU YANJIU ZHONGXIN (Population

Research Centre of the Academy of Social Sciences) (ed.), *Zhongguo renkou nianjian 1985* (Chinese Population Yearbook 1985). Beijing: Zhongguo shehui kexueyuan chubanshe.

ZGRKTJNJ (1988): ZHONGGUO GUOJIA TONGJIJU (ed.), *Zhongguo renkou tongji nianjian 1988* (Chinese Population Statistical Yearbook). Beijing: Zhongguo minchong chubanshe.

ZGTJNJ (1981): ZHONGGUO GUOJIA TONGJIJU (State Statistical Bureau) (ed.), *Zhongguo tongji nianjian 1981* (Chinese Statistical Yearbook 1981). Xianggang (Hong Kong): Xianggang jingji daobaoshe, 1982.

—— (1983): *Zhongguo tongji nianjian 1983* (Chinese Statistical Yearbook 1983). Beijing: Zhongguo tongji chubanshe.

—— (1985): *Zhongguo tongji nianjian 1985* (Chinese Statistical Yearbook 1985). Beijing: Zhongguo tongji chubanshe.

—— (1987): *Zhongguo tongji nianjian 1987* (Chinese Statistical Yearbook 1987). Beijing: Zhongguo tongji chubanshe.

—— (1988): *Zhongguo tongji nianjian 1988* (Chinese Statistical Yearbook 1988). Beijing: Zhongguo tongji chubanshe.

—— (1989): *Zhongguo tongji nianjian 1989* (Chinese Statistical Yearbook 1989). Beijing: Zhongguo tongji chubanshe.

ZHANG, G. F., and CENG, Y. S. (1984). 'Guanyu jianli yi Chongqing wei yituo de keshi zhongxin wei kaifa xinan jingji fuwu de tantao' (An Investigation into the Issue of Establishing Chongqing as a Science and Technology Centre Serving the Economy of South-West China), in Quanmin chengshi gongye guanli xueshi guolunhui (National Conference on Urban Industrial Management) (ed.), *Chengshi gongye guanli* (Urban Industrial Management), 150–64. Chongqing: Chongqing chubanshe.

ZHANG, G. Q. (1986). *Zhongguo tonghuo pengzhang shi 1937–1949* (A History of China's Inflation, 1937–1949). Beijing: Wenshi ziliao chubanshe.

ZHANG, X. M. (ed.) (1939). *Sichuan jingji cankao ziliao* (Reference Materials on Sichuan's Economy). Shanghai: Zhongguo guomin jingji yanjiusuo.

ZHANG, Y. Y. (ed.) (1957). *Zhongguo jindai nongye shi ziliao* (Materials on the History of Modern China's Agriculture), 3 vols. Beijing: Zhongguo kexueyuan jingji yanjiusuo.

ZHENG, D. Q. (1983). 'Minsheng gongsi chuanye jieduan ji lue' (A Brief Account of the Early Years of the Minsheng Company), in *Chongqing gongshang shiliao* (Historical Materials on Industry and Commerce in Chongqing), ii. 1–15. Chongqing: Chongqing chubanshe.

ZHONGGONG SICHUAN SHENG WEI DANGSHI GONGZUO WEIYUANHUI (CCP's Sichuan Committee for Work on Party History) (ed.) (1986). *Hongjun changzheng zai Sichuan* (The Red Army on the Long March in Sichuan). Chengdu: Sichuan sheng shehui kexueyuan chubanshe.

ZHONGGUO GUOJIA TONGJIJU (State Statistical Bureau) (ed.) (1987). *Guomin shouru tongji ziliao huibian* (Collection of National Income Statistics). Beijing: Zhongguo tongji chubanshe.

—— (ed.) (1989). *Zhongguo fenxian nongcun jingji tongji gaiyao 1980–1987*

(Outline Rural Economic Statistics for China's Counties). Beijing: Zhongguo tongji chubanshe.

—— (ed.) (1990). *Zhongguo fenxian nongcun jingji tongji gaiyao 1988* (Outline Rural Economic Statistics for China's Counties). Beijing: Zhongguo tongji chubanshe.

ZHONGGUO GUOMIN ZHENGFU ZHUJIJU TONGJIJU (National Government, Directorate of Statistics) (ed.) (1936). *Zhonghua minguo tongji tiyao 1935* (Statistical Abstract of the Republic of China). Nanjing: Zhengzhong shiju. Repr. Taibei: Xuehai chubanshe, 1973.

—— (ed.) (1940). *Zhonghua minguo tongji tiyao* (Statistical Abstract of the Republic of China). Chongqing: Zhengzhong shiju.

—— (ed.) (1946). *Zhongguo zutian zhidu zhi tongji fenxi* (A Statistical Analysis of Systems of Land Rent in China). Chongqing: Zhengzhong shiju.

Zhongguo jingji nianjian 1986 (Chinese Economic Yearbook 1986). Beijing: Jingji guanli chubanshe.

ZHONGGUO NONGMIN YINHANG (Farmers' Bank of China) (ed.) (1941). *Sichuan sheng jingji diaocha baogao* (Report of a Survey of Sichuan's Economy). Chongqing: Zhongguo wenhua fuwushu.

Zhongguo nongye nianjian 1983 (Chinese Agricultural Yearbook 1983). Beijing: Nongye chubanshe.

Zhongguo nongye nianjian 1986 (Chinese Agricultural Yearbook 1986). Beijing: Nongye chubanshe.

ZHONGGUO RENKOU XUEHUI (China Population Institute) (ed.) (n.d.). *Quanguo shaoshu minzu renkou lunwen ziliao xuanze* (A Compilation of Selected Materials on National Ethnic-Minority Populations Throughout China). Beijing.

ZHONGGUO XINAN MINZU YANJIU XUEHUI (South-West China Ethnic Research Institute) (ed.) (1986). *Xinan minzu diqu jingji gaikuang* (An Economic Survey of Ethnic-Minority Areas in South-West China). Chengdu: Sichuan sheng minzu yanjiusuo.

ZHONGHUA RENMIN GONGHEGUO NONGMUYUYE BU (Ministry of Farming, Livestock and Fisheries of the People's Republic of China) (ed.) (1985). *Anzhao shichang xuyao tiaozheng nongcun chanye jiegou* (Adjust the Structure of Rural Production in Accordance with Market Conditions). Beijing: Nongye chubanshe.

ZHONGYANG NONGYEBU JIHUASI (Ministry of Agriculture, Dept. of Planning) (ed.) (1952). *Liangnian lai de Zhongguo nongcun jingji diaocha huibian* (Collected Surveys of the Rural Economy of China over the Past Two Years). Beijing: Zhonghua shiju.

ZHOU, L. S., HOU, X. D., and CHEN, S. Q. (eds.) (1946*a*). *Sichuan jingji dituji* (An Economic Geography of Sichuan). Beibei (Sichuan): Zhongguo dili yanjiusuo.

—— —— —— (eds.) (1946*b*): *Sichuan jingji dituji shuoming* (An Annotated Economic Geography of Sichuan). Beibei (Sichuan): Zhongguo dili yanjiusuo.

ZIGONG SHI JINGJI YANJIUSUO (Zigong Municipality Economic Research Institute) (ed.) (1985). *Zigong shi qing*) (Conditions in Zigong Municipality). Zigong: no publisher.

ZIYANG XIAN NONGYE QUHUA WEIYUANHUI (Commission on Ziyang County's Agricultural Districts) (1985). *Sichuan sheng Ziyang xian zonghe nongye quhua baogao* (Summary of a Report on the Agricultural Districts of Sichuan Province's Ziyang County). Neijiang: no publisher.

ZKCDY (1980): ZHONGGUO KEXUEYUAN CHENGDU DILI YANJIUSUO (Chengdu Geographical Research Institute, Chinese Academy of Science) (ed.), *Sichuan nongye dili* (An Agricultural Geography of Sichuan). Chengdu: Sichuan renmin chubanshe.

ZSSWY (1984): ZHONGGONG SICHUAN SHENG WEI YANJIUSHI (Research Unit of the Sichuan Committee of the CCP) (ed.), *Sichuan sheng qing* (Conditions in Sichuan). Chengdu: Sichuan renmin chubanshe.

ZU, L. Y. (1985). 'Jiangsu sheng nongchanpin chengben fazhan qushi qianxi' (An Outline of Trends in Agricultural Production Costs in Jiangsu Province), in H. S. He (ed.), *Nongye jingji luncong* (Collected Essays on the Agricultural Economy), vi. 240–50. Beijing: Nongye chubanshe.

Western-Language Sources

Romanization of Chinese follows that used by the author/editor of the original.

ABDEL-FADIL, M. (1975). *Development, Income Distribution and Social Change in Rural Egypt 1952–70* (Dept. of Applied Economics Occasional Paper 45). Cambridge: Cambridge Univ. Press.

ADELMAN, I., and SUNDING, D. (1987). 'Economic Policy and Income Distribution in China', *Journal of Comparative Economics*, 11(3): 444–61.

Administrative Divisions of the People's Republic of China, The (1980). Beijing: Cartographic Publishing House.

ADSHEAD, S. A. M. (1984). *Province and Politics in late Imperial China*. London: Curzon Press.

AFANAS'YESKIY YE. A. (1960). 'Natural Conditions and Special Agricultural Features of the Province of Sichuan', in *The Geography of Agriculture in Communist China*, Joint Publications Research Service, Translation No. 3401; originally published in Russian by the Publishing House of Oriental Literature, Moscow, 1959.

—— (1962). *Szechwan*. New York: Joint Publications Research Service, Translation No. 15308; originally published in Russian by the Publishing House of Oriental Literature, Moscow.

AGANBEGYAN, A. (1988). *The Challenge: Economics of Perestroika*. London: Hutchinson.

ALAMGIR, M., and AHMED, S. (1988). 'Poverty and Income Distribution in Bangladesh' in Srinivasan and Bardhan (1988, 11–38).

AMSDEN, A. H. (1989). *Asia's Next Giant*. New York: Oxford Univ. Press.

ANAND, S. (1983). *Inequality and Poverty in Malaysia*. Oxford: Oxford Univ. Press.

ARRIGO, L. G. (1986). 'Landownership Concentration in China', *Modern China*, 12(3): 259–360.

ASH, R. F. (1976). *Land Tenure in Pre-Revolutionary China: Kiangsu Province in the 1920s and 1930s* (CCI Research Notes and Studies No. 1). London: School of Oriental and African Studies.

—— (1981). 'The Quest for Food Self-Sufficiency' in C. Howe (ed.), *Shanghai*, 188–221. Cambridge: Cambridge Univ. Press.

ASHTON, B., HILL, K., PIAZZA, A., AND ZEITZ, R. (1984). 'Famine in China 1958–61', *Population and Development Review*, 10(4): 613–45.

ATKINSON, A. B. (1975). *The Economics of Inequality*. Oxford: Oxford Univ. Press.

AVEDON, J. F. (1984). *In Exile from the Land of Snow*. London: Michael Joseph.

BACHMAN, D. (1991). *Bureancracy, Economy and Leadership in China: The Institutional Origins of the Great Leap Forward*. Cambridge: Cambridge Univ. Press.

BALASUBRAMANYAM, V. N. (1984). *The Economy of India*. London: Weidenfeld & Nicolson.

BANISTER, J. (1984). 'An Analysis of Recent Data on the Population of China', *Population and Development Review*, 10(2): 241–71.

—— (1987). *China's Changing Population*. Stanford, Calif: Stanford Univ. Press.

BARAN, P. A. (1957). *The Political Economy of Growth*. New York: Monthly Review Press.

BARKER, R., SINHA, R., and ROSE, B. (ed.) (1982). *The Chinese Agricultural Economy*. London: Croom Helm.

—— HERDT, R., and ROSE, B. (1985). *The Rice Economy of Asia*. Washington, DC: Resources for the Future.

BARNETT, A. D. (1963). *China on the Eve of Communist Takeover*. London: Thames & Hudson.

BECKER, E. (1986). *When The War Was Over*. New York: Simon & Schuster. *Beijing Review*, various issues.

BHADURI, A. (1977). 'On the Formation of Usurious Interest Rates in Backward Agriculture', *Cambridge Journal of Economics*, 1(1): 341–52.

BIANCO, L. (1986). 'Peasant Movements', in J. K. Fairbank and A. Feuerwerker (eds.), *The Cambridge History of China*, xiii(2): 270–328. Cambridge: Cambridge Univ. Press.

BIRD (BISHOP in original 1899 edn.), I. (1985). *The Yangtze Valley and Beyond*. London: Virago.

BOSERUP, E. (1981). *Population and Technology*. Oxford: Basil Blackwell.

BOWLES, S., GORDON, D. M., and WEISSKOPF, T. E. (1984). *Beyond The Wasteland*. London: Verso.

BRAMALL, C. (1989a). *Living Standards in Sichuan 1931–1978* (Contemporary China Institute Research Notes and Studies No. 8). London: School of Oriental and African Studies.

—— (1989*b*). 'Inequality and Poverty in Rural China: The Case of Sichuan Province, 1931–78'. Ph.D. dissertation, Univ. of Cambridge.

—— (1990). 'The Wenzhou "Miracle": An Assessment', in P. Nolan and F. R. Dong (eds.), *Market Forces in China*. London: Zed Books.

—— (1991). 'Collectivization', in T. Bottomore (ed.), *A Dictionary of Marxist Thought*, 2nd edn. Oxford: Basil Blackwell.

—— (1992). 'Economic Growth in China Between the Wars', *China Quarterly*, 131: 784–91.

BRANDT, L. (1989). *Commercialization and Agricultural Development*. Cambridge: Cambridge Univ. Press.

BRAY, F. (1986). *The Rice Economies*. Oxford: Basil Blackwell.

BROWN, H., and LI, M. L. (1926). 'A Survey of 25 Farms on Mount Omei, Szechwan, China', *Chinese Economic Journal*, 1(12): 1059–76.

—— —— (1928). 'A Survey of 50 Farms on the Chengtu Plain, Szechwan', *Chinese Economic Journal*, 2(1): 43–73.

BUCK, J. L. (1937). *Land Utilisation in China*, 3 vols. Oxford: Oxford Univ. Press.

—— (1943*a*). 'An Agricultural Survey of Szechwan Province', repr. in J. L. Buck, *Three Essays on Chinese Farm Economy* (London: Garland, 1980). (This is an English-language summary of Zhongguo nongmin yinhang, 1941 above.)

—— (1943*b*). 'Deflation: The Greatest Postwar Problem', *Economic Facts*, 24: 237–46, repr. in Dept. of Agricultural Economics, Univ. of Nanking (ed.), *Economic Facts*, iii, original pagination, Mar. 1943–June 1944 (London: Garland, 1980).

—— (1944).'Farm Tenancy in China', *Economic Facts*, 84; repr. in Dept. of Agricultural Economics, Univ. of Nanking (ed.), *Economic Facts*, iv. 481–97 (London: Garland, 1980).

—— (1947). 'Some Basic Agricultural Problems of China', repr. in J. L. Buck, *Three Essays on Chinese Farm Economy* (London: Garland, 1980).

—— and CHEN, D. T. (1944). 'The Most Capable Use of Land in Hwayang Hsien, Szechwan', *Economic Facts*, 38, repr. in Dept. of Agricultural Economics, Univ. of Nanking (ed.), *Economic Facts*, iv. 575–86 (London: Garland, 1980).

—— and HU, K. H. (1941). 'The Price of Rice and Its Determining Factors in Sichuan', *Economic Facts*, 15: 117–23, repr. in Dept. of Agricultural Economics, University of Nanking (ed.), *Economic Facts*, ii, original pagination, June 1938–Feb. 1943 (London: Garland, 1980).

—— and PAN, H. S. (1944). 'The Best Use of Land for the Welfare of the People of Penghsien', *Economic Facts*, 28, repr. in Dept. of Agricultural Economics, Univ. of Nanking (ed.), *Economic Facts*, iii (Mar. 1943–June 1944): 336–42 (London: Garland, 1980).

—— and SHAW, D. (1943). 'The Economic Position of Farmers in Penghsien, Szechwan in Relation to Other Classes of Society', *Economic Facts*, 22, repr. in Dept. of Agricultural Economics, Univ. of Nanking (ed.), *Economic Facts*, iii, original pagination, Mar. 1943–June 1944, 179–187 (London: Garland, 1980).

—— and YIEN, C. C. (1943). 'The Economic Effects of War upon Farmers in Penghsien, Szechwan', *Economic Facts*, 19, repr. in Dept. of Agricultural Economics, Univ. of Nanking (ed.), *Economic Facts*, iii (Mar. 1943–June 1944): 106–112 (London: Garland, 1980).

BURKI, S. J. (1988). 'Poverty in Pakistan: Myth or Reality?' in T. N. Srinivasan and P. K. Bardhan (eds.), *Rural Poverty in South Asia*, 69–88. New York: Columbia Univ. Press.

CAG (China Report, Agriculture) (1984). 'Meeting Views Experience in Supporting Poor Households' (translation of a radio broadcast made by the Sichuan Provincial Service, Chengdu, 25 July 1984). Joint Publications Research Service, CAG-84-025, 20 Sept.

CAY 1985: China Agriculture Yearbook 1985. Beijing: Agricultural Publishing House, 1986.

CH'AI, Y. (1964). 'Electrical Irrigation in Mountainous areas in Sichuan', *Jingji yanjiu*, 9. New York: Joint Publications Research Service Translation No. 27822 (14 Dec.).

CHAKRAVARTY, S. (1987). *Development Planning*. Oxford: Clarendon Press.

—— (1989). *Development Economics: Some Basic Issues* (Marshall Lecture, Univ. of Cambridge, May).

CHAN, A., MADSEN, R., and UNGER, J. (1984). *Chen Village*. Berkeley, Calif.: Univ. of California Press.

CHAN, S. W. (ed.) (1955). *Concise English–Chinese Dictionary*. Stanford, Calif.: Stanford Univ. Press.

CHANG, K. T. (1972). *The Rise of the Chinese Communist Party 1928–38*. Lawrence, Kan.: Univ. Press of Kansas.

CHATTOPADHYAY, M., and RUDRA, A. (1976). 'Size Productivity Revisited', in *Economic and Political Weekly*, 11(39).

CHAYANOV, A. N. (1966 edn.). *The Theory of Peasant Economy*, ed. B. Kerblay, D. Thorner, and R. E. F. Smith. Homewood, Ill.: Richard D. Irwin.

CHEN, J. S., CAMPBELL, T. C., LI, J. Y., and PETO, R. (eds.) (1990). *Diet, Lifestyle and Mortality in China*. Oxford: Oxford Univ. Press.

CH'EN, J. (1985). 'Local Government Finances in Republican China', in *Republican China*, 10(2): 42–53.

—— (1987). 'Reflections on the Long March', *China Quarterly*, 111: 450–65.

CHENG, X. M. (1984). 'A Survey of the Demographic Problems of the Yi Nationality in the Greater and Lesser Liang Mountains', *Social Sciences in China*, 5(3): 207–31.

CHEN, K., JEFFERSON, G., RAWSKI, T., WANG, H., and ZHENG, Y. (1988). 'Productivity Changes in Chinese Industry, 1953–1985', *Journal of Comparative Economics*, 12: 570–91.

CHI, C. T. (1939). *Wartime Economic Development in China*. New York: Institute of Pacific Affairs.

CH'I, H. S. (1982). *Nationalist China at War*. Ann Arbor, Mich.: Univ. of Michigan Press.

The China Handbook, 1937–43. London: Chinese Ministry of Information.

The China Handbook, 1939–45. London: Chinese Ministry of Information.

A Chinese–English Dictionary (1978). Beijing: Beijing Waiguoyu xueyuan Yingyuxi (Faculty of English, Beijing Foreign Languages Institute).

CHUAN, H. S., and KRAUS, R. A. (1975). *Mid-Ch'ing Rice Markets and Trade*. Cambridge, Mass.: Harvard Univ. Press.

CONQUEST, R. (1988; 1st edn. 1986). *The Harvest of Sorrow*. London: Arrow.

COWELL, F. A. (1977). *Measuring Inequality*. Oxford: Philip Allan.

CRAFTS, N. F. R. (1985). *British Economic Growth during the Industrial Revolution*. Oxford: Oxford Univ. Press.

CROOK, I., and CROOK, D. (1966). *The First Years of Yangyi Commune*. London: Routledge & Kegan Paul.

DELMAN, J., OSTERGAARD, C. S., and CHRISTIANSEN, F. (eds.) (1990). *Remaking Peasant China*. Aarhus: Aarhus Univ. Press.

DESAI, M. (1976). 'The Consolidation of Slavery', review article in *Economic History Review*, 29(3): 491–503.

DONG, F. R. (1982). 'Relationship Between Accumulation and Consumption', in D. X. Xu (ed.), *China's Search for Economic Growth*. Beijing: New World Press.

DONNITHORNE, A. (1967). *China's Economic System*. London: George Allen & Unwin.

—— (1984). 'Sichuan's Agriculture: Depression and Revival', *Australian Journal of Chinese Affairs*, 12: 59–86.

DORE, R. P. (1965). 'Land Reform and Japan's Economic Development', repr. from *Developing Economies*, 4, in T. Shanin (ed.), *Peasants and Peasant Societies*, 377–88 (London: Penguin, 1971).

DREZE, J., and SEN, A. (1989). *Hunger and Public Action*. Oxford: Clarendon Press.

EASTERLIN, R. (1971). 'Regional Income Trends, 1840–1950', in R. W. Fogel, and S. L. Engerman (eds.), *The Reinterpretation of American Economic History*. New York: Harper & Row.

EASTMAN, L. E. (1986). *Seeds of Destruction*. Stanford, Calif.: Stanford Univ. Press.

—— (1988). *Family, Fields and Ancestors*. Oxford: Oxford Univ. Press.

EF (1943): *Economic Facts*, 16. app. ii, pp. 51–4, repr. in Dept. of Agricultural Economics, Univ. of Nanking (ed.), *Economic Facts*, ii (June 1938–Feb. 1943) (London: Garland, 1980).

ELLMAN, M. (1989). *Socialist Planning*, 2nd edn. Cambridge: Cambridge Univ. Press.

ELVIN, M. (1973). *The Pattern of the Chinese Past*. Stanford, Calif.: Stanford Univ. Press.

ENDICOTT, S. (1988). *Red Earth*. London: I. B. Tauris.

EPSTEIN, I. (1949). *Notes on Labour Problems in Nationalist China*, repr. by Garland, London, 1980.

ESHERICK, J. W. (1981). 'Number Games', *Modern China*, 7(4): 387–411.

FAURE, D. (1989). *The Rural Economy of Pre-Liberation China*. Oxford: Oxford Univ. Press.

FEI, X. T. (1979). 'Sichuan: Calamity and Revival', *China Reconstructs*,

28(1): 59–63.

FEI, X. T. (1983). *Chinese Village Close-Up*. Beijing: New World Press.

FEUERWERKER, A. (1977). *Economic Trends in the Republic of China 1912–49* (Michigan Papers in Chinese Studies No. 31). Ann Arbor, Mich.: Univ. of Michigan Press.

FIELDS, G. S. (1980). *Poverty, Inequality and Development*. Cambridge: Cambridge Univ. Press.

FLOUD, R., WACHTER, K., and GREGORY, A. (1990). *Height, Health and History*. Cambridge: Cambridge Univ. Press.

FOGEL, R. W., and ENGERMAN, S. L. (1974). *Time on the Cross: The Economics of American Negro Slavery*. Boston: Little, Brown.

FREYN, H. (1941). 'China's Wartime Base', *China Quarterly* (Chongqing), 6(3): 417–35.

FRIEDMAN, M., and FRIEDMAN, R. (1980). *Free To Choose*. London: Penguin.

FRIEDMAN, F., PICKOWICZ, P. G., and SELDEN, M. (1991). *Chinese Village, Socialist State*. New Haven, Conn.: Yale Univ. Press.

FRIEDMANN, J. (1966). *Regional Development Policy*. Cambridge, Mass.: MIT Press.

GOMULKA, S. (1986). *Growth, Innovation and Reform in Eastern Europe*. Brighton: Wheatsheaf.

GOODMAN, D. S. (1986). *Centre–Province Relationships in the People's Republic of China: Sichuan and Guizhou 1955–65*. Cambridge: Cambridge Univ. Press.

GREEN, F. (ed.) (1989). *The Restructuring of the UK Economy*. Hemel Hempstead: Harvester Wheatsheaf.

GRIFFIN, K. (1974). *The Political Economy of Agrarian Change*. London: Macmillan.

—— (ed.) (1984). *Institutional Reform and Economic Development in the Chinese Countryside*. London: Macmillan.

—— and GRIFFIN, K. (1984). 'Institutional Change and Income Distribution', in Griffin (1984: 20–75).

—— and SAITH, A. (1982). 'The Pattern of Income Distribution in Rural China', *Oxford Economic Papers*, 34(1): 172–206.

GRUNFELD, A. T. (1987). *The Making of Modern Tibet*. London: Zed Books.

GUNDE, R. (1976). 'Land Tax and Social Change in Sichuan, 1925–35', *Modern China*, 2(1): 23–48.

HAHN, F. H. (1984). *Equilibrium and Macroeconomics*. Oxford: Basil Blackwell.

HAN, S. (1982). *Birdless Summer*. London: Triad/Panther.

HANLEY, S. (1988). 'The Material Culture: Stability in Transition', in M. B. Jansen, and G. Rozman (eds.), *Japan in Transition*, 447–70. Princeton, NJ: Princeton Univ. Press.

HANSON, P. (1981). *Trade and Technology in Soviet–Western Relations*. London: Macmillan.

HENIN, P.-Y. (1986). *Macrodynamics*. London: Routledge & Kegan Paul.

HINTON, W. (1966). *Fanshen*. New York: Monthly Review Press.

—— (1983). *Shenfan*. New York: Random House.

—— (1991). *The Privatization of China*. London: Earthscan.

HIRSCHMAN, A. O. (1958). *The Strategy of Economic Development*. New Haven, Conn.: Yale Univ. Press.

HOSIE, A. (1897). *Three Years in Western China*. London: G. Philip & Son.

HOWE, C., and WALKER, K. R. (eds.) (1989). *The Foundations of Chinese Planned Economy*. London: Macmillan.

HSIANG, C. Y. (1941). 'Mountain Economy in Szechwan', *Pacific Affairs*, 14: 448–62.

HSU, L. S.-L. (1935). *Silver and Prices in China*. Shanghai: Commercial Press.

HU, K.-H. (1943*a*). 'A Preliminary Study of the Cost of Living of the Military–Official–Educational Class in Chengtu', *Economic Facts*, 21: 163–9, repr. in Dept. of Agricultural Economics, Univ. of Nanking (ed.), *Economic Facts*, iii (Mar. 1943–June 1944) (London: Garland, 1980).

—— (1943*b*). 'A Preliminary Study of the Cost of Living of the Merchant–Storekeeper Class in Chengtu', *Economic Facts*, 22: 189–95, repr. in Dept. of Agricultural Economics, Univ. of Nanking (ed.), *Economic Facts*, iii (Mar. 1943–June 1944) (London: Garland, 1980).

—— (1943*c*). 'A Preliminary Study of the Cost of Living of the Laborer–Peddler Class in Chengtu', *Economic Facts*, 23: 221–6, repr. in Dept. of Agricultural Economics, Univ. of Nanking (ed.), *Economic Facts*, iii (Mar. 1943–June 1944) (London: Garland, 1980).

HUANG, P. C. C. (1975). 'Analyzing the Twentieth Century Chinese Countryside: Revolutionaries versus Western Scholarship', *Modern China*, 1(2): 132–60.

—— (1985). *The Peasant Economy and Social Change in North China*. Stanford, Calif.: Stanford Univ. Press.

—— (1990). *The Peasant Family and Rural Development in The Yangzi Delta, 1350–1988*. Stanford, Calif.: Stanford Univ. Press.

ISHIKAWA, S. (1971). 'Changes in the Structure of Agricultural Production in Mainland China', in W. A. D. Jackson (ed.), *Agrarian Policies and Problems in Communist and Non-Communist Countries*, 346–77. Seattle: Univ. of Washington Press.

JAIN, A. K., and VISARIA, P. (1988). *Infant Mortality in India*. London: Sage.

KALDOR, N. (1970). 'The Case for Regional Policies', in *Scottish Journal of Political Economy*, 17(3): 337–47.

KANE, P. (1988). *Famine in China*. London: Macmillan.

KAPP, R. A. (1973). *Szechwan and the Chinese Republic, 1911–38*. New Haven, Conn.: Yale Univ. Press.

—— (1974). 'Chungking as a Centre of Warlord Power, 1926–1937', in M. Elvin and G. W. Skinner (eds.), *The Chinese City Between Two Worlds*, 143–70. Stanford, Calif.: Stanford Univ. Press.

KATZMAN, M. T. (1977). *Cities and Frontiers in Brazil*. Cambridge, Mass.: Harvard Univ. Press.

KIRKBY, R., and CANNON, T. (1989). 'Introduction', in D. S. G. Goodman (ed.), *China's Regional Development*. London: Routledge.

372 *References*

Ko, F. T. (1943). 'Cost and Profits of Producing Rapeseed and Other Winter Crops in Szechwan', *Economic Facts*, 16: 14–19, repr. in Dept. of Agricultural Economics, Univ. of Nanking (ed.), *Economic Facts*, ii (Jan. 1938–Feb. 1943) (London: Garland, 1980).

Kosai, Y., and Ogino, Y. (1984). *The Contemporary Japanese Economy*. London: Macmillan.

Kueh, Y. Y. (1985). *Economic Planning and Local Mobilisation in Post-Mao China* (CCI Research Notes and Studies No. 7). London: School of Oriental and African Studies.

—— (1988). 'Food Consumption and Peasant Incomes in the Post-Mao Era', *China Quarterly*, 116: 634–70.

Kuo, S. W. Y., Fei, J. C. H., and Ranis, G. (1981). *The Taiwan Success Story*. Boulder, Colo.: Westview.

Lardy, N. R. (1983). *Agriculture in China's Modern Economic Development*. Cambridge: Cambridge Univ. Press.

Lavely, W., Xiao, Z. Y., Li, B. H., and Freedman, R. (1990). 'The Rise in Female Education in China', *China Quarterly*, 121: 61–93.

Lavely, W. R. (1984). 'The Rural Chinese Fertility Transition: A Report From Shifang *xian*, Sichuan', *Population Studies*, 35(3): 365–84.

Lee, C. H. (1986). *The British Economy since 1700: A Macroeconomic Perspective*. Cambridge: Cambridge Univ. Press.

Lee, K. C. (1939). 'Usury in the Rural Districts of Szechwan', in R. H. Tawney (ed.), *Agrarian China*. London: George Allen & Unwin.

Leeming, F. (1985). *Rural China Today*. London: Longman.

Lefebvre, A. (1979). *Le District de Guanghan au Sichuan*. Toulouse: Université Toulouse-le-Mirail.

Lenin, V. I. (1899; 1957 edn.). *The Development of Capitalism in Russia*. London: Lawrence & Wishart.

—— (1959 edn.). *Alliances of the Working Class and the Peasantry*. London: Lawrence & Wishart.

—— (n.d.). *Questions of the Socialist Organisation of the Economy*. Moscow: Progress Publishers.

Lewis, W. A. (1954). 'Economic Development with Unlimited Supplies of Labour', *Manchester School*, 22(2): 139–91.

Lin, F. D., and Zhou, Q. (1981). 'Shifang County: Family Planning', in Z. Liu (ed.), *China's Population*, 159–68. Beijing: New World Press.

Lin, L., and Gu, Z. C. (1985). 'The Course of Reform in Sichuan's Economic Structure', *Social Sciences in China*, 6(1): 179–205.

Liu, R. T. (1940). 'Cost of Producing Silk in Santai', *Economic Facts*, 14: 43–59, repr. in Dept. of Agricultural Economics, Univ. of Nanking (ed.), *Economic Facts*, ii (June 1938–Feb. 1943) (London: Garland, 1980).

Liu, S. N., and Wu, Q. G. (1986). *China's Socialist Economy: An Outline History*. Beijing: Beijing Review.

Liu, T. C., and Yeh, K. C. (1965). *The Economy of the Chinese Mainland*. Princeton, NJ: Princeton Univ. Press.

MA, H. (1983). *New Strategy for China's Economy*. Beijing: New World Press.

MACFARQUHAR, R. (1983). *The Origins of the Cultural Revolution*, ii: *The Great Leap Forward*. Oxford: Oxford Univ. Press.

MADSEN, R. (1984). *Morality and Power in a Chinese Village*. Berkeley, Calif.: Univ. of California Press.

MALLORY, W. H. (1926). *China: Land of Famine*. New York: American Geographical Society.

MAO, Z. D. (ed.) (1957). *Socialist Upsurge in China's Countryside*. Peking: Foreign Languages Press.

—— (1971). *Selected Reading from the Works of Mao Tsetung*. Peking: Foreign Languages Press.

MARITIME CUSTOMS, STATISTICAL DEPT. OF THE INSPECTOR-GENERAL OF CUSTOMS (1938). *Domestic Trade* (vol. iv of *Reports, Abstracts, Analysis and Imports and Exports and Domestic Trade*). Shanghai.

MARX, K. (1954 edn.). *Capital*, i. London: Lawrence & Wishart.

Mathews' Chinese–English Dictionary (1943). Rev. American edn. Cambridge, Mass.: Harvard Univ. Press.

MATHEWS, T. J. (1971). 'The Cultural Revolution in Sichuan', in East Asian Research Center, Harvard University (ed.), *The Cultural Revolution in the Provinces*, 94–146. Cambridge, Mass.: Harvard Univ. Press.

MATHIAS, P., and DAVIS, J. A. (ed.) (1989). *The First Industrial Revolutions*. Oxford: Basil Blackwell.

MENDES, R. B. (1987). 'The Rural Sector in the Socio-Economic Context of Brazil', *CEPAL Review*, 33: 39–59.

MINAMI, R. (1986). *The Economic Development of Japan*. London: Macmillan.

MORRISON, G. E. (1895; 1985 edn.). *An Australian in China*. Oxford: Oxford Univ. Press.

MOSHER, S. W. (1982). *Broken Earth*. London: Robert Hale.

MYERS, R. (1989). 'Review of Lippit', *China Quarterly*, 119: 640–1.

MYERS, R. H. (1967). 'The Usefulness of Local Gazetteers for the Study of Modern Chinese Economic History: Szechuan Province During the Ch'ing and Republican Periods', *Tsing Hua Journal of Chinese Studies*, 6(1, 2): 72–102.

—— (1970). *The Chinese Peasant Economy: Agricultural Development in Hopei and Shantung, 1890–1949*. Cambridge, Mass.: Harvard Univ. Press.

—— (1972). 'The Commercialization of Agriculture in Modern China', in W. E. Willmott (ed.) (1972). *Economic Organization in Chinese Society*. Stanford, Calif.: Stanford Univ. Press.

—— (1982). 'Land Property Rights and Agricultural Development in Modern China', in R. Barker, R. Sinha, and B. Rose (1982: 37–47) above.

—— (1986). 'The Agrarian System', in J. K. Fairbank and A. Feuerwerker (eds.), *The Cambridge History of China*, xiii(2): 230–69. Cambridge:

Cambridge Univ. Press.

MYERS, R. H. (1989). 'The World Depression and the Chinese Economy, 1930–36', in I. Brown (ed.), *The Economies of Africa and Asia in the Interwar Depression*. London: Routledge.

MYRDAL, G. (1957). *Economic Theory and Underdeveloped Regions*. London: Duckworth.

NARB (1936). *Crop Reporting in China, 1934*. Nanking: NARB, Ministry of Industry.

NAUGHTON, B. (1988). 'The Third Front: Defence Industrialization in the Chinese Interior', *China Quarterly*, 115: 351–86.

NICOL, W., and YUILL, D. (1982). 'Regional Problems and Policy', in A. Boltho (ed.), *The European Economy: Growth and Crisis*, 409–48. Oxford: Oxford Univ. Press.

NISHIKAWA, S. (1988). 'Grain Consumption: The Case of Choshu', in M. B. Jansen and G. Rozman (eds.), *Japan in Transition* (pb. edn.), 421–46. Princeton, NJ: Princeton Univ. Press.

NOLAN, P. (1976). 'Collectivisation in China: Some Comparisons with the USSR', *Journal of Peasant Studies*, 3(2): 192–220.

—— (1981). 'Rural Income in the People's Republic of China, 1952–57'. Ph.D. thesis, Univ. of London.

—— (1983*a*). *Growth Processes and Distributional Change in a South Chinese Province: The Case of Guangdong*. London: School of Oriental and African Studies.

—— (1983*b*). Sichuan Notebooks (interview notes and data collected in Sichuan in 1983). Unpublished.

—— (1988). *The Political Economy of Collective Farms*. Cambridge: Polity Press.

—— and DONG, F. R. (eds.) (1990*a*). *Market Forces in China*. London: Zed Books.

—— —— (eds.) (1990*b*). *The Chinese Economy and Its Future*. Cambridge: Polity Press.

PAGANO, U. (1985). *Work and Welfare in Economic Theory*. Oxford: Basil Blackwell.

PAI, Y. Y. (1939). 'Labour Tax in the Building of the Szechwan–Hunan Highway', in R. H. Tawney (ed.), *Agrarian China*, 110–112. London: Allen & Unwin.

PARISH, W., and WHYTE, M. K. (1978). *Village and Family in Contemporary China*. Chicago: Univ. of Chicago Press.

PATNAIK, U. (1976). 'Class Differentiation within the Peasantry', *Economic and Political Weekly*, 11(39): A82–101.

PECK, G. (1941). *Through China's Wall*. London: Collins.

PENG, X. Z. (1987). 'Demographic Consequences of the Great Leap Forward in China's Provinces', *Population and Development Review*, 13(4): 639–70.

PIAZZA, A. (1983). *Trends in Food and Nutrient Availability in China, 1958–1981* (Staff Working Paper 607). Washington, DC: World Bank.

—— (1986). *Food Consumption and Nutritional Status in the PRC*. Boulder, Colo.: Westview.

POPKIN, S. (1979). *The Rational Peasant*. Berkeley, Calif.: Univ. of California Press.

RAHMAN, A. (1986). *Peasants and Classes*. London: Zed Books.

RAMACHANDRAN, K. (n.d.). 'Food Consumption in Rural Indian Households', in C. Gopalan (ed.), *Combating Undernutrition*. New Delhi: Nutrition Foundation of India.

RAWLS, J. (1971). *A Theory of Justice*. Cambridge, Mass.: Harvard Univ. Press.

RAWSKI, T. G. (1989). *Economic Growth in Prewar China*. Oxford: Univ. of California Press.

REN, M. E., YANG, R. Z., and BAO, H. S. (1985). *An Outline of China's Physical Geography*. Beijing: Foreign Languages Press.

Rice Statistics (1941): Appendix to 'Rice Problem', special issue of *Economic Facts*, 15: 150–60, repr. in Dept. of Agricultural Economics, Univ. of Nanking (ed.), *Economic Facts*, ii (June 1938–Feb. 1943) (London: Garland, 1980).

RICHTHOFEN, F. VON (1903). *Baron von Richthofen's Letters 1870–72*. Shanghai: North China Herald Office.

RISKIN, C. (1987). *China's Political Economy*. Oxford: Oxford Univ. Press.

—— (1990*a*). 'Food, Poverty and the Development Strategy in the People's Republic of China', in L. F. Newman (ed.), *Hunger in History*. Oxford: Basil Blackwell.

—— (1990*b*). 'Where Is China Going?' in Nolan and Dong (1990*b*: 41–62).

ROEMER, J. E. (1982). *A General Theory of Exploitation and Class*. Cambridge, Mass.: Harvard Univ. Press.

—— (1986). 'Should Marxists Be Interested in Exploitation?' in J. E. Roemer (ed.), *Analytical Marxism*, 260–82. Cambridge: Cambridge Univ. Press.

ROLL, C. R. (1980). *The Distribution of Rural Incomes in China*. London: Garland.

ROZMAN, G. (1982). *Population and Marketing Settlements in Ch'ing China*. Cambridge: Cambridge Univ. Press.

RUDRA, A. (1988). 'Emerging Class Structure in Rural India' in Srinivasan and Bardhan (1988: 483–500).

SAG (1986). *Sichuan Agricultural Geography*, trans. from ZKCDY (1980), (above), in Joint Publications Research Service Translation No. CAG-86-026 (25 June).

SALISBURY, H. (1985: pb. edn. 1986). *The Long March*. London: Pan.

SCHUMPETER, J. A. (1951). *The Theory of Economic Development*. Cambridge, Mass.: Harvard Univ. Press.

SCOTT, J. C. (1976). *The Moral Economy of the Peasant*. New Haven, Conn.: Yale Univ. Press.

SELDEN, M. (ed.) (1979). *The People's Republic of China: A Documentary*

History of Revolutionary Change. New York: Monthly Review Press.
—— (1982). 'Cooperation and conflict: cooperatives and collective formation in China's countryside', repr. in Selden (1988: 54–100).
—— (1988). *The Political Economy of Chinese Socialism*. London: M. E. Sharpe.
SEN, A. (1981). 'Market Failure and Control of Labour Power', *Cambridge Journal of Economics*, 5(3): 199–228; 5(4): 293–318.
SEN, A. K. (1973). *On Economic Inequality*. Oxford: Clarendon Press.
—— (1981: pb. 1982). *Poverty and Famines*. Oxford: Clarendon Press.
—— (1987). *The Living Standard*. Cambridge: Cambridge Univ. Press.
—— (1988). 'Family and Food: Sex Bias in Poverty', in Srinivasan and Bardhan (1988: 453–72).
—— (1989). 'Food and Freedom', *World Development*, 17(6): 769–81.
SHAMBAUGH, D. (ed.) (1982). 'Zhao Ziyang's "Sichuan Experience": Blueprint for a Nation', *Chinese Law and Government*, 15(1): 3–126.
SHANIN, T. (1972). *The Awkward Class*: extract repr. in J. Harriss (ed.), *Rural Development*, 223–45 (London: Hutchinson, 1982).
—— (1985). *Russia as a 'Developing Society'*, i. London: Macmillan.
SHAWCROSS, W. (1985). *The Quality of Mercy*. London: Fontana/Collins.
SHUE, V. (1980). *Peasant China in Transition*. Berkeley, Calif.: Univ. of California Press.
Sichuan Ribao (1982). 'Exploration of Ways in which the Western Sichuan Plain can Develop Agriculture', trans. in Joint Publications Research Service, *China Report: Agriculture*, No. 227, 20 Sept., 38–41.
SICULAR, T. (ed.) (1989). *Food Price Policy in Asia*. Ithaca, NY: Cornell Univ. Press.
SKINNER, G. W. (1964–5). 'Marketing and Social Structure in Rural China', *Journal of Asian Studies*, 24(1): 3–43; 24(2): 195–228; 24(3): 363–99.
—— (1987). 'Sichuan's Population in the Nineteenth Century; Lessons from Disaggregated Data', *Late Imperial China*, 8(1): 1–79.
SMEDLEY, A. (1956). *The Great Road*. New York: Monthly Review Press.
SMETHURST, R. J. (1986). *Agricultural Development and Tenancy Dispute in Japan, 1870–1940*. Princeton, NJ: Princeton Univ. Press.
SMIL, V. (1988). *Energy in China's Modernization*. London: M. E. Sharpe.
SMITH, P. J. (1988). 'Commerce, Agriculture and Core Formation in the Upper Yangzi, 2 A.D. to 1948', *Late Imperial China*, 9(1): 1–78.
SNOW, E. (1972; 1st published 1937). *Red Star Over China*. London: Penguin.
SRINIVASAN, T. N., and BARDHAN, P. K. (eds.) (1988). *Rural Poverty in South Asia*. New York: Columbia Univ. Press.
STONE, B. (1988). 'Developments in Agricultural Technology', *China Quarterly*, 116: 767–822.
STROSS, R. E. (1986). *The Stubborn Earth*. London: Univ. of California Press.
SUKHATME, P. V. (1988). 'Energy Intake and Nutrition: On the Autoregulatory Homeostatic Nature of the Energy Requirement', in Srinivasan and Bardhan (1988: 365–88).

SUN, C. C. (1960). *Economic Geography of Southwestern China.* New York: Joint Publications Research Service trans. No. 15069 from the original Chinese, *Xinan diqu jingji dili* (Beijing: Kexue chubanshe).

SWB (1981). *Summary of World Broadcasts.* SWB FE/W115/A/1, 7 Jan. London: BBC.

TAWNEY, R. H. (1932). *Land and Labour in China.* London: George Allen & Unwin.

THORBECKE, E. (1979). 'Agricultural Development', in W. Galenson (ed.), *Economic Growth and Structural Change in Taiwan.* London: Cornell Univ. Press.

TOWNSEND, P. (1979). *Poverty in the United Kingdom.* Harmondsworth: Penguin.

TRAVERS, L. (1982). 'Bias in Chinese Economic Statistics: The Case of Typical Example Investigation', *China Quarterly*, 91: 478–85.

TREUDLEY, M. B. (1971). *The Men and Women of Chung Ho Ch'ang.* Taibei: Orient Cultural Service.

TSUI, R. T. (1944). 'Relation of Size of Farm to Farm Efficiency', *Economic Facts*, 36, repr. in Dept. of Agricultural Economics, Univ. of Nanking (ed.), *Economic Facts*, iv. 533–5 (London: Garland, 1980).

—— (1946). 'Correlation Analysis on Factors Affecting Farm Profits', *Economic Facts*, 51, repr. in Dept. of Agricultural Economics, Univ. of Nanking (ed.), *Economic Facts*, iv. 801–4 (London: Garland, 1980).

UNGER, J. (1984). 'The Class System in Rural China: A Case Study', in J. L. Watson (ed.), *Class and Social Stratification in Post-Revolutionary China*, 121–41. Cambridge: Cambridge Univ. Press.

UNICEF (1990). *The State of the World's Children 1990.* Oxford: Oxford Univ. Press.

VERMEER, E. B. (1982). 'Income Differentials in Rural China', *China Quarterly*, 89: 1–33.

—— (1988). *Economic Development in Provincial China.* Cambridge: Cambridge Univ. Press.

WADE, R. (1990). *Governing the Market.* Princeton, NJ: Princeton Univ. Press.

WALKER, K. R. (1965). *Planning in Chinese Agriculture.* London: Frank Cass.

—— (1984). *Food Grain Procurement and Consumption in China.* Cambridge: Cambridge Univ. Press.

WANG, G. C., and ZHOU, Q. R. (ed.) (1985). *Smashing the Communal Pot.* Beijing: New World Press.

WANG, L. X. (1988). 'Mao's Legacy in Anhui', *Kunlun*, 6, trans. by Joint Publications Research Service, CAR-89-079.

WANG, X. Q., and BAI, N. F. (1991). *The Poverty of Plenty.* London: Macmillan.

WANG, Y. Y. (1943). 'The Effect of Rising Prices on Different Social Classes', *Economic Facts*, 23: 207–11, repr. in Dept. of Agricultural Economics, Univ. of Nanking (ed.), *Economic Facts*, iii (Mar. 1943–June 1944) (London: Garland, 1980).

WATSON, A. (ed.) (1980). *Mao Zedong and the Political Economy of the Border Regime*. Cambridge: Cambridge Univ. Press.

—— (1984). 'Agriculture Looks for "Shoes that Fit": The Production Responsibility System and Its Implications', in N. Maxwell and B. McFarlane (eds.), *China's Changed Road to Development*, 83–108. Oxford: Pergamon.

—— (1989). 'Investment Issues in the Chinese Countryside', *Australian Journal of Chinese Affairs*, 22: 1–30.

WIENS, T. B. (1982). *The Microeconomics of Peasant Economy*. London: Garland.

WILKINSON, F. (1988). 'Where Do We Go From Here? Real Wages, Effective Demand and Economic Development', *Cambridge Journal of Economics*, 12(1): 179–91.

WILLIAMSON, J. G. (1965). 'Regional Inequality and the Process of National Development: A Description of the Patterns', *Economic Development and Cultural Change*, 13(4): 425–63, 3–45.

—— (1988). 'Migration and Urbanization', in H. Chenery and T. N. Srinivasan (eds.), *Handbook of Development Economics*, i. Amsterdam: North-Holland.

WOODHEAD, H. G. W. (ed.) (1926). *The China Yearbook 1925–26*. Tientsin (Tianjin): Tientsin Press.

—— (ed.) (1931). *The China Yearbook 1931*. Shanghai: North China Daily News & Herald.

WORLD BANK (1983). *China: Socialist Economic Development*, iii. Washington, DC: World Bank.

—— (1986a). *China: Long Term Issues and Options*. Washington, DC: World Bank.

—— (1986b). *World Development Report 1986*. Oxford: Oxford Univ. Press.

—— (1989). *India: Poverty, Employment and Social Services*. Washington, DC: World Bank.

XIN, W., TANG, G. Z., HE, Y. G., and LI, C. M. (1984). 'Tremendous Achievements, Bright Prospects', *Sichuan Ribao*, 26 Sept., trans. by Joint Publications Research Service, CEA-84-095 (*China Report, Economic Affairs*), 26 Nov., 29–37.

YANG, W. Y., and HU, K.-H. (1939). 'A Cost of Living Index for the Merchant–Storekeeper Class and for All Three Classes in Chengtu, Szechwan', *Economic Facts*, 13: 32–41, repr. in Dept. of Agricultural Economics, Univ. of Nanking (ed.), *Economic Facts*, ii (June 1938–Feb. 1943) (London: Garland, 1980).

—— and KAO, C. Y. (1940). 'Wartime Price Movements in China', *Economic Facts*, 14: 61–106, repr. in Dept. of Agricultural Economics, Univ. of Nanking (ed.), *Economic Facts*, ii (June 1938–Feb. 1943) (London: Garland, 1980).

YEH, K. C. (1979). 'China's National Income, 1931–36', in C. M. Hou and T. S. Yu (eds.), *Modern Chinese Economic History*, 95–128. Taibei: Institute of Economics, Academia Sinica.

ZELIN, M. (1988). 'Capital Accumulation and Investment Strategies in Early Modern China: The Case of the Furong Salt Yard', *Late Imperial China*, 9(1): 79–122.

ZGNYNJ (1981). *Chinese Agricultural Yearbook 1981*, partially trans. in Joint Publications Research Service, *China Report: Agriculture*, No. 255, 28 Apr., 170–80.

ZHENG, Y. Y. (1984). 'Sichuan's Basic Economic Development Situation', trans. from *Jingji Diaocha* (Economic Survey), No. 2, in Joint Publications Research Service, CEA-84-096, 29 Nov.

Index

Aba autonomous prefecture 16, 147, 198–9, 205–6, 300–1, 303, 310
agricultural:
  cultivated area 9, 165–6, 232
  double-wheeled plough 84
  economies of scale 128–9, 220–4
  growth 22–3, 90–3, 106, 188–214
  household generational mobility 131, 134–5
  interest rates 129, 229–30, 238–43
  labour mobilization 190, 204, 310–12, 321–2
  markets 128–31, 135–6, 226
  multiple cropping 91–2, 96, 195
  ownership of land 216–24, 235–7
  production costs 197–8
  socio-economic generational mobility 131, 134–5, 253–5
  sown area 91–2, 96, 195, 199–200, 318–19, 322
  surplus labour 66–7
  taxation 73, 134, 233–7
  technical change 84–5, 96, 107–8, 129, 189, 192–208, 211–13, 220–1
  tenancy 222–32, 243–4
  tractors 106, 189, 204
  wages 131, 243–53
  see also fertilizer; grain; irrigation; rural industry
Amsden, A. 69
Anhui province 247, 291–2, 303–4
anthropometric data 39–41
Ash, R. 125, 127 n., 189 n., 191, 193–4, 215

Ba county 228–9, 240, 289
Bangladesh 220, 284
Banister, J. 292, 294–5, 297
Batang county 219
Baxian prefecture 24, 143–4, 147, 151, 159, 160, 169, 181, 186, 199, 223, 240, 301
Bazhong county 252–4, 289
Beichuan county 156
birth rates 292–4, 296–7, 299
Brandt, L. 130–1, 135–6, 216, 243, 245–6
Brazil 176–7
Buck, J. L. 130, 132, 135, 195, 217, 222–6, 228–30, 239–40, 247–8
Bukharinism 3, 6, 79

Cangxi county 37, 50, 289, 290
capabilities 7, 49–54, 264–5

capital–output ratios 2, 4
cash crops 196–7, 199–203
central planning, see planning
Chakravarty, S. 68–9, 85
Changshou county 187, 199
Chayanov, A. 130
Chengdu:
  city 13, 18–19, 24, 35–6, 39–40, 42, 102, 109, 154, 168, 179, 240, 248, 301
  plain 15, 19, 93, 126, 143–6, 154–6, 189, 193, 195–7, 206–7, 227, 229, 243, 290
Chiang Kaishek 22, 77–8, 126, 201
Chinese Communist Party (CCP) 22, 78, 103, 119, 126, 188, 314
Chongqing:
  city 13, 18–19, 23–4, 36, 39–40, 42, 73, 102, 108, 146–7, 154–6, 168, 218–19, 236–7, 239, 248, 282, 299, 301, 306, 310
  county 146, 233 n., 236–7
coal industry 23, 43, 312, 315, 320–1
collectives:
  communes 325–30
  creation 22, 81, 274, 300, 309
  dissolution 4, 22–3, 170–1, 274
  performance 4, 81–4, 91, 221
commerce, see trade
consumption:
  of durables 46–8, 104, 275, 277–8
  of food 31–41, 52–4, 104, 147, 252, 282–4, 316–17
  requirements (calories) 38–9, 312
co-operatives 133–4
corruption, rural 273–8
cotton industry 54–5
crude birth rates, see birth rates
crude death rates, see death rates
Cultural Revolution 2, 22, 262, 269–70

Da county 239
Daxian prefecture 147, 160, 181, 186, 301
Dayi county 146, 236–7
Dazhai system 262–3
Dazu county 43
death rates 12, 104, 265, 289, 291–304, 306, 308–10, 312
defence industry 96, 99–103, 108–9, 250–3
decollectivization, see collectives
deforestation 91, 96, 321
Deng Xiaoping 2, 96, 255
Derong county 19
draught animals 83, 192, 210–11

Dujiangyan 55, 154–5, 192, 195
Dukou, *see* Panzhihua

East Asian NICs 3, 5, 56–7, 69, 88
Eastman, L. 73, 77, 132, 245
Ebian county 160
education 263, 265, 272
Egypt 220
electricity:
　production 23, 43, 87, 93
　rural consumption 193, 208
　hydro 54, 93
Elvin, M. 130–1
Emei:
　county 43
　mountain 13, 66
energy 2, 87, 93–4, 109, 185, 312
Esherick, J. 127 n., 216
ethnic minorities 15–16, 148, 154, 163, 180,
　183–5, 230–1, 299–300, 303
exploitation 115–19, 127–8

famine:
　in China 5, 10, 281, 291–6, 305
　in 1930s Sichuan 23, 89, 156, 179,
　　282–91, 303
　in Sichuan during the GLF 161, 182,
　　295–333
　in USSR 3, 281
farming, *see* agriculture
Feldman model 8, 59, 320
Fengdu county 154
Fengjie county 204
fertility, *see* birth rates
fertilizer, chemical 43–4, 97, 106, 193–208,
　212–13
Fields, G. 120, 122–5
food-processing industry 311
Fujian province 51, 270
Fuling:
　county 108, 154, 222, 229, 239, 289
　prefecture 16, 147, 151, 153–5, 159–61,
　　181, 186, 301, 303
Fushun county 240, 266–7

Gansu province 304
Garze autonomous prefecture 16, 147,
　300–1, 303, 310
Gomulka, S. 65–6
Goodman, D. 22, 83, 313, 327
grain:
　consumption 2, 31–41, 104, 184, 282–4
　export 32, 135–6, 324–5, 329
　procurement 192, 328–9
　production 24, 74–6, 79, 80–5, 90–3,
　　188–214, 284–5, 306–19, 328
　self-sufficiency policy 189–91, 198–204
　storage 249, 289, 329

　yields 193–8, 212–13, 222–4
Great Leap Forward (1958–62) 2, 5, 91,
　94–5, 207, 212, 270, 274, 281, 286–7,
　291–333
growth rates:
　after 1978, 4, 7, 23–4, 59–60, 103–11
　before 1949, 7, 56
　under Mao (1949–78) 29–32, 79, 314
Guan county 146, 155, 236
Guang'an:
　county 239, 255
　prefecture 160, 181, 186
Guangdong province 10, 189, 271, 276
Guanghan county 158, 167, 170, 182, 187,
　207–8, 240, 260–3, 265–6, 269–70, 319
Guangyuan:
　county 187, 208, 290
　prefecture 159, 160, 181, 185–6
Guizhou province 154, 159, 255, 282
Gulin county 219, 265
Gusong county 218

health care 1, 54
heavy industry:
　before 1930: 23
　during the 1930s 23, 57–8, 250–2
　during the 1950s 25, 87–9
　during the 1960s and 1970s 25, 41–9, 98–
　　103
　during the 1980s 105, 108–9
　during the Great Leap Forward 312, 315,
　　320–4
　during the Second World War 24, 58, 72,
　　76
　output share of 41–2
　'Third Front' and 30, 94, 98–103, 108
Hebei province 5, 320
Hechuan county 315
heights 39–41
Heilongjiang province 178
Himalayan plateau 10, 13, 162, 265, 300
Hongya county 235, 240
Hongyuan county 158, 162
Huang, P. 119, 125, 127 n., 134–5, 143,
　194, 215, 216
Huayang county 178–9, 224, 227, 240,
　244 n., 252, 271
Huaying county 158, 169
Hubei province 18, 21, 254
Hunan province 117, 254

India 32, 51, 112, 116–17, 118, 177, 220,
　285, 288, 305
industrialization 11, 12, 41–9, 56, 72–3,
　108–9, 145, 169, 185–8, 250–2, 312,
　314–16
inequality, in other countries 259–60
　see also intra-local; spatial

infant mortality 49–52, 104, 161–3, 265, 289
intra-local inequality:
  in China 2, 6, 10, 125–36
  and data problems 9, 125, 215–16, 262–78
  in 1950s Sichuan 80–2, 278
  in 1980s Sichuan 259–79
  in Republican Sichuan 125, 132, 215–57, 278
  theory 9, 115–25
investment:
  in agriculture 97, 106–8
  in industry 66–7, 88–9, 94–5, 99–102, 320–4
  in infrastructure 21, 30, 58–9, 86–7, 94, 109–11
  in regions of Sichuan 175–6, 183–8, 205–6
  share in NDMP 2, 99, 313, 320–4
irrigation 55, 85, 190, 192–208, 212

Japan 8, 19, 28, 32, 41, 77, 89, 151, 197, 221, 235, 245
Jiajiang county 235
Jiang'an county 218, 240
Jiangbei county 219, 240
Jiange county 290
Jiangjin county 219
Jiangsu province 11, 15, 19, 51, 111 n., 178, 198, 247
Jiangxi province 184
Jiangyou county 156, 236–7, 254
Jianyang county 179, 266
Jinghua county 148, 166
Jingyan county 182, 205–6, 211–13, 219, 290, 299, 310, 315, 318–19
Jintang county 146, 196
Junlian county 219

Kalecki, M. 37, 56, 320
Kampuchea 281, 298
Keynes, J. M. 144, 241
Kham 21, 309
Korea, South (ROK) 8, 57, 88
Kuomintang (KMT) 7, 11, 22, 103, 126, 168, 201, 252, 289, 332

land reform 118–19, 172, 254, 271, 278, 300, 309
Lardy, N. 190–1
Leibo county 160, 207–8, 265
Lenin, V. 82, 117, 127–8, 133
Leshan:
  county 208, 211, 235, 240, 266–7
  prefecture 24, 147, 151, 160, 169, 181, 185–6, 188, 301–2
Lewis, W. A. 65

Li county (Lifan) 218, 290
Liangshan autonomous prefecture 16, 92, 127, 147, 167, 170–1, 179, 198, 207, 230–1, 265, 301, 310
life expectancy 1, 49–50, 53, 104
literacy 50–1, 104, 111, 161–3, 265
Long county 255
Longchang county 85
Lu county (Luzhou) 43, 240
Luxian prefecture 151, 154, 160, 172, 181, 186

Mabian county 148, 160, 265
machine industry 88, 99–100
Malaysia 261
Maowen county 252
Mao, Zedong:
  Great Leap Forward and 281, 314–15, 320, 327–8, 332
  literature on Maoist development 1–6, 112–13
  speeches and writings 11, 29, 80–1, 117–18, 133–4, 189, 224–5, 314–15, 320, 327, 332
Marx, K. 115, 143
Mianyang:
  county 239
  prefecture 147, 153, 155, 160, 172, 181, 185–6, 301–2
Mianzhu county 182
Ministry of International Trade and Industry (MITI) 68, 89
mortality, *see* death rates; infant mortality
Muli county 180
Myers, R. 130–2, 215, 226, 245–6

Nanchong prefecture 147, 160, 172, 181, 186, 301
Nanchuan county 218, 266–7
Nanjiang county 219, 266–7, 289
Nanjing:
  city 13, 18, 22
  decade (1928–37) vii, 7–9
Neijiang:
  city 85, 239, 299, 306, 310, 315
  prefecture 76–7, 147, 161, 172, 181, 186, 196, 227, 301
neo-populism 130–6
net domestic material product (NDMP) 11, 12, 31, 79
Ningxia province 37
Nolan, P. vii, 1, 3–4, 6–9, 64, 81, 91, 177, 191, 260–1, 269
nuclear weapons:
  development of in China 96, 101–3, 105
  US and 98–103

opium 27, 89, 166, 199–200, 235

Pakistan 32
Panzhihua (Dukou) city 16, 24, 36, 43, 100–1, 180, 183, 301
Peng county 146, 228
Peng Dehuai 320, 327, 332
Pengshui county 154, 218
Pengxi county 266
Pi county 146, 218
pig:
   deaths during collectivization 83–4
   deaths during the Great Leap Forward 316
   stock 83, 283, 307–8
Pingwu county 156
planning:
   during the Great Leap Forward 90–5, 331–2
   during the 1940s 72–8
   during the 1950s 6, 78–90
   during the 1960s and 1970s 90–103, 273
   during the 1980s 103–11, 273
   failures 1–6, 64, 112–13
   Mao and 1–9, 99
   success of in China vii, 1–9, 100–3, 112–13
   theories of 8, 60–72
   USSR and 1, 3, 61, 63–6, 112
polarization 80, 82, 128–30, 133, 244
population:
   before 1900: 15
   censuses 1, 286–7, 291, 294, 296
   density 15–16, 17, 144–5, 181, 211
   during GLF 291–304, 306–10
   during late Maoism 187
   during Republic 153, 232, 282–4, 286–7, 290
   growth 180–2, 232
   migration 67, 175–82, 184
   urban 12, 16
   see also birth rates; death rates
poverty, rural:
   absolute 6, 27, 121, 169–73, 245–53
   in the 1930s 6, 132, 245–53
   in the 1970s 2–6
   in the 1980s 53–4
   relative 121, 169–73
   spatial 2, 3, 5, 169–74, 190
   theory 120–5
prices 73–6, 79, 202, 242–3, 248–9, 285, 290, 331
   see also terms of trade
production functions 70
Pujiang county 146

Qianwei county 235
Qijiang county 218
Qingchuan county 204, 254
Qionglai:

county 146, 167, 269, 315
   prefecture 161, 181, 186
Qu county 37, 50

railways 10, 18–19, 20 (map), 57, 86–7, 89, 109–11, 155–6
Rawski, T. 7–9, 234, 246–7
Red Army 22, 126, 152, 156, 180, 238, 251, 252–3, 288
Renshou county 179
Riskin, C. 1–3, 6–9, 53, 259–60, 294–5
rivers:
   Anning 13, 92, 180, 207, 265
   Jialing 18
   Jinsha 15, 21, 101
   Min 155–6
   in Sichuan 18–20 (map), 55, 59, 86, 110, 142
   Wu 154, 159
   Yangzi (Changjiang) 15, 18–21, 24, 72, 86, 126, 135, 151, 154, 250–1
roads 18, 57, 86, 109–11
Roemer, J. 115–16, 128
Rongchang county 85
rural industry 24, 186–7, 189–90, 212, 243–53, 265–7, 268–72, 281, 312

salt industry 23, 76–7
Santai:
   county 218
   prefecture 151, 160, 181, 186
Schumpeter, J. 63–4, 68
Selden, M. 1, 4–9, 81–2, 291
Sen, A. K. 7, 49, 52, 120, 124, 285, 305, 317–18
Sertar county 162
Serxu county 219
Shaanxi province 328
Shandong province 51, 142, 217
Shanghai 29, 44, 191, 193–4
Shanin, T. 130, 134–5
Shanxi province 276
Shapingba district 146–7
Shifang county 50–1, 83, 148, 155, 158, 167, 170–1, 182, 187, 197, 199, 203, 208, 211–13, 263–7, 274–6, 289, 298–9, 302, 306, 308, 310, 315, 318–19, 328
shipping 18–20, 23, 72, 95, 108–9, 154
Shu 13, 27, 86, 99
Shuangliu county 146
Sichuan:
   boundaries 10–11, 14 (map), 15, 21–2, 140–1, 171, 310–11
   economic geography 15–21, 57–9
   physical geography 10–15, 126, 152–5
   political change 21–2, 126–7, 215
   rainfall 288, 319–20

rebellion in (1956–8) 22, 300, 309–10
warlords 22, 126, 156, 215, 233–7, 241, 250–2, 254–5
sidelines 92–3, 243–53, 264, 268–72
silk industry 24, 46, 249
Skinner, W. 139–45, 154–5
slavery 127, 159–61, 230–1
Songjiang county (Jiangsu) 194, 197
Songpan:
  county 290
  prefecture 152–3, 160, 179–80, 186
spatial inequality:
  in China 2, 5–7, 158
  data problems 145–8, 152, 163–9, 171
  long-run changes in Sichuan 163–9, 174–214
  in 1980s Sichuan 156–69, 173, 262–8
  in other countries 150–1
  in Republican Sichuan 139–45, 148–56
Stalinism 3, 56
State Statistical Bureau 1, 95, 262, 291, 310–11
steel industry 43, 91, 281, 312, 320–1
sugar cane 196, 227
Suining county 205, 239–40

Taiwan 7–8, 19, 97–8, 221
Tawney, R. 225, 232, 238
terms of trade, intersectoral 4, 85–6, 97, 105, 188–9
textile industry 23, 45–6, 95
'Third Front' industrialization 25, 30, 94, 98–103, 183
tianfu zhiguo (the Heavenly Kingdom) 11, 13, 27, 282
Tianquan county 219
Tibet 10, 15, 21, 153, 180, 183–5, 300
Tongjiang county 289
trade, foreign 151, 155, 172, 245–53, 302, 324–5, 329–30, 332
trade, internal 47–8, 131, 135–6, 142–5, 216, 300, 302, 329–30
transport 2, 10, 18–21, 58–9, 86–7, 95, 109–11, 142, 155–6, 191, 288, 302, 313

United Kingdom 8, 10, 28, 40, 107, 314
USA:
  and 'threat' to China 25, 48, 98–103, 105, 188, 191–2
  and Vietnam 98–9, 101

USSR:
  aid to China 87, 324
  famine in 3, 281, 332
  split with China 98, 102 n.
  Tsarist Russia 134–5, 178

Vermeer, E. 127, 215, 259, 328

Wan county 108, 229, 236–7, 240
Wanxian prefecture 147, 160, 181, 186, 301
Wanyuan county 267
weights 40
welfare functions 120–5
Wenchuan county 153
Wenjiang:
  county 37, 50–1, 146, 207–8
  prefecture 147, 153–5, 161, 181, 186, 301–2
Wushan county 208, 265

Xichong county 319
Xikang province (1939–55) 21, 254
Xindu county 43, 146, 167, 219, 269
Xinfan county 228
Xinjiang province 15
Xinjin county 146
Xiushan county 161–3, 171, 187, 207–8, 254, 265, 300
Xuyong county 148

Ya'an:
  county 218, 236–7
  prefecture 147, 301
Yangzi Gorges 18–21, 55, 59, 89, 204, 288
Yibin:
  city 148, 199, 236–7, 240
  prefecture 147, 160, 172, 181, 186, 301
Yongchuan prefecture, *see* Baxian
Youyang county 161–3, 187, 205, 208, 219, 236–7, 254, 265, 300, 319
Yunnan province 13, 21, 37, 151, 270
Yunyang county 187, 208

Zhao Ziyang 31, 44–5, 96, 105, 198, 269
Zhaohua county 148
Zhejiang province 11, 19, 56, 111 n., 270
Zhong county 289
Zigong city 16, 23, 36, 76–7, 218, 301
Ziyang county 43, 315
Zoige county 162